Case Studies Within Psychotherapy Trials

Case Studies Within Psychotherapy Trials

Integrating Qualitative and Quantitative Methods

EDITED BY

DANIEL B. FISHMAN

STANLEY B. MESSER

DAVID J.A. EDWARDS

FRANK M. DATTILIO

OXFORD
UNIVERSITY PRESS

Oxford University Press is a department of the University of Oxford. It furthers
the University's objective of excellence in research, scholarship, and education
by publishing worldwide. Oxford is a registered trade mark of Oxford University
Press in the UK and certain other countries.

Published in the United States of America by Oxford University Press
198 Madison Avenue, New York, NY 10016, United States of America.

Library of Congress Cataloging-in-Publication Data
Names: Fishman, Daniel B., editor. | Messer, Stanley B., editor. |
Edwards, D. J. A., editor. | Dattilio, Frank M., editor.
Title: Case studies within psychotherapy trials : integrating
qualitative and quantitative methods / edited by Daniel B. Fishman,
Stanley B. Messer, David J.A. Edwards, and Frank M. Dattilio.
Description: Oxford ; New York : Oxford University Press, [2017] |
Includes bibliographical references and index.
Identifiers: LCCN 2016027783 (print) | LCCN 2016029927 (ebook) |
ISBN 9780199344635 | ISBN 9780199344642 (ebook)
Subjects: | MESH: Psychotherapy—methods | Research Design | Case Reports
Classification: LCC RC337 (print) | LCC RC337 (ebook) | NLM WM 40 |
DDC 616.89/140072—dc23
LC record available at https://lccn.loc.gov/2016027783

9 8 7 6 5 4 3 2 1

Printed by Edwards Brothers Malloy, United States of America

To Peter E. Nathan (1935–2016),

valued colleague, good friend, and innovative thinker

As a rule, when I have heard some slight indication of the course of events I am able to guide myself by the thousands of other similar cases which occur to my memory.

—Arthur Conan Doyle, "The Red-Headed League," 1891

What treatment, by whom, is most effective for this individual with that specific problem, and under which set of circumstances?

—Gordon Paul, 1967, p. 111

A public policy proposal is forwarded that no form of health intervention—physical or mental [including psychotherapy]—should be supported through third-party reimbursement and publicly supported training programs unless it has been demonstrated to be safe and effective. It is argued that randomized controlled clinical trials [RCTs] should be viewed as the most valid, though not exclusive, source of evidence.

—Gerald Klerman, 1983, p. 929

EBPP [Evidence-Based Practice in Psychology] promotes effective psychological practice and enhances public health by applying empirically supported principles of psychological assessment, case formulation, therapeutic relationship, and intervention.

—APA Task Force on Evidence-Based Practice, 2006, p. 271

Common to all experts, however, is that they operate on the basis of intimate knowledge of several thousand concrete cases in their areas of expertise. Context-dependent knowledge and experience are at the very heart of expert activity. Such knowledge and expertise also lie at the center of the case study as a research and teaching method or to put it more generally still, as a method of learning.

—Bent Flyvbjerg, 2006, p. 222

A psychotherapy case formulation is a hypothesis about the causes, precipitants, and maintaining influences of a person's psychological, interpersonal, and behavioral problems. A case formulation helps organize information about a person, particularly when that information contains contradictions or inconsistencies in behavior, emotion, and thought content. Ideally, it contains structures that permit the therapist to understand these contradictions and to categorize important classes of information within a sufficiently encompassing view of the patient. A case formulation also serves as a blueprint guiding treatment and as a marker for change.

—Tracy Eells, 2007, p. 4

[In] statistical hypothesis testing, . . . the scientist deduces one statement (or a few statements) from the theory and compares that statement with many observations [across different individuals]. If the observations tend to match the statement, . . . then the hypothesis is considered as confirmed. In contrast, . . . the theory-building case study strategy . . . compares many theoretically-based statements with correspondingly many observations [within the same individual] . . . [asking] how well the theory describes details of the case. . . . because many statements are examined . . . The gain in confidence in the theory from a close match may be as large as from a statistical hypothesis-testing study.

—William B. Stiles, 2009, pp. 11–12

Randomized clinical trials (RCTs) research has been touted for three decades as the gold standard for determining effective and optimal treatments in the mental health arena. Unfortunately, RCT designs have failed to advance the field of psychotherapy as much as initially expected, largely because they have not proven able clearly to identify either unique or specific treatments for different diagnostic conditions. . . . Aspects of treatment and patients that do distinguish among treatment effects are seldom incorporated in RCT designs because they lie outside of the realm of what are considered "interventions."

—Larry Beutler and Bryan Forrester, 2014, p. 168

CONTENTS

PREFACE AND ACKNOWLEDGMENTS

In psychotherapy research, the world of randomized clinical trials (RCTs) is one of elaborate logical designs to achieve experimental control; a focus on specific variables and discrete, normative, quantitative measures of them; a search for general laws; fidelity to therapy manuals; and extensive statistical analyses of the therapy results of groups of clients. In contrast, the world of case studies of individual psychotherapy sessions and courses of therapy is one of qualitatively rich patterns of human transactions; the narrative development of an emotionally important relationship between therapist and client; the complex interaction of a client's personality, life history, presenting symptoms and distress, and present life situation, leading the therapist to develop a guiding case formulation and treatment plan; and the personality, training, and expertise of the therapist. In short, one world focuses on *numbers about variables within groups,* and the other world focuses on *words about patterns within specific persons.* Up to this point, these worlds—sometimes seeming to be more associated with the physical sciences and the humanities, respectively, than with "social science" per se—have not unsurprisingly been separated, despite the fact that the methods associated with these worlds actually analyze the exact same data, consisting of psychotherapy interactions, and despite the fact that some mental health professionals like clinical psychologists are intensively trained in both of them.

This book is based on the premise that both of these worlds are of great value in psychotherapy research. Specifically, in Chapters 3–6 we present four psychotherapy research projects. In each there is a combination of a formal, quantitative RCT study of randomly assigned groups; two or three systematic, in-depth qualitative case studies of individual clients drawn from the experimental group of the RCT; and a discussion of how the two types of knowledge emerging from the RCT study and the case studies can be integrated and synthesized, with the sum of the two types of knowledge being greater than their parts. We believe one of the strengths of this book is that we systematically bring together these two different perspectives on the same psychotherapy interactions, and that readers thus have the opportunity to immerse themselves in each, side by side, and then to join the process of exploring how these two perspectives can complement one another.

In closing, the senior editor wants to first acknowledge one of the major inspirations and driving forces for this book, his valued friend and mentor, Peter E. Nathan, who passed away prior to the completion of the book. While one of the major figures in the world of psychotherapy RCTs—being the senior editor of Oxford's classic in this area, *A Guide to Treatments That Work*, first–fourth editions, Peter had the open-mindedness, sophistication, and vision to see that qualitative and case study research could expand on the knowledge generated by RCTs. With this mindset, Peter was instrumental as an Associate Editor in guiding my development as Editor-in-Chief of the journal *Pragmatic Case Studies in Psychotherapy* (http://pcsp.libraries.rutgers.edu), which helped set the stage for the present book.

Second, we would like to thank the contributing authors of the four projects at the heart of this book for devoting themselves to instantiate the new paradigm we are proposing, namely, to delve into the experimental condition of their randomized clinical trials and to openly and honestly, with incisive critical reflection, explore the clinical narrative details and theoretical meanings of specific clients. Third, we want to thank the chapter commentators for extending our understanding of the potentials and challenges of our "Cases Within Trials" paradigm. Last we want to thank our spouses, who supported us with grace and encouragement through this challenging but very satisfying editorial experience.

Daniel B. Fishman
Stanley B. Messer
David J.A. Edwards
Frank M. Dattilio

ABOUT THE EDITORS

Daniel B. Fishman, PhD, is Professor of Clinical Psychology at the Rutgers Graduate School of Applied and Professional Psychology, and he is its former Director of Psychological Services. Dr. Fishman is the founder and editor-in-chief of the peer-reviewed, quarterly, online journal *Pragmatic Case Studies in Psychotherapy* (http://pcsp.libraries.rutgers.edu). The journal is epistemologically grounded in Dr. Fishman's book, *The Case for Pragmatic Psychology* (1999). A licensed psychologist, Dr. Fishman is a Fellow of the American Psychological Association in the areas of psychotherapy, qualitative research, clinical psychology, philosophical psychology, and community psychology. Author of more than 100 articles and more than 100 invited addresses, Dr. Fishman is also the author or coauthor of six prior books and is on the editorial board of four prominent journals.

Stanley B. Messer, PhD, Dean of the Graduate School of Applied and Professional Psychology (GSAPP) at Rutgers University for 15 years, is now a Distinguished Professor there. A practicing clinical psychologist, he has published extensively on the application of psychodynamic theory and research to the brief and integrative therapies and on the issue of evidence-based practice. Dr. Messer has also lectured and given invited workshops about these areas in several international venues, including Argentina, Brazil, China, Israel, Norway, and Poland. He is president-designate of the international Society for the Exploration of Psychotherapy Integration.

David J.A. Edwards, PhD, is a Professor in the Department of Psychology at Rhodes University, Grahamstown, South Africa (part time). He is a practicing clinical psychologist with training in cognitive-behavior therapy and other modalities and a longstanding interest in psychotherapy integration. He is certified as a schema therapist for individuals and couples by the International Society of Schema Therapy. He has been the author or co-author of over 20 published clinical case studies and 11 articles or book chapters on case study methodology. His writing has reflected his ongoing concern about the way in which ruling paradigms have defined science in a way that has marginalized the actual experience of clinicians who need to be responsive to individual clients and the unique challenges each presents.

Frank M. Dattilio, PhD, ABPP, is a teaching associate in psychiatry (part-time) at Harvard Medical School and maintains a part-time faculty position with the Department of Psychiatry at the University of Pennsylvania Perelman School of Medicine, where he has taught for 27 years. Dr. Dattilio is a clinical psychologist and a fellow of the American Psychological Association in clinical psychology. A prominent, internationally recognized couple and family therapist, he is specifically known for his development of the cognitive-behavioral therapy model. With works translated into 30 languages, Dr. Dattilio has 300 professional publications and 22 books in the areas of couple and family therapy and clinical and forensic psychology. Dr. Dattilio has also been the recipient of numerous awards for outstanding achievement in the fields of psychology and psychotherapy.

CONTRIBUTORS

Kristian Bech Arendt, PhD
Department of Psychology and
    Behavioural Sciences
Aarhus University
Aarhus, Denmark

Jacques P. Barber, PhD
Gordon F. Derner Institute of
    Advanced Psychological Studies
Adelphi University
Garden City, NY

Sarah Bloch-Elkouby, MS
Gordon F. Derner Institute of
    Advanced Psychological Studies
Adelphi University
Garden City, NY

William M. Buerger, PsyM
Graduate School of Applied and
    Professional Psychology
Rutgers University–New Brunswick
Piscataway, NJ

Brian C. Chu, PhD
Graduate School of Applied and
    Professional Psychology
Rutgers University–New Brunswick
Piscataway, NJ

Harold Chui, PhD
Gordon F. Derner Institute of
    Advanced Psychological Studies
Adelphi University
Garden City, NY, and
Department of Educational
    Psychology
The Chinese University of Hong Kong
Shatin, New Territories, Hong Kong

John F. Clarkin, PhD
Department of Psychiatry
Joan and Sanford I. Weill Medical
    College of Cornell University
New York, NY

Tracy L. Clouthier, MS
Department of Psychology
Pennsylvania State University
University Park, PA

Frank M. Dattilio, PhD
Department of Psychiatry
Harvard Medical School
Boston, MA, and
Department of Psychiatry
University of Pennsylvania Perelman
    School of Medicine
Philadelphia, PA

Laura J. Dietz, PhD
Department of Psychology
University of Pittsburgh at Johnstown
Johnstown, PA

David J.A. Edwards, PhD
Department of Psychology
Rhodes University
Grahamstown, South Africa, and
Department of Psychiatry
University of Cape Town
Cape Town, South Africa

Daniel B. Fishman. PhD
Graduate School of Applied and
    Professional Psychology
Rutgers University–New Brunswick
Piscataway, NJ

Carlos A. Sierra Hernandez, MS
Department of Psychology
Simon Fraser University
Burnaby, British Columbia, Canada

Lauren J. Hoffman, PsyD
Division of Child and Adolescent
    Psychiatry
Columbia University Medical Center
New York, NY

Alejandro Interian, PhD
Mental Health & Behavioral Sciences
VA New Jersey Health Care System
Lyons, NJ

Otto F. Kernberg, MD
Department of Psychiatry
Joan and Sanford I. Weill Medical
    College of Cornell University
New York, NY

Sarah S. Kerner, PsyD
Department of Pediatric Psychiatry
Morgan Stanley Children's Hospital
    of New York Presbyterian/
    Columbia
University Medical Center
New York, NY

Mark F. Lenzenweger, PhD
Department of Psychology
The State University of New York at
    Binghamton
Binghamton, NY

Kenneth N. Levy, PhD
Department of Psychology
Pennsylvania State University
University Park, PA

Irene Lundkvist-Houndoumadi, PhD
Private practice
Frederiksberg, Denmark

Kevin B. Meehan, PhD
Department of Psychology
LIU-Brooklyn
Brooklyn, NY

Stanley B. Messer, PhD
Graduate School of Applied and
    Professional Psychology
Rutgers University–New Brunswick
Piscataway, NJ

John C. Norcross, PhD
Department of Psychology
University of Scranton
Scranton, PA, and
Department of Psychiatry
SUNY Upstate Medical University
Syracuse, NY

William E. Piper, PhD
Department of Psychiatry
University of British Columbia
Vancouver, British Columbia, Canada

Ariana Prawda, PsyD
Private Practice
Alexandria, VA

Silke Stjerneklar, PhD
Department of Psychology and
    Behavioural Sciences
Aarhus University
Aarhus, Denmark

Mikael Thastum, PhD
Department of Psychology and
  Behavioural Sciences
Aarhus University
Aarhus, Denmark

Frank E. Yeomans, MD, PhD
Department of Psychiatry
Joan and Sanford I. Weill Medical
  College of Cornell University
New York, NY

Jami F. Young, PhD
Graduate School of Applied and
  Professional Psychology
Rutgers University–New Brunswick
Piscataway, NJ

Elaina A. Zendegui, PsyD
Department of Psychiatry
Joan and Sanford I. Weill Medical
  College of Cornell University
New York, NY

PART I

Introduction

R andomized clinical trials (RCTs), based on quantitative group research, are considered the "gold standard" of psychotherapy research. However, an exclusive commitment to such research designs and write-ups has created a barrier in making RCT knowledge relevant for real-world psychotherapy practice. The rise of the mixed-methods movement—integrating quantitative and qualitative approaches—has created credibility and rigor in the area of qualitative research, especially in the arena of systematic case studies, providing a bridge to practice. The first two chapters describe how this book builds on the mixed-methods movement to illustrate the "value added" in research knowledge by combining RCT quantitative group results with the qualitative results of systematic case studies drawn from the RCT. This model is called the "Cases Within Trials," or simply the "CWT" method.

The Terrain

DANIEL B. FISHMAN AND DAVID J.A. EDWARDS ■

Over the past two decades, the field of psychotherapy research has been dominated by two contrasting and frequently conflicting perspectives: that of the nomothetic, experimental researcher, who conducts randomized clinical trials (RCTs) that emphasize quantitative, group data; and that of the idiographic, interpretative researcher, who emphasizes qualitative, individual data from clinical case studies (e.g., Division 12 Task Force, 1995; Fishman, 1999; Howard et al., 1996; Miller, 2004).

Recently there has been a major movement toward bridging these two perspectives and developing their potential for complementarity and synergy (e.g., Barkham, Hardy, & Mellor-Clark, 2010; Goodheart, Kazdin, & Sternberg, 2006; Norcross, Beutler, & Levant, 2006; Wolfe, 2012). This is the central theme of this book: to go beyond the historical dialectic and conflict between researchers and practitioners by presenting the rationale for and cogent examples of a new approach to the interface between research and practice. This new approach was introduced by three of this book's editors in an article a few years ago (Dattilio, Edwards, & Fishman, 2010), which helped to propel the development of this book, and is here called the "Case Studies Within Psychotherapy Trials" model, or the "Cases Within Trials" (CWT) model, for short. The CWT model seeks to integrate knowledge from RCTs with that from systematic case studies strategically drawn from the RCTs to expand the traditional gold standard of what constitutes best-practice psychotherapy research to include systematic case studies along with RCTs. In the following chapters, four project examples of this model in action are presented. Combining such knowledge creates synergy. The qualitative picture of the realities and complexities of therapy in the case studies provides a rich source of information that complements the often limited conclusions that can be drawn from the quantitative results of RCTs. The result is a more nuanced set of conclusions about the most effective methods for addressing the various mental health problems we are concerned with, conclusions that are practically useful to the managers and clinicians who must deliver the treatments at the front line.

GROUP-BASED, EXPERIMENTAL RESEARCH
IN PSYCHOTHERAPY

As is fully familiar to the scientific and professional communities, although not necessarily to the lay public, the experimental group researcher focuses on comparing groups of psychotherapy clients on a limited number of discrete, quantified variables—such as client characteristics and scores on self-report outcome questionnaires—while striving to control all of the other sources of variance. The goal is to derive statistically significant quantitative relationships among the independent and dependent variables studied and to provide empirical support for the generality of these relationships in the form of broad laws.

A particularly influential version of the experimental group perspective was set forth nearly three decades ago by Gerald Klerman (1983), a psychiatrist who offered the following plan after serving as the Director of the US Alcohol, Drug Abuse and Mental Health Administration under President Jimmy Carter:

> A public policy proposal is forwarded that no form of health intervention— physical or mental [including psychotherapy]—should be supported through third-party reimbursement and publicly supported training programs unless it has been demonstrated to be safe and effective. It is argued that randomized controlled clinical trials [RCTs] should be viewed as the most valid, though not exclusive, source of evidence. (p. 929)

Klerman drew this proposal from what was considered the scientifically most powerful model in psychopharmacology: the double-blind pharmaceutical study, whereby patients with a designated ailment, such as hypertension, cancer, or insomnia, were randomly assigned to either a particular experimental drug group or to a placebo group control. The random assignment was designed to control for all other variables that could impact on the ailment besides the experimental drug (for a history of the development of the RCT, see Wampold, 2015, pp. 11–16).

In 1995, more than a decade later, Klerman's call for RCT-based research served to inspire a group of clinical psychologists—from the Society of Clinical Psychology (Division 12 of the American Psychological Association)—to create a preliminary set of guidelines for identifying "empirically validated psychological treatments" (EVTs; Division 12 Task Force, 1993). The group created categories of EVTs. This term was later changed to "empirically supported treatments" (ESTs). Within the EST framework, the most rigorous category was that of a "well-established" treatment, which involved at least "two good group design studies [i.e., RCTs] conducted by different investigators," which showed the experimental treatment "superior to pill or psychological placebo or to another treatment" (1995, p. 6). Subsequent lists of psychotherapy treatments that met the RCT criteria of ESTs were published in 1998 in Nathan and Gorman's *Treatments That Work* (in its fourth edition in Nathan & Gorman, 2015), and in a continuously updated list of treatments that meet the EST criteria on Division 12's Web site under the title,

"Research-Supported Psychological Treatments" (Society of Clinical Psychology, 2015; see also proposals to update the methodology behind this and similar lists in Tolin et al., 2015).

According to Nathan and Gorman, the ideal study for demonstrating an EST involved at least the following elements: (a) a pool of clients who suffer from one and only one diagnostic category of psychopathology; (b) random assignment to an experimental or a control group; (c) in the experimental group, provision of a model of therapy that is operationally defined by a manual; (d) training therapists in the experimental group in how to administer the manualized treatment; (e) assessing therapist fidelity to the manual; and (f) objectively and quantitatively assessing the clinical status of the research clients on measures of symptoms relevant to the psychopathology being treated, both at the beginning and end of therapy, so that the statistical significance of the difference between symptoms before and after treatment can be determined. The logic of this design is to ensure that the only difference between the experimental and control groups is the experimental therapy program. This is achieved by (1) controlling all the client variables via random assignment, (2) standardizing the nature of the experimental therapy delivered by operationalizing it in a manual, and (3) using validated measures of the target symptoms before and after treatment and submitting them to rigorous statistical analysis. The Society of Clinical Psychology's requirement that a "well-established" treatment involve at least two independent RCTs was intended to assure that one of the keystones of science, replicability, was met. In short, the EST model was set forth as a scientifically rigorous method for determining the efficacy of a particular, manualized treatment method for a specific diagnostic category of psychopathology.

CASE-BASED, CLINICAL PRACTICE OF PSYCHOTHERAPY

In contrast, the other perspective in psychotherapy research is that which involves the practitioner, who is always dealing with a *particular case*—be it an individual client, a family, or a therapy group (Fishman, 1999). The practitioner addresses all the complexities of the particular client's history, present life circumstances, and the phenomenology of his or her experience, his or her vulnerabilities and strengths, and how these relate to what are often multiple presenting problems and difficulties (McLeod, 2010). The therapist also deals with and must be aware of the complexities involved in forming a relationship and building a working alliance with each client, often in the face of significant interpersonal difficulties that the client brings. Unlike the experimental researcher, who controls for the contextual complexities of the individual case by randomized assignment, the practitioner is committed to work with the individual client in full context (Fishman, 2005; Norcross, 2011; Wampold, 2015; Yin, 2014).

There are a number of methods for writing rigorous and systematic case studies. These have been categorized and described by McLeod, as presented below.

The approach employed in the case studies in this book is the pragmatic case study method described in Chapter 2 and summarized in Figure 2.1. Based on the work of Schon (1983) and Peterson (1991), the method builds on observationally established transtheoretical, best-practice ways in which professionals like psychotherapists apply theoretical knowledge effectively in the service of helping individual clients achieve their individual goals.

Briefly, the pragmatic case study method involves (a) grounding practice in a general, guiding theoretical conception of psychopathology and the processes by which it can be changed; (b) a systematic assessment of the client's problems; (c) the development of a case formulation and associated treatment plan (Eells, 2007), based on applying (a) to (b); (d) a detailed description of the subsequent course of therapy, including modifications of the case formulation and treatment plan based on the therapist being responsive to feedback from the client and the therapy process; and (e) at the conclusion of therapy, a formal evaluation of the therapy process, typically including both quantitative and qualitative data. Throughout, established procedures for ensuring methodological quality and reducing unintentional subjectivity are followed, for example in the case study design by using standardized quantitative measures in addition to qualitative data for outcome assessment and by recognizing methodological limitations (Kazdin, 1981); and in the case write-up, by making a clear distinction between descriptive clinical information and its interpretation, by grounding interpretations in examples, by owning one's perspective, by providing credibility checks, and by maintaining internal coherence throughout (Fishman, 2013; Elliott, Fischer, & Rennie, 1999).

THE ADVANTAGES AND DISADVANTAGES OF QUANTITATIVE AND QUALITATIVE METHODS

The advantage of the quantitative methods used by the experimental researcher is that a few variables can be rigorously measured and comparisons made using objective statistical tests of significance. The disadvantage of such methods, however, is that they reduce qualitatively complex phenomena to simple numbers with little context, and this in turn limits their value to (and credibility with) practitioners. Thus, clinical practitioners typically view qualitative research and case studies as more appropriate to the world of practice, since qualitative researchers strive to capture real-world human complexity and its narrative meanings on its own terms, using words rather than numbers. A recent study by Stewart and Chambless (2007) illustrates this. Doctoral-level clinical psychologists in private therapy practice were randomly assigned to receive (1) a research review of data from randomized controlled trials of cognitive-behavioral treatment (CBT) and medication for bulimia; (2) a case study, including CBT-informed therapy for a fictional patient with bulimia; or (3) both—to see the effect of this information on two dependent variables, a practitioner's likelihood of seeking training and of trying the new bulimia intervention. Stewart and Chambless found that for the practitioners, the introduction of the case study information had a significant positive impact on the dependent variables, whereas the introduction of random-ized RCT data had no such impact. This result was regardless of indicators of how research-oriented the practitioners were, such as being CBT oriented, coming from a graduate program that emphasized research outcome findings, or being recent graduates. In sum, it seemed to be their common role as full-time thera-pists that drew the participants to see the case study material as most relevant to their practice.

Since John Watson's behavioral manifesto in 1913, quantitative, experimen-tally oriented models have dominated academic psychology (Fishman, 1999). However, for at least four decades qualitative psychology has been staking out its claim to an important space in the field. For example, the American Psychological Association recently changed the name and focus of its Division 5, which is devoted to research methods, adding qualitative research to its previous exclu-sive focus on quantitative approaches. In the Division's new journal, *Qualitative Psychology*, Jackson (2015) documents the recent growth of qualitative meth-ods in psychological research. For example, in the research studies indexed in PsycINFO, 20 years ago search terms like "statistical OR measurement" were in a ratio of 1 to 14.55 compared to search terms like "qualitative OR naturalistic." That figure has changed today to a ratio of 1 to 2.77. There was a similar finding in a search of terms in syllabi of psychology methodology courses (p. 181). Moreover, Jackson points out that this growth in the relative equity of qualitative research in psychology is paralleled by the growth of qualitative research more broadly, with more than 100 scholarly journals today publishing qualitative studies (p. 181).

IDIOGRAPHIC VERSUS NOMOTHETIC: THE DIALECTIC

The marginalization of qualitative methods in psychological research in general, and clinical psychology in particular, led to a harmful rift between researchers wedded to a nomothetic approach and practitioners whose work is necessarily idiographic. This rift was noted three decades ago (Barlow, 1981; Kiesler, 1981; Safran, Greenberg, & Rice, 1988). On the one side, researchers argued that the private nature of psychotherapy practice has allowed most practitioners to be un-accountable and uncritical in their work, collecting and presenting no objective, "hard data" for evaluating their effectiveness and for making their therapy process accessible for critical evaluation. They also pointed out that the RCT provides a robust scientific way for determining the efficacy of a particular type of therapy for a specific type of problem. On the other side, practitioners pointed out that the RCTs involved in the EST research include patients with only a single diagnostic problem, eliminating relevance for many of the clients seen in routine practice. Practitioners also pointed out that ESTs leave a substantial number of patients un-changed. For example, even when a treatment is shown to be efficacious in an RCT, there are still a substantial number of poor-outcome clients (e.g., Dimidjian & Hollon, 2011). Also, even an effect size as strong as .80 means that 11% of the clients in the experimental group do no better than the average person who has not received psychotherapy (Cooper, 2009, p. 22), and a somewhat recent meta-analysis of 28 RCTs found that 40% of clients showed no clinically significant improvement (Hansen, Lambert, & Forman, 2002). Moreover, practitioners argue that they need flexibility in adapting treatment to the individual client—what Stiles and colleagues (e.g., Kramer & Stiles, 2015; Norcross, 2011; Stiles, Barkham, Connell, & Mellor-Clark, 2008) have referred to as "therapist responsiveness"—and that this is inconsistent with rigorously following a manual (see also Beutler & Forrester, 2014). In addition, practitioners anecdotally claim that they are able to achieve positive outcomes without using manualized procedures. (For a fuller and dramatic exploration of the dialectic, see the article by Barry Wolfe [2012], who presents a two-chair dialogue reflecting his conflicting, simultaneous professional roles: 20 years as a program manager of research on psychotherapy at the US National Institutes of Mental Health and his simultaneous role as a practicing therapist for almost 40 years.)

MIXED METHODS: A UNIFYING PARADIGM

The CWT model that we are recommending in this book serves as a vehicle for transcending this long-standing conflict between researchers and practitioners. It does this by adopting the mixed-methods model. This is an integrative research paradigm that has been gathering momentum in medicine, education, and the social sciences. It takes a pragmatic approach to our understanding of what research methods can provide valid knowledge and starts with the assumption that quantitative and qualitative data each have their own strengths but also weaknesses in validly describing the world. The mixed-methods model provides an epistemological rationale for combining research methods that generate what are in effect different kinds of knowledge, and it offers guidelines for integrating the two kinds of methods within a single research study. By combining both types of data, researchers gain a more differentiated and trustworthy overall picture of the phenomenon being studied (e.g., see Teddlie & Tashakkori, 2009). As alluded to earlier, the advantages of quantification are that they provide (a) stable meanings across time; (b) the ability to achieve quality control via established psychometric procedures that seek to achieve reliability among different observers; (c) the capacity to efficiently reduce large amounts of complex differences across the multiple individual cases included in group research designs; (d) the ability to obtain an objective, normative context for comparing individual clients; and (e) the capacity to create top-down deductive laws (Stiles, 2009).

However, these strengths are offset by significant disadvantages because in the process of oversimplifying information, much of what is valuable is discarded. It is just this type of "lost" information that words and qualitative description excel at: (a) by creating "thick" descriptions that include the detail, complexity, context, subjectivity, and the multifaceted nature of human

Table 1.1 Typical Outcome Structure of a Randomized Clinical Trial
for a Disorder Such as Depression

Experimental condition, e.g., CBT treatment for depression	**E01, E02, E03, E04, E05** **E06, E07, E08, E09, E10** **E11, E12,** *E13, E14, E15* *E16, E17, E18, E19, E20* **(60% successful)**
Control condition, e.g., "waiting list" control	**C21, C22, C23, C24, C25** *C26, C27, C28, C29, C30* *C31, C32, C33, C34, C35* *C36, C37, C38, C39, C40* **(20% successful)**

NOTE: Items in italics indicate unsuccessful resolution of depression, and items in roman text and bold indicate successful resolution of depression.
CBT, cognitive–behavioral therapy.

From D. B. Fishman (2013), The pragmatic case study method for creating rigorous and systematic, practitioner-friendly research, *Pragmatic Case Studies in Psychotherapy*, 9(4), p. 416. Copyright 2013 by Daniel B. Fishman.

knowledge; (b) by capturing the narrative, storytelling structures of human knowledge; and (c) by having the capacity to ground generalizations in particular instances, so that the generalizations are derived from the bottom up (Fishman, 1999; Stiles, 2009).

In psychotherapy outcome research, the complementary strengths of quantitative and qualitative data translate into the fact that they are positioned to answer different research questions (Creswell, Fetters, & Ivankova, 2004). This can be seen by examining the typical structure of an RCT, as shown in Table 1.1. The table illustrates this structure with a study comparing an experimental condition of CBT treatment for a problem such as depression with a control condition of a placement on a waiting list. The advantage of the quantitative group data is that it can answer a question like: Is the experimental condition *on average* more effective than the no-treatment control condition? Specifically, as shown in the table, since 60% of the clients in the experimental condition (E1-E12) were successful compared to 20% (C21-C24) in the no-treatment control condition, the answer to the question is yes, the experimental condition was *on average* more effective than the control condition.

In contrast, the advantage of the qualitative case study data is that they can answer questions like: Why did some *particular individual clients* in the experimental condition—like clients E01 and E02—have successful therapy outcomes, while other subjects in the experimental condition—like E13 and E14—did not? Were there different reasons for success between E01 and E02? Were there different reasons for the therapeutic failures in the cases of clients E13 and E14? Qualitative case studies can answer these and similar questions about the differences between patients in the control condition, like clients C21 and C22 who had successful outcomes compared with clients C25 and C26, who had unsuccessful outcomes.

In sum, analyses of quantitative group data are of value in describing general relationships across groups of subjects involving a few variables, while qualitative case data are of value in thickly describing processes within individual cases, revealing complex patterns in the ways that one patient differs from another. This means that to study psychosocial phenomena systematically in a manner that yields conclusions that are trustworthy (Lincoln & Guba, 1985; Morrow, 2005), it is important both (a) to fully assess the rich and varied details, contexts, and levels of the phenomenon—that is, by *capturing complexity*—as well as (b) to do this is in a precise, reliable, and explicit manner with definitions that are as clear as possible—that is, by *ensuring rigor*. There is a dialectical relationship between these two goals: as the information we gather encompasses more of the rich and varied details in a situation, it becomes less precise and reliable; and, likewise, as the information we gather becomes more and more precise and reliable, for example, through quantification, it encompasses less and less of these details and becomes more decontextualized.

There is an increasing number of theorists and researchers who are working to navigate this dialectic, rather than embracing an all-or-none position at one of the poles. This is the impetus behind the rising influence of mixed-methods research in general. One expression of this in psychotherapy research is the move from *"protocol-based" treatment manuals* that specify treatment procedures quite strictly on a session-by-session basis to the development of *"principle-based" treatment manuals* that incorporate a range of interventions that are delivered responsively on the basis of broad principles (e.g., Henggeler et al., 2009; Kendall & Beidas, 2007; Wolfe, 2012). Another is the development by some advocates of case studies—representing the complexity pole of the continuum—of methodologies for making case study description and interpretation more systematic, reliable, and insulated from unexamined bias (Elliott et al., 2009; Elliott, Fischer, & Rennie, 1999; Fishman, 1999, 2005; 2013; Messer, 2007; Stiles, 2009), sacrificing some of the richness and intricacies of individuals' lives in order to gain more reliability, transparency, and theoretical clarity in studying them.

OTHER EMERGING RESOLUTIONS OF THE PARADIGM DIALECTIC IN PSYCHOLOGY AND CLINICAL PRACTICE

In recent years a diverse collection of broader philosophical, scientific, methodological, political, economic, and organizational evolutionary movements have led to an environment that is supportive of a mixed-methods approach to psychotherapy research generally and to the CWT model specifically. These have resulted in the expansion of phenomena considered appropriate by mainstream researchers for investigation, moving from experimentally based, quantitative group data into areas that focus on qualitative research and case studies. In addition, these movements support the idea that knowledge derived from individual case study research makes an important contribution that complements the valuable, but limited knowledge gained from RCT-based group research. Examples of these developments are reviewed next.

The American Psychological Association: Expanding Best Practice Beyond Empirically Supported Treatments

THE AMERICAN PSYCHOLOGICAL ASSOCIATION'S EVIDENCE-BASED PRACTICE IN PSYCHOLOGY MODEL

The American Psychological Association (APA Presidential Task Force, 2006) has developed a model of best clinical practice called evidence-based practice in psychology (EBPP), which they define as "the integration of the best available research with clinical expertise in the context of patient characteristics, culture, and preferences" (p. 273).

EBPP means that clinicians are tasked with selecting and tailoring treatments to individual patients in light of the *best available evidence*. Such evidence includes the following:

- Clinical observation (including individual case studies) and basic psychological science [which] are valuable sources of innovations and hypotheses (the context of scientific discovery);
- Qualitative research [which] can be used to describe the subjective, lived experiences of people, including participants in psychotherapy;
- Systematic case studies [which] are particularly useful when aggregated— as in the form of practice research networks—for comparing individual patients with others with similar characteristics;. . . . [and]
- RCTs and their logical equivalents (efficacy research) [which] are the standard for drawing causal inferences about the effects of interventions (context of scientific verification). (p. 274)

THE AMERICAN PSYCHOLOGICAL ASSOCIATION'S EMPIRICALLY SUPPORTED (THERAPY) RELATIONSHIPS

The development of the concept of empirically supported relationships (ESRs) complements the development of empirically supported treatments (ESTs; now called "research-supported psychological treatments") by Division 12 of the American Psychological Association (APA), mentioned earlier. Division 29 (Psychotherapy) of the APA created a parallel task force on ESRs to examine and synthesize the research evidence on the nature and qualities of the therapeutic relationship that contribute to treatment effectiveness. Their results were first published in a 2002 book that is now in its second edition (Norcross, 2011).

Research on the development of ESTs focused on the efficacy of specific procedures for clinical intervention. This approach was based on the assumption that a psychological treatment is similar to the administration of a drug which may or may not be efficacious in treating a physical disease like malaria or pneumonia.

By contrast, researchers have long suggested that there may be *common factors* that impact on the effectiveness of treatment regardless of the specific treatment employed or the theory on which it is based. For example, these common factors relate to the nature of the relationship between therapist and client, the therapist's responsiveness and capacity for empathy, and the extent to which the client and therapist have a shared vision of the goals of therapy. These common factors are contrasted with the *specific factors* relating to the particular kind of treatment employed.

Historically, there have also been polarized debates between those who have argued that what is primary in treating mental disorders are specific therapy techniques that are efficacious relatively independent of how they are delivered, and those who have argued that techniques are largely irrelevant and that it is the quality of the relationship between client and therapist that brings about change. As Norcross and Lambert (2011) stated it:

> Do treatments cure disorders or do relationships heal people? Which is the most accurate vision for practicing, researching, and teaching psychotherapy? (p. 3)

The heated conflicts between the two sides are referred to by Norcross and Lambert as the psychotherapy "culture wars" and are the focus of Wampold's (2015) book, *The Great Psychotherapy Debate*.

In the spirit, discussed earlier, of growing pluralism and increasing recognition of the complexity of therapy, Norcross and Lambert (2011, p. 3) point out the need to go beyond the culture wars and for all to affirm that:

> decades of psychotherapy research consistently attest that the patient, the therapist, their relationship, the treatment method, and the context all contribute to treatment success (and failure). We should be looking at all of these determinants and their optimal combinations.

Central to the ESR project is the research on individualizing treatment in response to particular client behaviors. (See also the work of Jacqueline Persons [2008], discussed later, on conducting cognitive-behavioral therapy based upon an individualized case formulation of the client.) Norcross (2011) points out that this perspective is not new:

> The mandate for individualizing psychotherapy was embodied in Gordon Paul's (1967) iconic question: "*What* treatment, by *whom*, is most effective for *this* individual with *that* specific problem, and under *which* set of circumstances?" Every psychotherapist recognizes that what works for one person may not work for another. . . .
>
> The [goal] . . . of creating the optimal match in psychotherapy . . . is to increase treatment effectiveness by tailoring it to the individual and his/her singular situation. In other words, psychotherapists endeavor to create a new therapy for each patient. (pp. 9–10)

It is here that the CWT approach can make a valuable contribution because the individual case studies provide the data about the personality and characteristic behaviors of particular clients and how these impact on the process of delivering treatment. Thus, the CWT model provides a valuable means of addressing Norcross and Wampold's (2011) conclusion that an important goal for psychotherapists is to integrate idiographic and nomothetic perspectives by adapting psychotherapy "to the *particulars* of the individual patient according to *generalities* identified by research" (p. 429).

Adding "Practice-Based Evidence" to Evidence-Based Practice as a Source of Psychotherapy Research

Another source of evidence on the effectiveness of different forms of psychotherapy comes from naturalistic studies of therapists in practice. An important aspect of this practice-based evidence (PBE; Barkham, Hardy, & Mellor-Clark, 2010) involves qualitatively and quantitatively monitoring the course of therapy in everyday clinical settings using measures of process and outcome, frequently in the form of quantitative self-report scales. Wampold (2010) points out the important role of PBE:

> One of the problems with the dissemination of . . . [EST] treatments is that implementation of these treatments is not accompanied by outcome measurement. Thus how well treatments work "on the ground" in any given setting is unknown. . . . [PBE] is based on actual outcomes, creating accountability based on metrics in practice settings. (p. 270)

The practice-based evidence movement has spawned a number of methodologically rigorous, quantitative self-report questionnaire systems which each consist of a global survey that is clinically relevant for any client—across all diagnostic groups (e.g., the OQ-45 system [Lambert, 2010] and the CORE [Barkham, Hardy, & Mellor-Clark, 2010]). Each of these systems possesses a number of crucial common characteristics: psychometrically acceptable reliability and validity; sensitivity in detecting change over the course of therapy; and a very large database of responses for a variety of clinical populations. With the use of this database, it is possible to create ongoing feedback that predicts the expected course of treatment over time for a particular type of client. This feedback can be employed to warn clinicians of potentially poor outcomes if the present trends in the therapy continue, and to suggest ways of making changes for altering this negative course, using a method developed by Lambert (2010).

The practice-based evidence movement also encompasses the use of normatively established, problem-specific outcome measures drawn from RCTs that can be used to statistically benchmark the practitioner's case against the results of the RCT. Examples are Persons, Bolstrom, and Bertagnolli's (1999) clinical research on depression; and Clement's (2007) case study of obsessive-compulsive disorder, which also illustrates how the PBE can be integrated with systematic, qualitative case studies of the target clients.

Another dimension of practice-based evidence is contained in the "Two-Way Bridge Initiative" (Goldfried et al., 2014; Two-Way Bridge Web Site, http://www.stonybrook.edu/commcms/two-way-bridge/), developed by Marvin Goldfried, in conjunction with Division 12 (Clinical Psychology) and Division 29 (Psychotherapy) of the American Psychological Association. The Initiative is designed to parallel the two-way communication system that physicians in the United States use whereby they can offer feedback to the Food and Drug Administration (FDA) on problematic clinical variables they encounter in using a drug, even though its efficacy has been demonstrated by an RCT.

Specifically, therapists who are using ESTs are surveyed as to the barriers to treatment they have experienced. Goldfried and his team started out with cognitive-behavioral treatments and to date have published the results of such surveys for a variety of anxiety disorders. The variables explored typically fall into the following general categories, all independent of the EST procedures themselves: "variables associated with the patient's symptoms, other patient problems or characteristics, patient expectations, patient beliefs about symptoms, patient motivation, social system (home, work, other), problems/limitations with the intervention procedure, [and] therapy relationship issues" (Goldfried et al., 2014, pp. 5–6). As a more specific example, in therapists' feedback about barriers to implementing ESTs for obsessive-compulsive disorder, the most common variables identified included "limited premorbid functioning, chaotic lifestyles, controlling and critical families, OCD symptom severity, OCD symptom chronicity, and comorbidities" (Jacobson, Newman, & Goldfried, 2016, p. 75).

The Two-Way Bridge Initiative highlights the multiple, complex contexts that impact upon and can interfere with the application of an EST in real-world practice. The Initiative thus reinforces the value of the present book's CWT model, which systematically explores the facilitating and inhibiting contexts that impact upon whether the EST that defines the experimental condition of a therapy RCT is effective for a particular client.

The concept of PBE has become another vehicle for bridging the conflict between group-based researchers and case-based practitioners. As Wampold (2010) observes:

> Knowledge derived from practice-based evidence should not be antagonistic to those who conduct RCTs, but rather the top-down and bottom-up evidence will converge to create an amalgam that is richer and more useful than evidence from any one method. (p. ix)

This vision resonates strongly with the rationale behind the CWT model, which provides a new formal structure for bringing together the statistical results of group research with the qualitative and quantitative results of systematic case studies drawn from those RCTs.

Case Study Knowledge Comes of Age

John McLeod Pulls the Case Study Field Together

Narrative case studies, whether in extended form or in the form of short case examples, have played a central role in the development of approaches to psychotherapy. They have served as a vehicle for communicating the theories on which the treatment approach was based and for describing the kinds of ongoing processes that occur that can lead to clinical change. Examples are Freud's 1905 case of "Dora," for psychoanalysis; J. B. Watson's 1920 case of "Little Albert," for behavior therapy; Rogers's 1942 case of "Herbert Bryant," for client-centered therapy (the first fully transcribed case ever published); and Yalom's 1989 cases in his book *Love's Executioner*, for existential therapy. However, historically, within the academic mainstream, because of their narrative, relatively nontechnical nature, their easy accessibility to the general public, their focus on personal experience, and their lack of experimentally derived, group-based, quantitative data, case studies were viewed as being, by their very nature, unscientifically journalistic and subjectively biased, and they became marginalized in psychotherapy research.

In recent years, as discussed earlier, with the rise in psychology of a more pluralistic, mixed-methods approach to research designs, including the development of methodologies for making case study description and interpretation more systematic, reliable, and insulated from unexamined bias, there has been a reemergence of interest in the case study as a credible and useful vehicle for therapy research, complementing experimental group studies (Edwards, 2007). However, this reemergence has been fragmented geographically, conceptually, and methodologically, and it has been hidden from the view of many academic researchers and practicing therapists. John McLeod's (2010) book, *Case Study Research in Counselling and Psychotherapy* (2010), does the crucially important, scholarly job of pulling these fragments together into a persuasive and coherent whole (Fishman, 2010).

A particularly important part of McLeod's book is his differentiation of case studies into five distinct, complementary models. Each model has a distinct purpose, method of data design and collection, strategy for data summary and interpretation, and role in expanding the field's knowledge base, both practical and theoretical. The models include an emphasis upon using case studies as exemplars of best clinical practice; as settings for single-case, quantitative experiments; as vehicles for intensively evaluating efficacy via diverse types of data as analyzed by multiple judges; as a way to explore the narrative meaning of the therapy experience for both client and clinician; and as a means for theory building. In addition, Fishman (2012) has illustrated the advantages of combining different models within the same case study.

Theory Building Through Case Studies

Although it has often been suggested that case studies are useful for generating descriptions of and hypotheses about phenomena that are not well understood ("the context of discovery"), it has long been recognized that they can do more than that and can contribute to the "context of justification" (Giorgi, 1986; Flyvbjerg, 2006; Popper, 1934/2002). That is, under the right circumstances, they can provide rigorous tests of theory (Bromley, 1986; Edwards, 1998: Mitchell 1983; Shapiro, 1970; Stake, 1994). Indeed, a single case can be enough to show that an apparently well-established principle is wrong, or at least that it does apply universally. This is sometimes called a "crucial case study" (Mahrer, 1988). Eckstein (1975) gives a famous example of how a single case can settle a theoretical dispute. When the vacuum pump was invented in 1650, a single trial of dropping a coin and a feather simultaneously showed that they fell at the same rate. Galileo, who had predicted this in contradiction to Aristotle's belief that the feather would fall more slowly, was shown to be right. More recently, the importance of case studies for theory building have been emphasized by Stiles and Messer, as we examine next.

William Stiles on the Logic of the Theory-Building Case Study
Stiles (2009) compares the logic of group-based versus case-based theory building:

> [In] statistical hypothesis testing, . . . the scientist deduces one statement (or a few statements) from the theory and compares that statement with many observations [across different individuals]. If the observations tend to match the statement, . . . then the hypothesis is considered as confirmed, and confidence in the statement is substantially increased. This, inductively, yields a small increment of confidence in the theory. . . .
>
> In contrast, . . . the theory-building case study strategy . . . compares many theoretically-based statements with correspondingly many observations [within the same individual], . . . [asking] how well the theory describes details of the case. Importantly, observations of a case may address different manifestations of a theoretical tenet or different tenets. For reasons familiar to researchers in psychology . . . the change in confidence in any one statement may be small. However, because many statements are examined . . . the gain in confidence in the theory from a close match may be as large as from a statistical hypothesis-testing study. (pp. 11–12)

Stiles (2009) has concretely and extensively illustrated this model in his use of a variety of case studies in the development of his "assimilation" model. This theory focuses on the general process by which clients work through the thoughts and feelings associated with the problematic experiences that brought them into treatment. Stiles's work argues again for the "value-added" knowledge of combining case-based with group-based research, in this instance of building theory both from the "bottom up" and the "top down."

Stanley Messer on Theory Building by Instantiating Concepts
Another dimension of the use of case studies for theory building involves one of the functions that they serve: expanding the actual meaning of general theoretical

concepts by concretizing them with specific, contextually embedded, narratively structured examples of case material. On this topic, Stanley Messer (2011) writes:

> There is an interplay between the propositions of the theory and the facts on the ground; each informs and alters the other. This can be described by what is known as the hermeneutic circle wherein the parts of a theory take meaning from the individual statements and these derive their meaning from the whole. Similarly, there is a reciprocal relationship between clinical observations and the theory within which the practitioner operates, each informing and giving meaning to the other. For the psychotherapist, a theory is not merely an abstract device or an object of elegance and beauty, but is a way to think concretely about clinical cases. (p. 440)

To illustrate this aspect of how cases can aid theory building, Messer presents a vignette from the transcribed case of Ron, a patient with a narcissistic disorder seen by the therapist Michael Shoshani. The vignette illustrates how Shoshani used strategies drawn from two-person, relational psychodynamic theory, which includes a consideration of the therapist's own struggles and self-revelations in the therapy. After presenting the case vignette, Messer (2011) concludes:

> Because of the detail offered, the complexity, the interweaving of theory and practice, and the exposure of mistakes lending considerable credibility to the account, it gives one a much better understanding of the relational point of view as it is practiced, as compared to merely reading the theory. That is, it helps to elaborate and concretize the theory. (p. 445)

Development of Case-Study-Based Thinking Within the Cognitive-Behavioral Therapy Movement

With some notable exceptions in developing case-based approaches (e.g., Lazarus, 1985), the CBT field has historically had a strong commitment to and has taken leadership in the group-based EST movement. In this context, it is noteworthy that recently Jacqueline Persons, a leader in the CBT movement, has staked out a different, influential model based on case formulations individualized to the particular client. In her words in her well-known book (2008):

> Most EST protocols consist of a list of interventions that are to be carried out in order to treat the disorder targeted by the EST. The EST protocol assumes that the mechanisms causing and maintaining the symptoms of the patient who is being treated at that moment match the mechanisms that underpin the design of protocol. The protocol also assumes that the patient's goal is to treat the DSM disorder targeted by the protocol. These assumptions often appear to be incorrect. My solution to these problems . . . is to recommend

that clinicians examine the EST protocols to understand the [theoretical] formulations that under-pin them and how the interventions in the protocol flow out of the formulations. Then they can use that [theoretical] information (not the step-by-step procedures of the protocol itself) to guide their work. (p. vii)

As described earlier in the discussion of Stiles's work, Persons's work combines a "top-down" focus on employing general, experimentally derived principles with "bottom-up" examples of how those principles play out in case material, leading in turn to ideas for refining those principles.

Finally, it is important to note that Persons's individualized psychotherapy model (as well as the individualized case formulation movement generally [e.g., Eells, 2007]) parallels the development in health services of "personalized medicine," in which medical interventions are customized to the distinctive somatic characteristics of each individual patient (Hamburg & Collins, 2010).

Government-Funded Research Becomes More Pluralistic in the Type of Projects and Evidence It Supports

Government funding tends to set the priorities for what methods, theories, and types of psychopathology are valued and included in psychotherapy research. Recent developments in the funding priorities by governments in Europe and the United States are supportive of research employing a mixed-methods approach.

SUPPORTIVE DEVELOPMENTS IN EUROPEAN GOVERNMENTAL FUNDING OF PSYCHOTHERAPY RESEARCH: ADDING PRAGMATIC CLINICAL TRIALS TO EXPLANATORY CLINICAL TRIALS

Historically, RCTs have been designed to take place in highly controlled, laboratory-like conditions and to test causal research hypotheses. To conduct an RCT, patients and practitioners are highly selected, interventions are highly controlled, and there is relatively little concern with meeting the goal of applying the results to practice in routine settings. Schwartz and Lellouch (1967) first coined the term *explanatory* RCT for such a study. They contrast this with the term *pragmatic* RCT, one which is explicitly designed to generalize to usual practice by being carried out in routine practice conditions, for example, randomly assigning depressed clients to two different groups of psychotherapy practitioners in the same community with different theoretical orientations. Whereas the goal of an explanatory trial is understanding, the goal of a pragmatic trial is decision making. In the words of Schwartz and Lellouch:

> [A pragmatic trial] seeks to answer the question—which of . . . two treatments should we prefer? The definition of the treatments is flexible and usually complex; it takes account of auxiliary treatments and of the possibility of withdrawals.

The criteria by which the effects are assessed take into account the interests of the patients and the costs in the widest sense. The class of patients is predetermined as that to which the results of the trial are to be extrapolated. (p. 647)

A group of medical researchers associated with RCT research has developed a set of methodological criteria for conducting explanatory RCTs, including those with psychotherapy, which they call *Consolidated Standards of Reporting Trials*, or the "CONSORT Statement," for short (http://www.consort-statement. org/). More recently, a parallel group has been developed for establishing quality criteria for pragmatic RCTs. Funded by the European Union and called "Pragmatic Randomized Controlled Trials in HealthCare," or "Practihc" for short, it has its own website: http://www.practihc.org/. Practihc has teamed up with the CONSORT group to publish guidelines for reducing the risk of threats to internal validity in pragmatic trials and to improve the methodological quality in their reporting (Zwarenstein et al., 2008). Note that developing systematic case studies from cases drawn from an RCT is one strategy for making the RCT more pragmatic in the knowledge it yields.

SUPPORTIVE DEVELOPMENTS IN US GOVERNMENTAL FUNDING OF PSYCHOTHERAPY RESEARCH
Federal Quality Standards for Mixed-Methods Research
As mentioned earlier, in 1983 Gerald Klerman, former director of the US Alcohol, Drug Abuse, and Mental Health Administration, called for research in psychotherapy that focused on the efficacy of particular intervention techniques, as established by randomized clinical trials. This call dominated the funding priorities of US government-funded psychotherapy research for many years, and this focus helped to create the EST project of the APA's 1995 Division 12 Task Force described earlier.

As time passed, however, researchers came to realize that the EST model had limits and that it was important to look at other components of the therapy process, paralleling views about the larger process of healing interventions that were taking place in medicine. This broader view was encapsulated in the US Institute of Medicine's (2001) model of evidence-based practice, which posited three legs to the stool of practice: "the integration of best research evidence with clinical expertise and patient values" (p. 147); and this model led in turn to APA's (2006) evidence-based practice in psychology (EBPP) model, described earlier. Paralleling this change in conceptual frameworks regarding best clinical practice, funding priorities of the US government for mental health research have broadened. For example, the Office of Behavioral and Social Sciences Research of the NIH recently commissioned best-practice standards for evaluating the growing amount of mixed-methods research that NIH has been funding (Creswell, Klassen, Clark, & Clegg Smith, 2011).

Comparative Effectiveness Research
The US American Recovery and Reinvestment Act (ARRA) of 2009 created the Federal Coordinating Council for Comparative Effectiveness Research to manage

comparative effectiveness research (CER) across the federal government. CER is designed to address the gap between scientific knowledge derived from explanatory RCTs conducted in highly specialized, controlled settings, and the way in which practice actually takes place in real-world settings. The goal of CER is to improve the cost effectiveness of medical, mental illness, and substance abuse services as they are practiced throughout the United States. In the words of an Institute of Medicine (2009) report on "Initial National Priorities for Comparative Effectiveness Research," which sets the mission of CER:

> A patient has a right to expect the best possible care, and a health professional has a duty to provide it. But how can one know what is best? Scientific understanding of normal biology and pathological processes [based on explanatory RCTs] can provide a foundation, but scientific principles alone can go only so far. Studies that measure results in practice [e.g., using pragmatic RCTs and case studies] are the only way to learn what works, how well, for what groups of patients, and in what specific circumstances.
>
> Yet, for want of appropriate studies, innumerable practical decisions facing patients and doctors every day do not rest on a solid foundation of knowledge about what constitutes the best choice of care. One consequence of this uncertainty is that highly similar patients experience widely varying treatment in different settings, and these patients cannot all be receiving the best care. Comparative effectiveness research is a strategy that focuses on the practical comparison of two or more health interventions to discern what works best for which patients and populations. (p. xiii)

One example of the types of practice-based discrepancies that CER is designed to reduce is represented in the work of John Wennberg and his colleagues at The Dartmouth Institute for Health Policy and Clinical Practice. Over the past 40 years they have documented geographic variation in health care that patients in the United States receive, a phenomenon sometimes called "practice pattern variation" (e.g., see http://www.dartmouthatlas.org/). For example, Wennberg and his colleagues (e.g., Wennberg, 2010) have compared areas of the United States where there are low versus high expenditures for the same types of patients. They have concluded that since the medical care in the low-expenditure areas is not discernibly different in quality from that in the high-expenditure areas, it would be cost-effective to adopt the practices in the low-expenditure areas nationwide. Wennberg estimates that if this were done, the savings nationwide would be about 30% to 40% of the total now being spent on health care services. Because the United States now spends almost $4 trillion on medical care, the savings thus would be of great magnitude.

It should be noted that the dramatic findings and practical implications of Wennberg et al.'s work have in effect been the result of their adopting a case study perspective on national health practices. Instead of looking at groups of medical centers across the country and calculating means of *average* costs nationally per procedure and per diagnosis (the types of statistics frequently employed in setting reimbursement rates), Wennberg et al. have looked at each medical center as *a separate case*, and then compared and contrasted the differences among them. This is another example of the different types of important information that can be derived from a case-based versus a group-based approach to research.

A theme running throughout the rationale of pragmatic trials and comparative effectiveness research is the importance of studying clinical practice in context, including systematically investigating the role of context on the delivery of RCT-based interventions. As a result, the domain of relevant, credible physical and behavioral health knowledge has been expanded to include qualitative and case-study-based research designs.

CONCLUSION: BACK TO THE FUTURE

In sum, while much has been written about the basic incompatibility of the dominant quantitative research model in psychotherapy and the qualitative preferences of the practitioner community, the recent developments described earlier have resulted in a growing rapprochement on both sides in the service of pragmatically improving the effectiveness of psychotherapy.

The present book is designed to build on this growing rapprochement by formalizing the complementary relationship between RCT and case study data and knowledge via the CWT model described earlier. In Chapters 3–6, this model is illustrated with four RCT projects that include case studies drawn from the experimental condition of the RCT design. Chapter 2 presents a reader's guide to the method and format employed in the project chapters and the commentaries associated with them. (For a parallel approach to integrating group-based and case-based knowledge in the related field of complementary medicine, see the article "Assessing Efficacy of Complementary Medicine: Adding Qualitative Research Methods to the 'Gold Standard'" by Verhoef, Casebeer, & Hilsden, 2002.)

As a striking historical postscript to the present discussion, it should be noted that over 60 years ago, Carl Rogers and Rosalind Dymond (1954) published a book documenting a research project with the very characteristics represented here in the CWT model: (a) the use of both experimental group research designs and the analysis of positive-outcome and negative-outcome cases drawn from those designs; (b) case studies based on audio recordings and transcripts, to reduce the type of subjectivity that resided in earlier case studies like Freud's; (c) the use of a multimodal, mixed-methods design, involving the collection and analysis of multiple normed, quantitative self-descriptive questionnaires and multiple sources of qualitative data (e.g., clinical assessment interviews and follow-up interviews in addition to therapy transcripts); and (d) the use of case studies for theory development (e.g., in the positive-outcome case of Mrs. Oak, who became a prototype of Rogers's self-actualization theory). We are proud to "rediscover" a paradigm created by one of the discipline's most esteemed clinical psychologists.

REFERENCES

APA Presidential Task Force on Evidence-Based Practice (2006). *American Psychologist*, *61*, 271–285.

Barkham, M., Hardy, G.E., & Mellor-Clark, J. (2010). *Developing and delivering practice-based evidence: A guide for the psychological therapies.* Oxford, England: Wiley-Blackwell.

Beutler, L. E., & Forrester, B. (2014). What needs to change: Moving from "research informed" practice to "empirically effective" practice. *Journal of Psychotherapy Integration*, *24*, 168–177.

Bromley, D. B. (1986). *The case-study method in psychology and related disicplines.* New York: John Wiley.

Clement, P. W. (2007). Story of "Hope": Successful treatment of obsessive compulsive disorder. *Pragmatic Case Studies in Psychotherapy*, *3*(4), 1–36. Available at http://pcsp. libraries.rutgers.edu/. doi: http://dx.doi.org/10.14713/pcsp.v3i4.910

Creswell, J. W., Fetters, M. D., & Ivankova, N. V. (2004). Designing a mixed methods study in primary care. *Annals of Family Medicine*, *2*, 7–12.

Creswell, J. W., Klassen, A. C., Plano-Clark, V. L., & Smith, K. C. (2011). *Best practices for mixed methods research in the health sciences.* National Institutes of Health. Accessed on August 22, 2015 at http://obssr.od.nih.gov/mixed_methods_research

Dattilio, F. M., Edwards, D. J. A., & Fishman, D. B. (2010). Case studies within a mixed methods paradigm: Towards a resolution of the alienation between researcher and practitioner in psychotherapy research. *Psychotherapy Theory, Research, Practice, Training Practice, Training*, *47*, 427–441.

Dimidjian, S., & Hollon, S. D. (2011). Special Issue: What can be learned when empirically supported treatments fail? *Cognitive and Behavioral Practice*, *18*, 303–305.

Division 12 Task Force (1995). Training in and dissemination of empirically validated psychological treatments: Report and recommendations. *The Clinical Psychologist*, *48*, 3–23.

Eckstein, H. (1975). Case study and theory in political science. In F. I. Greenstein & N. W. Polsby (Eds.), *Handbook of political science: Volume 7. Strategies of enquiry* (pp. 79–137). Reading, MA: Addison-Wesley.

Edwards, D. J. A. (1998). Types of case study work: A conceptual framework for case-based research. *Journal of Humanistic Psychology*, *38*(3), 36–70.

Edwards, D. J. A. (2007). Collaborative versus adversarial stances in scientific discourse: Implications for the role of systematic case studies in the development of evidence-based practice in psychotherapy. *Pragmatic Case Studies in Psychotherapy*, *3*(1), 6–34. Available at http://pcsp.libraries.rutgers.edu/. doi: http://dx.doi.org/10.14713/pcsp.v3i1.892

Elliott, R., Fischer, C. T., & Rennie, D. L. (1999). Evolving guidelines for publication of qualitative research studies in psychology and related fields. *British Journal of Clinical Psychology*, *38*, 215–229.

Elliott, R., Partyka, R., Alperin, R., Dobrenski, R., Wagner, J., Messer, S. B., Watson, J. C., & Castonguay, L. G. (2009). An adjudicated hermeneutic single-case efficacy design study of experiential therapy for panic/phobia. *Psychotherapy Research*, *19*, 543–557.

Fishman, D. B. (1999). *The case for pragmatic psychology.* New York, NY: NYU Press.

Fishman, D. B. (2005). Editor's introduction to PCSP—From single case to database: A new method for enhancing psychotherapy practice. *Pragmatic Case Studies in Psychotherapy*, *1*(1), 1–50. Available at http://pcsp.libraries.rutgers.edu/. doi: http://dx.doi.org/10.14713/pcsp.v1i1.855

Fishman, D. B. (2013). The pragmatic case study method for creating rigorous and systematic, practitioner-friendly research. *Pragmatic Case Studies in Psychotherapy*, *9*(4), 403–425. Available at http://pcsp.libraries.rutgers.edu/. doi: http://dx.doi.org/10.14713/pcsp.v9i4.1833

Flyvbjerg, B. (2006). Five misunderstandings about case study research. *Qualitative Inquiry*, *12*, 219–245. http://dx.doi.org/10.1177/1077800405284363

Giorgi, A. (1986). The "context of discovery/context of verification" distinction and descriptive human science. *Journal of Phenomenological Psychology*, *17*, 151–166.

Goldfried, M. R., Newman, M. G., Castonguay, L. G., Fuertes, J. N., Magnavita, J. J., Sobell, L., & Wolf, A. W. (2014). On the dissemination of clinical experiences in using empirically supported treatments. *Behavior Therapy*, *45*, 3–6.

Goodheart, C. D., Kazdin, A. E., & Sternberg, R. J. (Eds.). (2006). *Evidence-based psychotherapy: Where practice and research meet*. Washington, D.C.: American Psychological Association.

Hamburg, M. A., & Collins, R. S. (2010). The path to personalized medicine. *The New England Journal of Medicine*, *363*, 301–304. doi: 10.1056/NEJMp1006304

Hansen, N. B., Lambert, M. J., & Forman, E. M. (2002). The psychotherapy dose-response effect and its implications for treatment delivery services. *Clinical Psychology: Science and Practice*, *9*, 329–343.

Henggeler, S. W., Cunningham, P. B., Schoenwald, S. K., Borduin, C. M., & Rowland, M. D. (2009). *Multisystemic therapy for antisocial behavior in children and adolescents* (2nd ed.). New York, NY: Guilford.

Institute of Medicine. (2001). *Crossing the quality chasm: A new health system for the 21st century*. Washington, DC: National Academies Press.

Institute of Medicine (2009). *Initial national priorities for comparative effectiveness research*. Washington, D.C.: The National Academies Press. Available at http://www.nap.edu/catalog.php?record_id=12648

Jacobson, N. C., Newman, M. G., & Goldfried, M. R. (2016). Clinical feedback about empirically supported treatments for obsessive-compulsive disorder. *Behavior Therapy*, *47*, 75–90.

Kazdin, A. E. (1981). Drawing valid inferences from case studies. *Journal of Consulting and Clinical Psychology*, *49*, 183–192.

Klerman, G. L. (1983). The efficacy of psychotherapy as the basis for public policy. *American Psychologist*, *38*, 929–934.

Lambert, M. J. (2010). *Prevention of treatment failure: The use of measuring, monitoring, and feedback in clinical practice*. Washington, DC: American Psychological Association.

Lazarus, A. A. (1985). *Casebook of multimodal therapy*. New York, NY: Guilford.

Mahrer, A. R. (1988). Discovery-oriented psychotherapy research: Rationale and aims. *American Psychologist*, *43*, 694–702.

McLeod, J. M. (2010). *Case study research in counselling and psychotherapy*. London, UK: Sage.

Messer, S. B. (2007). Psychoanalytic case studies and the pragmatic case study method. *Pragmatic Case Studies in Psychotherapy*, *3*(1), 55–58. Available at http://pcsp.libraries.rutgers.edu/. doi: http://dx.doi.org/10.14713/pcsp.v3i1.894

Messer, S. B. (2011). Theory development via single cases: A case study of the therapeutic relationship in psychodynamic therapy. *Pragmatic Case Studies in Psychotherapy*, *7*(4), 440–448. Available at http://pcsp.libraries.rutgers.edu/. doi: http://dx.doi.org/10.14713/pcsp.v7i4.1112

Miller, R. B. (2004). *Facing human suffering: Psychology and psychotherapy as moral engagement*. Washington, D.C.: American Psychological Association.

Mitchell, J. C. (1983). Case and situation analysis. *Sociological Review*, *31*(2), 187–211.

Nathan., P. E., & Gorman, J. M. (2015). *A guide to treatments that work* (4th ed.). New York, NY: Oxford University Press.

Norcross, J. C. (Ed.) (2011). *Psychotherapy relationships that work: Evidence-based responsiveness* (2nd ed.). New York, NY: Oxford University Press.

Norcross, J. C., Beutler, L. E., & Levant, R. F. (2006). *Evidence-based practices in mental health: Debate and dialogue on the fundamental questions*. Washington, D.C.: American Psychological Association.

Norcross, J. C., & Wampold, B. E. (2011). Evidence-based therapy relationships: Research conclusions and clinical practices. In J. C. Norcross (Ed.), *Psychotherapy relationships that work: Evidence-based responsiveness* (2nd ed.), pp. 423–430. New York, NY: Oxford University Press.

Paul, G. L. (1967). Strategy of outcome research in psychotherapy. *Journal of Counseling Psychology*, *31*, 109–118.

Persons, J. B. (2008). *The case formulation approach in cognitive behavior therapy*. New York, NY: Guilford.

Persons, J. B., Bostrom, A., & Bertagnolli, A. (1999). Results of randomized controlled trials of cognitive therapy for depression generalize to private practice. *Cognitive Therapy and Research*, *23*, 535–548.

Peterson, D. R. (1991). Connection and disconnection of research and practice in the education of professional psychologists. *American Psychologist*, *40*, 441–451.

Popper, K. (1934/2002). *The logic of scientific discovery, 2nd ed.* New York: Routledge.

Rogers, C. R., & Dymond, R. F. (Eds.). (1954). *Psychotherapy and personality change*. Chicago, IL: University of Chicago Press.

Schon, D. A. (1983). *The reflective practitioner: How professionals think in action*. New York, NY: Basic Books.

Schwartz, D., & Lellouch, J. (1967). Explanatory and pragmatic attitudes in therapeutical trials. *Journal of Chronic Diseases*, *20*, 637–648.

Shapiro, M. B. (1970). Intensive assessment of the single case: An inductive-deductive approach. In P. Mittler (Ed.), *The psychological assessment of mental and physical handicaps* (pp. 645–666). London, UK: Methuen.

Stake, R. E. (1994). Case studies. In N. K. Denzin & Y. S. Lincoln (Eds.), *Handbook of qualitative research* (pp. 236–247). Thousand Oaks, CA: Sage.

Stewart, R. & Chambless, D. H. (2007). Does psychotherapy research inform treatment decisions in private practice? *Journal of Clinical Psychology*, *63*, 267–281.

Stiles, W. B. (2009). Logical operations in theory-building case studies. *Pragmatic Case Studies in Psychotherapy*, *5*(3), 9–22. Available at http://pcsp.libraries.rutgers.edu/ doi: http://dx.doi.org/10.14713/pcsp.v5i3.973

Stiles, W. B., Barkham, M., Connell, J., & Mellor-Clark, J. (2008). Responsive regulation of treatment duration in routine practice in United Kingdom primary care settings: Replication in a larger sample. *Journal of Consulting and Clinical Psychology*, *76*, 298–305.

Teddlie, C. B., & Tashakorrie, A. (2009). *Foundations of mixed methods research: Integrating quantitative and qualitative approaches in the social and behavioral sciences*. Thousand Oaks, CA: Sage.

Verhoef, M. J., Casebeer, A. L., & Hilsden, R. J. (2002). Assessing efficacy of complementary medicine: Adding qualitative research methods to the "gold standard." *The Journal of Alternative and Complementary Medicine*, *8*, 275–281. doi: 10.1089/10755530260127961.

Wampold, B. E. (2010). Foreword. In M. Barkham, G. E. Hardy, & J. Mellor-Clark (Eds.). *Developing and delivering practice-based evidence: A guide for the psychological therapies* (pp. xvii–xix). Oxford, England: Wiley-Blackwell.

Wennberg, J. E. (2010). *Tracking medicine: A researcher's quest to understand health care*. New York, NY: Oxford University Press.

Wolfe, B. E. (2012). Healing the research–practice split: Let's start with me. *Psychotherapy*, *49*, 101–108.

Zwarenstein, M.,Treweek, S., Gagnier, J. J., Altman, D. G., Tunis, S., Haynes, B., Gent, M., Oxman, A.D., & Moher, D. (2008). Improving the reporting of pragmatic trials: An extension of the CONSORT Statement. *British Medical Journal*, *337*, a2390. Available at http://bmj.com/cgi/content/full/337/nov11_2/a2390#BIBL

2
—

Navigating the Projects

DANIEL B. FISHMAN ∎

THE PROJECTS: CHAPTERS 3–6

In Chapters 3–6 the Cases With Trials (CWT) model is illustrated with four randomized clinical trial (RCT) projects: cognitive-behavioral therapy (CBT) for youth anxiety; interpersonal therapy (IPT) for preventing adolescent depression; psychoanalytic, transference-focused psychotherapy (TFP) for adult borderline personality disorder; and motivational interviewing for adult depression, respectively.

Table 2.1 shows various characteristics of the RCT components of the four chapters. Reflecting its methodological quality, each RCT component in the four studies was published in a peer-reviewed research journal, with the journal and year of publication listed in the first row. (Note that to capture the established format and standards for formally reporting RCT results, Chapters 3–6 employ the style and focus of the original RCT publications.)

As mentioned earlier and as shown in the second through fourth rows of Table 2.1, the four projects sample a diversity of theoretical orientations, clinical problem areas, and therapy modalities. The other rows also show how the four projects vary along a variety of dimensions, like client characteristics (e.g., differing percentages of minority individuals); lengths of therapy (from 3 to about 100 sessions); follow-up times (from none to 18 months); and research designs (e.g., experimental condition compared to waitlist, on one hand, and experimental condition compared to other evidence-based therapies, on the other). The diversity among the four projects shown in Table 2.1 allows for the examination of the connection between RCT and case study knowledge to be viewed across a range of clinical and research contexts.

The RCT Section of the Project Chapters

Contrasting with the diversity of the project content, a common set of headings is built into each project chapter, to provide a single conceptual framework that

Table 2.1 CHARACTERISTICS OF THE RANDOMIZED CONTROLLED TRIAL (RCT) STUDIES

Characteristic	Chapter 3 (Thastum et al.)	Chapter 4 (Kerner & Young)	Chapter 5 (Levy et al.)	Chapter 6 (Interian et al.)
Authors, journal, and year of original publication of the RCT study*	Arendt, Thastum, & Hougaard, *Acta Psychiatrica Scandinavica*, 2015	Young, Mufson, & Gallop, *Depression and Anxiety*, 2010	Clarkin, Levy, Lenzenweger, & Kernberg, *American Journal of Psychiatry*, 2007	Interian, Lewis-Fernández, Gara, & Escobar, *Depression and Anxiety*, 2013
Theoretical model	Cognitive-behavioral therapy (CBT)	Interpersonal psychotherapy (IPT)	Psychoanalytic, transference-focused psychotherapy (TFP)	Client-centered, motivational interviewing (MI); here called "motivational enhancement therapy for antidepressants" (META)
Clinical problem area addressed	Anxiety	Depression	Borderline personality disorder	Depression
Therapy modality	Group	Group	Individual	Individual
Case studies drawn from same RCT therapy group	No	Yes	Not applicable	Not applicable
Number of clients selected for case studies	2	2	2	3
Client age	Youth	Adolescent	Adult	Adult

(continued)

Table 2.1 CONTINUED

Characteristic	Chapter 3 (Thastum et al.)	Chapter 4 (Kerner & Young)	Chapter 5 (Levy et al.)	Chapter 6 (Interian et al.)
Client % female	57%	60%	92%	76%
Greater than 50% minority	No	Yes	No	Yes
Amount of therapy in the experimental condition (EC)	8 group sessions over 8 weeks	2 individual plus 8 group sessions over 10 weeks	Twice weekly individual sessions over 1 year (about 100 sessions)	2 sessions over 5 weeks, then a booster session within 5 months
Follow-up times after posttherapy assessment	3 months, 12 months	6 months, 12 months, 18 months	None	None
Experimental design	Experimental condition (EC) vs. waiting list: superiority trial	EC vs. treatment as usual (TAU): superiority trial	EC vs. a more empirically established therapy and vs. a theoretically contrasting therapy: both a noninferiority trial and a superiority trial, respectively	EC+TAU vs. TAU only: superiority trial
Total number randomized into conditions (number in experimental condition)	109 (56)	57 (36)	90 (31)	50 (26)

*In the book's text, we sometimes refer to the RCT by the authors of the book chapter in which the RCT is contained rather than by the authors of the separately published version of the RCT.

facilitates comparisons among them. These headings are outlined in Table 2.2, and are connected to Figure 2.1, described below. As seen, there are four sections to each project chapter: The RCT Study, The Case Studies, Synthesis, and Commentary. Each is described next.

The first section describes the RCT, and it follows the categories typically associated with the publication of an RCT study: Introduction, Method, Results, and Discussion.

Table 2.2 OUTLINE OF THE HEADINGS IN COMMON
FOR THE PROJECT CHAPTERS 3–6

Component in Figure 2.1	HEADING LEVEL 1	Heading Level 2	HEADING LEVEL 3
	THE RCT STUDY		
		Introduction	
		Method	
		Results	
		Discussion	
	THE CASE STUDIES*		
		The Nature and Rationale for Specific Cases Selected for the Case Studies	
A		The Clients	
B and C		Guiding Conception With Research	
		Positive-Outcome Client's Therapy: Assessment, Formulation, and Course	
D			ASSESSMENT OF THE POSITIVE-OUTCOME CLIENT'S PROBLEMS, GOALS, STRENGTHS, AND HISTORY

(continued)

Table 2.2 CONTINUED

Component in Figure 2.1	HEADING LEVEL 1	Heading Level 2	HEADING LEVEL 3
E			POSITIVE-OUTCOME CLIENT'S FORMULATION AND TREATMENT PLAN
F			POSITIVE-OUTCOME CLIENT'S COURSE OF THERAPY
		Negative-Outcome Client's Therapy: Assessment, Formulation, and Course	
D			ASSESSMENT OF THE NEGATIVE-OUTCOME CLIENT'S PROBLEMS, GOALS, STRENGTHS, AND HISTORY
E			NEGATIVE-OUTCOME CLIENT'S FORMULATION AND TREATMENT PLAN
F			NEGATIVE-OUTCOME CLIENTS'S COURSE OF THERAPY
G, H, I		Therapy Monitoring and Use of Feedback Information	
J, K, L		Concluding Evaluation of the Therapy Process and Outcome	

Table 2.2 CONTINUED

Component in Figure 2.1	HEADING LEVEL 1	Heading Level 2	HEADING LEVEL 3
	SYNTHESIS OF THE FINDINGS FROM THE RCT AND CASE STUDY APPROACHES		
	COMMENTARY		

'In the project chapters there are three exceptions in the format of the Case Studies sections in this outline. First, in Chapter 4 on interpersonal group therapy with adolescents, the term "therapy" is changed to "intervention," to emphasize the preventive nature of the project (see text). Second, cases are presented within sections, so that the headings then refer to:

- Assessment of a Positive-Outcome Client, and of a Negative-Outcome Client,
- Formulation, Goals, and Intervention Plan for the Two Clients, and
- Course of Intervention for the Two Clients.

Second, in Chapter 6, there is also a third, Mixed-Outcome client, whose headings parallel those of the Positive-Outcome and Negative-Outcome clients.

The Case Studies Section of the Project Chapters

PETERSON'S DISCIPLINED INQUIRY MODEL CREATES THE CONCEPTUAL FOUNDATION FOR THE CASE STUDIES

The second section describes the Case Studies, and they follow Schon's (1983) empirically derived model of best practice across a variety of professions, including psychotherapy, engineering, architecture, management, and town planning. Called "reflective practice," this model distinguishes between novice and expert practitioners. Novices follow the rules and procedures they were taught in their training in a cookbook-type manner, while experts rework these procedures to meet the unique nature of a particular applied situation. Thus, there is a type of dialogue between the expert's repertoire of cognitive understanding and his or her responsiveness to the environmental cues in the case at hand. Practitioners learn from each case situation, and over time part of their developing expertise comes from the database of cases and case situations that they remember and are then able to apply to new practice situations (see also Flyvbjerg, 2006, on this issue).

In further developing Schon's reflective practice model for psychotherapy practice, Peterson (1991) conceptualizes and labels therapy as "Disciplined Inquiry," as shown in Figure 2.1, as adapted by Fishman (2013). As can be seen, the Disciplined Inquiry model starts with a consideration of the *client* and his or her presenting problems (component A in the figure), as seen within the theoretical, *guiding conception* (component B) and related *experience and research* background (component C) that the practitioner brings to the case. The practitioner begins

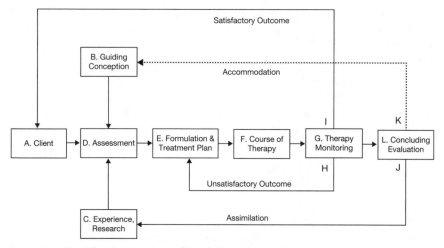

Figure 2.1 Best Therapy Practice as "Disciplined Inquiry."
Adapted by Fishman (2013) based on Peterson, 1991.

treatment with an individualized *assessment* (component D) of the client and his
or her problems. This includes the systematic gathering of qualitative and of normative, quantitative data to form the basis of an assessment. The individualized
assessment data are then conceptualized within the guiding conception, leading
to an *individualized formulation* (component E) for the case. The formulation is
a theory about the particular client based on the assessment, and as such it is an
individualized version of the guiding conception. The formulation is then used to
develop a *treatment plan* for the individual, which in turn leads to a *course of therapy* (component F). This clinical process is consistently subjected to *therapy monitoring* (component G), generating feedback loops. If the therapy is not proceeding
well, possible changes in the formulation and treatment plan might be required
(see component H); whereas if the case is going well and meeting the needs of
the client, arrangements for termination in consultation with the client might be
made (component I). If the *therapy monitoring* results in showing that the client
has been successful and/or the therapist and client agree that further therapy will
not be productive, therapy is terminated and a *concluding evaluation* (component
L) is conducted. This can yield feedback for either confirming—via *assimilation*—
the original *guiding conception* (component J), or revising that theory through
accommodation (component K). As shown in Table 2.2, the components A-L in
Figure 2.1 can be arrayed into a linear set of headings within each of the case studies in the 4 projects. To aid the reader in following the case study structure, the
fonts of the heading-level columns in Table 2.2 parallel those in the text.

Fishman (1999), Miller (2004), Dattilio et al. (2010), Stiles (2009), and others have presented epistemological rationales for the value of rigorous, systematic
case studies in the development of a scientific knowledge base in psychotherapy. Fishman (2005) has used the Disciplined Inquiry model in Figure 2.1—
and its associated headings in Table 2.2—as the conceptual foundation of a

peer-reviewed, online, open-access journal of case studies and case study method titled *Pragmatic Case Studies in Psychotherapy* (PCSP; pcsp.libraries.rutgers.edu). (Note that the term "pragmatic" emphasizes a focus in therapy case studies on connecting therapy process to outcome rather than to the development of clinical theory or technique per se.)

Three related ventures include (a) another peer-reviewed, online journal of therapy case studies titled *Clinical Case Studies* (Hersen, 2002), which uses heading categories generally parallel to those listed in Heading Level 2 of Table 2.2 and thus follows the Disciplined Inquiry model in a broad sense; (b) the St. Michael's College Clinical Case Study List (Miller, 2004), a critically collated collection that, as of 2004, included over 350 individual systematic case studies published in peer-reviewed psychotherapy journals after 1967 and more than 125 published psychotherapy casebooks (Miller, 2004); and (c) the Single Case Archive (Mattias et al., 2013; http://singlecasearchive.com), a database of over 440 published psychoanalytically oriented case studies drawn from journals whose quality is screened by their being included in the Institute of Scientific Information (ISI) journal list of the Thomson Publishing Company.

All four of these endeavors—the *PCSP* and the *Clinical Case Studies* journals, the St. Michael's List, and the Single Case Archive—have together generated over 1,200 scholarly publications of psychotherapy case studies. They all share the same goals: to establish rigorous criteria of quality in the case study method and to publish examples of case studies that exemplify this quality, in the process building a large, integrated database of systematic case studies in psychotherapy. This database is created on the logic that the larger the number of high-quality case studies, the greater the potential for developing generalizable knowledge through cross-case comparisons—what Iwakabe and Gazzola (2009) call "meta-synthesis," as a parallel to the meta-analysis of multiple RCT studies. This same logic applies specifically to the case studies presented in this book. Each of the four project chapters presents a good-outcome and a poor-outcome client. Based on the limitations of the contextual specificity of case studies, the editors recognize that two case studies are a type of "proof of concept," which is only the beginning of an ideal design process of creating many more case studies within each RCT and then comparing across case studies, both within each RCT and across RCTs.

THE HEADINGS IN THE CASE STUDIES SECTION

As mentioned above, the common headings for the case study section in each of the project chapters is presented in Table 2.2. Also shown in the Table is how the various common headings relate to each of the components in the Disciplined Inquiry model outlined in Figure 2.1. In other words, the structure of the case studies in Chapters 3–6 is designed to reflect the structure of the best practice, Disciplined Inquiry model in Figure 2.1.

Note that the second subsection, The Clients, provides a brief capsule of each of the clients involved. This material is somewhat redundant with the more expanded material in later subsections on Assessment of the client. However, the goal of the second subsection is to emphasize that the Disciplined Inquiry model starts with the client and his or her presenting problems (see Fig. 2.1), and to introduce the clients to the reader early on as a context for all that follows in the case study. Also note in Table 2.2 that all the projects present at least two case studies, a positive-outcome client and a negative-outcome client, both drawn from the experimental condition.

In Table 2.2, the positive-outcome client's assessment, formulation, and course of therapy is first presented, and this is followed by the negative-outcome client's assessment, formulation, and course of therapy. The advantage of this organization is that it presents a holistic picture of each client's therapy. On the other hand, there is one exception to this arrangement. In Chapter 4, on interpersonal group therapy, the two cases are presented by subsection, that is, first the assessment of both clients, then the formulation and treatment plan of both clients, and then the course of therapy for both clients. This type of organization was chosen because the two cases were both in the same group, and thus their presentation follows the process of the group.

One other exception to the outline in Table 2.1 is that in Chapter 6 on motivational enhancement therapy, a third, mixed-outcome client is also presented.

The Method in Each Case Study Section

In a typical systematic case study, the method employed to collect and analyze data is presented. Because each of the case studies in Chapters 3–6 used the same method, to avoid redundancy, we are presenting the method here.

In each project, all the therapy sessions were audio- or videotaped, and the same quantitative data were collected on every participant. In addition, the therapists in the RCT who conducted the therapy were carefully supervised by senior clinicians steeped in the theoretical model and clinical problem area involved. After all the data had been collected, the quantitative results were employed to choose a representative client with a positive outcome and one with a negative outcome (in the motivational interviewing project, a mixed-outcome client was also chosen). The tapes, clinical session notes, supervision session notes, and the quantitative data available for each of the clients were used as the basis for creating a case study on the selected clients. In some instances the therapist in the case was involved in reviewing and contributing to the case write-up, but in none was the therapist the primary writer of the case studies. In each instance, the authors of the project chapter and this book's editors were involved in critically reviewing the material presented in the case studies and in their interpretation.

A Note About the Length of Different Sections in the Project Chapters

The length of the RCT sections in the project chapters is about the same length or somewhat shorter than a journal-published RCT study. Because an RCT is a quantitative study, this can run in the range of 35 or so double-spaced manuscript pages because quantitative core material can typically be summarized very succinctly in a small number of statistical tables. On the other hand, the qualitative material in a systematic case study involves narrative text that requires a good deal more space to capture the concrete details of the case's background, therapy process, and outcome. Moreover, in a systematic case study the goal is to separate, to the extent possible, much of the descriptive assessment and therapy process material from formulations of it so that (a) what is primarily description can be differentiated from what is primarily interpretation; and (b) readers with other theoretical perspectives can make an argument for an alternative interpretation of the descriptive data. For these reasons, and based on my experience in editing systematic case studies in the *PCSP* journal, the case studies sections in each of the project chapters tend to be twice or more times as long as the RCT sections of the chapters.

The Synthesis Section of the Project Chapters

The Synthesis section focuses on how the knowledge set forth in the RCT and Case Studies sections relates to and complements each other, from the perspectives of theory development, empirical research methodology, and clinical practice improvement.

The Commentary Section of the Project Chapters

Each chapter has a Commentary written by an outside expert (and in one instance, the expert's team) who specializes in the clinical topic area. Like the Synthesis section, each Commentary focuses on the implications of the project chapter's RCT and Case Studies knowledge from a variety of perspectives. Commentators were not constrained to a particular format, in order to encourage a wide variety of viewpoints on the project chapters.

REFLECTIONS AND NEXT STEPS: CHAPTERS 7 AND 8

Chapter 7 presents an outside commentary on the four project chapters as a whole by the RCT researcher Jacques Barber and his research team. Finally, Chapter 8 by the editors discusses the themes and "lessons learned" from the four project chapters and the commentaries.

REFERENCES

Dattilio, F. M., Edwards, D. J. A., & Fishman, D. B. (2010). Case studies within a mixed methods paradigm: Towards a resolution of the alienation between researcher and practitioner in psychotherapy research. *Psychotherapy Theory, Research, Practice, Training Practice, Training, 47*, 427–441.

Desmet, M., Meganck, R., Seybert, C., Willemsen, J., Geerardyn, F., Declercq, F., Inslegers, R., Trenson, E., Vanheule, S., Kirschner, L., Schindler, I., & Kächele, H.

(2013). Psychoanalytic single cases published in ISI-ranked journals: The construction of an online archive. *Psychotherapy and Psychosomatics, 82,* 120–121. http://dx.doi.org/10.1159/000342019

Fishman, D. B. (1999). The case for pragmatic psychology. New York, NY: NYU Press.

Fishman, D. B. (2005). Editor's introduction to PCSP—From single case to database: A new method for enhancing psychotherapy practice. *Pragmatic Case Studies in Psychotherapy, 1*(1), 1–50. Available at http://pcsp.libraries.rutgers.edu/. doi: http://dx.doi.org/10.14713/pcsp.v1i1.855

Fishman, D. B. (2013). The pragmatic case study method for creating rigorous and systematic, practitioner-friendly research, *Pragmatic Case Studies in Psychotherapy, 9*(4), 403–425. Available at http://pcsp.libraries.rutgers.edu/. doi: http://dx.doi.org/10.14713/pcsp.v9i4.1833

Flyvbjerg, B. (2006). Five misunderstandings about case study research. *Qualitative Inquiry, 12,* 219–245. http://dx.doi.org/10.1177/1077800405284363

Hersen, M. (2002). Rationale for clinical case studies: An editorial. *Clinical Case Studies, 1,* 3–5.

Iwakabe, S. & Gazzola, N. (2009). From single case studies to practice-based knowledge: Aggregating and synthesizing case studies. *Psychotherapy Research, 19,* 601–611.

Miller, R. B. (2004). *Facing human suffering: Psychology and psychotherapy as moral engagement.* Washington, D.C.: American Psychological Association.

Peterson, D. R. (1991). Connection and disconnection of research and practice in the education of professional psychologists. *American Psychologist, 40,* 441–451.

Schon, D. A. (1983). The reflective practitioner: How professionals think in action. New York, NY: Basic Books.

Stiles, W. B. (2009). Logical operations in theory-building case studies. *Pragmatic Case Studies in Psychotherapy, 5*(3), 9–22. Available at http://pcsp.libraries.rutgers.edu/. doi: http://dx.doi.org/10.14713/pcsp.v5i3.973

PART II

The Projects

The next four chapters—varying across dimensions such as theoretical orientation and type of mental disorder—illustrate the Cases Within Trials (CWT) method. To facilitate comparison across projects, each is organized in three main sections, including findings gained from the RCT, findings gained from the case studies, and a synthesis of the two types of knowledge. Each project concludes with a commentary by an outside expert (or expert team) in the theoretical and disorder focus of the project.

"Cool Kids/Chilled Adolescents"

Cognitive-Behavioral Therapy for Youth With Anxiety Disorders in Denmark

MIKAEL THASTUM, IRENE LUNDKVIST-HOUNDOUMADI,
KRISTIAN BECH ARENDT, SILKE STJERNEKLAR,
AND DANIEL B. FISHMAN ∎

Commentary by Lauren J. Hoffman,
Elaina A. Zendegui, and Brian C. Chu

THE RCT STUDY

Introduction

Anxiety disorders are debilitating conditions, which recent research has shown to be extremely common among children and adolescents (henceforth referred to as "youths," unless age differences specifically are considered). A recent epidemiological meta-analysis by Costello, Egger, Copeland, Erkanli, and Angold (2011) estimated their prevalence to be 12.3% for children (ages 6–12 years) and 11.0% for adolescents (ages 13–18 years).

Without treatment, anxiety disorders among youth often take a chronic course and may lead to additional problems (Keller et al., 1992). Anxiety disorders in youth have been associated with social and academic impairment (Essau, Conradt, & Petermann, 2000), as well as increased risk of developing substance abuse (Costello, Mustillo, Erkanli, Keeler, & Angold, 2003), depression (Roza, Hofstra, van der Ende, & Verhulst, 2003), and other anxiety disorders (Pine, Cohen, Gurley, Brook, & Ma, 1998). It is for this reason that considerable efforts have been invested toward developing and evaluating psychotherapeutic interventions for childhood anxiety disorders over the past two decades. Cognitive-behavioral therapy (CBT) is the most studied psychotherapy for youth with anxiety disorders, and the past two decades have witnessed an increasing number of studies in this area. Two recent meta-analyses identified 48 (Reynolds, Wilson, Austin,

& Hooper, 2012) and 41 (James, James, Cowdrey, Soler, & Choke, 2013) randomized controlled trials of CBT for youth anxiety, and they concluded that CBT
is an efficacious intervention for youth anxiety disorders. However, independent
replications of specific CBT protocols are still warranted, particularly in cultures
different from those in which they were developed, and this is the focus of the
present RCT study.

Specifically, one CBT treatment for youth anxiety, called the "Cool Kids/
Chilled Adolescents" (CK/CA) program and structured in group format, was
developed and shown to be efficacious in Australia by Rapee and associates
(Hudson et al., 2009; Rapee, 2000, 2003; Rapee, Abbott, & Lyneham, 2006).
The aim of the present study was to evaluate the efficacy of a Danish version
of the CK/CA programs for youth anxiety disorders. While this version had
demonstrated promising results in previous systematic case studies (Lundkvist-
Houndoumadi & Thastum, 2013a, 2013b), this is the first independent RCT
evaluation of the programs by researchers other than its developers in Australia,
and the first RCT evaluation of a CBT protocol for youth anxiety disorders in
Denmark.

Method

For a more in-depth description of the method and results than is presented
below, see Arendt, Thastum, and Hougaard (2015).

PARTICIPANTS
Participants were 109 youth with anxiety disorders, recruited from the training and research clinic for youth with anxiety disorders at the Department of
Psychology, Aarhus University, Denmark ("the University Clinic"), in the period
from January 2011 to April 2012. The youth were between the ages of 7–16 years
($M = 11.78$, $SD = 2.74$), with 62 (57%) girls and 47 (43%) boys. The inclusion
criterion was an anxiety disorder as the primary diagnosis. Exclusion criteria
were psychosis, untreated attention-deficit/hyperactivity disorder (ADHD),
intellectual disability, and severe behavior disorders. Participants were diagnosed
according to the *Diagnostic Statistical Manual of Mental Disorders*, 4th edition
(*DSM-IV*; American Psychiatric Association, 1994) with the "ADIS-IC, C/P" (see
later). Youth fulfilling the enrollment criteria were randomly allocated into either
a treatment or a wait-list control condition. Table 3.1 shows demographic information in the two conditions.

ASSESSMENTS
Three primary (1–3, described here) and six secondary assessment measures
(4–9) were administered to the Treatment and Waiting List groups. Measures
1–8 were administered pre and post therapy and at 3-month follow-up. In addition, measures 2–4 were administered at 12-month follow-up. As part of another

Table 3.1 Demographic and Diagnostic Characteristics

	GCBT (*n* = 56)	Wait-List (*n* = 53)
Youth mean age in years	11.82 (2.49 SD)	11.73 (2.47 SD)
Females	31 (55.5%)	31 (58.5%)
Living with two parents	47 (83.9%)	42 (79.2%)
On psychopharmacological medication	5 (8.9%)	4 (7.5%)
HIGHEST COMPLETED EDUCATION OF MOTHERS/FATHERS		
Further and higher education	48/31 (85.7%/56.4%)	37/24 (69.9%/47.1%)
Vocational education	5/22 (8.9%/40.0%)	8/22 (15.1%/43.1%)
Elementary- or high-school equivalent	3/2 (5.4%/3.6%)	8/5 (15.0%/9.8%)
PRIMARY DIAGNOSIS		
SAD	16 (28.7%)	20 (37.7%)
GAD	14 (25.0%)	12 (22.6%)
SoP	7 (12.5%)	10 (18.9%)
SP	11 (19.6%)	5 (9.4%)
OCD	4 (7.1%)	4 (7.6%)
PD with AP	0 (0.0%)	1 (1.9%)
AP without PD	4 (7.1%)	1 (1.9%)
COMORBID DIAGNOSES		
Anxiety disorders	42 (75.0%)	35 (66.0%)
No comorbidity	7 (12.5%)	10 (18.9%)
Externalizing disorders	6 (10.7%)	7 (13.2%)
Mood disorder	4 (7.1%)	6 (11.3%)
Other	3[a] (5.4%)	4[b] (7.5%)
Mean number of anxiety disorders per youth	2.73	2.66

AP, agoraphobia; CSR, Clinician Severity Rating (ADIS C/P-IV). a: 1 enuresis, 1 sleep terror disorder, 1 selective mutism; b: 3 sleep terror disorder, 1 enuresis; GAD, generalized anxiety disorder; GCBT, group cognitive-behavioral treatment; OCD, obsessive-compulsive disorder; PD, panic disorder; SAD, separation anxiety disorder; SoP, social phobia; SP, specific phobia.

study, youth who had not responded to treatment at the 3-month follow-up were offered further individualized treatment. Consequently, nonresponding participants were excluded from the 12-month follow-up. Finally, measure 9, consumer satisfaction, was administered only post treatment. Figure 3.1 illustrates the flow of participants through the study.

1. *The Anxiety Disorder Interview Schedule for DSM-IV, Parent and Child Versions (ADIS-IV C/P; Albano & Silverman, 1996).* This semistructured interview assesses youth anxiety disorders according to *DSM-IV* criteria, based on information from separate interviews with the youth and the youth's parents. It also allows for evaluations of other disorders often associated with anxiety,

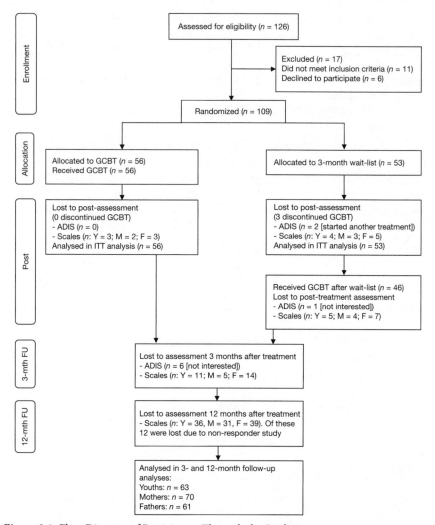

Figure 3.1 Flow Diagram of Participants Through the Study.
Note. GCBT = group cognitive-behavioral treatment; ITT = intention to treat;
F/U = follow-up; ADIS = Anxiety Disorder Interview Schedule for DSM-IV;
Y = youth scale; M = mother scale; F = father scale.

including affective and disruptive behavior disorders. A *Clinician Severity Rating* (CSR) is given, ranging from 0 (no interference) to 8 (extreme interference). A CSR of 4 or above indicates a disorder, while a CSR of less than 4 is considered subclinical. Separate CSRs are made by youth, parents, and clinician. The clinician CSR is based on the parents' and youth's ratings and clinical judgment. Only the clinicians CSRs are reported here. The most impairing, clinician-provided ADIS-IV diagnosis was considered the primary anxiety diagnosis. Diagnostic interviews were conducted by psychologists or graduate students trained in the use of ADIS-IV C/P.

ADIS-IV C/P has demonstrated good to excellent test-retest reliability over 7–14 days for the presence of specific diagnoses and the CSR (Silverman, Saavedra, & Pina, 2001), as well as strong concurrent validity (Wood, Piacentini, Bergman, McCracken, & Barrios, 2002). In the present study, an interrater reliability check was conducted by letting two trained assessors watch and rate 22 (20.2%) of the video-recorded baseline interviews. The interrater reliability (Cohen's Kappa) for the primary anxiety diagnosis was 0.77. The intraclass coefficient for the CSR of the primary anxiety diagnosis was .69.

2. *The Spence Children's Anxiety Scale (SCAS).* This measure is a self-report rating scale for youth to assess their anxiety symptoms (Spence, 1997). It consists of 44 items (including six positive filler items) rated from 0 (never) to 3 (always). The scale consists of six subscales for specific anxiety diagnoses: social phobia (SoP), panic disorder (PD) and agoraphobia (AP), generalized anxiety disorder (GAD), obsessive–compulsive disorder (OCD), separation anxiety disorder (SAD), and specific phobias (SP [e.g., fear of physical injury]). The scale yields subscale scores and a full scale score. The Danish translation of the SCAS has demonstrated good psychometric properties in a Danish sample (Arendt, Hougaard, & Thastum, 2014). Internal consistency for the total scale in the current sample was excellent ($\alpha = .90$).

3. *The Spence Children's Anxiety Scale—Parent Version (SCAS-P).* This measure contains the same items as the youth version (without the six filler items) and is scored in the same fashion (Nauta et al., 2004). The Danish translation of SCAS-P has demonstrated good psychometric properties in a Danish sample (Arendt, Hougaard, & Thastum, 2014). Internal consistency for the total scale in the current sample was excellent for both the mother report (SCAS-Pm; $\alpha = .89$) and the father report (SCAS-Pf; $\alpha = .87$).

4. *The Child Anxiety Life Interference Scale (CALIS)* assesses life interference and impairment associated with youth anxiety (e.g., school, leisure time, and getting along with friends and family), rated by both the youth (9 items) and the parents (9 items) (Lyneham et al., 2013). Parents also rate interference with their own life (e.g., career; stress; and relationship with spouse, friends, and family) attributed to the youth's anxiety (seven items). All items are rated on 5-point Likert scales from 0 (not at all) to 4 (a great deal). CALIS consists of subscales measuring interference with the youth's life at home and outside of home, but in the current study they were combined into a single measure of overall interference. The scale has demonstrated satisfactory internal consistency on subscales for both the youth and parent ratings (α range = .70–.90), and moderate stability for a 2-month retest period (r range = .62–.91; Lyneham et al., 2013). In the current study, Cronbach's α was .81 for youth-reported, and .83 for both mother- and father-reported overall interference with the youth's life. Internal consistency for interference on parent life was .87 for mothers and .89 for fathers.

5. *The Short Version of Mood and Feelings Questionnaire (S-MFQ)* consists of 13 items rated from 0 (not true) to 2 (true) to assess child and adolescent depressive symptoms within the last 2 weeks, as rated by both the youth and the parents (Angold et al., 1995). The S-MFQ has shown good internal consistency in the youth self-report ($\alpha = .85$) and the parent-report ($\alpha = .87$) (Angold et al., 1995).

In the current study, internal consistency was excellent (youth version, α = .89; mother-report, α = .88; father-report, α = .88).

6. *The Beck Youth Inventories of Emotional and Social Impairment, Self-Concept Scale (BYI-S)*. The Beck Youth Inventories (BYI) is a youth self-report inventory consisting of five separate scales for anxiety, depression, anger, disruptive behavior, and self-concept (Beck, Beck, & Jolly, 2001). Each scale consists of 20 items rated from 0 (never) to 3 (always) on how well they describe the youth. In the current study, only the scale for self-concept (BYI-S) was used. BYI-S assesses the youth's self-perceived competences and self-worth. The Danish translation of BYI has demonstrated good internal consistency (α = .87–.89) for BYI-S (Thastum, Ravn, Sommer, & Trillingsgaard, 2009). In the current study, Cohen's α was .93.

7. *The Clinical Global Impression-Improvement of Anxiety Scale (CGI-I) (Guy, 1976)*. This is a single rating (1–7) of the youth's present condition in comparison to his or her condition prior to the initiation of treatment. It is based on all of the quantitative and qualitative information available concerning behaviors, symptoms, and functioning in all aspects of the youth's life. Youth scoring 1 (very much improved) or 2 (much improved) were considered as *responders* in the present study, and those with scores of 3 and above as *nonresponders* (3 = minimally improved with little or no clinically meaningful reduction of symptoms and little change in clinical status and functional capacity; 4 = no change; and 5–7 = worse in increasing degrees).

8. *Children's Global Assessment Scale (CGAS; Shaffer et al., 1983)*. An adaptation of the DSM Global Assessment Scale for adults, the CGAS is a measure of overall severity of disturbance. It is a rating of 1 to 100 made by a clinician independent of specific mental health diagnoses. CGAS ratings were used as a summary source of clinical functioning in the youth in the present research and will be referred to in the case studies of Lisa and Marius that follow. In the clinician's rating of the CGAS, all available quantitative and qualitative data were used. The rating categories that are relevant for the present study include the following: 91–100, superior functioning; 81–90, good functioning in all areas; 71–80, no more than slight impairments in functioning; 61–70, some difficulty in a single area but generally functioning well; 51–60, variable functioning with sporadic difficulties or symptoms in several but not all social areas; and ratings 50 and below reflecting more disturbed functioning. Scores above 70 on the CGAS are designated as indicating normal function.

9. *Experience of Service Questionnaire (ESQ)*. An ESQ for youth (ESQ-C) and for parents (ESQ-P) was constructed to measure satisfaction with treatment (Attride-Stirling, 2002). The ESQ-C consists of 7 items and the ESQ-P of 10 items, with both rated 1 ("Certainly True"), 2 ("Partly True"), and 3 ("Not True"); and with three free-text sections inquiring into what the respondent liked about the service, what he or she felt needed improving, and any other comments.

CASE-FINDING PROCEDURES

All families referred themselves to the University Clinic in response to the Clinic's webpage, newspaper advertisements, or recommendations from local community health services. Families were required to send an e-mail or a letter to the Clinic describing the youth's anxiety symptoms and problems, and relevant families were invited to the Clinic for an initial diagnostic assessment, consisting of the ADIS-IV-C/P. Electronically administrated rating scales were sent by e-mail to the families to complete prior to their appearance at the clinic.

INTERVENTIONS

Two manualized CBT programs were employed in the present randomized clinical trial: the *Cool Kids* (CK) program, for ages 6–12, and the corresponding *Chilled Adolescents* (CA) program adapted for ages 13–18, mentioned earlier (hereafter called the "CK/CA" programs when referred to together.) Like other CBT programs such as the Coping Cat (Kendall, 1990) and Friends for life (Barratt, 2004), the CK/CA programs are transdiagnostic, addressing youth with all types of anxiety disorders. The rationale behind this is that because of the high degree of comorbidity among anxiety disorders (Rapee, Schniering, & Hudson, 2009), transdiagnostic anxiety programs improve the programs' effectiveness and applicability. The potential advantages of a group program are the addition of group processes among youth and their parents to facilitate change and the possibility of more cost-effectiveness over an individual therapy program.

CK and CA each has a separate workbook adapted to the respective ages for which it is targeted, and these were translated in Danish and handed out at the first session. The workbooks outlined the theme for each session and assignments to be carried out in and between sessions.

The CBT components of both programs are the same. First, there is a focus on teaching children and adolescents to recognize their emotions like fear, stress, and anxiety. Second, it helps youth to challenge beliefs associated with feeling anxious and to generate alternative, more realistic thoughts via cognitive restructuring (*detective thinking*). Third, it encourages youth to gradually engage with feared activities in more positive ways; exposure to anxiety-provoking situations is gradually achieved through the joint creation of *stepladders* with the youth and parents. Fourth, the youth are offered *social skills training, problem solving,* and *worry surfing,* which aim at building tolerance to the anxious feelings and helping the youth to refocus attention on everyday activities so as to prevent worries from interfering in the day-to-day functioning. Finally, there is an additional component for parents that informs them of the treatment principles and teaches them alternate ways of interacting with their youth.

The CK/CA programs include a relatively high degree of parental involvement, as both parents are prompted to participate in every session, during which 45–60 minutes are dedicated to parental psychoeducation.

In the present trial the treatment consisted of 10 two-hour weekly group sessions with six to seven youth and their parents in each group. There was a mean of 74.44 (SD = 7.44) days between the first and the last session. The mean number of sessions attended by youth, mother, and father were 9.25 (SD = 0.84), 8.82 (SD = 1.64), and 7.45 (SD = 3.01), respectively. In most cases (91.07%), both parents participated in the treatment.

The in-vivo exposure assignments, suggested in the CK/CA manual at session 8, took place at a local shopping mall. Three months after the end of treatment, participants were offered a 1-hour booster group session.

Each group was led by one of two psychologists who were trained and supervised in the use of the CK/CA program by the first author, who had considerable experience with the program having trained with Australian developers of the program. The role of the therapist is to coach and teach youth and their parents about issues related to anxiety and coping skills through role playing, therapist modeling, working through hypothetical examples provided in the workbook, games, in vivo exposure, and interactive discussions. The importance of the work that the family does between sessions is also stressed.

In addition, three students participated in each group, assisting the youth and/ or parents during the in-session assignments. The students were part of a graduate clinical psychology training program at the University Clinic, where they learned about the theories behind CBT. They received weekly group supervision for their participation in the treatment program.

The control condition was a 3-month wait-list. All participants in the wait-list condition were offered treatment after the waiting period and 46 (86.79%) accepted, of which 42 (79.25%) completed the treatment. All participants in both conditions were encouraged not to engage in other forms of treatment or change their medication during the treatment or wait-list period. At postassessment, three participants in the treatment condition and two participants in the wait-list condition had reduced or stopped their use of psychopharmacological medication.

Statistical Analysis

All pre-post comparisons between conditions were based on intention to treat (ITT) analyses using the *last observation carried forward* approach (which means that for each individual, missing values were replaced by the last observed value of that variable). Analyses assessing stability of outcome from posttreatment to follow-up were conducted only on data from those who completed the questionnaires. A last-observation-carried-forward approach may overestimate the stability of treatment gains due to a likely higher dropout rate among relapsing participants. All follow-up analyses were conducted on the pooled data from participants in the CBT condition and the wait-list condition (after they had received treatment). Such an approach is viewed as acceptable, since there were neither significant differences on outcome measures between the two conditions at posttreatment, nor interaction effects in the follow-up period.

Results

Baseline Comparisons (Table 3.1)

Table 3.1 presents the means and standard deviations of the CBT and the wait-list groups on demographic and diagnostic characteristics at baseline; and Table 3.2

Table 3.2 Pre- and Post-Measures of Outcome for Treatment and Wait-List Conditions

		Pre-*M* (*SD*)	Post-*M* (*SD*)	Time-by-Condition Effect	Pre to Post Effect Size*
ADIS CSR primary diagnosis	CBT	6.09 (1.07)	2.16 (2.59)	$F(1, 107) = 57.49, p < .001,$ $\eta_p^2 = 0.35$	$p < .001, d = 1.98$
	WL	6.25 (1.14)	5.45 (1.90)		$p = .004, d = 0.40$
ADIS CSR all diagnoses	CBT	12.54 (5.99)	5.21 (5.19)	$F(1, 107) = 29.46, p < .001,$ $\eta_p^2 = 0.22$	$p < .001, d = 1.31$
	WL	12.55 (6.16)	10.75 (5.63)		$p = .018, d = 0.31$
SCAS youth	CBT	39.16 (18.06)	21.57 (14.42)	$F(1, 107) = 22.76, p < .001,$ $\eta_p^2 = 0.18$	$p < .001, d = 1.08$
	WL	39.19 (15.00)	32.55 (15.64)		$p < .001, d = 0.43$
SCAS-P mother	CBT	39.79 (16.97)	22.25 (12.59)	$F(1, 107) = 34.13, p < .001,$ $\eta_p^2 = 0.24$	$p < .001, d = 1.17$
	WL	40.11 (13.63)	37.04 (16.95)		$p = .058, d = 0.20$
SCAS-P father	CBT	37.15 (13.80)	23.56 (13.87)	$F(1, 104) = 23.65, p < .001,$ $\eta_p^2 = 0.19$	$p < .001, d = 0.98$
	WL	34.92 (14.45)	32.63 (16.17)		$p = .099, d = 0.15$
CALIS youth	CBT	11.89 (7.35)	7.55 (6.46)	$F(1, 107) = 7.23, p = .008,$ $\eta_p^2 = 0.06$	$p < .001, d = 0.63$
	WL	12.09 (6.88)	10.94 (7.20)		$p = .153, d = 0.16$
CALIS mother	CBT	17.79 (7.19)	10.61 (7.28)	$F(1, 107) = 17.25, p < .001,$ $\eta_p^2 = 0.14$	$p < .001, d = 0.99$
	WL	19.92 (7.75)	17.94 (9.07)		$p = .041, d = 0.23$
CALIS father	CBT	16.05 (6.84)	10.96 (7.72)	$F(1, 104) = 12.45, p < .001,$ $\eta_p^2 = 0.11$	$p < .001, d = 0.70$
	WL	18.35 (7.52)	17.14 (9.16)		$p = .116, d = 0.14$
CALIS-P mother	CBT	11.07 (6.91)	6.82 (6.28)	$F(1, 107) = 9.24, p = .003,$ $\eta_p^2 = 0.08$	$p < .001, d = 0.64$
	WL	12.13 (6.19)	11.21 (6.58)		$p = .251, d = 0.14$

(*continued*)

Table 3.2 Continued

		Pre-M (SD)	Post-M (SD)	Time-by-Condition Effect	Pre to Post Effect Size*
CALIS-P father	CBT	7.85 (6.09)	5.71 (5.46)	$F(1, 104) = 44.39, p = .029,$	$p < .001, d = 0.37$
	WL	9.12 (5.69)	8.80 (6.16)	$\eta_p^2 = 0.05$	$p = .632, d = 0.05$
S-MFQ youth	CBT	6.51 (6.02)	2.96 (3.84)	$F(1, 106) = 5.57, p = .020,$	$p < .001, d = 0.70$
	WL	6.66 (5.00)	5.19 (5.32)	$\eta_p^2 = 0.05$	$p = .012, d = 0.28$
S-MFQ mother	CBT	5.88 (4.96)	3.34 (3.78)	$F(1, 107) = 4.15, p = .044,$	$p < .001, d = 0.56$
	WL	6.70 (5.22)	5.79 (5.51)	$\eta_p^2 = 0.04$	$p = .110, d = 0.17$
S-MFQ father	CBT	5.05 (4.50)	2.85 (4.03)	$F(1, 104) = 3.82, p = .053,$	$p < .001, d = 0.52$
	WL	6.33 (4.88)	5.73 (5.92)	$\eta_p^2 = 0.04$	$p = .316, d = 0.11$
BYI-S youth	CBT	40.09 (10.77)	44.33 (9.01)	$F(1, 106) = 5.13, p = .026,$	$p < .001, d = 0.43$
	WL	37.60 (10.14)	38.75 (10.86)	$\eta_p^2 = 0.05$	$p = .180, d = 0.11$

*Positive effect sizes indicate improvement.

ADIS, Anxiety Disorder Interview Schedule for *DSM-IV*; BYI-S, Becks Youth Inventory (self-concept subscale); CALIS, Child Anxiety Life Interference Scale; CALIS-P, Child Anxiety Life Interference Scale—interference on parent life; CBT, cognitive-behavioral therapy; CSR, Clinician Severity Rating (ADIS); $\eta_p^2 =$ partial eta squared; SCAS, Spence Children's Anxiety Scale; S-MFQ, Mood and Feelings Questionnaire (short version); WL, wait-list condition.

presents similar statistics for the continuous outcome measures at baseline. No significant differences between groups were found in any of these measures at baseline.

ANALYSES OF VARIANCE OF OUTCOME VARIABLES BY TREATMENT CONDITION AND TIME (TABLE 3.2)

Table 3.2 also shows analyses of variance (ANOVA) for each of the outcome variables in terms of the condition (treatment versus wait-list) by time (pretreatment versus posttreatment) effect. If the F value is significant, it means that the change from pretreatment to posttreatment significantly differs between the treatment and wait-list groups. The partial η^2 value is a measure for the effect size for use in ANOVA. As a general rule, values of 0.009–0.04 indicates small effect sizes, 0.05–0.13 medium, and 0.14 and above large effect sizes (Cohen, 1990). In the last column, the effect size (d) of the paired samples t-tests for the pre-post treatment for both the treatment and the wait-list condition are found (in general, values of 0.2–0.5 indicate small effect sizes, 0.5–0.8 medium, and 0.8 and above, large effect sizes; Cohen, 1990).

As can be seen in Table 3.2, youths in the treatment condition had significantly greater improvement compared with the wait-list condition across all raters on the primary outcome measures (ADIS CSR and SCAS), as well as on the secondary outcome measures of depression (S-MFQ), life interference (CALIS), and self-concept (BYI-S).

ADIS RESULTS

At posttreatment, significantly more youths (37 [66.1%]) in the intervention condition were free of their primary diagnosis, compared with youths (4 [7.5%]) in the wait-list condition, with a χ^2 (1) = 39.74, $p < 0.001$. Also, significantly more youths (27 [48.2%]) in the intervention condition were free of all anxiety diagnoses, compared with youths (3 [5.7%]) in the wait-list condition, χ^2 (1) = 24.72, $p < 0.001$.

CLINICAL AND STATISTICALLY SIGNIFICANT CHANGE ON SCAS/SCAS-P FROM PRE TO POST FOR THE TREATMENT VERSUS WAIT-LIST CONDITIONS (TABLE 3.3)

Table 3.3 shows clinical changes over time on the SCAS ratings by the youth, mother, and father data, using Jacobson and Truax's (1991) Reliable Change Index method. In the analysis, we employed Danish community and clinical norms split into gender and age groups (7–12 and 13–17 years) (Arendt et al., 2014). Four types of change are shown in Table 3.3, as described in the table note. As shown, in all the change categories the treatment group had considerably higher percentages of success. For example, on the most rigorous indicator—"Clinically Significant Change"—42.9%, 51.8%, and 41.8% of the treatment met this criterion in terms of the youth, mother, and father ratings, respectively, while the parallel ratings for the Waiting List group were 11.3%, 11.3%, and 9.8%, respectively. A chi-square analysis of each of these three sets of differences was statistically significant at the .001 level.

Table 3.3 Reliable (Statistically Significant) and Clinically Significant Change on SCAS/SCAS-P from Pre to Post in Treatment Group Versus Wait-List Group

	Child		Mother		Father	
	Treatment $n = 56$	Wait-List $n = 53$	Treatment $n = 56$	Wait-List $n = 53$	Treatment $n = 55$	Wait-List $n = 51$
[a]Unchanged	33.9%	64.1%	48.2%	75. 5%	41.8%	74.5%
[b]Reliable deterioration	0%	5.7%	0%	13.2%	3.6%	5.9%
[c]Reliable improvement	66.1%	30.2%	51.8%	11.3%	54.6%	19.6%
[d]Clinically significant change	42.9%	11.3%	51.8%	11.3%	41.8%	9.8%

[a]"Unchanged," no change in status regarding the clinical cutoff point and no statistically significant change.

[b]"Reliable deterioration," statistically significant worsening of symptoms.

[c]"Reliable improvement," statistically significant improvement of symptoms.

[d]"Clinically significant change," above clinical cutoff at pre and below at post, and reached reliable improvement.

Treatment Satisfaction

Both youth and parents were highly satisfied with the treatment. For example, 79.6% of the youth agreed that the treatment helped them, and only 5.4% disagreed; 81.7% would recommend the treatment to a friend with similar problems; and 86% trusted the therapist. Among parents, 72.9% of the mothers and 69.6% of the fathers agreed that the treatment helped their youth, and only 2% disagreed. Seventy-five percent of mothers and 53.3% of fathers agreed that they were able to change their behavior toward their youth in a positive way during treatment; and 96.9% of mothers and 89.1% of fathers trusted the therapist. In the comments on what could be improved in the program, one of the most frequent was that the program was too short or that there was too little time between sessions, reported by 40 (36%) of the mothers and 21 (19%) of the fathers.

Diagnosis-Specific Results

For each of the different primary diagnoses in the pooled sample, the number of youths free of their primary diagnosis at posttreatment (in terms of an intent-to-treat analysis) were as follows: SAD = 20 (62.5%), GAD = 20 (87.0%), SoP = 5 (29.4%), SP = 11 (68.8%), OCD = 5 (62.5%), PD with AP 1 (100%), and AP without PD 3 (60.0%). A chi-squared test with four groups (i.e., ignoring the three small diagnostic groups of OCD, PD with AP, and AP without PD) revealed that there was a significant association between the type of primary diagnosis at pretreatment and whether or not participants were free of their primary diagnosis at posttreatment, χ^2 (3) = 14.21, p = .003. Comparing SoP with all other primary diagnoses merged together revealed that participants with a primary SoP diagnosis were significantly less likely to be free of their primary diagnosis at posttreatment than youths with any other primary diagnosis, χ^2 (1) = 10.39, p < .001.

Post-hoc ANOVA revealed that there was significant difference in mean age between different primary diagnoses F (6, 95) = 7.38, p < .001, partial η^2 = 0.32, with social phobic youth being significantly older (M = 13.96, SD = 1.55) than youths with SAD (M = 10.46, SD = 1.76) and GAD (M = 11.56, SD = 2.14). Youths with primary social phobia were also significantly more likely to have a comorbid affective disorder (47.1%) compared to youths with any other primary diagnosis (5.9%), p < .001 (Fisher's Exact Test). However, there was still a significant interaction effect between time and primary diagnosis on ADIS CSR of the primary diagnosis when controlling for age and comorbid affective disorder, F (6, 90) = 2.80, p = .015, partial η^2 = 0.16, with social phobic youth improving significantly less. The same was true when excluding youths with comorbid affective disorders from the analysis.

Results at Follow-Up (the Pooled Data; Table 3.4)

ANOVA results. Table 3.4 presents means, standard deviations, test statistics, and effect sizes (Cohen's *d*) for all outcome measures from posttreatment to 3-month and 12-month follow-ups based on the pooled data of participants from both conditions. Table 3.4 shows that all of the variables—with one exception—show a statistically significant effect in terms of improvement over time from posttreatment

Table 3.4 Follow-Up Data for the Pooled Sample

	Post	3-Month Follow-Up	12-Month Follow-Up	Test Statistics	Effect Sizes*
ADIS CSR primary ($n = 95$)	2.43 (2.58)	1.93 (2.60)		$t(94) = 2.18, p = .032$	$d = 0.19$
ADIS CSR sum ($n = 95$)	5.44 (5.04)	4.37 (4.36)		$t(94) = 2.57, p = .012$	$d = 0.23$
SCAS youth ($n = 63$)	20.43 (13.20)	14.90 (10.78)	15.65 (12.10)	$F(2, 124) = 17.72, p < .001$	a: $p < .001, d = 0.46$ b: $p < .001, d = 0.38$ c: $p = 1.0, d = -0.07$
SCAS mother ($n = 70$)	20.93 (11.53)	17.90 (12.49)	17.11 (14.93)	$F(1.7, 115.4) = 5.50, p = .008$	a: $p = .004, d = 0.25$ b: $p = .021, d = 0.29$ c: $p = 1.0, d = 0.06$
SCAS father ($n = 61$)	21.08 (13.68)	17.07 (10.53)	16.84 (13.46)	$F(1.7, 99.7) = 7.82, p < .001$	a: $p < .001, d = 0.33$ b: $p = .012, d = 0.31$ c: $p = 1.0, d = 0.02$
CALIS youth ($n = 63$)	7.86 (7.00)	4.14 (3.87)	5.71 (7.59)	$F(1.6, 96.1) = 6.70, p = .004$	a: $p < .001, d = 0.66$ b: $p = .272, d = 0.29$ c: $p = .345, d = -0.26$
CALIS mother ($n = 69$)	10.30 (6.67)	8.25 (7.23)	7.59 (8.57)	$F(1.5, 102.4) = 4.85, p = .017$	a: $p = .003, d = 0.29$ b: $p = .032, d = 0.35$ c: $p = 1.0, d = 0.08$

Table 3.4 CONTINUED

	Post	3-Month Follow-Up	12-Month Follow-Up	Test Statistics	Effect Sizes*
CALIS father ($n = 61$)	10.13 (7.29)	8.31 (6.92)	6.80 (7.25)	$F (1.7, 104.1) = 9.06, p < .001$	a: $p = .013, d = 0.26$ b: $p < .001, d = 0.46$ c: $p = .273, d = 0.21$
CALIS-P mother ($n = 69$)	6.65 (5.59)	5.22 (6.08)	3.87 (5.27)	$F (2, 136) = 15.39, p < .001$	a: $p = .008, d = 0.24$ b: $p < .001, d = 0.51$ c: $p = .022, d = 0.24$
CALIS-P father ($n = 61$)	5.74 (5.45)	4.39 (4.76)	3.80 (4.84)	$F (2, 120) = 7.23, p < .001$	a: $p = .032, d = 0.26$ b: $p = .002, d = 0.38$ c: $p = .751, d = 0.12$
S-MFQ youth ($n = 88$)	2.77 (3.31)	2.57 (3.85)		$t (87) = 0.69, p = .493$	$d = 0.06$
S-MFQ mother ($n = 95$)	3.07 (3.82)	2.87 (4.04)		$t (94) = 0.59, p = .558$	$d = 0.05$
S-MFQ father ($n = 86$)	2.63 (4.27)	2.33 (3.76)		$t (85) = 0.83, p = .408$	$d = 0.07$
BYI-S youth ($n = 88$)	42.94 (10.07)	44.59 (10.90)		$t (87) = 2.47, p = .016$	$d = 0.16$

*Positive effect sizes indicate improvement.

ADIS, Anxiety Disorder Interview Schedule for *DSM-IV*; BYI-S, Becks Youth Inventory (self-concept subscale); a = post treatment to 3-month follow-up; b = post treatment to 12-month follow-up; c = 3- to 12-month follow-up; CALIS, Child Anxiety Life Interference Scale; CALIS-P, Child Anxiety Life Interference Scale interference on parent life; CSR, Clinician Severity Rating (ADIS); SCAS, Spence Children's Anxiety Scale; S-MFQ, Mood and Feelings Questionnaire (short version).

to 3-month follow-up. Only changes in the MFQ ratings were not significant. These improvements were maintained at 12-month follow-up, with the exception of mother rating on CALIS-P, which significantly improved even further from the 3-month to the 12- month follow-up.

ADIS results. On the ADIS for the pooled sample, 60 (63.2%) youths were free of their primary anxiety diagnosis, and 42 (44.2%) were free of all their anxiety diagnoses at posttreatment, while at 3-month follow-up 70 (73.7%) youths were free of their primary anxiety diagnosis and 55 (57.9%) were free of all their anxiety diagnoses.

Discussion

THE EFFICACY OF THE CK/CA PROGRAMS

The aims of this RCT were to conduct the first evaluation of the CK/CA programs independent of their Australian founders, and the first evaluation of a CBT program for youth anxiety disorders in Denmark. The Danish versions of the CK/CA programs were found to be efficacious. Youths in the treatment condition had significantly greater improvement compared with the wait-list condition across all raters on the primary outcome measures (ADIS CSR and SCAS), as well as on the secondary outcome measures of depression (S-MFQ), life interference (CALIS), and self-concept (BYI-S) (see Table 3.2). Also, significantly more youth in the treatment condition were free of their primary anxiety diagnosis (66.1%) or all anxiety diagnoses (48.2%), compared to the number of youth in the wait-list condition (primary, 7.5%; all, 5.7%). Similarly, compared to the wait-list condition, significantly more youth in the treatment condition reached clinically significant change on SCAS and SCAS-P at postassessment (see Table 3.3).

Results (see Table 3.4) at follow-up assessments indicated that youth improved even further from posttreatment to 3-month follow-up (pooled sample) with increased remission rates and significantly reduced anxiety symptoms and life interference across all raters, although with no changes in youth depressive symptoms. Youth anxiety symptoms (SCAS) and anxiety-related life interference (CALIS) were stable from 3- to 12-month assessment, although mothers reported significantly reduced interference in their own everyday life in the same period.

COMPARISON OF THE RESULTS WITH OTHER STUDIES

The results of the present study support the existing evidence on the CK/CA program as an efficacious treatment for youth anxiety disorders (e.g., Hudson et al., 2009; Rapee, Lyneham, et al., 2006). Compared to the prior studies of the CK/CA programs, the remission rates of the current study are similar to that of a study by Rapee, Lyneham, et al. (2006), in which 48.9% were free of all anxiety diagnoses at posttreatment (compared to 48.2% in the present study); and 61.1% at 3-month follow-up (compared to 57.9% in the present study). However, our remission rates were higher than those that Hudson et al. (2009) report: free of all: 33.3% (post) and 49% (3-month follow-up).

The most recent Cochrane review of CBT studies of youths with anxiety disorders (James et al., 2013) found a remission rate of 59.4% for any anxiety diagnosis at posttreatment, which is somewhat higher than the remission rate in the present study at posttreatment (48.2%). However, when comparing remission rates of CBT to wait-list control, the odds ratio for nonremission was 0.13 in James et al. (2013), compared to 0.11 in the present study (lower figures indicate higher effect size).

Effect sizes from pretreatment to posttreatment on youth-reported anxiety measures (SCAS) were larger in the current trial compared to those reported in the meta-analyses of Reynolds et al. (2012). This group found a d (CBT relative to passive control) of 0.77, compared to 0.94 in the current trial). Furthermore, the within-group effect size of the intervention group in our study was $d = 1.08$, and thus also larger than that of .98 found in the meta-analysis of James et al. (2013) and those calculated from prior studies of CK/CA, including 0.40 in Rapee, Lyneham, et al. (2006) and 0.70 in Hudson et al. (2009).

The numerically lower remission rate in the present study (48.2%) compared to that of 59.4% in the meta-analysis of James et al. (2013) may be due to a more severely disordered sample in the present study, with 75% of youth having at least one comorbid anxiety disorder compared to approximately 40% (range 33%–65%) in the James et al.'s sample of studies. Although it has been shown that the presence of comorbid anxiety diagnoses does not reduce the rate at which CBT improves youth anxiety symptoms (Rapee et al., 2013; Rapee, 2003), it may reduce end-state functioning, resulting in fewer participants free of anxiety diagnoses after treatment.

The relatively large treatment effect sizes found on self-report anxiety measures (SCAS) in the present study may be influenced by the statistical phenomenon of "regression toward the mean" due to the high pretreatment scores reported by youths and parents. Participants in the present study had higher total scores on SCAS (M = 39.16) and SCAS-P (M = 39.79) compared to norms for anxiety-disordered youths in North America (SCAS = 35.82 and SCAS-P = 29.70; Whiteside & Brown, 2008) and Australia (SCAS-P = 31.8; Nauta et al., 2004). Another factor that may have increased the efficacy of the program may be the presence of the three graduate students in each group who functioned as cotherapists.

THE GENERIC FORMAT OF THE CK/CA PROGRAMS

The generic format of the CK/CA programs offer some advantages, as youths with any kind of primary anxiety disorder and comorbid anxiety disorders can be included and mixed together in the same group. This may reduce the waiting period from assessment to treatment start for youths with particular anxiety diagnoses. Furthermore, a single generic program for anxiety disorders may be easier to implement in the public health care system than a number of different, diagnosis-specific programs. These advantages are being recognized in the field generally under the rubric of "transdiagnostic interventions," in which "eclectic treatment strategies to address multiple diagnostic problem sets [are] linked by common underlying etiological maintaining mechanisms" (Chu, 2012, p. 1). In line with our experience, Chu points out that some of the advantages over traditional approaches that transdiagnostic treatments offer include "increased efficiency, practicality, efficaciousness, and effectiveness" (2012, p. 1).

However, while the generic format may offer a number of advantages, the meta-analysis of Reynolds et al. (2012) found smaller effect sizes for generic CBT programs ($d = 0.53$) than for diagnosis-specific programs for OCD, SoP, and post-traumatic stress disorder ($d = 0.77$).

Although the present study found overall large effect sizes for the generic program evaluated here, the results for the specific diagnoses in the present study indicated that the generic group format of CK/CA may be less effective for SoP. Other studies (e.g., Crawley et al., 2008; Hudson et al., 2015) have also found that youths with a primary SoP diagnosis have poorer treatment response to generic CBT programs compared to other primary anxiety diagnoses. These findings are also consistent with the present guidelines recommended by the National Institute for Health and Care Excellence (NICE, 2013) that diagnosis-specific and/or individual treatment programs appear better suited for youths with primary SoP.

LIMITATIONS AND CONCLUSION

The study has some limitations. The treatment is compared to a passive wait-list control and not another active treatment control. Also, no assessment of therapist competence or adherence to protocol was conducted. Furthermore, a majority of ADIS interviews were conducted by students with moderate prior assessment experience. Finally, it is uncertain if the addition of three student assistants in each group could have influenced treatment outcome and diminished generalizability.

In conclusion, this first independent evaluation indicates that the generic CK/CA program is an efficacious treatment for youth anxiety disorders, with youths with a primary diagnosis of social phobia having relatively poorer outcomes. These results are in line with those found in recent meta-analyses of CBT for youth anxiety disorders.

THE CASE STUDIES

The Nature and Rationale for Specific Cases Selected for the Case Studies

To better understand the factors and processes associated with the successful and unsuccessful cases, two clients were chosen for case study from the RCT project described earlier: Lisa, a 13-year-old girl who experienced successful elimination of her primary anxiety diagnosis of generalized anxiety disorder; and Marius, a 12-year-old boy who did not experience successful elimination of his primary anxiety diagnosis of social phobia. These two clients were chosen because, besides outcome, both were similar in a variety of ways: both were about the same age, 13 and 12 years, respectively; and both came from relatively stable, well-educated, middle-class families of a Danish ethnic background.

Another factor in our choice was Lisa and Marius's differences in gender and initial diagnosis. In a recent large multisite trial of clinical and genetic predictors of response to CBT in pediatric anxiety disorders (Hudson et al., 2015), and consistent in part with our results that we described earlier, female gender and social phobia were associated with poorer outcomes. We therefore thought it would be particularly informative for case study to select a female responder with a GAD diagnosis, and a male nonresponder with a social phobia diagnosis.

The Clients

LISA, A CLIENT WITH A POSITIVE OUTCOME

Lisa (13 years old) lived with her mother, her stepfather, and two blood-related siblings in a relatively small town. She had not been in contact with her biological father for 7 years and thought of and referred to her mother's new husband as her father. Both siblings had been diagnosed earlier, with Lisa's older brother suffering from ADHD and Asperger's disorder, now austistic spectrum disorder, and her older sister suffering from ADD and nonverbal learning disorder (NLD). It should be noted that her older sister had been a victim of rape.

Some years previously, Lisa had participated in a sibling's course for youth with ADHD. After the course was completed, she continued to participate with individual consultations with the family counselor up until last year, when she was referred to individual therapy sessions with a psychologist. In addition, Lisa suffers from asthma and has been attending a special asthma school, where the youths learn to deal with the physical symptoms of the disease. In relation to the asthma, the family has had extra focus on Lisa's weight and general health.

MARIUS, A CLIENT WITH A NEGATIVE OUTCOME

When Marius (12 years old) began the therapy program, he was attending the sixth grade and lived with his parents. He came from a well-educated middle-class family of a Danish ethnic background. Marius lived with both his parents, who had been separated for some time, but had moved back together 4 months before therapy started. Both parents suffered from social phobia, while his older brother suffered from autism spectrum disorder and was in a residential treatment facility. Marius had been diagnosed with social phobia and Tourette's syndrome a year prior to starting therapy, but he had not yet received any treatment for his anxiety disorder.

Guiding Conception With Research Support

Earlier in the RCT section under the headings of "Introduction" and "Interventions," the wide prevalence and negative impact of youth anxiety disorders are documented, along with a description of the established efficacy of CBT for treating such disorders and a presentation of the basic structure of the CK/CA programs. Next, we first briefly consider the theory underlying the CK/CA programs and next provide some more details about their structure to provide more context for helping the reader follow the flow of the therapy.

THEORY

In the CK/CA CBT Group model, anxiety is assumed to be a tripartite construct involving physiological, cognitive, and behavioral components. Physiological arousal occurs in the form of autonomic nervous system activity, which prepares the individual for "fight or flight." The cognitive component involves a narrowing of attention or a shift in focus toward the threat cues in the situation. This is accompanied by certain thoughts and images that are followed by behaviors, which are a response to the perception of the situation as dangerous (Barlow, 2002). A distinction between normal adaptive fear and maladaptive fear, according to Ollendick, King, and Yule (1994), is that adaptive fear is based on a realistic appraisal of the potential threat. In contrast, maladaptive fear is based on an unrealistic appraisal of the threat that the specific stimulus poses to the individual.

It is normal and expected for youth to have certain fear and anxiety reactions during development, with the focus of anxiety changing at different ages and cognitive developmental levels (Muris & Field, 2011). From a clinical psychological perspective, youth are frequently referred for anxiety treatment when the fear interferes with the activities that would be expected at their specific developmental level (Carr, 2006).

An understanding of the factors involved in the etiology and maintenance of youth anxiety can be described through the model of Rapee (2001), which is grounded in the empirical literature on genetic and environmental factors associated with youth anxiety disorder. The model starts with a recognition of *genetic factors*, which determine that some youth are born with *anxious vulnerability*, which may be manifested through the youth's temperament and evidenced by high levels of *arousal and emotionality*, as well as *avoidance* and *cognitive processing bias*. This vulnerability to anxiety may elicit in others, such as parents, behaviors that maintain or exacerbate anxiety.

Parental anxiety, which is also likely responsible for the genetic factors that the youth inherited in the first place, may also influence parents' behavior, which becomes overprotective, thus providing *environmental support of avoidance* of feared situations by the youth, whose temperament serves to maintain that overprotection. *Parental anxiety* also interferes with the parents' ability to cope in difficult situations, thereby exacerbating the possible adverse *effects of the social environment* that is reciprocally influenced by the youth's vulnerability to anxiety.

THE INCLUSION OF THE FAMILY IN CBT

Given the potential role that parents play in the maintenance of anxiety disorders in children (e.g., Creswell, Murray, Stacey, & Cooper, 2011; Hudson & Rapee, 2009; Bögels & Brechman-Toussaint, 2006), it makes sense to include parents as a central part of the treatment. Although the evidence from studies comparing child-focused treatment to family-focused treatment does not lead to clear conclusions regarding their relative effectiveness (Breinholst, Esbjorn, Reinholdt-Dunne, & Stallard, 2012; Cobham, Dadds, & Spence, 1998; Shortt, Barrett, & Fox, 2001; Silverman et al., 1999; Spence, Donovan, & Brechman-Toussaint, 2000), findings from those reviews and treatment studies suggest that family-based CBT is either as effective or more effective than individual CBT. Parent inclusion is particularly effective in the case of younger children (7-10 year-olds) and girls. This may be the case because most family-based treatments for child anxiety teach parents to model coping behaviors and successful problem solving. However, while younger children regularly view their parents as models, adolescents are usually more influenced by their peers.

Parental anxiety has been found to interfere with the development of the parents' adaptive coping skills and leads to behaviors that may exacerbate the anxiety of their children, thereby adding an additional risk factor in the maintenance of childhood anxiety. There is actually some evidence indicating that a family-based treatment may be more effective for children whose parents also have an anxiety disorder (Cobham et al., 1998), and that CBT with active parental involvement emphasizing contingency management and transfer of control may support long-term maintenance of treatment gains (Manassis et al., 2014).

Fathers are often included less than mothers in the treatment of developmental psychopathology (Lazar, Sagi, & Fraser, 1991), and childhood anxiety disorders are no exception. Research on normal development indicates that fathers play an important and different role than mothers in the protection of children against severe anxiety (Bogels & Phares, 2008), and studies of various types of developmental psychopathology reveal better long-term effects when fathers are included in treatment (e.g., Bagner & Eyberg, 2003). Studies of treatment of anxious children with parental involvement typically only include mothers (e.g., Silverman, Kurtines, Jaccard, & Pina, 2009), or do not report whether fathers participated in the therapy sessions (e.g., Kendall, Hudson, Gosch, Flannery-Schroeder, & Suveg, 2008; Schneider et al., 2011).

A recent study included both parents in a family CBT program for anxious youth and both parents were expected to participate in all treatment sessions. Parents were involved in the treatment as co-clients, e.g., the parents learned skills to modify maladaptive parental beliefs and expectations, to reduce negative reinforcement of their child's anxious behavior, to support the child's mastery, and to increase effective communication. It was found that both mother and father attendance and engagement in the treatment were associated with child gains (Podell & Kendall, 2011). Although little is known about fathers' specific role in child anxiety treatment, these findings may indicate that their role should not be overlooked.

Structure of the Therapy

As mentioned earlier, the families met on a weekly basis for 10 sessions, each session lasting 2 hours. A detailed description of the content of each session is presented in Table 4 of Lundkvist-Houndoumadi and Thastum (2013a). Generally, all sessions used a combination of group and individual work and proceeded along the following steps for each group of about six families:

1. The families gathered in one room and each family spoke with the student therapist (referred to as the *ST*) assigned to them about what they had accomplished during the previous week, as well as possible problems they may have had while implementing the homework.
2. The clinical psychologist (referred to as the *psychologist*) introduced the goal for the overall session. The youth and the STs went to another room, where the psychologist presented the content of each session based on the manual of the CK-CA Program, using the youth's workbook as a supplement.
3. The psychologist and all but one of the STs returned to the group of parents, while the remaining ST stayed behind and played with the youth. Parents were informed about the principles that had been presented to the youth and in an interactive way taught the treatment principles and alternate ways of interacting with their youth using the parents' workbook of the CK/CA Program.
4. The youth came into the room and sat with their parents and STs. Youth told their parents what they had learned, and along with the parents and STs, the youth helped decide on the assignments for the following week.

(For more details on the structure of the therapy, see Table 3.7 in Lundkvist-Houndoumadi and Thastum [2013a]).

Lisa's Positive-Outcome Therapy: Assessment, Formulation, and Course

Assessment of Lisa's Problems, Goals, Strengths, and History

Having learned about the Anxiety Clinic through Lisa's caseworker, her mother and stepfather sent an email to the clinic, describing Lisa's social inactivity, her resistance toward new and unfamiliar situations, and her extreme tendency to worry:

> [. . .] For example she needs to take the bus alone from her home to the family counselor. It's nowhere near possible for her to take the wrong bus, she has a clip card to pay for the ride and she knows where to get off. Still she worries a lot about other things like people in the bus talking to her, looking at her, sitting next to her or smelling. [. . .] Situations like this happen a lot with her. No matter what we tell her, she seems to have her own personal opinion about it.
>
> She gets scared from the things she sees on TV, even things you wouldn't expect to be frightening. She worries about a lot of things, family illnesses, and war and so on. She's a girl who likes to be cuddled, kissed and touched and she has an enormous need for adult contact.
>
> We hope that you are able to help us so that the family has a chance to function properly.

Developmental History

A few weeks later, at an assessment interview, Lisa's mother described her pregnancy and birth by Caesarean as proceeding within normal range. Except from her asthma, Lisa was in good health during most of her childhood and her mother remembered her being developmentally advanced for her age in relation to both motor skills and language development. Her mother and stepfather described her as being a very caring and cheerful person, who could appear stubborn at times but was neither shy nor behaviorally inhibited.

Lisa's problems began at age 9–10 months when she would be dropped off at day care. Though apparently very fond of her child care provider, she would cry for 5 to 10 minutes after being left with her. This pattern was repeated all the way through kindergarten, where she mostly behaved in a self-sufficient manner and would only on rare occasions seek adult help or guidance.

On request and encouragement from her kindergarten teacher, Lisa started school at the age of 6, although her mother had argued that she should wait another year. Lisa is academically average, and she states that she sometimes experiences trouble concentrating, but her teachers have not been concerned about her or felt she needed to be assessed for possible learning difficulties. However, she becomes distressed when she does not do well at a particular task, and over the last few years she has stopped playing with her friends after school.

Her mother reported that Lisa has anxiety attacks that can last up to several hours during which she feels dizzy and experiences being outside of her own body. The parents had thought the attacks were related to Lisa's asthma but concluded that they were related to anxiety when an increase in the dosage of her asthma medication had no effect on the recurrent attacks. The family is now convinced that the attacks are primarily related to Lisa's anxiety.

Family History

Lisa lived with her mother, stepfather, and brother (16 years old) and sister (17 years old). Several years previously Lisa's biological father had been deprived of his right of access to all three youth because he was physically abusing Lisa's brother, and Lisa had not been in contact with him for the last 7 years.

Lisa's older brother, diagnosed with ADHD and Asperger's syndrome, had just returned home after staying 2 years at a lower-secondary-level boarding school for 14- to 17-year-olds. His transition to home has been difficult for the entire family. Lisa's mother showed up at the interview with a black eye, because the son had recently hit her. This had distressed Lisa so much that she had slept most nights since with her mother.

Lisa's sister had been raped several times recently by older men, of whom one was her handball coach. The family were still distressed about this because the perpetrators were never sentenced because of missing evidence. She had recently been diagnosed with nonverbal learning disorder and attention-deficit disorder.

Two other past events had been distressing for Lisa: her grandparents' divorce when Lisa was 9, and the death from cancer of her stepfather's father, to whom she had been close. Furthermore, her mother assumed that Lisa might be predisposed to psychological disorders from her biological father, since both he and several others on this side of the family struggled with alcohol abuse. Adding to this, the father's new child with another woman had recently been diagnosed with ADHD.

Although Lisa's mother describes the family as "abnormal" due to the youth's disabilities, she also stated that she believed they as a family had the necessary resources to deal with the many challenges they faced.

Status at the Time of Referral

Based on the ADIS conducted with Lisa and her mother, as well as self-report questionnaires, information was gathered on Lisa's anxiety issues and their degree of impact on the family's life and general functionality. The results from the assessment at pretreatment can be seen in Tables 3.5 and 3.6.

Lisa was physically mature for her age. During the interview she was at ease and appeared honest, open, and easy to talk to. Lisa reported that she had come because she among other things was afraid of scary movies, which made her want to sleep in her parents' bed. She was also afraid that something would happen to her, for example, that she would be raped like her sister.

Lisa's mother described Lisa's difficulties as primarily centering around social themes, but from the diagnostic interviews it appeared that worrying was a major source of Lisa's anxiety. This included fear of humiliation in a range of social settings. She feared others pointing to or laughing at her in places like school and restaurants, as a result of, for example, stumbling or falling. She feared not being good enough, saying something wrong, or being boring, and she felt anxious

Table 3.5 OUTCOME MEASURES FOR LISA

	Pretreatment	Posttreatment	Follow-Up
ADIS-C	GAD: 6 Social phobia: 5 Separation anxiety: 4 Specific phobia, disabled people: 4	Social phobia: 5	—
ADIS-P	GAD: 7 Specific phobia, people in costumes: 7 Separation anxiety: 6 Specific phobia, dogs: 5 Social phobia: 4 Specific phobia, disabled people: 4	Social phobia: 7 Specific phobia, dogs: 2	—
ADIS-Clinician	GAD: 7 Separation anxiety: 5 Social phobia: 4 Specific phobia, dogs: 4 Specific phobia, disabled people: 4	Social phobia: 4	—
CGAS	51	66	85
CGI-I	—	2	1

Table 3.6 QUANTITATIVE DATA AT THREE POINTS IN TIME FOR LISA

Scale	Pretreatment			Posttreatment			3-Month Follow-Up		
	Mother	Father	Child	Mother	Father	Child	Mother	Father	Child
BYI									
Self-concept			28			34			42§#¤[ab]¤[ab]
SCAS									
Panic/agoraphobia	12	4	4	1 §#¤	1 §	2 §¤	1 §#¤[a]	2 §	1 §¤[a]
Generalised anxiety	21	10	6	1 §#¤	1 §#¤	0 §#¤	0 §#¤[a]	1 §#¤[a]	0 §#¤[a]
Social phobia	17	8	6	4 §#¤	3 §¤	5 §	4 §#¤[a]	2 §#¤[a]	4 §
Anx. physical injury	16	8	9	3 §#¤	3 §#¤	2 §#¤	2 §#¤[a]	2 §#¤[a]	2 §#¤[a]
OCD	11	4	9	0 §#¤	0 §¤	2 §#¤	1 §#¤[a]	0 §¤[a]	1 §#¤[a]
Separation anxiety	18	7	6	5 #¤	3 §¤	3 §#¤	3 §#¤[a]	2 §¤[a]	3 §#¤[a]
TOTAL	95	41	40	14 §#¤	11 §#¤	14 §#¤	11 §#¤[a]¤[a]	9 §#¤[a]¤[a]	11 §#¤[a]¤[a]
CALIS									
Child interference	31	24		15 #¤	14 #¤		8 #¤[ab]	5 #¤[ab]	
Family Interference	35	10		6 #¤	1 #¤		1 #¤[a]	1 #¤[a]	
Child reported			15			9			4 #¤[a]

Nature or size of change: §, clinical change; #, statistically significant change; ¤, large effect, compared to: [a] pretreatment, [b] posttreatment.

answering questions at school, attending sports, eating in front of others, and talking to unknown people. Lisa worried about family finances, whether her mother and stepfather would separate or if her stepfather would get cancer as his father did. She had specific phobias of snakes, heights, the dark, dogs, insects, thunder, people in costumes, riding on a bus, and choking and getting sick. However, it was only dogs and people in costumes that she avoided because of her fear.

At the interview Lisa also explained that she worried a great deal about being away from her parents. She was afraid that something would happen to them or to her while they were apart. Although the fear of rape, physical attack, and robbery was present even when Lisa was with her parents, it was magnified when she did not have the protection of her mother. At times, when Lisa's older brother had been aggressive toward their mother, Lisa wanted to sleep with her parents, and she worried constantly about the safety of her mother. The only times Lisa was able to spend the night outside the home was when she and her mother had made very clear agreements about it beforehand, especially with respect to her mother being available on her cell phone. At one occasion Lisa sent 250 text messages to her mother during a sleepover.

Additional information emerged from the family's completion of the standardized measures. On the Spence Youth's Anxiety Scale (SCAS), Lisa's report regarding different anxiety disorders was within normal range (defined as ratings below one standard deviation over the mean for a community sample) except for her report of anxiety for physical injury and for OCD, which were both in the clinical range—the latter being a new clinical feature that emerged. In contrast, on the SCAS-P, Lisa's parents both reported symptoms within the clinical range for all the anxiety disorders present in the scale with no exceptions. Notably, Lisa's mother reported extremely high levels of symptoms for all the disorders; in fact, all higher than two and three standard deviations of the mean of the clinical sample. For both parents, ratings on GAD, social phobia, and anxiety over physical injury were the highest compared to the normal and clinical range.

On the questionnaire measuring the impact of anxiety in everyday life (CALIS), Lisa reported interference within the clinical norm. On the other hand, Lisa's mother reported very high interference (twice the mean for a clinical sample) with both the youth's life and the family's life.

Finally, on the self-concept scale of the Beck Youth Inventory (BYI), Lisa scored considerably below the mean—that is, as having a poor self-concept—for Danish girls at her age (Thastum, 2009).

Overall Lisa was greatly affected by her anxiety. She could not sleep over at her friends' houses or go to the mall. Periodically she stayed home from school and avoided all social activity; experienced sleep disturbances; and had trouble being alone, finishing homework, and eating. As a result, she became easily irritated and was often very tired. Following the clinician's assessment, Lisa was diagnosed with generalized anxiety disorder (GAD) as her primary diagnosis with a CSR severity rating of 7. The clinician's global assessment of functioning, measured through Children's Global Assessment Scale (CGAS) was 51, indicating variable functioning with symptoms on several but not all social areas.

LISA'S FORMULATION AND TREATMENT PLAN

Case Formulation

Information obtained in Lisa's assessment interview was integrated into a case formulation, in line with Carr's (1999) model.

A number of *personal predisposing factors* were present in the case of Lisa, which presumably increased her vulnerability in developing anxiety. Her mother's descriptions of Lisa as a girl who found it hard to be in new and unknown situations and who cried every time she was dropped off at daycare or kindergarten suggested that Lisa might have an inhibited temperament. Lisa herself had many descriptions as well of reactions indicating a tendency to withdraw. Biologically, the multiplicity of family members with mental health issues; that is, the siblings' developmental and behavioral disorders and the presence of alcohol abuse in the biological fathers' family, all pointed to Lisa being genetically predisposed.

Also present are a number of complementary *contextual predisposing factors* consisting of the prevalence of intergenerational trauma experienced by Lisa and the impact of disturbed attachment relationships from one generation to another. Specifically, these include Lisa's biological father's violence against her mother and his absence primarily due to his violent behavior toward Lisa's older brother; parental divorce; death of a loved grandparent; divorce of the grandparents; the ADHD and Asperger's syndrome of Lisa's brother; and the impact of sexual abuse of Lisa's sister on the sister herself as well as on the rest of the family. From the view of the parents, all of these events created a chaotic home environment and led to the mother feeling overburdened.

With respect to the *personal maintaining factors*, Lisa was a girl with a great sense of responsibility. This often led her to be involved in the many conflicts between her mother and siblings, worrying and assuming responsibility for her mother. Often she would send out text messages to her mother just to check if she was alright and to make sure that her older brother behaved. When her older sister was preparing to leave home, Lisa worried about how to help her with the future distance between them. Related to the fact that Lisa had been involved in many of the family conflicts, one hypothesis was that she had developed a fear of chaos. She constantly worried that the current relatively calm period would soon transform into family difficulties, chaos, and uncertainty, and she seemingly did not know how to handle this possibility. Her recurrent concern about the family's private finances and the parent's potential divorce also fit well into this hypothesis along with the thought that Lisa had a tendency to ruminate. The fact that Lisa always had been scared of and intimidated by new and unknown situations in combination with the present family conditions may also have contributed to the development of a low uncertainty tolerance. Accordingly, Lisa often asked the question "what if . . . ?" and she explained her fear of people in costumes and disabled people with reference to their unpredictable behavior. Adding to the list of possible personal maintaining factors, Lisa often experienced life as controlled by external elements of which she had no control, strongly indicating an external locus of control.

With respect to *maintaining factors*, the context of the great uncertainty and insecurity characteristic of the family was seen as both predisposing Lisa to and maintaining her anxiety. Furthermore, her mother often acted in an overprotective manner, sending Lisa text messages to see how she was and asking her if she was able to manage the school day. Adding to this, the mother and the stepfather both helped maintain Lisa's anxiety by supporting her avoidant behavior and making reassurances whenever they felt it necessary.

A number of *protective factors* were presumably also present in the case of Lisa. She was perceived to be of normal intelligence and functioned overall at an average academic level in class. She expressed a great sense of motivation for the therapy, as did her parents, and they all seemed to grasp the cognitive-behavioral treatment principles. In relation to the contextual protecting factors, Lisa's stepfather functioned as a stable attachment figure and had done so for a long time. The family as a whole seemed motivated for and optimistic about the course of therapy; they were easy learners and eager to do a lot of homework. Moreover, the family used humor as a positive coping mechanism and had a loving and caring way of relating to one another. Socially they were very outgoing, and although Lisa did not have many friends, she felt closely connected to the few she had. Furthermore, she had been attending the same school throughout all of her school years, which according to the parents made her feel safe and relatively at ease.

Treatment Goals
Based on the assessment information and the case formulation, together with the therapist, the family developed five treatment goals. Lisa appeared somewhat withdrawn in the process, but with moderate pressure from her mother, she agreed to the following:

1. To be able to stay at home alone in the evening when mom and dad are going out.
2. To be able to be with many other people, for example, at festivals and concerts.
3. To want to go with other people from home and to actually do it.
4. To fall asleep in my own room in less than 30 minutes.
5. To be able to spend the night at other people's houses and send a maximum of five text messages a day to mom. "I can call her in case I need vital information such as when and where to pick me up."

LISA'S COURSE OF THERAPY
Sessions 1–2: Introduction, Psychoeducation, and Realistic Thinking
At the first therapy session Lisa appeared open and dedicated, and was quick to participate. Asked about things to be afraid of in the youths' lives, she was the first to answer "Being raped." She also elaborated on how this fear could affect their lives by stating that one would not be able to go out alone if it was dark outside. All in all she worked hard on the tasks that she was given and responded well to the rewards.

During the sessions dealing with realistic thinking, Lisa participated eagerly and raised her hand on many occasions. She generally seemed to have an understanding of the principles behind realistic thinking, but she struggled when she was asked to use them on her own anxiety. Despite this, Lisa volunteered when the group was asked to write on the board an example of a frightening situation that had actually happened for her within the last week:

What happened?	Lying in bed, couldn't sleep
What were you thinking?	My sister can't take care of herself (worry rating: 7)
Evidence:	
What facts do you have about the situation?	She does some crazy things
Is there anyone else who can help her?	She talks a lot with mom; it helps She gets help from her boyfriend and the psychologist
Has she been in a similar situation before?	She has proven earlier that she can take care of herself
What could also happen?	She will be all right and she'll be happy
Realistic thought:	If anything goes wrong, a lot of people are there to help (worry rating: 5)

The other youth in the group acted as detectives and asked Lisa questions to which she answered as best she could. She managed to stay very positive during the work, and she often smiled when she realized how unrealistic her thoughts were. She later expressed that she thought the detective's way of questioning her thoughts was very helpful, especially when she could get the help from other group members.

Commenting on the process of doing homework, Lisa's parents explained that they already used realistic thinking at home, but also that they sometimes felt Lisa's resistance toward the different homework tasks. Sometimes she would withdraw from filling out the detective worksheets when asked and encouraged by her parents.

Session 3: Child Management Training for the Parents
At session 3, in which the parents learned about child management strategies, both the mother and the stepfather listened actively and contributed with several examples of their own inappropriate parental behavior toward Lisa, for example, by giving Lisa too much attention when she went to bed at night by asking: "Do you want me to put you to bed," or "I hope that you will sleep well tonight." Also they realized that they had a tendency to let Lisa avoid potentially anxiety-provoking situations. They said that in the future they wanted to take on more "confrontations" with Lisa, to pressure her to do things that she previously had been shielded from, for example, to participate in family get-togethers. At the

end of the session, the mother asked the psychologist about whether it would be a good idea to examine Lisa for ADHD. The psychologist answered that she did not see any signs of ADHD in Lisa, and she recommended that the mother reevaluate the situation after the end of the CK/CA treatment.

Sessions 4–8: Graduated Exposures, Assertive Communication, Worry Surfing, and Problem Solving

At session 4, Lisa worked with making gradual stepladders (exposure hierarchy) based on her goals. It was difficult for her, since several of her goals were about being more social and spending more time with friends. By carefully exploring her social relationships, it appeared that Lisa had several friends, but that she avoided having contact with them and visiting them. Therefore, sleeping at a friend's house was decided to be the goal for the first stepladder, although Lisa was a bit reluctant in the beginning because she thought it was an unattainable goal.

Goal	Activity
Step 10	Sleep with Alma at her house
Reward	Five stickers
Step 9	
Reward	
Step 8	
Reward	
Step 7	Visit Alma for an evening and go back to sleep at her own house
Reward	A new DVD film
Step 6	Eat dinner at Alma's house
Reward	A sticker
Step 5	Take the bus to Alma's house and be picked up by her father
Reward	A sticker
Step 4	Be at Alma's house for a while and then go to the cinema
Reward	Two tickets for the cinema
Step 3	Be at Alm's house for 5 minutes when the dog is there
Reward	A sticker
Step 2	Be at Alma's house for 5 minutes when the dog is not there
Reward	A sticker
Step 1	Talk to Alma
Reward	A sticker

NOTE: Lisa only thought she needed eight steps, and thus the blank steps 8 and 9.

It rapidly emerged that what prevented Lisa from starting with the steps was that she was afraid of dogs, and that there was a dog in Alma's house. Therefore, Lisa decided to make another stepladder where the goal was to be able to stay in a house with a big dog. The first step was to pat a dog while somebody else was holding the dog, and the final goal was that it would feel OK to be together with big dogs. (Lisa was later successful with the "sleeping-over" and "big dogs" stepladders, as described later.)

When making both stepladders, Lisa seemed rather sulky and withdrawn, and she needed a lot of help. It became clear that this withdrawal was in response to Lisa's parents being overly pushy in helping her. They wanted Lisa to face her anxiety more, and they made a lot of suggestions for steps. Despite this, Lisa was happy when the stepladders were finally constructed. (Note that Lisa's parents were very engaged in making the stepladders; they wanted Lisa to face her anxiety more, and they came with a lot of suggestions for steps. The parents very-involved behavior probably reinforced Lisa's tendency to withdraw in the process. However, the mother had been especially aware of the effects of her own behavior toward Lisa. For example, the mother reported that she had experienced the positive effect on Lisa when occasionally the mother was less active and had given more responsibility to Lisa. Lisa responded well to rewards, and the family had made a reward system in which Lisa collected stickers that later could be exchanged for things, such as DVDs, cinema tickets, or books.)

Lisa was skeptical about the worry-surfing technique, and she refused to use it. However, she participated actively in the session on problem solving, and she volunteered to solve a problem in public in the youth session. She often skipped sports classes, and after her stepfather talked to the teacher, Lisa had been excused from sports for a month. What particularly worried her was going into the shower with the other kids and feeling humiliated when she did not understand the rules of the games. The stepfather had talked to the teacher, and Lisa had been excused from sports for a month. However, Lisa wanted to participate, and she felt left out when she was not involved. The problem that she wanted help to solve was thus, "How can I participate in sports?" The other kids in the group contributed with several suggestions. Those that Lisa considered the best were doing detective thinking and doing a stepladder. In the end Lisa made a stepladder with the goal of participating in sports.

Gradually Lisa progressed in working with her anxiety. She also slowly became more courageous in relation to facing the things she feared. For example, her parents went to spend the night in another city while Lisa was taken care of by her older brother. She also took the train alone in order to visit her sister. On both occasions her parents were proud to tell the therapist that Lisa and her mother only sent a few text messages to each other. Around session 6, the number of messages sent between the two were within normal range, and the entire family seemed happy about this progress. Lisa and her mother had at this point in therapy apparently realized the extremity of their text message communication, and they were able to smile and laugh at their old habits.

In session 8, which took place at a shopping mall, the family at the start of the session happily reported that since the last session Lisa had slept with a friend (Alma) in her house, had tried to expand her group of friends by talking to several kids in the school, and had participated in sports at school. Also she had been more comfortable with big dogs.

The student therapist (ST) and the family made a list of possible exposures for Lisa in the mall: (1) to be close to noisy youth, (2) to be close to handicapped people, and (3) to do something embarrassing, for example, buying something without having enough money. Although Lisa was very reluctant about the last suggestion, the ST and Lisa went to a shop where Lisa was supposed to buy cough drops with not enough money, and with an Icelandic coin. She was very nervous about it, but with a little encouragement she completed the task, and afterward the ST and Lisa laughed about how embarrassing it had been.

When returning to the cafeteria where the parents were waiting, a handicapped man had arrived. Lisa and the ST sat at a table next to him. Lisa told the ST that what particularly scared her about handicapped people was the unpredictability, that she did not know what to say, and that she was scared about what the person might do. Also she felt a lot of compassion with these people and felt sorry for them. Suddenly the man stood up and sat down at the table behind Lisa. He was rather unstable in his walk and almost tumbled over Lisa. Lisa was afraid but stayed at her place despite the fact that the man's chair touched Lisa and that he talked to her and complained. Although Lisa practiced doing other embarrassing activities in the mall, she found these relatively easy, with the situation with the handicapped man being the most educational and challenging for Lisa at the mall.

Sessions 9–10: Reviewing Goals, Maintenance, and Setbacks

Before session 9, the ST and the psychologist made a revised case formulation based on material and clinical thinking that had emerged in the therapy. The case formulation brought into focus Lisa's excessive sense of responsibility for others, for example, regarding her sister's and mother's situations, and her tendency to worry. At the same time, the formulation emphasized that Lisa has many personal and contextual protective factors. At the start of session 9, the ST and the psychologist presented the case formulation to Lisa's parents. There were three components: (a) the Problem, which was worry and anxiety; (b) What Initiated the Anxiety: grandfather dying from cancer; and (c) Things That Were Keeping the Anxiety Going, which included (i) anxiety about reality-based family disruptions, such as her sister leaving home, her brother hitting her mother, her parents threatening a divorce, and challenges in the family finances; (ii) the unpredictability in Lisa's life; (iii) Lisa taking too much responsibility; and (iv) Lisa thinking too much about things.

In reviewing the case formulation, the parents recognized several of the factors and their connections with Lisa's anxiety. They agreed that Lisa had taken too much responsibility for things that had happened in the family, and that this probably had led to her constant worrying. In that connection, Lisa mentioned that she presently was functioning as a support person for a friend in her class who had some personal problems. The psychologist emphasized that it is nice that Lisa was kind and empathetic, but that it also is important that she did not take on responsibility for her friend's problems and worries. It seemed that Lisa became more aware that worries do not help (e.g., "worrying does not prevent my brother from hitting my mother"; see the GAD model in Kertz & Woodruff-Borden, 2011). Generally, it was difficult for the family to identify factors that initiated the anxiety. The mother described Lisa as a girl who always had a tendency to worry and had difficulties with new things happening.

In the youth session there was a discussion of what had changed since the start of the therapy. Lisa completed a list of previous and present worries:

Previous worries: Many people, meeting new friends, war, giving a speech, being home alone, being mobbed, being away from home, dogs, school.
Present worries: Meeting new friends, giving a speech, being away from home, dogs, school.

Asked about what she had achieved during the therapy, Lisa answered: "A lot, for example getting rid of embarrassment, participating in sports, and being home with others."

At session 10, the family reported that the last week Lisa had been at a friend's house and, in general, she had worried less. Consistent with this, Lisa thought that her anxiety and worries had diminished, she showed insight in recognizing that she still had things to work with, for example less fear of dogs and getting more self-confidence in social relations. The parents expressed satisfaction with the therapy and enthusiastically expressed how proud they had been of Lisa's efforts during the therapy. They were interested in keeping contact with the other families after the therapy, because they experienced the group as an important positive factor in the therapy. At the end of the last session, they invited the other families to an activity day in a climbing hall. Overall, Lisa seemed satisfied with the therapy and optimistic about coping with her anxiety in the future.

Booster Session: 3 Months After the End of Therapy
Lisa and her mother came to this session. Lisa was still maintaining progress: She did not experience excessive anxiety anymore, her self-confidence had increased, and she was now a happy and social teenager. Previously Lisa was medicated due to her asthma, but her asthma had remitted, and she was no longer taking medication—something her mother attributed to the CK/CA program. When asked if anything had gotten worse than before over the last 3 months, Lisa could not think of anything.

Marius's Negative-Outcome Therapy: Assessment, Formulation, and Course

ASSESSMENT OF MARIUS'S PROBLEMS, GOALS, STRENGTHS, AND HISTORY
Marius's parents contacted the Anxiety Clinic after reading about the Cool Kids program in the local newspaper, sending the following e-mail:

We have a son who will soon be 12 years and who after assessment at a child psychiatric clinic was given the diagnosis of social phobia. What is the possibility of him attending a Cool Kids intervention, as described in the newspaper yesterday?

Information presented in the following section was gathered through a case history interview conducted with the father, since the mother was sick that day.

Developmental History
Overall, Marius reached the developmental milestones as expected, with some minor deviations in that he walked a bit later than usual (15 months), but developed language earlier.

His father described him as an infant who was not very interested in exploring his environment. In kindergarten Marius was a very shy child, who preferred playing one to one and would rather not participate in social arrangements. He had difficulties meeting new people, but he was eager to learn things and had a good sense of humor. At 5 years of age he began showing some tics. After kindergarten there was an increase in motor tics (grimaces) and vocal tics.

Marius's social difficulties became most apparent in school; the teachers described him as being very quiet, reserved, and insecure, prone to exhibit a defeatist attitude. He managed well academically, but he had difficulty following instructions and rules, and it was hard for him to do group work. According to the father, Marius experienced difficulties with problem solving, being somewhat lazy, and tiring easily. Marius's parents had been concerned about his social anxiety, which seemed to them more than "just being shy." When they tried to encourage him to take initiatives for social arrangements, he would react with intense anxiety, making statements like "I will die if I do it."

Approximately a year prior to starting the CK/CA program, Marius was assessed psychiatrically following a referral by the school counselor, who was concerned about possible obsessions, concentration difficulties, and autism spectrum disorder. It was concluded that Marius suffered from Tourette's syndrome and social anxiety. He also suffered from epilepsy, which was controlled by medication. Despite this, intellectually he performed as expected for his age.

Family History
Both of Marius's parents suffered from social phobia. The mother's social phobia had been severe, and for a period of time, when Marius was 2 years old, she did not leave the house. She received CBT, which helped her, and later on she chose to get further education as a life coach. The father's anxiety was not as severe, and he had not received treatment for it. However, he had chosen to work as a freelancer, so that he would not be confronted with anxiety-provoking social situations on a daily basis.

The parents had had many quarrels in which they would shout at each other in Marius's presence. Four years prior to referral, they separated and Marius lived with his mother. The father had moved back in with the family 4 months prior to the assessment, but there had been further conflict. Following the mother's training as a life coach, which resulted in her better expressing thoughts and feelings, the marital relationship improved. Her communication with Marius also improved. Marius was closer to his mother, as he would turn to her with things that troubled him. Even after the father had moved back, it was mostly the mother who was engaged in Marius's difficulties.

When Marius was 6 years old, his 18-year-old half-brother (from the mother's side) who lived with them became psychotic and was admitted to a psychiatric facility for a period of time. This impacted on Marius, as much of the parents' attention and resources were channeled toward the half-brother. The half-brother returned home but was later readmitted and was living at the facility for 3 years prior to the family starting the CK/CA therapy, and the mother would often worry about how he was doing there.

The father emphasized the positive, stating that in his view, they had a lot of resources as a family, mentioning education and knowledge.

Status at the Time of Referral

On the basis of the ADIS diagnostic interviews conducted with the father and Marius, as well as self-report questionnaires, information was gathered on Marius's anxiety difficulties and the degree to which they had an impact on the family's life. The results from the assessment at pretreatment can be seen in Tables 3.7 and 3.8.

Marius was very shy during the diagnostic interview and did not report any symptoms. He would avoid eye contact, and it was apparent to the interviewer that he felt very uncomfortable in the situation. According to the father, Marius's difficulties were centered on social situations and the evaluation of others, as he was afraid of doing something embarrassing in front of them. His anxiety was primarily apparent in school, where he could not do presentations, read aloud, raise his hand in class, or answer questions the teacher would pose. In case the teachers insisted on an answer, he would turn red and while looking down he would say: "I don't know." As a consequence, special arrangements had been made for him in school, so that he was not obliged to do presentations and did not need to participate actively in class.

Marius experienced difficulties meeting new people, youth as well as adults, and he did not seem to be interested in making new friends. He had two good friends he would "hang out" with in school and other settings, and he would attend social events if the friends did. When his parents tried to set some rules at home, he could sometimes react with intense anger. In contrast, when not at home, he would be very cautious, talk very quietly, and avoid eye contact. He avoided situations in which his performance could be evaluated, or he would try to direct attention away from himself. Furthermore, he was very self-critical and was preoccupied with what others thought of him.

The clinician's assessment was that Marius had a primary diagnosis of social phobia with an ADIS severity CSR rating of 5, which was the same rating the father made. Marius's social anxiety was generalized, as his fear was related to most social situations. Besides social anxiety, the father reported that Marius showed some symptoms of OCD. Marius would count things or do things a specific number of times. The compulsions were not for longer than an hour a day, and the clinician was unsure whether they could be better attributed to the Tourette's syndrome, but ended up including compulsions as a diagnosis. The clinician's global assessment of functioning, measured through the Children's Global Assessment Scale, was 58, indicating that Marius showed variable functioning with symptoms on several but not all social areas.

Table 3.7 OUTCOME MEASURES FOR MARIUS

	Pre-Group Treatment	Post-Group Treatment	3-Month Follow-Up to Group Treatment	Post-Individual Treatment	3-Month Follow-Up to Individual Treatment
ADIS-C	—	—	Social phobia: 4	Social phobia: 4	—
ADIS-P	Social phobia: 5	Social phobia: 4	Social phobia: 5 (father) Social phobia: 6 (mother)	Social phobia: 4 (mother and father)	Social phobia: 4. OCD: 6 (mother and father)
ADIS-Clinician	Social phobia: 5 Compulsions: 4	Social phobia: 4	Social phobia: 5	Social phobia: 4	— OCD: 4
CGAS	58	66	55	61	64
CGI-I	3	3	3	2	2

Table 3.8 Quantitative Data at Three Points in Time for Marius

Scale	Pretreatment			Posttreatment			3-Month Follow-Up		
	Mother	Father	Child	Mother	Father	Child	Mother	Father	Child
BYI									
Self-concept			46			45			44
SCAS									
Panic/ agoraphobia	0	0	0	0	1	0	1	1	0
Generalized anxiety	4	3	2	5	4	2	4	3	4
Social phobia	8	5	4	8	7	3 §	10	5	3 §
Anx. physical injury	6	4	2	2 §# ¤	3	3	3 §¤[a]	3	1 ¤[b]
OCD	6	5	2	6	3	0	5	4	0
Separation anxiety	0	3	0	0	1	0	1	2	0
TOTAL	**24**	**20**	**10**	**21**	**19 §**	**8**	**24**	**18 §**	**8**
CALIS									
Child interference	8	12		10	9		13	6 ¤[a]	
Family interference	5	6		3	4		6	4	
Child reported			7			0 ¤			0 ¤[a]

§clinical change, #statistically significant change, ¤large effect, compared to: [a]pretreatment, [b]posttreatment.

On the Self-Concept scale on the Beck Youth Inventories (BYI), Marius reported a rather high self-concept, perhaps overcompensating for his clear problems in the area of social phobia. Information was gathered on the family's perception of Marius's anxiety difficulties using the Spence Children's Anxiety Scale (SCAS and SCAS-P), which is the primary self-report instrument measuring anxiety. Marius's report of anxiety symptoms was overall very limited, with his report of social phobia being the highest, but still within the normal range. According to the mother, social phobia was the primary difficulty, while the father's rating was lower than the mother's and as high as his report of OCD symptoms. On the questionnaire measuring the impact of anxiety in everyday life (CALIS), Marius and both his parents overall reported rather low interference, with all reports being under the norm. The father gave the highest ratings, which indicated interference in Marius's life due to his anxiety.

Overall, Marius and his parents appeared to underreport the extent of Marius's problems, as compared with the behavioral manifestations of his difficulties. Perhaps their experience with Marius's much more severely disturbed half-brother led to this underreporting.

MARIUS'S FORMULATION AND TREATMENT PLAN
Case Formulation

Information obtained at the assessment was integrated in a case formulation, in line with Carr's (1999) model. First, a number of *personal predisposing factors* were present in the case of Marius, which increased his vulnerability in developing an anxiety disorder. There were indications of Marius being genetically predisposed, since both of his parents suffered from social phobia and additional psychopathology was present in the family (especially on the mother's side). From the descriptions of Marius during infancy and his early school years as a shy child who was reluctant to explore his surroundings, it seems he had an inhibited temperament. Furthermore, despite his relatively high score on the BYI self-concept scale, there were indications of Marius having low self-esteem, since he was described as having a defeatist attitude and a tendency to be very self-critical, which was evidenced during therapy, when he would make statements such as: "I will never learn this." In addition, his Tourette's syndrome may have induced his fear of rejection and ridicule from others.

Contextual predisposing factors included Marius's early exposure to parental anxiety, as Marius, for instance, became more shy after the period in which the mother did not leave the house. In addition, the brother's problems contributed to the mother worrying more about how Marius was doing. These issues may have influenced the parent–child relationship during childhood, since probably the parents did not always have the resources to be emotionally available for Marius. Furthermore, when Marius was 8 years old, his parents separated and he was witness to a lot of conflicts between the parents that could have contributed to an unsafe atmosphere at home.

The separation of the parents together with the brother's psychotic episode could have functioned as precipitating factors, as these two events were described as very stressful for Marius and seemed to have triggered the onset of his anxiety problems.

Several *maintaining factors* became apparent during therapy and were added to the case formulation. Marius had a tendency to avoid anxiety-provoking social situations, as for instance actively participating in class and talking to new people. He would attribute his successes to external factors and explain his failures by referring to internal stable factors. Marius also had difficulties expressing thoughts and feelings. (This later made therapy work more difficult, as it was not possible to practice cognitive restructuring with him.)

Moreover, Marius was not motivated to attend therapy and do homework. Besides, the parents had a somewhat critical stance toward the psychologist at the beginning, and the father was afraid that therapy was too hard for Marius.

The parents' somewhat negative beliefs concerning therapy could have influenced their degree of engagement in therapy and, in turn, might have influenced Marius.

The parents' own social phobia could have maintained Marius's anxiety through modeling avoidance of social situations, the father, for instance, choosing to be a freelancer in order to avoid too much contact with others. The mother had a tendency to answer on Marius's behalf and thereby would support his avoidance, while the father would set high demands and was unable to take a graduated approach to exposures. The parents' worrying related to Marius's brother, and the family conflicts related to the father having moved back, drew off family resources from Marius, suggesting that this could be a problem in the upcoming CK/CA treatment, with a lack of full support from the parents. Lastly, the special arrangements for Marius in school could have contributed to the maintenance of Marius's avoidance of anxiety-provoking situations, in that he did not need to participate actively in class, and also there seemed to be communication difficulties between the school and the family.

A number of *protective factors* were also apparent in Marius's case. He was assessed to be of normal intelligence and managed well academically in school. Additionally, he had two good friends and would play handball with other youth of his age in his leisure time. The father had described the family as educated and knowledgeable, which may be seen as important resources. In addition, the parents were motivated for receiving therapy, acknowledging that Marius needed professional help.

In addition, the parents had an understanding of Marius's difficulties, as they also experienced social anxiety. The mother's previous attendance of therapy and her further education as a life coach had given her some skills that contributed to her understanding of the therapy principles and her being able to talk with Marius about his anxiety difficulties. It seemed that Marius had a secure attachment to his mother in that he would turn to her in case he needed support. Finally, the family had a social network, which supported them.

Treatment Goals
In the first session, Marius was asked to circle the pictures of things he was afraid of and thought were a problem for him. He circled pictures of the following themes: "meeting new friends," "giving a speech," "being shy," and "heights." The parents noted that they hoped Marius would achieve the following through therapy: "take part in social arrangements," "dare to meet new people," "talk in a relaxed way to youth and adults in social settings," "talk in front of others in class," "call friends," and "ask things from the neighbor." The parents said that they would like Marius to no longer "stay away from presentations in school, or become silent in social situations." With this background, the following five goals were set:

1. Talk in front of others in class
2. Participate actively in social arrangements (e.g., start a conversation)

3. Meet new friends
4. Call friends
5. Talk in a relaxed manner with new people (youth and adults)

Treatment Plan
The treatment was planned to follow the Cool Kids program manual (see Table 3.4 in Lundkvist-Houndoumadi & Thastum, 2013a). The case formulation for Marius was taken into account in the treatment plan, and as information regarding maintaining factors was gathered, the therapists tried to address those. The treatment plan had to be revised when it became apparent how the group format of therapy was too anxiety provoking for Marius. In order for him to be able to attend the group setting with the other youth, some components of therapy needed to be introduced to him earlier than usual. Detective thinking (i.e., cognitive restructuring) and stepladders (i.e., gradual exposures) were therefore presented already in sessions 2 and 3, respectively. Furthermore, the family could not come to sessions 1 and 6, and they therefore got two individual sessions instead, where the material was presented to the family by the ST. Finally, the family received a home visit between sessions 8 and 9.

Marius's Course of Therapy
Sessions 1–2
Issues of motivation for therapy. Marius and his parents were unable to attend the first session, and they were offered an individual session instead. When Marius showed up with his father, he had red eyes and looked very nervous. His father explained how Marius had resisted attending, due to the prospect of meeting the other youth. Marius's ST introduced him to the connection between thoughts and feelings, and he got engaged in the material, suggesting good examples. Even though he seemed nervous and did not talk a lot, he would smile once in a while and gladly received praise and stickers.

As the second session approached, Marius became very anxious again about meeting the other youth. He refused to go to the room with the other families and sat down in the corridor, hiding his face in his arms. Marius lightly banged his head against the wall and had turned red, showing great difficulty answering the ST's questions on his thoughts and feelings. He managed to reply that his fear reached 10 on the anxiety scale (1–10) and gave statements such as "I would only go in there if I were invisible or wore a mask," "I will die if I go in there," and "I will hit my dad when we get home for bringing me here." Nevertheless, the ST succeeded in gradually getting Marius closer to the room, so that he could look in at the other youth. He did not enter the room at this session.

In response to Marius's severe anxiety related to the group format of therapy, his father commented: "It is not helpful when the cure is worse than the problem," but he also seemed to become aware of how severe Marius difficulties were. Despite this, his father agreed to come again next time, to the third session, as he could see it was important for Marius to attend therapy.

Phone call: After the ST had obtained supervision, she called the family. The father called the mother to the phone, mentioning that Marius had talked with her about it, and the mother explained how they had not prepared Marius adequately on what would happen. She said that "Marius got a shock when realizing he had to be with the other youth," but "Marius agreed to attend on his own terms." Marius said he would go with his parents, as long as he did not have to attend the session with the other youth alone. The ST explained to the mother how a gradual stepladder of exposure could be made, in order for Marius to be able to attend the group; and the mother agreed to talk to Marius about that. The phone call illustrated that it was the mother who had the primary role in the anxiety work related to the program.

Session 3

Introduction to cognitive restructuring and the gradual stepladder. Marius seemed less nervous than the previous session, and he and both his parents showed up earlier, in order to have time to plan a stepladder with the ST. Marius had been introduced at home to cognitive restructuring and completed exercises in the workbook with his mother. Even though Marius understood the technique, he could not identify his own thoughts, perhaps because he had not been confronted with anxiety- provoking situations during the week.

The ST introduced Marius to the principles of the gradual stepladder and tried to brainstorm with the family on possible rungs of a stepladder with the following goal: "to sit at the big table with the other kids and be asked about something." Marius did not have any suggestions for possible steps and reacted to the suggestions with "that could be . . .," while the mother supported the ST's proposals. The father suggested that Marius could "take a deep breath and step into the room," which was the technique the father would use in situations he feared.

Marius did not seem very anxious about taking the first steps on the stepladder and was cooperative, setting anxiety ratings before, during, and after the steps. However, he was unable to identify any thoughts in order to do cognitive restructuring and rejected the ST's suggestion that he was worried because he might have been thinking that others would laugh at him, by commenting, "This is highly unlikely and silly." Even though Marius did not seem to profit from cognitive restructuring, his anxiety dropped after the exposures, and he succeeded in reaching step 7 at the stepladder: "sitting at a table next to the others."

The parents were somewhat critical of the psychologist during the parents' session, commenting on her choice of words and her expecting specific answers. Nevertheless, the parents seemed motivated to come to the next session and so did Marius, who received praise from the parents for his brave behavior at the session.

Session 4

Difficulties with implementing techniques between sessions. During the week Marius had once more not been confronted with situations he feared and had therefore not been anxious. Furthermore, he would forget to do cognitive restructuring on his own, and when practicing with his mother, he could not identify any thoughts.

Exposure work in sessions. During the youth's session, the ST and Marius continued working on the stepladder and he succeeded in reaching his goal: "to sit at the table with the other kids and answer the psychologist's question." Even though he turned red and was very nervous, he claimed he would not be as nervous next time. At this point in therapy Marius had shown engagement in the exposures done in the sessions, and despite the initial resistance, he had overcome his intense fear to attend the group (rated as a anxiety-provoking, maximum score of 10).

Marius managed to achieve one goal in session 4, namely to call a friend.

Sessions 5 and 6

Difficulties with implementing techniques between sessions. The family had planned a stepladder, in order for Marius to be able to borrow things from the neighbor. One evening, when the father realized they were short of butter, he asked Marius to go to the neighbor and get some, since: "any way he should practice this." In retrospect, the parents did not think they had handled the situation in a very pedagogical manner, since they did not follow the planned stepladder. Nevertheless, the mother had taken over in that specific situation, supporting Marius in order for him to be able to do the step. Marius wrote in his workbook that he had learned that the neighbor was kind and willing to lend things, and his anxiety had dropped from 4 to 0. Even though the father once more modeled a "just face the feared situation" approach, the exposure had been effective with his anxiety dropping and allowing cognitive restructuring to occur.

Exposure work in sessions. Marius sat at the table with the other kids from the beginning and was able to answer a question the psychologist posed.

Motivation for therapy. At this session the mother talked about how Marius was not motivated to attend therapy, as it took time from other activities. He did not see the purpose of the program, since he did not believe he had difficulties, and none of the goals they had set were things he was motivated to reach. He felt the whole day was gone, when they were back home, and he had not learned anything from what the psychologist had said at the last session: "It went in through one ear and out from the other." While the mother discussed these issues, the ST tried to come in contact with Marius, but he would look away and when asked about something, he would answer: "I don't know." The mother tried to help by saying to Marius: "She is trying to ask you something," and "Try to tell her what you told me."

During the youth's session, Marius showed interest in the worry-surfing technique, which was introduced to the youth by them walking around in the clinic, commenting on what they saw. At the end of the session the mother mentioned how they would not be able to attend the next session due to vacation. They were motivated to continue the work, but the mother also commented that "Marius needs a good break from everything."

Marius's belief in the program seemed to be low, and there were indications of a weak alliance with the ST, which did not allow for a successful discussion and challenge of that belief. Marius seemed to be overwhelmed by the work he had to put into the program, and the mother responded to this by acting in a somewhat overprotective manner, stating that he needed a break. It is possible that the intense anxiety he experienced in the group made it difficult to follow the psychologist's instructions. Interestingly, he showed more interest when he was introduced to the techniques that involved the most active experiential involvement, such as worry surfing requiring Marius to tolerate his anxious feelings consciously.

Session 7

Difficulties with implementing techniques between sessions. The family had made some new stepladders with few steps and rewards that were related to school situations, as for instance raising his hand in class. Marius did not think the opportunity appeared to practice the step. Marius did not look at the ST while she tried to talk to him, and his mother answered on his behalf either directly when the questions were posed or after he had answered: "I don't know." The ST talked with the parents about including the school in the anxiety work, and the mother referred to cooperation difficulties with the teachers. Marius expressed an unwillingness to have his teachers involved and knowing about his social difficulties (although of course they already knew because of the special arrangements the teachers had made for him.)

Marius would not be confronted with anxiety-provoking situations due to his avoidance, and the mother had a tendency to support his avoidance, as illustrated with her answering on his behalf.

Motivation for therapy. The family came earlier to the session in order for them to learn about problem solving. The problem that was presented as an example was that of a child accidentally breaking his mother's vase. Marius's suggestions for possible solutions to this problem were as follows: "Move out from home" or "Hit mom unconscious and buy a new vase." His approach can be perceived as deliberately provocative and an indication of his continuing resistance to the program and his lack of interest in cooperating with the ST.

Exposure work in sessions. Mother brought a mini-stepladder they had prepared at home, in order for Marius to raise his hand and say something at the youth's session, which he had rated as 4 on the anxiety-provoking scale. Before Marius had the opportunity to practice this, the following dialogue occurred:

PSYCHOLOGIST: What is the hardest thing you have done during the week?
MARIUS: I don't know. . .
P: Were you nervous about coming today?
M: Yes.
P: It is very brave of you coming despite your anxiety. What is your anxiety rating now that you talk in front of the other youth?
M: Seven.

P: Are your thoughts related to being afraid that others would think you act in an embarrassing manner?

M: [nods]

P: Do you think Marius is acting in an embarrassing manner?

YOUTH: No.

P: How do you think Marius should be rewarded for his brave behavior today?

YOUTH: Four stickers!

Following this sequence, the ST reminded Marius of his mini-stepladder to which he commented that his anxiety for raising his hand and saying something had increased to seven and he could not do it. The group format allowed the therapist to do some exposure work in the session, while using the other youth's feedback. However, the dialogue with the psychologist had provoked an anxiety reaction in Marius, the intensity of which possibly took him by surprise (a rating of 7 instead of a previous rating of 4), while the ST had not allowed the anxiety levels to lower before asking him to do more exposures.

Later, the youth in the group were encouraged to do some role playing as a way of practicing assertiveness skills. Marius did not want to take part and therefore only observed. The psychologist tried talking with Marius, and he reported his anxiety was still at seven. When she continued talking to him, he went to the wall and slightly banged his head toward the wall and turned red. Afterward he told the ST that he had no intention of practicing the social skills, as he had difficulties seeing what he could use them for.

Marius became overwhelmed in the session and showed an angry, immature, defensive reaction, rejecting the program and stating that he could not see the use of social skills. The ST talked with him about how he would be able to tackle his anxiety if he continued trying. The following dialogue occurred, which illustrates his fear of failing that led him to avoid the situation altogether:

MARIUS: I will not raise my hand, if I am not 100% sure of the answer.

ST: When are you 100% sure you know the answer?

MARIUS: I am never 100% sure.

Session 8

Difficulties with implementing techniques between sessions. Marius claimed that there had not been any possibility for him to practice social skills with his teacher, and the mother still felt unsure about how to work with the stepladders in practice.

Exposure work in sessions. The family needed to leave earlier for the handball team's annual party and therefore met with the ST before the other families arrived at the shopping mall, where the session was planned to take place. Marius was red in his face, avoided eye contact, and did not answer the questions posed to him. The parents had thought of possible exposures for Marius, as for instance asking for something in a shop. When the ST walked around with him in the shopping mall and tried to prepare him for the exposures, Marius avoided looking at her and rated all the suggested exposures as being anxiety provoking with an 8 or 10 rating.

The ST gave Marius some cards with what he should ask for, in case he forgot. They practiced the cards together and she asked people about the time, while Marius observed. Marius's anxiety would not decrease, and it was not possible to identify thoughts that made him anxious, rejecting all the ST's suggestions. The psychologist suggested they try to do some passive behavior experiments, where the ST demonstrated potential embarrassing social interactions. Before each experiment Marius was supposed to make hypotheses about what would happen, and after the experiment evaluate what he observed. There was only time for one passive behavior experiment, in which the ST asked a stranger for information about the mall but the ST forgot what to ask about. In this instance, Marius's negative expectation in response to the ST's behavior (that the stranger would be angry) was challenged successfully, and the parents were encouraged to practice more situations with him at home.

From the beginning of the in-vivo session in the mall, Marius showed signs of being very anxious and was therefore unwilling to do exposures. He had experienced intense anxiety at the previous session and possibly the in-vivo session was not within his zone of proximal development at this point in therapy. The continuous focus on him identifying the thoughts that made him anxious also appeared to have been very stressful, since he was unable to do so.

Between Sessions 8 and 9, Phone Call and Home Visit Focusing on Motivation in Therapy

Phone call: Marius's mother called the ST and talked with her about how Marius had given up after the session at the shopping mall, with statements such as "I will never learn this; it is too hard." Even though they did not demand that Marius do a lot of homework for the program, the mother still found it difficult to motivate him. When asked whether he would like to be able to say things in front of others, he answered affirmatively. Therefore, it seemed that Marius *did* wish to overcome his anxiety. It is likely that the previous session had been too demanding for him, and he therefore found it difficult to believe he would succeed in fighting his fears.

Responding to the ST's question about what she believed was needed for Marius to become more motivated, the mother answered, "Clarity, structure, realistic and small goals, and energy from both parents." They decided to make the practice of stepladders easier by choosing one focus area per week. At the end of the phone call, the mother commented how happy she was for their talk, being more hopeful and ready to implement the tasks they had talked about.

Home visit: At the home visit the parents talked with the ST about how Marius got very surprised that there were only two sessions left and told them, "But then there won't be enough time for me to be cured!" The mother explained how Marius perceived the CK/CA program homework as a "bitter obligation," similar to homework for school and would always prefer doing something else than the program homework. Nevertheless, the father described how they had practiced detective thinking and done behavioral experiments spontaneously. Once more it seemed as if Marius wanted to get over his anxiety, but he had resistance toward the program. The father's spontaneous approach seemed to be effective in getting Marius to work on his anxiety, as it did not have the characteristics of homework.

The parents talked with the ST about how difficult it was for them to know how much they should pressure Marius. This might be related to the mother's identification with Marius's problems, as illustrated in her following comment:

I experience Marius as shut out from the world, as if he is closed in his own little shell, which is difficult to break through. I can so easily put myself in his place, since I myself have felt exactly like this.

The father added that he could also understand Marius's difficulties. This might have held the parents back from engaging Marius in work between sessions. It was noted by the ST how the parents no longer referred to what each of them did, but how they as "parents" tackled Marius's difficulties, indicating that a shift had occurred, where the parents cooperated in the anxiety work. To help the parents structure the work in between sessions, the ST provided them with sheets of different focus areas they could work on per week, which they were thankful for. Here is an example of one of the possibilities that the ST provided involving "Becoming More Active in Class":

Week 1: Marius raises his hand once per day, when a minimum of two other students have their hand raised. It is arranged with the teacher that Marius will not be chosen.
Week 2: Marius raises his hand once per day, when a minimum of one other student has his or her hand raised. It is arranged with the teacher that Marius will not be chosen.
Week 3: Teacher asks Marius a question once per day.
Week 4: Marius prepares one question every day, which the teacher gets to ask the following day. Marius raises his hand in class in order to answer the question.
Week 5: Marius raises his hand once per day and answers a question without having prepared the answer.

Meanwhile, another ST attached to the group tried to do problem solving with Marius related to his fear that others at school would know of his anxiety. Marius proposed some very extreme options and was clearly not interested in the more realistic options. To the idea that the teacher could tell the class that he was training to raise his hand, he reacted by throwing himself on the floor, rolling around and banging his head lightly, saying: "No, no, no, that is too stupid! That is not gonna happen, forget it!" Marius was clearly not ready for the others in his class to know and would show his rage and resistance to this in an extreme, immature manner.

Session 9
Difficulties with implementing techniques between sessions. Marius had taken a ride on an airplane, and he was no longer afraid of heights, although it was not clear if this was related to the CK/CA program. The parents had not practiced passive behavior experiments, and they talked about Marius having difficulties in implementing the techniques, even though he understood them. Nevertheless, it seemed that Marius used elements of them, as for instance he had started looking

people in the eyes more than he did earlier. The mother reported how one teacher had now been informed of the program, but Marius did not get to raise his hand in class. Marius was concerned about what his best friend would think of this, adding though that his friend might understand it, stating: "He is also handicapped." Marius continued avoiding and seemed to perceive his difficulties as a handicap, which possibly indicated some shame related to his anxiety that could explain his secrecy.

Exposure in the session. The psychologist started the youth's session by throwing a ball to the youth, with the one grabbing it having to answer a question. Marius was not expected to take part in this, but he surprised everyone by grabbing the ball that was meant for another youth and answering the questions posed to him. The ST had made cards, as reminders to Marius of how many times he should raise his hand during the session, and provided him with the correct answer to a question he was expected to answer. Unfortunately, Marius was unable to raise his hand, because he thought it looked weird if he would not be picked, when he was the only one raising his hand. When the psychologist got to the question he was supposed to answer, he turned red, folded his hands in front of himself, and sank in his chair, drawing sad "smileys" in his workbook. The psychologist asked other youth the question and afterward addressed Marius, who was able to answer the question he had written down. The psychologist continued to talk with him a bit and afterward praised him and gave him stickers. Marius was blushing, but he responded with a slight smile to the praise and looked proud of his achievement. Afterward he took part in role playing in order to practice social skills and raised his hand twice while playing Hangman with the other youth.

Marius showed signs of progress in this session. The stepladder was not well planned, since it demanded him acting in a manner that could be perceived as "weird," which probably also partly explained why he did not wish to practice this in school. When a more natural situation occurred, he was able to do so and he seemed to draw learning experiences from this, looking proud of his accomplishment.

Session 10: Evaluating Progress in Therapy
Marius had continued practicing social skills techniques during the week and had succeeded in raising his hand three times in class. The family thought this was a huge step, as it had taken a long time to overcome Marius's avoidance of this. The mother explained how it had been a great help to structure the program and accommodate the techniques for Marius's needs. She commented that "now something is happening," and the father thought they had gotten better at giving Marius the push he needed. The family seemed to experience a breakthrough after getting help to structure the techniques for Marius's needs. However, the help from the ST came too close to the end of the therapy for them to profit much.

Booster Session, 3 Months After the End of Therapy
During the summer, Marius had started taking more responsibility related to social situations and remembered to look others in the eyes and speak clearly. However, the mother mentioned they really had not used the techniques.

The family acknowledged it was important to continue the anxiety work in school, but they expressed many worries related to how they should tackle this, since Marius would not use the techniques and a new teacher team had to be involved.

Individualized Therapy for Marius as a Nonresponder

Because Marius was a nonresponder, according to our project protocol 3 months after the end of therapy he and his family were offered 10 individualized therapy sessions, based on the same principles and concepts as the CK/CA program. Specifically, the procedure for our nonresponder treatment project was the following. Youth who at the 3-month follow-up assessment after the RCT had a score greater than 2 on the CGI-I and who still had anxiety as their main problem were defined as "nonresponders" and offered further individualized treatment. The nonresponders were discussed at a clinical conference, in terms of the following questions: (1) Which factors had been effective in therapy? (2) What were the hypotheses for the reasons behind the nonresponse? and (3) If the family was offered case-based treatment, what should be worked on and how?

Afterward, an individualized case formulation was created for those to whom additional treatment would be offered. The families were then invited to a meeting, where the thoughts concerning possible reasons for the youth's nonresponse and suggestions for targets of the additional treatment sessions were presented. The families' perspectives were integrated into the design of the final individualized treatment plan. The additional treatment was grounded in CBT principles and consisted of up to 10 sessions, with a possibility for extension. Treatment was individualized, informed by the therapist's previous knowledge of the specific youth and family and by the particular factors that seemed important to facilitate the individual youth's positive response to treatment. The new case formulation and treatment plan that guided the subsequent individualized treatment of Marius focused on five areas:

- "What Is Needed More by Marius?"—for example, "setting more realistic goals," "using simpler stepladders," "practicing verbalizing worry thoughts," and "reducing avoidance behavior"
- "What Is Needed More by Parents?"—for example, "learning more about anxiety," "learning more about the methods by practicing on themselves," "better planning for Marius's homework," and "consistent rewards"
- "What Is Marius Good at Doing?"—for example, "doing spontaneous exposures such as raising his hand in school," "practicing his social skills by himself," "profiting from structure and clear tasks," "calling his best friends," and "being brave and disciplined in his stepladder practicing"
- "What Are the Parents Good at Doing?"—for example, "using rewards and praise," "helping Marius with structuring tasks," and "both actively participating in the therapy"

- "What Are Marius's General Strengths?" for example, "friends, humor, doing well in school, healthy hobbies (handball), good relationships with parents, and supportive parents"

Marius and both parents participated in all sessions, except sessions 3, 4, and 8, in which the mother was not able to attend due to meetings concerning Marius's older brother. At the first session the combined case formulation and treatment plan was presented for the family. The family agreed with the case formulation and added that it was also important to work with Marius's motivation, although it seemed unrealistic that they could do homework every day. After the school holiday Marius had gotten new teachers, with whom the parents met. The teachers were willing to help, and after receiving the CK/CA manuals, they asked Marius academic questions in class that were designed to make it easier for him to answer. The parents reported that they were very happy and motivated for the offer of the nonresponder treatment. Marius did not respond either way when asked if he was interested in continuing treatment.

During Marius's nonresponder treatment the work was focused on creating simple stepladders with few steps, for example, shopping at the grocery store, asking a neighbor about something, asking questions in school, and presenting in school. Also, there was a focus on continuing homework; in-session exposures (e.g., buying a youth magazine in a shop); preventing overprotecting parental behaviors; and generally working with the parents' "blind spots" due to their own social anxiety.

In the first two sessions there was a focus on Marius learning to be aware of and verbalizing his anxious thoughts. This was based on the psychologist's hypothesis that Marius's resistance to verbalizing was an avoidance behavior. Marius reacted in an extremely resistant fashion to these demands; for example, at home he desperately shouted to his father that "There is no thought, can't you grasp it!" Therefore in session 3 this strategy was terminated, to the great relief of both the parents and Marius. The therapy was focused afterward on exposures only.

Between sessions 5 and 6 the psychologist had a telephone contact with the child psychiatrist who was treating Marius for his Tourette's syndrome with medication, in order to coordinate their treatments.

After session 8 the father wrote an email in which he reported that Marius was insisting that he only wanted to come to the clinic once more. Session 9 was therefore cancelled.

At session 10 the therapy was evaluated. The parents were satisfied with the results of the therapy. In their opinion Marius had matured and had become braver and more self-confident. He could now raise his hand in class, ask teachers questions, present in class with a friend, buy things in shops, and borrow things from the neighbor. The mother did not speak on Marius's behalf anymore. The family had developed a common language to talk about the anxiety. These and other positive changes were written down for the family. In this session, Marius seemed more relaxed, had good eye contact, and was responsive in answering questions.

A month after the last session the psychologist participated in a meeting at the child psychiatric hospital, with participation of a representative from the hospital, three of Marius's teachers, and the parents. The conclusion of the meeting was that there was no longer any reason for Marius to be attached to the hospital, since Marius's Tourette's syndrome was now quite unproblematic and he no longer required medication. In school Marius was now treated as everyone else; that is, he would answer if questioned. Also, he had done presentations in class, and he had developed good social relationships with friends.

In line with the observations, an assessment by the ADIS revealed that Marius's social phobia at the end of therapy had decreased to a CSR of 4, and it had disappeared as a clinical diagnosis at the follow-up 3 months later. In addition to the exposures that were helpful for Marius to overcome his social phobia, the following procedures were found useful in meeting this goal: (1) the more structured therapy, with focus on helping the parents doing homework; (2) in-vivo exposures during the therapy sessions; (3) collaborating with the school; (4) more psychoeducation with the parents, with a focus on their own maladaptive overprotective attitudes toward Marius; and finally (5) the decision to stop insisting that Marius verbalize his thoughts, and instead to focus on realistic exposures.

Therapy Monitoring and Use of Feedback Information

For all the treatment cases, there were two ways in which therapy was monitored during each session, yielding important feedback that was folded into the ongoing therapy process. After each session, there was a supervision group, including both the group psychologist and the student therapists. Having multiple clinicians who were experiencing the group was very helpful in eliciting differing perceptions and different perspectives on the therapy process for each youth and for each group. Also, a variety of session-to-session ratings provided information regarding the therapy process. The earlier discussion of Lisa's and Marius's therapy process provides examples of the use of feedback information in ongoing treatment planning.

Concluding Evaluation of the Therapy Process and Outcome

LISA'S POSITIVE OUTCOME

Therapy outcome was measured through diagnostic interviews and self-report questionnaires. As shown in Table 3.5, based on the clinician's ADIS ratings, at pretreatment Lisa had a primary diagnosis of generalized anxiety disorder, with secondary diagnoses of separation anxiety, social phobia, and specific phobias for dogs and disabled people. At posttreatment, only the social phobia was present; and at 3-month follow-up, no diagnoses were present. The parallel ADIS-child and ADIS-parent ratings showed a very similar pattern.

As shown in Table 3.5 and consistent with the earlier discussion, at posttreatment the *Children's Global Assessment Scale* (CGAS) score was 66, close to clinical cutoff of 70, and at 3-month follow-up it had increased further to 85, in the "Good Functioning in All Areas" category. Also, at posttreatment the *CGI-I* was 2, indicating that Lisa was much improved, with a significant reduction of symptoms, although some remained. At 3-month follow-up the *CGI-I* was 1, indicating that Lisa was very much improved, had good functioning with no diagnoses met, had only minimal/subclinical symptoms, and had substantial change.

Table 3.6 presents Lisa's and her parents' self-report scores on the Beck Youth Inventory Self-Concept (BYI) measure; the Spence Children's Anxiety Scale (SCAS) measures; and the Child Anxiety Life Interference Scale (CALIS) measures. As shown in Table 3.6, except from the more positive self-report ratings from pre to post than found in the clinician ratings, the ratings on the self-report scales confirm the aforementioned findings. Both Lisa's and her parents' self-report of GAD symptoms on the SCAS measure revealed a clinical and statistically significant change from pre to post and at 3-month follow-up, with large effect sizes. The same pattern was seen for the Total SCAS scores and for the other SCAS subscales. On the CALIS measure, clinically and statistically significant change from pre to post and 3-month follow-up, with large effect sizes, were found for both Lisa and her parents. Especially the mother evaluated that Lisa's anxiety affected the family significantly less after the therapy ($d = 3.28$). Lisa's score on the Self-Concept Scale of the BYI changed clinically and statistically significantly from pre to 3-month follow-up, with a large effect size ($d = 1.41$).

LISA'S THERAPY PROCESS IN THE GROUP THERAPY

Lisa's view. Although it was Lisa's parents who initially insisted that Lisa should have therapy, Lisa seemed motivated for the therapy from the beginning. Already in the first session she was engaged, shared her worries in the youth group, worked actively with the tasks in the workbook, and accepted the in-session rewards. At the end of session 1, Lisa seemed happy and optimistic. The group format seemed to suit Lisa well and to increase her motivation.

Lisa understood quickly the concepts of realistic thinking and gradual exposure. According to the ST, Lisa and her parents had a humor-oriented approach to each other and to the work of dealing with Lisa's anxiety; and the ST also actively used humor in her work with Lisa, for example, by use of exaggerations in working with both detective thinking and stepladders. For example, when Lisa did exposures in the mall, the ST asked her whether the clerk would force her to buy things she did not want to buy; and when Lisa was learning realistic thinking, the ST asked her whether she was married to Justin Bieber (her big idol) or if she just thought that she was. Lisa was able to laugh at these absurdities. According to the ST, use of humor was a powerful coping strategy for Lisa, and she was able to use humor increasingly during the therapy. Occasionally during the therapy Lisa was reluctant and withdrawn, but when she was then helped by the therapists to complete her tasks, she usually was happy. She did homework with support from her parents and quickly experienced that the techniques had a positive effect on her worries, which motivated her to continue. Her self-confidence thus increased during the therapy. In the questionnaire the family completed at posttreatment, Lisa wrote, "At the start I did not want to go to therapy, but now I can see that it helped a lot. I am glad about that my mum and dad pressured me a bit to do the things I could not do. I am happy now."

Lisa's parents' view. Both Lisa's mother and her stepfather were motivated for the therapy from the beginning, and they were eager to start working with Lisa's anxiety. In session 3 on parent management, they became aware of their tendency to overprotect and avoid anxiety-provoking situations, and they started working with their own behaviors. They were both very open and reflective about their anxiety. At session 3 the mother brought several bracelets she had bought through an Internet site with the text "Openness about anxiety" written on them; and to the question about what a fly on the wall would observe in their home, the mother answered that "The fly would observe a lot of reassurance and overprotective behavior." Parents supported Lisa in doing her homework, they understood the principles of the therapy, and they seemed to agree and work well together. They were happy about being in the parent group and believed that the group format contributed to the success of the therapy.

Factors contributing to positive outcome. There was a good therapeutic alliance between the ST and Lisa, with agreement on the goals of the treatment and tasks, and the development of a personal bond made up of reciprocal positive feelings. This was enhanced by the ST's emphasis on humor in the cognitive restructuring and exposure. The manualized and graduated, step-by-step format of the therapy seemed to suit the family well, and they all responded well to the exercises in cognitive restructuring, graded exposure, and the parent management psychoeducation. Also, the group format suited both Lisa and her parents well, with Lisa being motivated by the group and the response from the other youth, and the parents benefiting from the contact with the other parents.

MARIUS'S NEGATIVE OUTCOME
Therapy outcome was measured through diagnostic interviews and self-report questionnaires. As shown in Table 3.7, based on the clinician's ADIS ratings, at pretreatment Marius had a primary diagnosis of social phobia, with a secondary diagnosis of compulsions. The social phobia diagnosis persisted through post group treatment, 3-month follow-up to group treatment, and post individual treatment, but finally disappeared at 3-month-follow-up to individual treatment. The parallel youth rating was somewhat in agreement with the clinician's, while the parents saw less reduction in diagnostic difficulties.

As also seen in Table 3.7, Marius's CGAS score did not change that much over the course of his treatments. It did end up at 6 points higher than when he started (64 versus 58), but still all his scores were below 70 and thus in the clinical range. Marius's CGI at the end of individual therapy and at 3-month, group-therapy follow-up was a 3 (minimally improved with little or no clinically meaningful reduction of symptoms and little change in clinical status and functional capacity); however, this improved at the end of individual therapy and at 3-month follow-up to a 2 (much improved).

Table 3.8 presents Marius's and his parents' self-report scores on the same measures shown for Lisa and her parents in Table 3.6 at the beginning, the end, and 3-month follow-up of the group treatment. Comparing Table 3.6 for Lisa and Table 3.8 for Marius, it can be seen that while there were a few significant improvements for Marius in the group treatment, generally there was little change as compared with Lisa. These figures reflect the difference in the CGI scores of Lisa and Marius at the 3-month follow-up to the group treatment, consisting of a 1 (very much improved) versus a 3 (minimally improved), respectively. A further comparison of Lisa's and Marius's results is presented in the "Synthesis" section.

MARIUS'S THERAPY PROCESS IN THE GROUP THERAPY

Marius's view. Marius perceived the work with the CK/CA program as a "bitter obligation," showing resistance to the program because he felt therapy took time from other activities he enjoyed. Even though he was motivated to overcome his social phobia, he was not always engaged in the work that was needed. This might be related to the fact that he experienced such intense anxiety that he could not stand the anxiety and often chose instead to avoid anxiety-provoking situations.

Marius seemed to have low self-esteem and react as defeated, giving up when things seemed very difficult, with statements like "It is too hard I will never learn this." His inability to identify the thoughts that were related to his anxiety also made it impossible to practice cognitive restructuring with him. As a result, he did not acquire a technique that could help him prepare for conducting exposures by lowering his anxiety level.

Also, Marius seemed to view himself as "handicapped" and did not wish others at school to know of his anxiety difficulties. This secrecy impaired the anxiety work at school and his feelings of being accepted by his classmates.

Marius's parents' view. At the beginning of therapy the parents seemed somewhat critical of the therapist, and the father was in doubt whether the therapy would be effective for Marius's difficulties, saying, "It is not helpful when the cure is worse than the problem." This might have influenced the parents' engagement in therapy and Marius's motivation for therapy, as well as his belief in his capabilities.

The parents were not very engaged in therapy, as they did not attend two of the sessions and did not do a lot homework, with the mother acknowledging they lacked the energy needed. They were unsure how much they should pressure Marius, and they did not prepare and support him as much as he needed before starting therapy and when implementing the first stepladder. The parents acknowledged they had difficulties implementing exposures in practice.

The fact that the parents had great understanding of Marius's difficulties and possibly identified themselves with him could have made it difficult to set demands. This identification with Marius also seemed to contribute to the mother being overprotective, talking on Marius's behalf and stating that he needed a break from the program.

Factors related to therapy. Therapy was conducted in a group format, which was very anxiety provoking for Marius, as a social phobic. It made the start of therapy very difficult for him, and this also could have had an impact on his motivation to attend therapy and most likely hindered his learning of techniques.

Also, the parents needed more guidance from the therapist, as at session 8 they were still uncertain about how to implement stepladders in practice. That became apparent when the student therapist's help in "clarifying and structuring," which the mother mentioned as important, contributed to the mother contacting the school and starting to implement the therapy principles. This led the mother to say that "now something is happening," but this was unfortunately at a very late stage in therapy.

Therapy was manualized, which did not target Marius's social phobia specifically. It was through the extra interventions (phone call and home visit) that the mother felt understood and the techniques were accommodated to Marius's needs. The intervention seemed to be too short for Marius's difficulties.

MARIUS AND HIS PARENTS' INDIVIDUAL, INDIVIDUALIZED THERAPY AFTER MARIUS WAS A "NONREPONDER" IN THE GROUP TREATMENT

As described earlier, Marius was offered an additional 10 sessions of nonresponder treatment. This treatment was moderately successful at posttreatment, based on a number of quantitative indicators as shown in Table 3.7, discussed earlier, and summarized by his 3-month follow-up rating of 2 (much improved).

At the 3-month assessment interview after the individual therapy, the parents evaluated Marius as functioning fairly well in his daily life, and they reported that he feels safe. He was attending school and sports and spent time with friends. He did not seem anxious while engaging in any of these activities. However, at the time the family was is in a difficult and stressful situation, since Marius's grandmother had been ill, and Marius's older brother had developed a new mental disorder and was presently being admitted to the psychiatric hospital. Marius's compulsions had escalated lately, perhaps due to his Tourette's condition. The family made an appointment with the child psychiatrist who had previously treated Marius. These changes are indicated by the appearance of OCD diagnoses at 3-month follow-up in the ADIS ratings by the clinician and the mother and father. Notably, at this follow-up Marius continued to maintain his positive CGAS score and to remain a "responder" on the CGI-I rating, along with the clinician not rating him as formally having social phobia.

SYNTHESIS OF THE FINDINGS FROM THE RCT AND CASE STUDY APPROACHES

The Effectiveness of the Cool Kids/Chilled Adolescents Program in Denmark

The results of the RCT showed that the implementation of the manualized, 10-session group CK/CA programs for treatment of youth anxiety disorders in Denmark was successful, with the results comparable to, and for the self-report measures, even better than, previous RCTs in other countries. At postassessment 66.1% of the youth in the intervention group were free of their primary anxiety diagnosis compared to 7.5% in the waitlist group. Furthermore, when compared to the waitlist group, youth, mothers, and fathers in the treatment group reported significantly more reduction in self-reported anxiety symptoms, everyday life interference due to anxiety, and depression. All of the changes were accompanied by large effect sizes. Youth also reported a significantly higher increase in self-confidence.

A more conservative measure of improvement is the percent of youth who demonstrated clinically significant change at the SCAS, that is, those who were above the clinical cutoff at pre and below at post, and whose change was statistically significant. This analysis shows that in terms of the youth, mother, and father ratings, respectively, 42.9%, 51.8%, and 41.8% of the youth in the treatment group demonstrated this type of improvement, compared with 11.3%, 11.3%, and 9.8%, respectively, in the waiting-list group (Table 3.2). Moreover, as described in the RCT results section, the reported satisfaction with the treatment at the postevaluation was high, both among youth and parents, and none of the youth or the parents thought that the treatment had made them or their youth worse. Three months after the treatment youth had improved even further with 73.0% being free of their primary diagnosis and 57.9% free of all anxiety diagnoses, and both self-reported anxiety symptoms and interference having further decreased significantly.

The Cultural Context of Replicating the CK/CA Program Across Countries

On the face of the situation, it would seem that there should be relatively few cultural issues is translating the CK/CA program from Australia to Denmark. First, there are many commonalities between the two countries: Both are affluent and industrialized, with a moderate to high percentage of the population being of European ancestry. Second, the sites of the program's implementation in both countries were similar, that is, in a large urban area. Thus, it is not a surprise that the two main participants in the development of the programs—Ronald Rapee in Australia and Mikael Thastum in Denmark—experienced almost no cultural differences in how the program was implemented. In the words of Thasum:

In 2008 [I] . . . was at a 6 month research stay at the Centre for Emotional Health at Macquarie University, Sydney, to study the evidence-based, cognitive-behavioral "Cool Kids" program for treating anxiety disorders in children developed by Ronald Rapee and his colleagues. . . . Returning to Denmark in August 2008, [I] . . . adapted and translated the manual and workbooks for the CF/CA program into Danish, and conducted an uncontrolled pilot test of the feasibility and preliminary efficacy of the Cool Kids program in Denmark. In the translation of the program almost no cultural adaptations were made, and all the illustrations were retained. From the material it seemed that the Danish and Australian culture is very similar. The feedback from the children and parents in the pilot study did not result in further adaptations of the material. (2013, p. 116)

And here are the words of Rapee and his colleagues (Perini, Wuthrich, & Rapee, 2013) in reading extended case studies based on Thastum's pilot study:

Of particular interest were the clear similarities from these anxious Danish children to our own experiences with childhood anxiety disorders in Australia. Aside from some minor cultural differences, the descriptions could easily have been taken from the case files of our own clients. There was an immediate sense of recognition, especially as we read about some of the treatment challenges encountered—each difficulty reminded us of obstacles we face regularly in our Clinic. The response rate reported, with four out of the six children making significant progress, is also consistent with the outcomes that we typically achieve within group-based treatment in Australia. (p. 363)

Increasing Remission Rates From Posttreatment to Follow-Up

As discussed previously, the increasing remission rate and anxiety reduction from the posttreatment assessment to the 3-month follow-up compared to other similar treatment programs may be explained by the fact that the treatment program was short and compressed, and that the families therefore continued working with the methods after the treatment ended. In line with this, in the qualitative evaluation at the posttreatment assessment, the most common comment to the question as to whether anything in the program could be improved, was that there should have been more time, for example, 2 weeks, between each session for more at-home practice, and that the program was too short.

Furthermore, a unique feature of our design was that in connection with the 3-month follow-up, there was a scheduled booster session, where youth and parents met with the therapists to discuss their progress and to problem-solve possible obstacles to progress. The youth's and their parents' expectations of the booster session may have increased their motivation to continue with the work associated with the therapy.

In the present study both parents participated in the treatment in 91% of the cases, and the mean number of sessions attended by the mother (8.82) versus the father (7.45) was very similar. As previously discussed, inclusion of fathers in treatment is associated with youth gains, both posttreatment and in the long term (Bagner & Eyberg, 2003; Podell & Kendall, 2011). The high participating rate of the fathers may therefore also distinguish this study from previous similar studies, and it may partly explain the high success rate. One year after treatment the self-reported symptoms were stable, which indicates a long-term effect of the treatment.

In sum, our RCT provides valuable information concerning the efficacy of CBT for youth with anxiety disorders in a Danish context, and it meets the generally accepted standards for causal inference and internal validity (e.g., random selection, homogeneous groups, a specified intervention, standardized outcome measures, and interrater reliability checks).

What the Cases of Lisa and Marius Tell Us

Although the RCT yielded successful results overall, at 3-month follow-up, 27.0% of the youth still suffered from the primary anxiety diagnosis with which they presented before treatment, and 42.1% of the youth suffered from other anxiety diagnoses. Thus, even though the treatment for many of the youth was successful, a large minority did not get sufficient help.

Consequently, the knowledge from the RCT *that* the treatment generally worked is not very informative about a range of important questions, such as practical knowledge for the clinician that is applicable to and effective in the individual case (Flyvbjerg, 2006), what characterizes nonresponders to the evidence-based treatment of anxious youth, under what conditions treatment works, and how the evidence-based treatment mechanisms of change may be enhanced to improve the outcome of this group, that is, the questions of with whom, under what conditions, and how treatment works (Weisz, Ng, Rutt, Lau, & Masland, 2013).

In a recent systematic review of clinical and demographic, pretreatment youth and family predictors of treatment outcome in CBT for anxiety disorders in youth, we concluded that few clinically relevant youth or family characteristics predicting treatment outcome were found, with our main finding being that the more severely disturbed patients both begin and end treatment at a higher level of disturbance than the less severely disturbed, but with at least as large a degree of improvement (Lundkvist-Houndoumadi, Hougaard, & Thastum, 2013). As mentioned earlier, a more recent study (Hudson et al., 2015)—to date, the largest multisite trial of clinical and genetic predictors of response to CBT in pediatric anxiety disorders—included a sample of 1,942 youth aged 5–18 years with a primary anxiety diagnosis who received CBT across 11 sites. Findings indicated that poorer response to CBT was associated with social phobia, high initial severity, nonanxiety comorbidity, female gender, and parental psychopathology.

In a review of the anxiety therapy literature with adults involving predictors of nonresponse, Taylor, Abramowitz, and McKay (2012) conclude that no predictor of treatment outcome has been consistently supported in the literature, and that more research is needed to develop criteria about methods for selecting optimal treatments, and strategies for improving outcome if initial treatment does not lead to clinical improvement. One of their suggestions is to reevaluate the case formulation in case of nonresponse, as we did in the case of Marius, as described earlier.

Research into mediators of change in evidence-based treatments for anxiety disorders in youth is also scarce, and findings confirming a temporal precedence for the mediators, relative to changes in anxiety symptoms, which is necessary for mediators to be considered true mechanisms of change (Weisz et al., 2013), is to our knowledge almost nonexistent. Prognostic variables of anxious youth's differential response to CBT and mechanisms of change probably form complex interactional patterns of causal relationships that may best be investigated either through large samples or multiple case studies that can investigate the complex, idiographic patterns of patient prognostic variables (Dattilio, Edwards, & Fishman, 2010; Fishman, 2005).

The two case studies drawn from our RCT were, as previously described, chosen to provide such idiographic knowledge of the therapeutic course of a typical client with good response (Lisa) and a typical poor-outcome client (Marius).

Lisa with GAD as primary diagnosis, and with SoP, SAD, and SP as comorbid diagnoses, was one of the 57.0% of the youth in the total treatment sample who at the 3-month follow-up was free of all anxiety diagnoses. One hundred percent of the 23 youth in the RCT with a primary diagnosis of GAD were free of this diagnosis at 3-month follow-up, although 26% still had other anxiety diagnoses, so in that way Lisa's positive outcome (e.g., see Table 3.5) represents a typical case.

In the previously mentioned multisite study by Hudson et al. (2015), where the treatment mainly was generic, it was also found that youth with GAD had high remission rates for the primary diagnosis (64% at post and 78% at 3-month follow-up). Lisa and her parents were in many ways ideal clients and instantiate, that is embody, some of the mediators of positive change in CK/CA therapy. Both Lisa and her parents were from the beginning motivated for the therapy. Lisa understood quickly the main principles of the therapy, realistic thinking and gradual exposure; she used the central therapeutic methods, including doing her homework; and she participated actively in the group. Her parents worked actively to combat their tendency toward overprotection, they drew support and help from the other parents in the group, and they were happy about the group setup. In addition, the alliance between the graduate ST and the family seemed very good.

In current models GAD is assumed to be maintained by (1) a low tolerance for uncertainty; (2) dysfunctional beliefs about worry; (3) negative problem orientation; and (4) dysfunctional strategies to reduce distress (Kertz & Woodruff-Borden, 2011; Payne, Bolton, & Perrin, 2011). The ST was inspired by these models and specifically worked with Lisa's low tolerance for uncertainty both by cognitive restructuring and by gradual exposure. Also the modified client-centered case formulation that was presented to the family at session 9 was inspired by this model (e.g., by emphasizing Lisa's anxiety as precipitated by chaos and unpredictability, and her excessive worrying). Only a few disorder-specific CBT programs for youth with GAD have been published, and none with a controlled design (Clementi & Alfano, 2014; Payne et al., 2011). Furthermore, the results for these programs do not present evidence for the rates of success being superior compared with those from generic treatment programs like ours and the earlier-mentioned Hudson et al. (2015) study.

Marius, with SoP as a primary diagnosis, and with OCD and Tourette's syndrome as comorbid diagnoses, was one of the 27.1% of the youth who still suffered from their primary anxiety diagnosis at 3-month follow-up. Since 58.8%

of the youth with SoP in the RCT still had their primary diagnosis at 3-month follow-up, Marius's poor outcome also represented a rather typical case. Similar results have been found in other studies. In the Hudson et al. (2015) study, youth with SoP had the poorest outcomes, as they were five times more likely than youth with GAD to still have a diagnosis at the end of the study. Also, in the large-scale "Child/Adolescent Anxiety Multimodal Study" (CAMS; Ginsburg et al., 2011), absence of an SoP diagnosis was a predictor of remission at posttreatment in all treatment conditions (sertraline, CBT, or a combination).

From the start of the treatment Marius experienced intense anxiety in the therapy sessions, probably because the group format seemed to overwhelm him with fear. He was not able to identify his anxious thoughts, and cognitive restructuring was therefore not very helpful for him. In a previous case study (Lundkvist-Houndoumadi & Thastum, 2013a), Erik, a 12-year-old boy with cognitive difficulties and multiple anxiety disorders, including SoP, who also participated in a CK/CA group treatment program, had similar problems with cognitive restructuring (although both he and his parent in many other respects were very different from the Marius case). One of the conclusions of the successful Eric case study was the necessity of accommodating the treatment to Erik's cognitive developmental level, such that Erik's cognitions were initially successfully challenged only through graduated exposures and only later addressed with cognitive restructuring, aided by the parents' guidance and with Erik's advancing cognitive maturation. This was possible within the manualized group treatment format.

In Marius's case, there might have been too much focus on cognitive restructuring, with the therapy therefore not meeting Marius developmental level. Marius reacted with great resistance to the therapist's and parents' attempts to make him verbalize his feelings and thoughts. It was apparently not before the therapists gave up this endeavor in the beginning of the nonresponder treatment course that positive change began to emerge. Thus, to treat Erik and Marius successfully, a modification of the CK/CA manual was required, where more focus was on exposures as a less direct means to challenge their maladaptive cognitions. Both youth were either not motivated or not able to engage in cognitive restructuring as an exercise detached from the exposure. When doing exposures, it was possible to challenge their erroneous cognitions, as they could more readily see the relevance of having realistic thoughts during anxiety-provoking situations.

In Lisa's case, it seemed to be possible to individualize her treatment without the therapist losing fidelity to the manualized treatment protocol. For example, this was achieved by working with her GAD symptoms, drawing guidance from current models of GAD, and by introducing a modified client-centered case formulation. A common critique of manual-based treatments is that manuals inhibit therapists' creativity and their sensitivity to individual needs (Kendall, Gosch, Furr, & Sood, 2008). Following Kendall, Chu, et al. (1998), Lisa's case exemplifies how both creativity and clinical skills can be components of manual-based treatment, and that it is possible to be flexible within fidelity. In a related way, in the case of Marius, the therapists may have been following the manual too inflexibly in the group treatment, without adapting it to the specific needs of Marius, which would have involved focusing more on exposures that were relevant for him and not insisting that he should practice cognitive restructuring and verbalize his emotions according to the manual.

Another issue that might have been related to Marius's nonresponse to treatment was that both of his parents suffered from SoP. The mother especially identified with Marius's problems and was very overprotective. Previous studies have found, albeit inconsistently, that parental psychopathology reduces the efficacy of treatment for anxious youth (Knight, McLellan, Jones, & Hudson, 2014; Lundkvist-Houndoumadi, Hougaard, & Thastum, 2014), and in the recent, large Hudson et al. (2015) study, youth whose parents manifested elevated anxiety and depression symptoms showed poorer rates of remission and response at the latter stages of therapy. Results from the case study of Erik (Lundkvist-Houndoumadi & Thastum, 2013a) and the case study of Marius may illuminate some of the inconsistent findings in previous research concerning the efficacy of parental involvement (Breinholst et al., 2012) and the influence of parental psychopathology (Lundkvist-Houndoumadi et al., 2014).

As with Marius's mother, Erik's mother suffered from anxiety herself. During therapy we actively worked on reducing the influence of the anxiety of Erik's mother on her behavior toward Erik and her perception of him. Treatment therefore may have contributed to transforming the mother from being a maintaining factor (an anxious parent) to a "mechanism of change" (an anxious parent who during therapy changed her behavior toward her youth in a manner that facilitated change). There is also the dynamic that both of these youth normalized their parents' behavior by mimicking the same disorder. It is a way of drawing close to them as well. Initial parental anxiety may thus in some cases, when successfully worked through, actually enhance treatment outcome. On the contrary, Marius's parents did not have the resources and/or did not get enough support to change their maladaptive behavior toward Marius during the manualized group treatment. In this case, parental anxiety therefore may have decreased the efficacy of the therapy.

Marius's parents were critical of the therapist from the beginning of the treatment, probably as a reaction to Marius's initial dramatically negative response to the group format. Furthermore, it was hard for Marius's parents to help with his homework and to implement exposures between sessions. In addition, the parents' social anxiety may have made it difficult for them to participate in a group with other parents. It thus seemed that the manualized group program did not suit the needs of the family. It was only during the home visit and the phone calls between sessions that the mother felt understood and where the necessary clarification and structuring of the therapy was initiated.

In a previous embedded case study of a similar CK/CA group of six youth (Lundkvist-Houndoumadi & Thastum, 2013b), we explored the differences between the four responders and the two nonresponders and found that seven factors differentiated the nonresponders. These included (1) lack of motivation; (2) that the youth seemed not to be aware of the negative consequences of their anxiety because their parents had supported their avoidance; (3) difficulties of using the treatment components; (4) lack of parental engagement; (5) low self-efficacy both in youth and parents; (6) not being able to use the group format positively, and (7) parental anxiety. In contrast, responders were characterized as being (1) motivated; (2) their parents were engaged and supportive and transferred skills to their youth; (3) the group treatment format was experienced as supportive by both youth and parents; (4) the support provided by parents reinforced youth's motivation, and the positive parenting style facilitated the practice and use of the treatment components; (5) youth integrated the anxiety coping skills and enhanced their self-efficacy, while their anxiety was gradually lowered; (6) the parents changed their expectations about their youth's ability to deal with anxiety, altered their own behavior (e.g., no longer overprotecting them), and acquired skills becoming more confident about handling future anxiety in their youth. These findings are very parallel to what was learned from Lisa's and Marius's cases.

Individualized Treatment Offered Nonresponders to Manualized Group CBT Increases the Response Rates

As previously described, a unique feature of our research design was the additional study of individualized CBT treatment for the nonresponders in the RCT, that is, youth with a CGI-I of 3–7 at the end of treatment. Of the 24 nonresponders (23% of the total number of youth treated), at the 3-month follow-up assessment of the RCT, 6 were excluded from the study because their primary problems were assessed not to be anxiety (2 with an eating disorder, 3 with autism spectrum disorder, and 1 other). Of the 18 who were offered nonresponder treatment, 4 did not wish additional treatment at the clinic, due to their being offered treatment elsewhere (2), having moved (1), or not believing additional treatment was needed (1). Thus, 14 youth (58% of the nonresponders) received case-based nonresponder treatment. Therapy usually consisted of 10 sessions, unless otherwise was considered suitable when planning treatment. The number of sessions ranged from 6 to 20 (M = 11.4, SD = 4.2). At the 3-month follow up assessment of the RCT, the primary diagnoses of the nonresponders were SoP (6), SAD (4), GAD (1), OCD (1), SP (1), and agoraphobia (1). The mean CSR of the primary diagnosis was 5.9, and the mean CGAS was 52.

At the post nonresponder treatment assessment, 57% were free of their primary diagnosis and 43% were free of all diagnoses. The mean CGAS was 63, and 86% were responders judged by the CGI-I. At the 3-month nonresponder follow-up assessment, 79% were free of their primary diagnosis and 64% were free of all diagnoses. The mean CGAS was 66, and 86% were responders judged by the CGI-I. Thus, a large number of youth with anxiety disorders who did not respond to manualized CBT improved with a subsequent case-based approach. At the 3-month nonresponder follow-up, of the total sample that had completed the RTC treatment including the nonresponders, 89% were free of their primary diagnosis, and 67% were free of all anxiety diagnoses (compared to 73.7% versus 57.9%, respectively, 3 months after the RCT, and provided that none of the responders from the RCT relapsed between the 3-month RCT follow-up assessment and the 3-month nonresponder follow-up assessment).

It seems that what was needed in the treatment was "more of the same" CBT treatment elements, but with individualized dosage and choice of the various CBT modules to address the individual difficulties of each particular youth and family. This could, for example, involve working with difficulties with motivation; with completion of homework; with diagnosis-specific treatment in the case of, for example, social phobia; with helping the youth identify his or her anxious cognitions; with taking comorbidity into consideration; or with working with parental anxiety. (For a full qualitative and quantitative description of the nonresponder study, see Lundkvist-Houndoumadi, Thastum, & Hougaard, 2015.)

Findings From a Mixed-Methods Approach Converge: Generic Manualized Group CBT May Not Be the Best Treatment of Choice for Youths With Social Phobia as a Primary Diagnosis

As reported herein, the majority of nonresponders had a primary SoP diagnosis. SoP may differ from other anxiety disorders in several ways. SoP involves a fear of social and/or performance situations, where youth with other disorders such as GAD or SAD are less concerned with the opinion of others (Crawley, Beidas, Benjamin, Martin, & Kendall, 2008). Youth with SoP also both have been found to rate themselves and to be less socially competent compared to youth with other disorders (Spence, Donovan, & Brechman-Toussaint, 1999). Although there is a tradition for generic treatment programs for treatment of youth anxiety, several trials have been conducted with specific programs for youth with SoP (e.g., Beidel, Turner, & Morris, 2000; Melfsen, Kuhnemund, & Schwieger, 20111 Spence, Donovan, & Brechman-Toussaint, 2000). Most programs are based on traditional CBT principles, but with an additional focus on social skills training. In the meta-analysis of Reynolds et al. (2012), nine trials that evaluated CBT for SoP in youth were included, all of them of group CBT, with a controlled effect size of youth pre-post self-reports of .79, compared to .53 for generic programs. Consistent with these findings, the NICE (2013) best practice guidelines include in their recommendations for youth with SoP the following treatment components: "Psychoeducation, exposure to feared or avoided social situations, [and] training in social skills and opportunities to rehearse skills in social situations" (p. 30).

Considering Marius, the manualized group treatment seemed not to allow a specific focus on his social anxiety and on social skills training. The group consisted of youth with a variety of diagnoses, most not involving fear of social situations, which may have exacerbated his low self-confidence and his negative evaluation of his social performance. Although the group ideally could have provided good opportunities for Marius to rehearse social interaction, this format was too anxiety provoking for him. However, in the following nonresponder treatment much more focus was on training Marius social skills. Since treatment now was individual, in the treatment sessions it was possible to plan in-vivo exposures that were not too anxiety provoking for Marius, for example, buying a magazine in a shop. The nonresponder treatment was an example of the benefits of reviewing and revising the original case formulation in the light of nonresponse and developing a new one that can lead to new interventions (Persons, 2013). However, we do not know whether Marius would have profited from being in a group consisting only of youth with SoP.

Conclusion

The combined RCT and case studies of the Danish CK/CA treatment program for anxious youth yield a number of important conclusions. First, the manualized-group CK/CA program can be very helpful for many youth, specifically in the Danish setting, at least through 3-month and 12-month follow-up. This finding is strengthened by one aspect of the design of the study: assessing the outcome of the waiting list control group when they were offered the same therapy 3 months into the project. The positive results of this therapy were similar to the results of the original treatment group, thus suggesting a type of informal replication of the findings with the original treatment group. (Note, of course, that this is not a full, independent replication of the results, since the subjects were part of the same study, in the same setting, conducted by the same researchers, and so forth.).

Second, for those youth who were nonresponders to this treatment, follow-up individual therapy that was tailored to the needs and contexts of each particular youth and his or her parents was able to increase the percentage of youth who can be helped. For example, while at 3-month follow-up the manualized group treatment was successful in yielding a rate of 73.7% of the youth being free of their primary diagnosis and 57.9% being free of all anxiety diagnoses, those rates were increased to 89% and 67%, respectively, when the effects of the individual therapy—based on the same CBT principles as the group manualized therapy but adapted to each client—were added.

Third, the reasons for the general success of the manualized treatment are exemplified in the case study of Lisa, who, along with her parents, demonstrated many of the factors associated with the capacity to benefit from the group therapy. These included Lisa's motivation for therapy, her willingness to share her worries in the youth group, her engagement with homework tasks, her understanding of the concepts of realistic thinking, her openness to the exposure tasks, and her parents, who were motivated for therapy, reflective, open to learning about the best way for them to help Lisa, and able to use humor to ease the challenge of Lisa trying new and difficult behaviors.

Fourth, the reasons for the limitations of the group therapy were exemplified by the case study of Marius, whose social phobia "scared him off" from participating in and benefitting from the group, a process exacerbated by his parents' overprotectiveness. The follow-up individualized therapy with

Marius showed how the same CBT principles behind the manualized therapy could be adapted and tailored to the needs of Marius and his parents to yield a positive result.

Finally, the overall design of the study can be likened to the concept of "stepped care," in which those clients like Marius who do not profit from the first step (manualized group therapy), then proceed to a second step of care (tailored individual therapy). While conducting only two case studies clearly has built-in limitations in the process of creating generalized knowledge, we believe that the insights and additional knowledge offered by the cases of Lisa and Marius argue strongly for devoting resources to numerous case studies as a routine part of conducting randomized clinical trials.

ACKNOWLEDGMENTS BY MIKAEL THASTUM ET AL.

We would like to acknowledge the special contribution to the RCT study that was made by Lisbeth Jørgensen and Signe Maria Schneevoigt Matthiesen, who were the two psychologists who ran most of the groups in the study; and also by Helle Karoline Andreassen and Nanna Marie Mortensen, the two student therapists who worked with the two cases, Lisa and Marius, respectively.

Funding for the study was provided by Trygfonden, a Danish Foundation.

REFERENCES

Albano, A. M., & Silverman, W. K. (1996). *Anxiety disorders interview scedule for DSM-IV. Child version.* Oxford, UK: Oxford University Press.

American Psychiatric Association (1994). *Diagnostic and statistical manual of mental disorders.* Washington, DC: Author.

Angold, A., Costello, E. J., Messer, S. C., Pickles, A., Winder, F., & Silver, D. (1995). Development of a short questionnaire for use in epidemiological studies of depression in children and adolescents. *International Journal of Methods in Psychiatric Research, 5*, 237–249.

Arendt, K. B., Hougaard, E., & Thastum, M. (2014). Psychometric properties of the child and parent versions of Spence Children's Anxiety Scale in a Danish community and clinical sample. *Submitted.*

Attride-Stirling, J. (2002). Development of methods to capture users' views of child and adolescent mental health services in clinical governance reviews. http://www.corc.uk.net/wp-content/uploads/2012/03/CHI-evaluation-report-Attride-Stirling-J1.pdf

Bagner, D. M. & Eyberg, S. M. (2003). Father involvement in parent training: when does it matter? *Journal of Clinical Child and Adolescent Psychology, 32*, 599–605.

Barrett, P. M. (2004). *Friends for life - Group leader's manual* (4th ed.). Brisbane: Australian Academic Press.

Barrett, P. M., Lowry-Webster, H., & Turner, C. M. (2014). *FRIENDS program for children: Group leaders manual.* Brisbane: Australian Academic Press.

Beck, J. S., Beck, A. T., & Jolly, J. (2001). *Beck youth inventories™ of emotional and social impairment.* Washington, DC: The Psychological Corporation.

Beidel, D. C., Turner, S. M., & Morris, T. L. (2000). Behavioral treatment of childhood social phobia. *Journal of Consulting and Clinical Psychology, 68,* 1072–1080.

Bogels, S. M., & Brechman-Toussaint, M. L. (2006). Family issues in child anxiety: Attachment, family functioning, parental rearing and beliefs. *Clinical Psychology Review, 26,* 834–856.

Bogels, S., & Phares, V. (2008). Fathers' role in the etiology, prevention and treatment of child anxiety: A review and new model. *Clinical Psychology Review, 28,* 539–558.

Breinholst, S., Esbjorn, B. H., Reinholdt-Dunne, M. L., & Stallard, P. (2012). CBT for the treatment of child anxiety disorders: A review of why parental involvement has not enhanced outcomes. *Journal of Anxiety Disorders, 26,* 416–424.

Carr, A. (2006). *The handbook of child and adolescent clinical psychology* (2nd. ed.) Nw York, NY: Routledge.

Clementi, M. A., & Alfano, C. A. (2014). Targeted behavioral therapy for childhood generalized anxiety disorder: A time-series analysis of changes in anxiety and sleep. *Journal of Anxiety Disorders, 28,* 215–222.

Cobham, V. E., Dadds, M. R., & Spence, S. H. (1998). The role of parental anxiety in the treatment of childhood anxiety. *Journal of Consulting and Clinical Psychology, 66,* 893–905.

Cohen, J. (1990). *Statistical power analysis for the behavioral sciences.* Hillsdale, NJ: Lawrence Erlbaum Associates.

Costello, E. J., Egger, H. L., Copeland, W., Erkanli, A., & Angold, A. (2011). The developmental epidemiology of anxiety disorders: Phenomenology, prevalence, and comorbidity. In W. K. Silverman & A. P. Field (Eds.), *Anxiety disorders in children and adolescents* (2nd. ed., pp. 56–75). Cambridge, UK: Cambridge University Press.

Costello, E. J., Mustillo, S., Erkanli, A., Keeler, G., & Angold, A. (2003). Prevalence and development of psychiatric disorders in childhood and adolescence. *Archives of General Psychiatry, 60,* 837–844.

Crawley, S. A., Beidas, R. S., Benjamin, C. L., Martin, E., & Kendall, P. C. (2008). Treating socially phobic youth with CBT: Differential outcomes and treatment considerations. *Behavioural and Cognitive Psychotherapy, 36,* 379–389.

Creswell, C., Murray, L., Stacey, J., & Cooper, P. (2011). Parenting and child anxiety. In W. K. Silverman & A. P. Field (Eds.), *Anxiety disorders in children and adolescents* (2nd. ed., pp. 299–321). Cambridge, UK: Cambridge University Press.

Dattilio, F. M., Edwards, D. J. A., & Fishman, D. B. (2010). Case studies within a mixed methods paradigm: Toward a resolution of the alienation between researcher and practitioner in psychotherapy research. *Psychotherapy, 47,* 427–441.

Eley, T. C., Napolitano, M., Lau, J. Y., & Gregory, A. M. (2010). Does childhood anxiety evoke maternal control? A genetically informed study. *Journal of Child Psychology and Psychiatry, 51,* 772–779.

Essau, C. A., Conradt, J., & Petermann, F. (2000). Frequency, comorbidity, and psychosocial impairment of anxiety disorders in German adolescents. *Journal of Anxiety Disorders, 14,* 263–279.

Fishman, D. B. (2005). From single case to database: A new method for enhancing psychotherapy practice. *Pragmatic Case Studies in Psychotherapy, 1*(1), 1–50. Available at http://pcsp.libraries.rutgers.edu/. doi: http://dx.doi.org/10.14713/pcsp.v1i1.855

Flannery-Schroeder, E., Sieberg, C. B., & Gosch, E. (2007). Cognitive-behavior group treatment for anxiety disorders. In R. W. Christner, J. L. Stewart, & A. Freeman (Eds.), *Cognitive-behavior group therapy with children and adolescents* (pp. 199–222). New York, NY: Routledge.

Flyvbjerg, B. (2006). Five misunderstandings about case-study research. *Qualitative Inquiry, 12*, 219–245.

Ginsburg, G. S., Kendall, P. C., Sakolsky, D., Compton, S. N., Piacentini, J., Albano, A. M., . . . & March, J. (2011). Remission after acute treatment in children and adolescents with anxiety disorders: findings from the CAMS. Journal of Consulting and Clinical Psychology, 79, 806–813.

Guy, W. (1976). *Clinical global impression (CGI). ECDEU assessment manual for psychopharmacology—revised* (pp. 218–222). Rockville, MD: National Institute of Mental Health.

Hudson, J. L., Keers, R., Roberts, S., Coleman, J. R. I., Breen, G. Arendt, K., . . . & Eley, T. C. (2015). Clinical predictors of response to cognitive-behavioral therapy in pediatric anxiety disorders: The Genes for Treatment (GxT) study. *Journal of the American Academy of Child & Adolescent Psychiatry, 54*, 454–463. doi: http://dx.doi.org/ 10.1016/j.jaac.2015.03.018

Hudson, J. L., Doyle, A. M., & Gar, N. (2009). Child and maternal influence on parenting behavior in clinically anxious children. *Journal of Clinical Child and Adolescent Psychology, 38*, 256–262.

Hudson, J. L., Rapee, R. M., Deveney, C., Schniering, C. A., Lyneham, H. J., & Bovopoulos, N. (2009). Cognitive-behavioral treatment versus an active control for children and adolescents with anxiety disorders: A randomized trial. *Journal of the American Academy of Child and Adolescent Psychiatry, 48*, 533–544.

James, A. C., James, G., Cowdrey, F. A., Soler, A., & Choke, A. (2013). Cognitive behavioural therapy for anxiety disorders in children and adolescents. *The Cochrane Database of Systematic Reviews, 6*, CD004690.

Keller, M. B., Lavori, P. W., Wunder, J., Beardslee, W. R., Schwartz, C. E., & Roth, J. (1992). Chronic course of anxiety disorders in children and adolescents. *Journal of the American Academy of Child and Adolescent Psychiatry, 31*, 595–599.

Kendall, P. C. (1990). *Coping cat woorkbook*. Ardmore, PA: Workbook Publishing.

Kendall, P.C., Chu, B.C., Gifford, A., Hayes, C., & Nauta, M. (1998). Breathing life into a manual: Flexibility and creativity with manual-based treatments. *Cognitive and Behavioral Practice, 5*, 177–198.

Kendall, P. C., Gosch, E., Furr, J. M., & Sood, E. (2008). Flexibility within fidelity. *Journal of the American Academy of Child and Adolescent Psychiatry, 47*, 987–993.

Kendall, P. C., Hudson, J. L., Gosch, E., Flannery-Schroeder, E., & Suveg, C. (2008). Cognitive-behavioral therapy for anxiety disordered youth: A randomized clinical trial evaluating child and family modalities. *Journal of Consulting and Clinical Psychology, 76*, 282–297.

Kertz, S. J. & Woodruff-Borden, J. (2011). The developmental psychopathology of worry. *Clinical Child and Family Psychology Review, 14*, 174–197.

Knight, A., McLellan, L., Jones, M., & Hudson, J. (2014). Pre-treatment predictors of outcome in childhood anxiety disorders: A systematic review. *Psychopathology Review, 1*, 77–129.

Lazar, A., Sagi, A., & Fraser, M. W. (1991). Involving fathers in social-services. *Children and Youth Services Review*, *13*, 287–300.

Lundkvist-Houndoumadi, I., Hougaard, E., & Thastum, M. (2014). Pre-treatment child and family characteristics as predictors of outcome in cognitive behavioural therapy for youth anxiety disorders. *Nordic Journal of Psychiatry*, *68*, 524–535.

Lundkvist-Houndoumadi, I. & Thastum, M. (2013a). A "Cool Kids" cognitive-behavioral therapy group for youth with anxiety disorders: Part 1, the case of Erik. *Pragmatic Case Studies in Psychotherapy*, *9*(2), 122–178. Available at: http://pcsp.libraries.rutgers.edu/. doi: http://dx.doi.org/10.14713/pcsp.v9i2.1817

Lundkvist-Houndoumadi, I. & Thastum, M. (2013b). A "Cool Kids" cognitive-behavioral therapy group for youth with anxiety disorders: Part 2, analysis of the process and outcome of responders versus nonresponders. *Pragmatic Case Studies in Psychotherapy*, *9*(2), 178–274. Available at: http://pcsp.libraries.rutgers.edu/. doi: http://dx.doi.org/10.14713/pcsp.v9i2.1818

Lundkvist-Houndoumadi, I., Thastum, M., & Hougaard, E. (2015). Effectiveness of an individualized case formulation-based CBT for nonresponding youths with anxiety disorders. *Journal of Child and Family Studies*, *25*, 503–517. doi:10.1007/s10826-015-0225-4

Lyneham, H. J., Sburlati, E. S., Abbott, M. J., Rapee, R. M., Hudson, J. L., Tolin, D. F., & Carlson, S. E. (2013). Psychometric properties of the Child Anxiety Life Interference Scale (CALIS). *Journal of Anxiety Disorders*, *27*, 711–719.

Manassis, K., Lee, T. C., Bennett, K., Zhao, X. Y., Mendlowitz, S., Duda, S., ... & Wood, J. J. (2014). Types of parental involvement in CBT with anxious youth: A preliminary meta-analysis. *Journal of Consulting and Clinical Psychology*, *82*, 1163–1172.

Melfsen, S., Kuhnemund, M., & Schwieger, J. (2011). Cognitive behavioral therapy of socially phobic children focusing on cognition: A randomised wait-list control study. *Child and Adolescent Psychiatry and Mental Health*, *5*, 1–12.

Muris, P., & Field, A. P. (2011). The "normal" development of fear. In W. K. Silverman & A. P. Field (Eds.), *Anxiety disorders in children and adolescents* (2nd ed., pp. 76–89). Cambridge, UK: Cambridge University Press.

Nauta, M. H., Scholing, A., Rapee, R. M., Abbott, M., Spence, S. H., & Waters, A. (2004). A parent-report measure of children's anxiety: Psychometric properties and comparison with child-report in a clinic and normal sample. *Behavior Research and Therapy*, *42*, 813–839.

NICE (National Institute for Health and Care Excellence) (2013). Social anxiety disorder: Recognition, assessment and treatment. http://www.nice.org.uk/guidance/cg159/resources/guidance-social-anxiety-disorder-recognition-assessment-and-treatment-pdf

Payne, S., Bolton, D., & Perrin, S. (2011). A pilot investigation of cognitive therapy for generalized anxiety disorder in children aged 7–17 years. *Cognitive Therapy and Research*, *35*, 171–178.

Perini, S.J., Wuthrich, V.M., & Rapee, R.M. (2013). "Cool Kids" in Denmark: Commentary on a cognitive-behavioral therapy group for anxious youth. *Pragmatic Case Studies in Psychotherapy*, *9*(3), 359–370. Available at http://pcsp.libraries.rutgers.edu/. http://dx.doi.org/10.14713/pcsp.v9i3.1828

Persons, J. B. (2013). Who needs a case formulation and why: Clinicians use the case formulation to guide decision-making. *Pragmatic Case Studies in Psychotherapy, 9*, 448–456.

Pine, D. S., Cohen, P., Gurley, D., Brook, J., & Ma, Y. (1998). The risk for early-adulthood anxiety and depressive disorders in adolescents with anxiety and depressive disorders. *Archives of General Psychiatry, 55*, 56–64.

Podell, J. L., & Kendall, P. C. (2011). Mothers and fathers in family cognitive-behavioral therapy for anxious youth. *Journal of Child and Family Studies, 20*, 182–195.

Rapee, R. M. (2000). Group treatment of children with anxiety disorders: Outcome and predictors of treatment response. *Australian Journal of Psychology, 52*, 125–129.

Rapee, R. M. (2001). The development of generalized anxiety. In M. Vasey & M. R. Dadds (Eds.), *The developmental psychopathology of anxiety* (pp. 481–503). Oxford, UK: Oxford University Press.

Rapee, R. M. (2003). The influence of comorbidity on treatment outcome for children and adolescents with anxiety disorders. *Behaviour Research and Therapy, 41*, 105–112.

Rapee, R. M., Abbott, M. J., & Lyneham, H. J. (2006). Bibliotherapy for children with anxiety disorders using written materials for parents: A randomized controlled trial. *Journal of Consulting and Clinical Psychology. 74*, 436–444.

Rapee, R. M., Lyneham, H. J., Hudson, J. L., Kangas, M., Wuthrich, V. M., & Schniering, C. A. (2013). Effect of comorbidity on treatment of anxious children and adolescents: Results from a large, combined sample. *Journal of the American Academy of Child and Adolescent Psychiatry, 52*, 47–56.

Rapee, R. M., Lyneham, H. J., Schniering, C. A., Wuthrich, V. M., Abbott, M., & Hudson, J. (2006). *Cool Kids therapist manual: For the Cool Kids child and adolescent anxiety programs*. Sydney: Centre for Emotional Health, Macquarie University.

Rapee, R. M., Schniering, C. A., & Hudson, J. L. (2009). Anxiety disorders during childhood and adolescence: Origins and treatment. *Annual Review of Clinical Psychology, 5*, 311–341.

Reynolds, S., Wilson, C., Austin, J., & Hooper, L. (2012). Effects of psychotherapy for anxiety in children and adolescents: A meta-analytic review. *Clinical Psychology Review, 32*, 251–262.

Roza, S. J., Hofstra, M. B., van der Ende, J., & Verhulst, F. C. (2003). Stable prediction of mood and anxiety disorders based on behavioral and emotional problems in childhood: A 14-year follow-up during childhood, adolescence, and young adulthood. *American Journal of Psychiatry, 160*, 2116–2121.

Schneider, S., Blatter-Meunier, J., Herren, C., Adornetto, C., In-Albon, T., & Lavallee, K. (2011). Disorder-specific cognitive-behavioral therapy for separation anxiety disorder in young children: A randomized waiting-list-controlled trial. *Psychotherapy and Psychosomatics, 80*, 206–215.

Shaffer, D., Gould, M. S., Brasic, J., Ambrosini, P., Fisher, P., Bird, H., & Aluwahlia, S. (1983). A children's global assessment scale (CGAS). *Archives of General Psychiatry, 40*, 1228–1231.

Shortt, A. L., Barrett, P. M., & Fox, T. L. (2001). Evaluating the FRIENDS program: A cognitive-behavioral group treatment for anxious children and their parents. *Journal of Clinical Child Psychology, 30*, 525–535.

Silverman, W. K., Kurtines, W. M., Ginsburg, G. S., Weems, C. F., Lumpkin, P. W., & Carmichael, D. H. (1999). Treating anxiety disorders in children with group cognitive-behaviorial therapy: A randomized clinical trial. *Journal of Consulting and Clinical Psychology, 67,* 995–1003.

Silverman, W. K., Kurtines, W. M., Jaccard, J., & Pina, A. A. (2009). Directionality of change in youth anxiety treatment involving parents: An initial examination. *Journal of Consulting and Clinical Psychology, 77,* 474–485.

Spence, S. H. (1997). Structure of anxiety symptoms among children: a confirmatory factor-analytic study. *Journal of Abnormal Psychology, 106,* 280–297.

Spence, S. H., Donovan, C., & Brechman-Toussaint, M. (1999). Social skills, social outcomes, and cognitive features of childhood social phobia. *Journal of Abnormal Psychology, 108,* 211–221.

Spence, S. H., Donovan, C., & Brechman-Toussaint, M. (2000). The treatment of childhood social phobia: The effectiveness of a social skills training-based, cognitive-behavioural intervention, with and without parental involvement. *Journal of Child Psychology and Psychiatry, 41,* 713–726.

Taylor, S., Abramowitz, J. S., & McKay, D. (2012). Non-adherence and nonresponse in the treatment of anxiety disorders. *Journal of Anxiety Disorders, 26,* 583–589.

Thastum, M. (2013). The Anxiety Disorder Clinic for Children and Adolescents (TADCCA) at the University of Aarhus in Denmark. *Pragmatic Case Studies in Psychotherapy, 9*(2), 115–121. Available at http://pcsp.libraries.rutgers.edu/. doi http://dx.doi.org/10.14713/pcsp.v9i2.1816

Thastum, M., Ravn, K., Sommer, S., & Trillingsgaard, A. (2009). Reliability, validity and normative data for the Danish Beck Youth Inventories. *Scandinavian Journal of Psychology, 50,* 47–54.

Weisz, J. R., Ng, M. L., Rutt, C., Lau, N., & Masland, S. (2013). Psychotherapy for children and adolescents. In M. Lambert (Ed.), *Handbook of psychotherapy and behavior change* (6th ed., pp. 541–586). Hoboken, NJ: John Wiley.

Whiteside, S. P., & Brown, A. M. (2008). Exploring the utility of the Spence Children's Anxiety Scales parent- and child-report forms in a North American sample. *Journal of Anxiety Disorders, 22,* 1440–1446.

Wood, J. J., Piacentini, J. C., Bergman, R. L., McCracken, J., & Barrios, V. (2002). Concurrent validity of the anxiety disorders section of the Anxiety Disorders Interview Schedule for DSM-IV: Child and parent versions. *Journal of Clinical Child and Adolescent Psychology, 31,* 335–342.

COMMENTARY
International Implementation of CBT: Universal Principles Meet Local Needs

Lauren J. Hoffman, Elaina A. Zendegui, and Brian C. Chu

The work of Thastum and his colleagues (this volume) presents exciting new directions for improving the robustness and accessibility of evidence-based services. Their chapter describes efforts to replicate evidence-based cognitive-behavioral therapy (CBT) treatment programs from one country, Australia, to another, Denmark, which contributes to the ever-expanding evidence base for global applicability of CBT for youth anxiety. We comment on the contributions of this replication trial and its implications for further dissemination of evidence-based practice across the globe, in addition to the unique role that mixed methods can play in this effort.

YOUTH ANXIETY ON A GLOBAL SCALE

Globally, mental health and substance use disorders are the leading cause of all of the "nonfatal burden" of disease, that is, in terms of disease that causes years of living with disability (Whiteford et al., 2013). Anxiety disorders are second among mental health disorders in contributing to functional impairment, next to depressive disorders. For both, the height of burden peaks early, prior to the age of 25 years. Specifically in Europe, anxiety disorders rank sixth as a top cause of disability across all ages, and they rank seventh as a leading cause of disability in Denmark (Murray et al., 2013).

CBT has a robust evidence base that supports its efficacy for treating anxiety in youth in controlled research settings (Silverman, Pina, & Viswesvaran, 2008) and has a growing evidence base for its effectiveness in more naturalistic settings (e.g., Southam-Gerow et al., 2010). Yet generally only a minority of those who require services to address psychological impairment actually receive treatment (Alonzo et al., 2004; WHO, 2004) and this is particularly true in children and adolescent populations. In developing countries, common barriers include a lack of well-established mental health care policies and coverage. Moreover, in both higher-income and lower- and middle-income countries, access to care remains a challenge due to lack of skilled treatment providers and acceptability of treatments across cultures (Patel, Chowdhary, Rahman, & Verdeli, 2011).

USING MIXED METHODS TO IMPROVE
TREATMENT EFFICACY

Despite CBT's established efficacy, approximately 40% of youth retain their anxiety diagnoses following treatment (James, James, Cowdrey, Soler, & Choke, 2013). Thastum et al.'s research offers an important next phase in improving this rate of success. Using a stepped-care approach, the authors employed a follow-up, individualized booster treatment posttrial for nonresponders like Marius. They found that after the originally nonrespondent youth had received these individualized sessions, remission rates went from 0% to 57%, and improved further at 3-month follow-up to 79%. When the results of the total group were combined, the 3-month follow-up remission rate went from 73% after the group therapy to 89% after the individualized therapy.

Thastum et al.'s case study of Marius highlights the authors' finding that socially phobic youth in the study responded less well to treatment than youth with other anxiety disorders. Marius's case demonstrates how social phobia can impact treatment in a variety of ways, primarily as it led to his particular resistance to participate in the group treatment. In addition, as Marius exhibited significant, debilitating anxiety preventing him from engaging in the first group session, it is possible that Marius's therapist did not have enough time to assess and provide coping skills for the particular behavioral patterns and/or cognitive distortions that maintained his distress. Thus, while cognitive restructuring and gradual exposures were introduced to Marius earlier than others in the group, those skills may not have specifically targeted Marius's unique anxiety response, particularly regarding entering and participating in the group. Subsequently, as merely sitting at the group table was anxiety provoking for Marius, his anxiety may have limited his ability to concentrate on the skills being taught, as well as his willingness to actively engage in the treatment process (e.g., answer questions, provide examples, etc.).

Furthermore, the group format may have been unable to provide Marius with enough dosage of exposure time to habituate to his anxiety, disconfirm his anxious cognitions, and practice all of his coping skills. The stepped-care approach allowed Marius's clinicians to combine information from the literature with Marius's unique experience to develop a second individualized case formulation. Marius's nonresponder treatment was then provided in an individual format and focused more on completing simple "stepladders" to reach exposure goals.

Marius's case illustrates several ways that his parents' anxiety may have maintained his anxiety and impacted treatment outcome. For example, in the group therapy phase, the family missed two sessions and failed to complete homework on several occasions, which may indicate parental avoidance of elements of the therapy. Parental avoidance may have been related to his parents' anxiety in group situations and their difficulty tolerating Marius's distress during group sessions and between-session exposures. Group therapists attempted to decrease avoidance by scheduling individual sessions to replace group sessions and giving the family additional support in troubleshooting barriers to homework completion.

In the post-group, individual treatment phase for Marius and his family, the individualized case formulation helped to improve treatment by revealing his parents' histories of social phobia and ways their continued avoidance behaviors may have contributed both to the etiology and the maintenance of Marius's anxiety. The therapist addressed these maintaining factors by scheduling individual sessions during times at which the family had no scheduling conflicts and providing large amounts of psychoeducation and individual support to decrease homework avoidance.

Individual formulation also revealed that parental beliefs may have maintained Marius's anxiety. Within the group format, problematic parental beliefs were illustrated when Marius's mother expressed that he needed a break from therapy and when his father expressed that the therapy was too hard for Marius and his concern that "the cure is worse than the problem." The sentiments expressed by both parents point to possible overprotectiveness, low belief in Marius's coping ability, and belief that distress may be threatening. Within the individual work, therapists addressed such beliefs with psychoeducation aimed at increasing his parents' awareness of the ways in which their behavior may contribute to the maintenance of Marius's anxiety.

This study provides a compelling example of how group-based controlled research, integrated with a working knowledge of the literature, and merged with individualized case formulation, can improve outcomes for local patients. Successful outcomes can then be used to develop future iterations of the general treatment protocol to maximize success at the start. In addition, by using both RCT and single case design, the authors created a stepped-care approach to managing nonresponse. Stepped-care approaches are seen as critical systemic interventions to increase access to care in a health care environment of continually declining resources (Collins, Westra, Dozois, & Burns, 2004). The authors' particular approach should be lauded because its initial group format is relatively resource minimal, and the individual case formulation component provides a systematic process of self-correction (Bower & Gilbody, 2005). This kind of systematic feedback that elevates clients for "step-up" care can help conserve resources while protecting individual health outcomes.

Together, individualized case analysis helps to identify cases in need of step-up care when treatment outcomes are unsatisfactory. Over the long run, cumulative reflection on these case formulations can also provide valuable ideas for iterative protocol improvement that can help increase efficacy and reach for already efficacious treatments.

EXTENDING THE REACH OF CBT AROUND THE GLOBE

Improving efficacy in CBT is only one battle in the war to improve access and effectiveness of care worldwide. Disseminating evidence-based practice around the globe is essential, but successful generalization to diverse settings cannot be guaranteed. Implementation of any protocol in new geographic regions requires consideration for local cultures, treatment settings, and clientele. Initial efforts have been promising. As a start, CBT for youth anxiety has since been applied in multiple Western countries and demonstrated successful outcomes in Australia (Hudson et al., 2009; Rapee, 2000); Germany (Essau, Conradt, Sasagawa, & Ollendick, 2012); Canada (Rose, Miller, & Martinez, 2009); and Sweden (Ahlen, Breitholtz, Barrett, & Gallegos, 2012). In general, compared to control conditions, CBT in those countries has resulted in greater likelihood of diagnostic remission, fewer symptoms of anxiety and depression, higher self-esteem, and lower perfectionism.

One particular group-based CBT program, similar in content to Thastum et al.'s CK/CA treatment, is the Friends for Life Program (Barrett, Lowry-Webster, & Holmes, 1999), which was initially developed in Australia—like CK/CA—and has since been extensively researched throughout the world. FRIENDS is a 10-week group-based anxiety intervention/prevention program that aims to build resilience in youth and to develop skills in managing anxiety (e.g., problem solving, relaxation, cognitive restructuring, graduated exposure). A closer review of the FRIENDS literature reveals considerable variability regarding the degree to which cultural adaptations have been made or described by researchers. In particular, studies of the use of FRIENDS in Mexico (Gallegos-Guajardo, Ruvalcaba-Romero, Garza-Tamez, & Villegas-Guinea, 2013), Canada (Rose et al., 2009), and Sweden (Ahlen et al., 2012) did not explicitly describe any cultural adaptations or considerations that were made. Other researchers have highlighted small modifications, including a Canadian study that changed the number of sessions to fit within the particular school setting (Mifsud & Rapee, 2005) and a German study that replaced animal images with more culturally relevant pictures (Essau et al., 2012). Only a few studies have thoroughly described significant cultural adaptations.

For example, Miller and colleagues (2011) described extensive modifications of the FRIENDS program for use with Aboriginal youth in Canada. Those authors specified important aspects of the treatment development process, including enlisting help from Aboriginal school board consultants and support workers to develop engaging, meaningful, and attractive materials for Aboriginal students. They also made considerable adaptations to the treatment content, such as writing scripts for the beginning and end of each lesson to encourage the use of storytelling techniques, introducing a new character to serve as a "guide" throughout the treatment, and including additional craft projects, such as a "medicine pouch" and a modified medicine wheel.

In addition, Siu (2007) also described cultural adaptations of the FRIENDS program for use in Hong Kong. Based on their knowledge of the local culture, they changed the treatment structure to be more acceptable and feasible to school settings (e.g., 10 sessions were reduced to 8) and families (e.g., parent sessions reduced from 4 sessions to 2). Adaptations were also made to the treatment content, including giving characters traditional Chinese names, incorporating pictures, examples, and homework assignments that better reflected the experiences of Chinese youth (e.g., increased emphasis on academic pressure), and replacing the original relaxation exercise with a more well-known Chinese relaxation script. Though the latter studies did not compare the original FRIENDS program with their culturally enhanced versions, the authors hoped that youth would be more engaged in treatment that utilized more culturally relevant materials, which would then translate into enhanced learning and greater program effectiveness.

CBT IN DENMARK

Notably, the study by Thastum and colleagues is the first evaluation of a CBT program for youth anxiety in Denmark, cross-nationally replicating the Cool Kids program that was originally developed by Rapee and colleagues (2000) in Australia. The Thastum et al. study contributes to the literature by continuing to study CBT in different settings, across different countries and continents. The authors' mixed-methods approach was particularly informative, as supplementing their rigorous RCT design with exemplary case studies provided valuable analyses at both the group and individual level. Specifically, while the quantitative methods help readers to understand the overall effectiveness of this particular international translation, the qualitative discussion helps to explain important treatment processes, which can improve our understanding of mechanisms of change and ways to enhance and/or adapt our treatments.

THE NEXT GENERATION OF DISSEMINATION: IMPLEMENTING CBT IN NON-WESTERN, DEVELOPING COUNTRIES

To date, most formalized clinical trials of CBT for anxiety have been conducted in higher income, Western countries. However, the loci of greatest unmet need likely exist in developing, lower- and middle-income countries (LMIC), on such continents as in Africa, Asia, and the Middle East (Patel, Flisher, Hetrick, & McGorry, 2007). Key challenges to addressing mental health needs in these countries include the shortage of mental health professionals, the fairly low capacity and motivation of nonspecialist health workers to provide quality mental health services, and the stigma associated with mental disorders. These national health policy barriers are beyond the scope of this commentary, but good recommendations do exist to guide adaptation of CBT across diverse nations and cultures.

Since evidence has supported the use of CBT across cultures, most recommendations focus on adapting specific content or delivery features of the intervention while leaving the core principles and strategies intact (Chowdhary et al., 2014; Patel et al., 2011). In a meta-analysis of 16 studies of adaptations of treatments for depressive disorders, authors noted that most changes occurred with the implementation of the interventions or were efforts to enhance the acceptability of the treatments (Chowdhary et al., 2014). For example, most adaptations were made in respect to language (e.g., replacing technical terms with colloquial expressions), context (e.g., reducing practical barriers to access, scheduling flexibility, etc.), and the therapist delivering the treatment (e.g., therapist–patient matching, cultural competence; Chowdhary et al., 2014). Many changes also involved incorporating local practices into treatment, extending goals of treatment to include family, attention to somatic models of illness, and simplifying treatment or using non-written materials (Chowdhary et al., 2014).

It is important to include details about the adaptation process because it aids in the replication of treatment delivery across new groups and facilitates consensus about the optimal methods of adaptation. Traditional reports of efficacy do not provide sufficient guidance in how to implement evidence-based interventions because they often leave out details about culturally responsive methods (Huey & Polo, 2008). In a meta-analysis of evidence-based treatments for ethnic-minority youth, Huey and Polo (2008) recommend that authors include a description of efforts to make a treatment culturally responsive, and, when methods are not explicit, authors should evaluate the extent to which culturally related content emerges as a natural element of the treatment process. It is notable that adaptations may not always be necessary. Despite the popularity and likely importance of cultural adaptation, evidence is mixed as to whether or not culturally responsive treatments are more beneficial than standard treatments (Huey & Polo, 2008; Chowdhary et al., 2014). Nevertheless, it helps scientific and implementation efforts for researchers to explain their decision regarding specific adaptations, even where no adaptations were made or were needed.

One common approach that guides cross-cultural adaptation is the Medical Research Council's (MRC) framework for complex interventions (Chowdhary et al., 2014; Patel et al., 2011). The MRC's framework involves four phases: development (identifying the evidence base, identifying and developing a theory, modeling process and outcomes); feasibility and piloting; evaluation; and implementation (Craig et al., 2008). In the Chowdhary et al. study (2014), common elements in adaptation processes tended to be selection of a theory-driven psychological treatment, consultation with a variety of stakeholders in the adaptation process, the use of mixed methods to assess feasibility and acceptability, pilot studies to evaluate barriers to the delivery of the treatment, and, finally, evaluation in a controlled study. In this way, Thastum et al.'s mixed-methods approach could be used to assess formally for feasibility and acceptability issues that may facilitate or impede further implementation across Danish sites and populations.

USING MIXED METHODS TO FURTHER CROSS-CULTURAL DISSEMINATION AND IMPLEMENTATION

Mixed-methods research, making use of some combination of quantitative and qualitative data and analysis, seems to have an essential role to play in dissemination and implementation science and, therefore, in cultural adaptations

(Southam-Gerow & Dorsey, 2014). Qualitative methods, deemphasized in recent years with the prominence of behaviorism and empiricism, may be the most appropriate methodological approach for early-stage research, particularly when trying to understand a treatment's potential uptake in diverse contextual settings with many potentially influencing factors (Southam-Gerow & Dorsey, 2014). Case study is a type of qualitative data that allows a richness of detail about individuals or groups and their context (Palinkas, 2014). Qualitative data can help one understand the process and context of an RCT, including helping to understand ways to better target study participants, account for unexplained findings in quantitative data, and determine reasons for the success or failure of a treatment (Palinkas, 2014; Southam-Gerow & Dorsey, 2014). Qualitative data are very useful in "translational" research when one wants to know how to proceed with the translation optimally (Palinkas, 2014). In cross-cultural adaptations, qualitative data are not only used to assess the experience of direct participants (i.e., clients) as they receive the intervention, but they are also used to assess the opinions of important stakeholders (e.g., health care administrators, policy makers, nonpatient families) through focus groups and interviews (Chowdhary et al., 2014).

Qualitative data are particularly helpful when making cultural adaptations because they allow one to consider context at various levels. Many dissemination and implementation models account for various levels of the ecology, including child, family, therapist, treatment team, and broader system (Southam-Gerow & Dorsey, 2014). Complexity at various levels must be considered in order to implement treatments effectively across diverse settings. Considering cultural differences among countries in their family systems and in their parenting styles is particularly important when conducting clinical work with children, who rely heavily on their parents. Qualitative data may be especially helpful in teasing out cultural differences between families, as such differences may be particularly subtle. Furthermore, relying solely on quantitative approaches to assess a priori constructs may risk missing important differences in treatment implementation (e.g., understanding important cultural differences in intergenerational relations before implementing parenting management and functional assessment techniques).

CLIENT, CONTEXT, TREATMENT, AND COMMUNITY FACTORS THAT MAXIMIZE GLOBAL DISSEMINATION

To maximize efficacy and effectiveness by creating culturally sensitive CBT, Hinton and Jalal (2014) propose parameters that account for context at multiple levels when implementing CBT in global settings. Hinton and Jalal (2014) suggest that several key client, context, treatment, and community features must be specified to facilitate cross-national implementation. Key client factors to consider include the language of the intended client and the treatment (while including degree of language fluency of the client base); key demographic variables (e.g., socioeconomic status, education, literacy); and religious background of the group (including specific denominations of larger religions).

Key culturally specific contextual factors include typical traumas that the intended client population has experienced; typical external stressors; local community problems; pragmatic barriers in how or where treatment is provided; what kinds of case management resources are available to the client outside of the presiding therapist; and how and where the patient was recruited.

Key treatment and treatment-model factors that implementers are encouraged to think about include how and whether *DSM/ICD* disorders are considered; what underlying biopsychosocial mechanisms maintain the observable problem; and what target problems the client relates to. These factors then help the provider develop a working case conceptualization of how the disorder is maintained and how treatment targets those mechanisms as contextualized by culture.

To make CBT techniques tolerable and credible for diverse cultural groups, Hinton and Jalal further encourage implementers to consider several community issues, including therapist–client matching and how concerns may differ across the individual and community. They also encourage implementers to utilize local sources of resilience and recovery in order to address stigma about the disorder and the seeking of treatment; to address structural barriers to treatment; and to attend to social demand characteristics and economic incentives of the treatment. Any individual dissemination effort may not have the resources to identify or address comprehensively all concerns that derive from such an analysis. However, the degree to which implementers are mindful of the aforementioned factors may very well predict success for local, regional, and national uptake and sustainability of the intervention or program.

CONCLUSIONS AND FUTURE DIRECTIONS

This commentary has reviewed the Thastum et al. study and its broader implications vis-à-vis past and current efforts to disseminate and evaluate CBT for youth anxiety across different countries. To date, formal clinical trials have provided substantial evidence for the generalizability of treatment effects across most higher-income Western societies. In this context, we discussed how the study by Thastum et al. provides further evidence that CBT can be implemented in one such country—Denmark—with relatively limited adaptation needed from prior models of the Cool Kids/Chilled Adolescents protocol, originally developed in Australia. We also pointed out how the Thastum et al. study demonstrates the power of a mixed-methods approach integrating the quantitative data of an RCT with the qualitative data of case studies to better understand in depth the process of change in successful cases and the need for and nature of additional, individualized, "stepped-up" therapy for unsuccessful cases.

We then described how the use of mixed methods, more generally, can be applied to the task of extending dissemination efforts to lower- and middle-income developing countries. For example, in successfully disseminating treatments in these countries, qualitative data are required to assess and adapt the treatments to the different, challenging local conditions in these areas, such as the shortage of mental health professionals, the lack of access to formal CBT when it is needed, and the significant cultural differences that lead to stigma for treatment. This individualization deserves special attention as the field tries to increase access to evidence-based care globally. Such efforts present new challenges, but with these come unique opportunities to learn more about how and why evidence-based care works, for whom, in what settings, and under what circumstances. We look forward to the challenge.

REFERENCES

Ahlen, J., Breitholtz, E., Barrett, P. M., & Gallegos, J. (2012). School-based prevention of anxiety and depression: A pilot study in Sweden. *Advances in School Mental Health Promotion, 5*(4), 246–257.

Alonso, J., Angermeyer, M. C., Bernert, S., Bruffaerts, R., Brugha, T. S., Bryson, H., . . . & Vollebergh, W. A. M. (2004). Use of mental health services in Europe: Results from the European Study of the Epidemiology of Mental Disorders (ESEMeD) project. *Acta Psychiatrica Scandinavica, 109*(s420), 47–54.

Barrett, P. M., Lowry-Webster, H., & Holmes, J. (1999). The FRIENDS Group Leader's Manual for Children (Edition II).

Bower, P., & Gilbody, S. (2005). Stepped care in psychological therapies: Access, effectiveness, and efficiency. *British Journal of Psychiatry, 186*, 11–17.

Chowdhary, N., Jotheeswaran, A. T., Nadkarni, A., Hollon, S. D., King, M., Jordans, M. J. D., . . . Patel, V. (2014). The methods and outcomes of cultural adaptation of psychological treatments for depressive disorders: A systematic review. *Psychological Medicine, 44*, 1131–1146.

Collins, K. A., Westra, H. A., Dozois, D. J. A., & Burns, D.D. (2004). Gaps in accessing treatment for anxiety and depression: Challenges for the delivery of care. *Clinical Psychology Review, 24*, 583–616.

Craig, P., Dieppe, P., Macintyre, S., Michie, S., Nazareth, I., & Petticrew, M. (2008). Developing and evaluating complex interventions: the new Medical Research Council guidance. *BMJ, 337*, 979–983.

Essau, C. A., Conradt, J., Sasagawa, S., & Ollendick, T. H. (2012). Prevention of anxiety symptoms in children: Results from a universal school-based trial. *Behavior Therapy, 43*(2), 450–464.

Gallegos-Guajardo, J., Ruvalcaba-Romero, N. A., Garza-Tamez, M., & Villegas-Guinea, D. (2013). Social validity evaluation of the FRIENDS for Life program with Mexican children. *Journal of Education and Training Studies, 1*(1), 158–169.

Hinton, D. E., & Jalal, B. (2014). Parameters for creating culturally sensitive CBT: Implementing CBT in global settings. *Cognitive and Behavioral Practice, 21*(2), 139–144.

Hudson, J. L., Rapee, R. M., Deveney, C., Schniering, C. A., Lyneham, H. J., & Bovopoulos, N. (2009). Cognitive-behavioral treatment versus an active control for children and adolescents with anxiety disorders: A randomized trial. *Journal of the American Academy of Child & Adolescent Psychiatry, 48*(5), 533–544.

Huey, S. J., & Polo, A. J. (2008). Evidence-based psychosocial treatments for ethnic minority youth. *Journal of Clinical Child & Adolescent Psychology, 37*(1), 262–301.

James, A. C., James, G., Cowdrey, F. A., Soler, A., & Choke, A. (2015). Cognitive behavioural therapy for anxiety disorders in children and adolescents. *Cochrane Database of Systematic Reviews,* (2).

Mifsud, C., & Rapee, R. M. (2005). Early intervention for childhood anxiety in a school setting: Outcomes for an economically disadvantaged population. *Journal of the American Academy of Child & Adolescent Psychiatry, 44*(10), 996–1004.

Miller, L. D., Laye-Gindhu, A., Bennett, J. L., Liu, Y., Gold, S., March, J. S., ... & Waechtler, V. E. (2011). An effectiveness study of a culturally enriched school-based CBT anxiety prevention program. *Journal of Clinical Child & Adolescent Psychology, 40*(4), 618–629.

Murray, C. J., Richards, M. A., Newton, J. N., Fenton, K. A., Anderson, H. R., Atkinson, C., ... & Davis, A. (2013). UK health performance: Findings of the Global Burden of Disease Study 2010. *The Lancet, 381*(9871), 997–1020.

Palinkas, L. A. (2014). Qualitative and mixed methods in mental health services and implementation research. *Journal of Clinical Child & Adolescent Psychology, 43*(6), 851–861.

Patel, V., Chowdhary, N., Rahman, A., & Verdeli, H. (2011). Improving access to psychological treatments: Lessons from developing countries. *Behavior Research and Therapy, 49*, 523–528.

Patel, V., Flisher, A. J., Hetrick, S., & McGorry, P. (2007). Mental health of young people: A global public-health challenge. *The Lancet, 369*(9569), 1302–1313.

Rapee, R. M. (2000). Group treatment of children with anxiety disorders: Outcome and predictors of treatment response. *Australian Journal of Psychology, 52*(3), 125–129.

Rose, H., Miller, L., & Martinez, Y. (2009). "FRIENDS for Life": The results of a resilience-building, anxiety-prevention program in a Canadian elementary school. *Professional School Counseling, 12*(6), 400–407.

Silverman, W. K., Pina, A. A., & Viswesvaran, C. (2008). Evidence-based psychosocial treatments for phobic and anxiety disorders in children and adolescents. *Journal of Clinical Child & Adolescent Psychology, 37*(1), 105–130.

Siu, A. F. (2007). Using FRIENDS to combat internalizing problems among primary school children in Hong Kong. *Journal of Evidence-Based Psychotherapies, 7*(1), 11.

Southam-Gerow, M. A., & Dorsey, S. (2014). Qualitative and mixed methods research in dissemination and implementation science: Introduction to the special issue. *Journal of Clinical Child & Adolescent Psychology, 43*(6), 845–850.

Southam-Gerow, M. A., Weisz, J. R., Chu, B. C., McLeod, B. D., Gordis, E. B., & Connor-Smith, J. K. (2010). Does cognitive behavioral therapy for youth anxiety outperform usual care in community clinics? An initial effectiveness test. *Journal of the American Academy of Child & Adolescent Psychiatry, 49*(10), 1043–1052.

Whiteford, H. A., Degenhardt, L., Rehm, J., Baxter, A. J., Ferrari, A. J., Erskine, H. E., ... & Vos, T. (2013). Global burden of disease attributable to mental and substance use disorders: Findings from the Global Burden of Disease Study 2010. *The Lancet, 382*(9904), 1575–1586.

WHO World Mental Health Survey Consortium (2004). Prevalence, severity, and unmet need for treatment of mental disorders in the World Health Organization World Mental Health Surveys. *JAMA: The Journal of the American Medical Association, 291*(21), 2581–2590.

The Efficacy of Interpersonal Psychotherapy – Adolescent Skills Training (IPT-AST) in Preventing Depression

SARAH S. KERNER AND JAMI F. YOUNG ■

Commentary by Laura J. Dietz

THE RCT STUDY

Introduction

Adolescent depression is a serious mental health concern. The numbers are telling: Approximately 15% of adolescents experience a major depressive episode (Kessler & Walters, 1998). Depression in adolescence is associated with significant impairment in functioning (Puig-Antich et al., 1993) and an increased risk for developing a future major depressive episode (Lewinsohn, Rohde, Klein, & Seeley, 1999) and other psychiatric disorders (Fergusson & Woodward, 2002). Although psychotherapy and psychopharmacology are efficacious in treating depression, approximately 40% of adolescents fail to meet criteria for remission at the end of treatment in clinical trials (e.g., Brent et al., 1997; Clarke et al., 2005; Clarke, Rohde, Lewinsohn, Hops, & Seeley, 1999; Emslie et al., 1997; Kennard et al., 2006; Lewinsohn, Clarke, Hops, & Andrews, 1990; Mufson, Weissman, Moreau, & Garfinkel, 1999; Mufson, Dorta, Wickramaratne, et al., 2004; Treatment for Adolescents with Depression Study [TADS] Team, 2004). Furthermore, community studies indicate that many adolescents who meet criteria for a depressive disorder do not receive an adequate course of treatment (Lewinsohn & Clarke, 1999; Weisz, McCarty, & Valeri, 2006). Thus, although many adolescents experience depression, few receive services, and among those who do, many do not improve.

As a result of these concerns, there is a growing interest in the development of programs for the prevention of depression, particularly programs that can be delivered in schools where children and adolescents are most likely to receive services (e.g., Hoagwood & Olin, 2002; President's New Freedom Commission on Mental Health, 2003; Weist & Paternite, 2006). Preventive interventions can reach a larger portion of the population and, if efficacious, can prevent the onset of depressive episodes.

Preventive interventions are classified as universal, selective, and indicated (Gordon, 1983). Universal interventions are provided to the entire population; selective interventions, to a subsample with a known risk factor, such as parental divorce or parental depression; and indicated interventions, to individuals with subsyndromal depression. Elevated depressive symptoms are one of the biggest risk factors for developing a future depressive episode (Fergusson, Horwood, Ridder, & Beautrais, 2005; Horwath, Johnson, Klerman, & Weissman, 1992; Lewinsohn et al., 1994; Pine, Cohen, Cohen, & Brook, 1999). Furthermore, elevated depressive symptoms are persistent over time (Garrison, Jackson, Marsteller, McKeown, & Addy, 1990) and are associated with considerable impairment in psychosocial functioning (Gotlib, Lewinsohn, & Seeley, 1995; Judd, Paulus, Wells, & Rapaport, 1996; Lewinsohn, Solomon, Seeley, & Zeiss, 2000). In recognition of the considerable risk and impairment associated with "subsyndromal depression" (a clinical state meeting some but not all the criteria for major depression), there has been a call for indicated prevention programs, targeting adolescents with elevated depression symptoms (Hollon et al., 2002; Mrazek & Haggerty, 1994; US Public Health Service, 2000).

Based on the need for innovative indicated programs, Young and Mufson (2003) developed Interpersonal Psychotherapy – Adolescent Skills Training (IPT-AST), a school-based group prevention program for youth with elevated symptoms of depression. The rationale for developing IPT-AST came from two related lines of work: interpersonal theories of depression and empirical studies of interpersonal psychotherapy. Interpersonal theories of depression posit that certain individuals possess enduring interpersonal vulnerability factors, such as maladaptive interpersonal behaviors and/or chronic impairment in interpersonal relationships, which make them susceptible to the deleterious impact of interpersonal stressors on depression (Coyne, 1976; Hammen, 1992; Joiner & Coyne, 1999; Rudolph, Flynn, & Abaied, 2008). Consistent with these theories, prospective studies have found that increases in depressive symptoms in adolescents are associated with (1) maladaptive interpersonal behaviors (e.g., Connor-Smith, Compas, Wadsworth, Thomsen, & Saltzman, 2000; Rudolph, Hammen, & Burge, 1994); and (2) high levels of conflict and low levels of perceived support in family, peer, and romantic relationships (e.g., Allen et al., 2006; Eberhart & Hammen, 2006; Joyner & Udry, 2000; La Greca & Harrison, 2005; Sheeber, Davis, Leve, Hops, & Tildesley, 2007; Stice, Ragan, & Randall, 2004; Sweeting, Young, West, & Der, 2006). These findings highlight the value of an intervention that develops interpersonal skills to address problematic relationships and promote positive relationships to decrease the risk for depression.

Interpersonal psychotherapy (IPT) was developed for and tested with depressed adults and is based on the premise that depression occurs in an interpersonal context (Weissman, Markowitz, & Klerman, 2000). The focus of treatment is on the patient's depressive symptoms and the interpersonal context in which these symptoms occur. A large number of studies have demonstrated the efficacy of IPT with depressed adults (e.g., Elkin et al., 1989; Frank et al., 2007; Frank, Kupfer, Wagner, McEachran, & Cornes, 1991; Luty et al., 2007; Sloane, Stapes, & Schneider, 1985; Weissman et al., 1979) and depressed adolescents (Mufson et al., 1999; Mufson, Dorta, Wickramaratne, et al., 2004; Rosselló & Bernal, 1999). Given the interpersonal literature and the success of IPT for depressed adolescents, Young and Mufson (2003) posited that teaching interpersonal techniques might avert the interpersonal difficulties that have been shown to contribute to the onset of depression in adolescence and thereby effectively prevent depression over time.

Three studies have examined the efficacy of IPT-AST. In a pilot controlled trial, 41 adolescents with elevated depression symptoms were randomized to receive IPT-AST, as delivered by research clinicians, or usual school counseling (SC), as delivered by school counselors. Adolescents who received IPT-AST reported significantly fewer depressive symptoms and better overall functioning than adolescents in SC post-intervention and up to 6-month follow-up (Young, Mufson, & Davies, 2006). IPT-AST adolescents reported significantly fewer depression diagnoses (3.7%) during the follow-up period than adolescents in SC (28.6%). Adolescents in IPT-AST also showed significantly greater reductions in mother–child conflict than SC adolescents from baseline through the 1-year follow-up (Young, Mufson, & Gallop, 2009). In addition, baseline mother–child conflict moderated the programs' effects on depression symptoms. Adolescents in IPT-AST who had high baseline conflict showed significantly greater decreases in depression symptoms than adolescents in SC who had high conflict. IPT-AST appeared to be particularly effective for those youth with high baseline conflict as these youth showed more rapid decreases in depression symptoms than youth in IPT-AST with low baseline conflict. This study provides preliminary evidence of the efficacy of IPT-AST and points to parent–child conflict as a possible moderator of intervention effects.

Horowitz, Garber, Ciesla, Young, and Mufson (2007) compared IPT-AST, a cognitive-behavioral prevention (CB) group, and no intervention control in a universal sample of ninth-grade students. The IPT-AST program was modified for this study so that the program could be delivered as part of a health class. Unlike previous indicated prevention studies, youth did not participate in any pre-group sessions and the group size was considerably larger than in those other studies. At post-intervention, students in both CB and IPT-AST reported significantly lower levels of depressive symptoms than did those in the no-intervention control group; the two intervention groups did not differ significantly from each other. Differences between control and intervention groups were largest for adolescents with high levels of depressive symptoms at baseline. There were no significant differences between the three conditions at 6-month follow-up. Regarding possible moderators of intervention effects, the authors found that higher levels of baseline sociotropy (i.e., placing a high value on interpersonal relationships) predicted lower levels of depressive symptoms in the IPT-AST group as compared to the CB or control groups. This suggests that interpersonally oriented youth may benefit from a prevention program that focuses on social relationships.

The third randomized controlled trial, authored by the second author (J.F.Y.) and forming the basis for the mixed-method study presented here in this chapter, compared IPT-AST to usual school counseling (SC) for adolescents with elevated symptoms of depression. The following section describes its methods and additional details, and the main outcomes are provided in Young, Mufson, and Gallop (2010).

Method

CASE-FINDING PROCEDURES

Adolescents with elevated symptoms of depression were identified through a two-stage screening procedure. The first stage was a classroom-based screening in three single-sex high schools. Parents of students in the 9th and 10th grades were sent a letter about the screening from school administrators. Parents sent back a notice of refusal if they did not want their child to participate. On the day of the screening, adolescents were informed of the procedures and those who wanted to participate signed a screening assent form.

The screening consisted of the Center for Epidemiologic Studies-Depression Scale (CES-D) (Radloff, 1977), a 20-item measure that assesses depressive symptoms over the past week. A score of 16 or higher has been shown to be indicative of elevated depressive symptoms in adult populations (Radloff, 1977), but more variable cutoff scores have been recommended for adolescents (e.g., Garrison, Addy, Jackson, McKeown, & Waller, 1991). The current study used a cutoff score of 16 to identify as many adolescents as possible who may be experiencing depressive symptoms. Thus, adolescents with a CES-D score between 16 and below the criterion of 39 indicating likely full depression were eligible to be approached for the prevention project; those with a score of 40 or higher were seen by the principal investigator (PI) to assess clinical severity and determine potential eligibility. Eligible adolescents and their caregivers were contacted by the research staff to describe the prevention project. Interested families came to the school to learn about the project and provide informed consent and assent (see Fig. 4.1 for further details).

Adolescents who consented to the prevention project completed the Schedule for Affective Disorders and Schizophrenia for School-Age Children (K-SADS-PL) (Kaufman, Birmaher, Brent, & Rao, 1997) and the Children's Global Assessment Scale (CGAS) (Shaffer et al., 1983) to determine eligibility. Adolescents were eligible to participate in the study if they had at least two subthreshold or threshold depression symptoms on the K-SADS-PL and did not meet criteria for a current depressive episode. Adolescents were also required to have a CGAS score of 61 or higher, indicating that they had some minor impairments but were generally functioning well (Shaffer, Gould, Bird, & Fisher, 1983). Adolescents were excluded from the prevention component if they had a current diagnosis of depression, dysthymia, bipolar disorder, psychosis, panic disorder, obsessive-compulsive

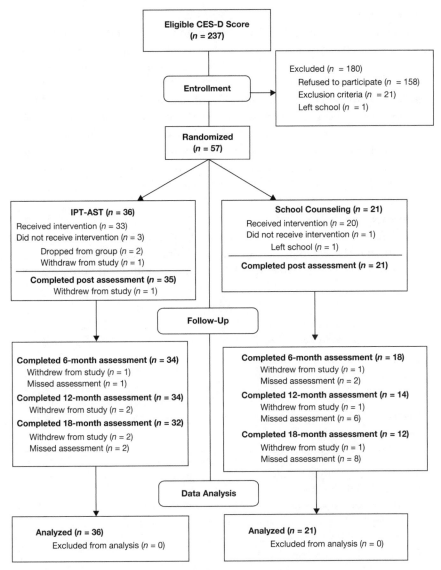

Figure 4.1 Consort Flowchart.

disorder, posttraumatic stress disorder, oppositional defiant disorder, conduct disorder, or untreated attention-deficit/hyperactivity disorder.

RANDOMIZATION

Fifty-seven adolescents were eligible to participate in the prevention component of the study and were randomly assigned to receive IPT-AST or SC using a table of random numbers. To ensure enough adolescents in the IPT-AST groups, the random-number table was generated so that approximately two thirds of adolescents in each school would be randomized to IPT-AST, resulting in 36 adolescents randomized to IPT-AST and 21 to SC.

Participants

Participants were aged 13 to 17 in the 9th and 10th grades. The average age was 14.5 (SD = 0.8) years, and the sample was 59.7% female. A majority of the adolescents (73.7%) identified themselves as Hispanic. Regarding race, 61.4% of the adolescents identified as white, 35.1% as African American, and 3.5% as biracial. Seventy percent of the sample lived in a single-parent household, and 29% reported a gross household income of $25,000 or less. Several of the adolescents met criteria for a current nonaffective *DSM-IV* diagnosis, but the majority (84.2%) had only subthreshold depression symptoms with no current diagnosis. Four adolescents had a past diagnosis of major depression or dysthymia (two in each condition). None of these adolescents had received prior treatment.

Assessments

Table 4.1 presents a summary of the various standarized assessment instruments employed, and the schedule and structure of contacts for the IPT-AST condition are summarized in Table 4.2. Adolescents in both conditions completed

Table 4.1 Assessment Instruments

GENERAL INFORMATION
o Demographic Instrument (DEM)
o General Medical History (GMH)
PARENTAL REPORTS OF PSYCHOPATHOLOGY
o Center for Epidemiological Studies-Depression Scale (CES-D)
o Family History Screen (FHS)
ADOLESCENT REPORTS OF PSYCHOPATHOLOGY AND FUNCTIONING
o Schedule for Affective Disorders and Schizophrenia for School-aged Children— Present and Lifetime Version (K-SADS-PL)
o Children's Depression Rating Scale-Revised (CDRS-R)
o Center for Epidemiological Studies-Depression Scale (CES-D)
o Screen for Child Anxiety Related Emotional Disorders (SCARED)
o Children's Global Assessment Scale (CGAS) #
INTERPERSONAL MEASURES
o The Conflict Behavior Questionnaire (CBQ)
o Perceived Social Support (PSS) #
o Social Adjustment Scale-Self Report (SAS-SR) #
INTERVENTION MEASURES
o Attitude Toward Intervention Questionnaire (ATI) #
SCHOOL MEASURES
o Student's Achievement Relevant Actions in the Classroom (SARAC) #
o Self-Efficacy in School (SES) #

#Where relevant, all the measures were scored so that higher scores indicate poorer functioning.

Table 4.2 Structure of Contacts for IPT-AST Condition

Contact Type	Time from Initial Contact	Assessment or Intervention	Group or Individual	Duration (minutes)	Instruments Administered
1. Screening	0 weeks	Assessment	NA	A: 15	A: CES-D
2. Consent meeting	1–2 weeks	NA	Individual	A: 30	P: Demographics, General Medical, CES-D, FHS, CBQ, FMSS
3. Eligibility evaluation	2–3 weeks	Assessment	Individual	A: 90–120	A: K-SADS-PL, CGAS
4. Baseline evaluation	4 weeks	Assessment	Individual	P: 60 A: 60	A: CDRS-R, SCARED, SAS-SR, CBQ, PSS, CASA, SARAC, ICI-S, Self-Efficacy
5. Individual pre-group sessions	5–6 weeks	Intervention	Individual	A: 45 (2x)	NA
6. IPT-AST groups	7–15 weeks	Intervention	Group	A: 90 (8x)	A: Depression Checklist, Mood Rating Scale
7. Mid-group evaluation	11 weeks	Assessment	Individual	A: 10	A: CES-D
8. Post-group evaluation	16 weeks (4 m)	Assessment	Individual	P: 20 A: 150	P: CES-D, CBQ, FMSS, ATT A: K-SADS-PL, CDRS-R, CES-D, SCARED, CGAS, SAS-SR, CBQ, PSS, CASA, ATT, SARAC, ICI-S, Self-efficacy

(continued)

Table 4.2 CONTINUED

Contact Type	Time from Initial Contact	Assessment or Intervention	Group or Individual	Duration (minutes)	Instruments Administered
9. 6-month evaluation	40 weeks (10 m)	Assessment	Individual	P: 10 A: 150	P: CES-D, CBQ A: K-SADS-PL, CDRS-R, CES-D, SCARED, CGAS, SAS-SR, CBQ, PSS, CASA, SARAC, ICI-S, Self-efficacy
10. 12-month evaluation	64 weeks (16 m)	Assessment	Individual	P: 10 A: 150	P: CES-D, CBQ A: K-SADS-PL, CDRS-R, CES-D, SCARED, CGAS, SAS-SR, CBQ, PSS, CASA, SARAC, ICI-S, Self-efficacy
11. 18-month evaluation	88 weeks (22 m)	Assessment	Individual	P: 10 A: 150	P: CES-D, CBQ A: K-SADS-PL, CDRS-R, CES-D, SCARED, CGAS, SAS-SR, CBQ, PSS, CASA, SARAC, ICI-S, Self-efficacy

A, adolescent; P, parent.

assessments at baseline, post-intervention, and at 6, 12, and 18 months post-intervention. Adolescents also completed the CES-D mid-intervention. The evaluations were conducted by independent evaluators, masters-level psychologists or social workers, who were blind to intervention condition. Adolescents were given $15 for completing each assessment. Each assessment consisted of the K-SADS-PL, CGAS, CES-D, and the Children's Depression Rating Scale-Revised (CDRS-R; Poznanski & Mokros, 1996), a 17-item clinician-rated instrument of depressive symptoms. At each of the follow-up assessments, the Longitudinal Interval Follow-up Evaluation (LIFE; Keller et al., 1987) was used in conjunction with the K-SADS-PL to provide more accurate information about symptoms and disorders since the last assessment. Changes in depressive symptoms (CES-D and CDRS-R) and overall functioning (CGAS) and rates of depression diagnoses in the follow-up period were the primary outcomes of the study.

Other measures were included to assess secondary outcomes, including anxiety symptoms and social functioning. Anxiety symptoms were assessed using the Screen for Child Anxiety Related Emotional Disorders (SCARED; Birmaher et al., 1999), a 41-item self-report instrument of anxiety symptoms. The SCARED has a total score and five subscales that assess subtypes of anxiety: panic/somatic, generalized anxiety, separation anxiety, social anxiety, and school phobia. We focused on the panic/somatic, generalized anxiety, and social anxiety subscales since these subscales were most relevant for our adolescent participants who were regularly attending school. The Social Adjustment Scale – Self-report (SAS-SR; Weissman & Bothwell, 1976) is a self-report measure that assesses overall social functioning as well as functioning in four domains: friends, school, family, and dating.

INTERVENTIONS

IPT-AST. IPT-AST teaches communication strategies and interpersonal problem-solving skills that adolescents can use to improve their relationships, with the expectation that these improvements will lead to reductions in depressive symptoms and a decreased likelihood of developing depression. IPT-AST involves two initial individual sessions and eight weekly 90-minute group sessions. During the pre-group sessions, the leader meets with each adolescent to assess depressive symptoms, provide a framework for the group, and conduct the interpersonal inventory to identify specific interpersonal goals for the group. In the treatment group sessions, adolescents learn about the symptoms of depression, discuss the relationship between feelings and interpersonal interactions, and learn different communication and interpersonal strategies. First, these communication and interpersonal strategies are taught through didactics and role-plays. Then, group members are asked to apply the skills to different people in their lives, practicing first in group and then at home (Young & Mufson, 2003; Young, Mufson, & Schueler, 2016). The group leaders were masters- or doctoral-level psychologists or child psychiatrists who were trained and supervised by Dr. Young. Group size ranged from four to six adolescents.

School counseling. The remaining adolescents were referred to the school counselor to be seen at a frequency determined by the adolescent and the counselor. SC was not intended to be an equivalent intervention to IPT-AST. It was chosen as the comparison group because it approximates what normally occurs in the schools when an adolescent is identified as having mild emotional difficulties. This comparison allowed us to determine if IPT-AST was more effective than the counseling that normally occurs in these schools. The SC sessions were 30–45 minutes in duration and consisted of supportive individual counseling. The most commonly discussed topics in sessions were caregiver relationships (35.1%) and academic issues (24.3%).

Results

The main outcomes, focusing specifically on depressive symptoms, overall functioning, and depression diagnoses, are described in Young et al. (2010). A summary of these results are provided next.

Improvement

- From baseline to post-intervention, IPT-AST adolescents showed significantly greater improvements than adolescents in SC on depressive symptoms (CES-D: $t(215) = -2.56$, $p = 0.01$; CDRS-R: ($t(169) = -3.09$, $p < 0.01$) and overall functioning (CGAS: $t(168) = 3.24$, $p < 0.01$).
- In the 18 months following the intervention, there were no significant differences in rates of change on the CDRS-R ($t(91) = 0.92$, $p = 0.36$). However, there were significant differences in rates of change on the CES-D ($t(102) = 2.51$, $p = 0.01$) and the CGAS ($t(76) = -2.31$, $p = 0.02$), with SC adolescents showing greater improvements during the follow-up period than IPT-AST adolescents.

Mean Differences

- Regarding mean differences, IPT-AST adolescents had significantly lower CES-D (IPT-AST: 10.86, SC: 16.24; $F(1, 52) = 8.66$; $p < .001$; ES = .81), CDRS-R (IPT-AST: 44.24, SC: 49.90; $F(1, 52) = 8.82$; $p < .001$; ES = .80), and CGAS (IPT-AST: 76.63, SC: 70.95; $F(1, 52) = 22.28$; $p < .001$; ES = 1.27) scores than SC adolescents post intervention.
- At 6-month follow-up, there was a significant difference in CGAS scores (IPT-AST: 78.41, SC: 75.44; $F(1, 52) = 4.86$; $p = .03$; ES = 61), and a trend toward significance on the CES-D (IPT-AST: 12.55, SC: 16.22; ES = .51) and the CDRS-R (IPT-AST: 40.10, SC: 44.47; ES = .54).
- There were no significant differences between the groups at 12-month or 18-month follow-up, although the effects sizes were in the small to medium range at both time points (.17–.50).
- At the 12-month follow-up, the mean scores were as follows on the CES-D (IPT-AST: 10.76, SC: 13.64), CDRS-R (IPT-AST: 44.01, SC: 49.82), and CGAS (IPT-AST: 77.62, SC: 75.36).
- At the 18-month follow-up, the mean scores were as follows: CES-D (IPT-AST: 9.53, SC: 7.00), CDRS-R (IPT-AST: 39.47, SC: 40.67), and CGAS (IPT-AST: 79.38, SC: 78.58).

DEPRESSION DIAGNOSES

- None of the adolescents in either condition met criteria for a depressive disorder at the post-intervention assessment.
- By the 6-month follow-up, four SC adolescents (19.1%) met criteria for a diagnosis (three for major depression, one for dysthymia). No IPT-AST adolescents met criteria for a depressive disorder. This difference in rates is significant (Fisher's Exact Test, $p < .05$).
- By the 18-month follow-up, no additional adolescents in SC developed a depressive diagnosis (cumulative percent, 19.1%), while three IPT-AST adolescents reported a new diagnosis (three for major depression) (cumulative percent 8.3%). The difference in rates is no longer significant (Fisher's Exact Test, $p = .40$) (Young et al., 2010).

OTHER ANALYSES

Subsequent analyses from this RCT have examined the effects of IPT-AST on other relevant outcomes, in particular social functioning and anxiety outcomes. These analyses indicate that adolescents in IPT-AST report significantly greater improvements in total social functioning and friend functioning (Young, Kranzler, Gallop, & Mufson, 2012) and greater reductions in total anxiety symptoms, panic/somatic complaints, and generalized anxiety symptoms during the intervention than SC adolescents (Young et al., 2012). There were no significant differences between the two intervention conditions in rates of change on social anxiety symptoms; adolescents in both groups showed small, but significant, reductions in social anxiety scores.

Young et al. (2012) also looked at whether baseline anxiety symptoms predicted or moderated intervention outcomes. Adolescents with lower levels of baseline anxiety showed significantly greater improvements in depressive symptoms during the course of the preventive interventions than adolescents with higher levels of baseline anxiety. However, by post-intervention, the two anxiety groups had similar levels of depressive symptoms. Interestingly, adolescents with high baseline anxiety showed a continued decrease in depressive symptoms during the follow-up period, whereas adolescents low in anxiety showed a stabilization of depressive symptoms. These findings suggest that youth with comorbid depressive and anxiety symptoms may experience delayed intervention effects but that IPT-AST is still an effective intervention for these youth.

Discussion

The findings from earlier studies and this RCT point to the promise of IPT-AST as an effective prevention program for youth depression and anxiety. IPT-AST significantly reduces depressive and anxiety symptoms during the course of the intervention. The post-intervention and 6-month follow-up effect sizes for depression and anxiety are moderate to large, which are larger than those found in other depression prevention studies (see Horowitz & Garber, 2006; Stice et al., 2009;

Barrett et al., 2006; Gillham et al., 2006; Lock & Barrett, 2003; Lowry-Webster et al., 2001, 2003; Roberts et al., 2003). In addition, IPT-AST prevents the onset of depressive disorders in the 6 months to a year following the intervention, which is a rare finding in the depression prevention literature (Horowitz & Garber, 2006). Furthermore, IPT-AST has a positive effect on other domains of functioning, including overall functioning, social functioning, and parent–child conflict.

Unfortunately, the benefits of IPT-AST are less consistent beyond 6 months following the intervention. It is important to note that the lack of significant differences at the 12- and 18-month follow-up evaluations is not because the IPT-AST adolescents show an increase in depressive symptoms or a decrease in functioning over time. The symptom and functioning scores in the IPT-AST condition show small fluctuations but remain relatively stable during the follow-up period, suggesting a sustained impact of the prevention program.

Notably, the SC adolescents show continued improvements during the follow-up period. There are a number of possible explanations for this finding with differing implications. The first explanation is that a disproportionate number of SC adolescents were lost during the follow-up period. At the 12-month follow-up, 94.44% of IPT-AST youth completed the assessment as compared to 66.67% of SC youth. At 18-month follow-up, 88.89% of IPT-AST adolescents and 57.14% of SC adolescents completed the evaluation. Subsequent analyses found that a significantly greater proportion of youth in SC than in IPT-AST were asked to leave school during the follow-up period because of academic or behavioral problems (Young et al., 2012), and many SC youth did not complete assessments after they left the schools. Thus, the 12-month and 18-month data from the SC condition may not be representative of the group that began the study and may be inflated. It will be important for future studies to retain an equal proportion of youth in both conditions, particularly those who leave school, to better understand the long-term effects of prevention programs.

Another possible explanation for the lack of significant findings at follow-up is that SC adolescents continued to access services from the school counselors in the months following the intervention and that these additional services led to continued improvements, whereas the IPT-AST youth did not have any additional contact with the group leaders. It would be valuable to conduct individual systematic pragmatic case studies with representative members of the SC group to better understand whether continued services and/or other specific factors led to their improvement over time. As a result of these findings, we are including booster sessions in subsequent studies of IPT-AST to see if this can enhance the long-term preventive effects of IPT-AST. This potential explanation also points to the importance of training school counselors to deliver IPT-AST as these counselors can continue to support youth in the schools in the months and years following the intervention, providing informal booster sessions as needed to sustain effects over time.

Quantitative analyses from prior IPT-AST studies and the randomized controlled study described in this chapter suggest a number of possible moderators and predictors of intervention effects that are worthy of additional study. In particular, there is evidence that youth with high parent–child conflict may do particularly well in IPT-AST (Young et al., 2009), as well as youth who are high on sociotropy or affiliativeness (Horowitz et al., 2007). Regarding nonintervention specific predictors, analyses suggest that youth with comorbid anxiety symptoms show slower rates of change in depressive symptoms, although there are no significant differences in depressive symptoms at post-intervention or follow-up between youth high and low in baseline anxiety.

Given the promising findings from this study and earlier studies, additional research on IPT-AST is warranted. The two systematic case studies presented in the next section provide a unique opportunity to examine whether the identified moderator and predictor candidates influence individual outcomes within the RCT and to provide information about other variables that may impact intervention outcomes. These variables can then be systematically investigated in ongoing and future studies of IPT-AST. Within the literature on the prevention of mental health disorders, little is still known about the participant characteristics that influence intervention effects or the mechanisms through which these programs work. In line with the priorities identified by the Institute of Medicine (2009) and the President's New Freedom Commission on Mental Health (2002), ongoing studies of IPT-AST have sufficient sample size to more systematically examine moderators and mediators of IPT-AST. This will guide the further development of IPT-AST to ensure that the program is beneficial for a wide range of youth from diverse backgrounds.

Additionally, ongoing studies of IPT-AST are poised to answer other important questions about the intervention and the prevention field more generally. In current studies, in part based on results from this study, IPT-AST includes booster sessions with the aim of enhancing the long-term effects of the program. If IPT-AST can demonstrate sustained effects over time, efforts can be made to train school counselors to deliver this intervention. To date, IPT-AST has been compared to individual counseling, delivered at a frequency determined by school counselors. Current studies are comparing IPT-AST to control groups that are matched on modality, frequency, and duration of sessions. This will provide a more rigorous test of the efficacy of IPT-AST and will also provide important information about the efficacy of other types of prevention groups.

Despite the development of a number of efficacious prevention programs, the effect sizes for these programs are small to moderate (Horowitz & Garber, 2006; Stice et al., 2009). One explanation for the relatively modest impact of depression prevention programs is the interventions have not been designed for individualization. For example, IPT-AST, which focuses on interpersonal issues, may be less relevant for adolescents with positive relationships. To boost effects, there may be value in developing strategies for matching adolescents to prevention programs. In an ongoing study, we are comparing IPT-AST to a cognitive-behavioral prevention program for youth at high and low interpersonal risk and cognitive risk for depression. This will allow us to determine whether prevention programs that match youth to programs that address their vulnerabilities are beneficial.

Past research has informed the development and modification of this effective prevention program. Similarly, current and future quantitative and qualitative research on IPT-AST, such as the systematic case studies that follow, will continue to inform the intervention, future research questions, and the eventual implementation and dissemination of this model. The continued development and dissemination of IPT-AST and other effective prevention programs will allow more adolescents to receive help before they meet criteria for depression, with its associated impairments and societal costs.

THE CASE STUDIES

The Nature and Rationale for Specific Cases Selected for the Case Studies

The results from the RCT reviewed earlier indicate that overall, IPT-AST has a positive impact at posttreatment and short-term follow-up, but not at long-term follow-up. By selecting a positive-outcome client and a negative-outcome client from the treatment condition for systematic case study, we planned to further investigate these findings by exploring these questions: (1) What types of client characteristics, group therapy processes, and their interactions differentiate youth who respond to the treatment positively versus negatively? and (2) What are the processes whereby a client with positive outcome at posttreatment continues to maintain or increase her positive functioning over time?

The cases selected for the pragmatic case studies were identified through careful examination of assessment data. Only students who participated in the IPT-AST condition of the RCT were considered. Students who attended fewer than five IPT-AST group sessions (the average number of group sessions attended by participants in the RCT) were not considered for the pragmatic case studies. This decision was made not only because these students were partial completers of the intervention, but also because we felt that a qualitative analysis of group and individual components of the intervention would be less fruitful if students were absent from a majority of group sessions. Once these cases were excluded, we identified groups that included both students classified as "non-responders" and "responders" to intervention. Students were considered non-responders if they received a depressive diagnosis (major depressive disorder or dysthymia) during the intervention or follow-up period. Three participants out of the 36 youth in the IPT-AST condition met criteria for a depressive diagnosis during the project and two of this subset attended five or more groups. "Responders" were defined as students whose symptoms consistently decreased to below the clinical cutoff on the CES-D (16) over the course of the intervention and follow-up period and who did not meet criteria for a depressive diagnosis at any time point. Nineteen participants in the IPT-AST condition met response criteria, four of who were excluded because they were missing one or two data points. Thirteen of this subset attended five or more sessions. The authors also prioritized groups whose members completed all assessments for the study so that group quantitative and qualitative data could be considered in the analyses. Table 4.3 illustrates the specific criteria met by each IPT-AST group in the case selection process.

Table 4.3 CRITERION FOR GROUP SELECTION

Group	Completed __% of Evaluations	Included Responder With All Assessments Completed	Included Nonresponder With All Assessments Completed	Responder and Nonresponder Attended At Least 5 Group Sessions
1	100	X	X	X
2	100	X		
3	86	X	X	
4	100	X		
5	92	X		
6	97	X		
7	100	X	X	X

As shown in Table 4.3, three out of seven IPT-AST groups in the study met these conditions and two groups (Group 1 and Group 7) had all evaluations completed. Group 1 was not selected because, despite meeting criteria for a depressive diagnosis in the follow-up, the non-responder in this group did not have consistently elevated CES-D scores. Thus, we felt that this would not be as rich of a case to discuss. In addition, Group 1 was co-led by one of the authors, so Group 7 was also selected to minimize subjectivity. Group 7 consisted of five 9th grade female students. One student dropped out of the group after the two individual pre-group sessions, but she participated in all assessments. The other four members participated in all individual pre-group sessions and attended between three and eight group sessions. The selected case that benefited from the intervention (Menorka) participated in all individual and group sessions. The "non-response" case (Shelly) attended both individual sessions and six of the eight group sessions (Figure 4.2). Two doctoral-level psychologists led the group and were trained and supervised by the developer of the IPT-AST intervention.

Group 7 consisted of five ninth-grade female students. One student dropped out of the group after the two individual pre-group sessions, but she participated in all assessments. The other four members participated in all individual pre-group sessions and attended between three and eight group sessions. The selected case that benefited from the intervention (Menorka) participated in all individual and group

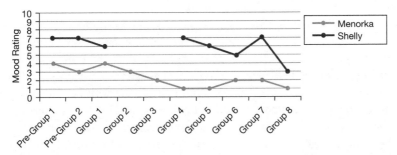

Figure 4.2 Profile Plots for Mood Ratings Over the Course of the Intervention.

sessions. The "nonresponse" case (Shelly) attended both individual sessions and six of the eight group sessions. Two doctoral-level psychologists led the group and were trained and supervised by the developer of the IPT-AST intervention (J.F.Y., the second author).

The clinical evaluations and the intervention sessions were audiotaped to assess adherence to intervention techniques and to better address clinical issues. Qualitative data from progress notes and from these audio recordings of the assessments and intervention sessions were used in conjunction with quantitative data from self-report measures to examine the experiences of the selected individuals over the course of the study.

To protect clients' identities and maintain confidentiality, certain information has been modified, including names, biographical information, and the phrasing of quotations (which remain in quotes) from the intervention sessions. Nevertheless, the clinical authenticity of these cases has been preserved.

The Clients

As context for the two cases, the demographics and baseline symptom profiles of members in the selected group are summarized and compared to means of participants in the IPT-AST condition in Table 4.4.

MENORKA, A CLIENT WITH A POSITIVE OUTCOME

Menorka was a 14-year-old, Latina female in a ninth-grade regular education class. She resided with her biological mother who had full-time employment. Menorka and her mother were on Medicaid and received food stamps; Menorka also reported that she was homeless for a brief period of time when she was younger. Menorka's parents separated when she was 5 years old and she had irregular contact with her biological father, who was incarcerated. Prior to his arrest, Menorka reported witnessing her father beat her mother as well as other partners on several occasions, but Menorka denied that her father physically abused her. Menorka described herself as "self-conscious," "quiet," and "lonely." She indicated that she had one best friend who did not attend her school and several school friends to whom she did not feel particularly close. She received mainly A's and B's in school and enjoyed attending church and competing on a gymnastics team.

SHELLY, A CLIENT WITH A NEGATIVE OUTCOME

Shelly was a 15-year-old, African American ninth-grade student in regular education. She resided with her biological mother and stepfather, both of whom she generally got along with well. Shelly's mother had a college education and worked as a paralegal (they did not receive government assistance). Shelly's parents separated before she was born and she had not had contact with her father for several years. Shelly elaborated that she was not interested in having a relationship with her father because he had let her down on several occasions and he "never lived up to his promises." Shelly reported that she felt behavioral and emotional

Table 4.4 Pre-intervention Demographics and Symptom Profiles of Group Members Compared to IPT-AST Condition Means

Case	Sex	Age	Ethnicity	Race	CES-D	CDS-R	CGAS	SCARED TOTAL
1 (Shelly)	F	15	Not Hispanic	African American	19	70	68	18
2 (Menorka)	F	14	Hispanic	White	29	62	73	20
3	F	14	Not Hispanic	African American	19	55	75	23
4	F	14	Hispanic	White	33	44	65	11
5	F	14	Hispanic	African American	27	63	75	11
IPT-AST Condition	55.60%	14.57	69.40%	41.70%	26.56%	51.75%	70.75%	22.53%
Mean (SD)	F	(.68)	Hispanic	African American	(6.72)	(11.17)	(4.12)	(9.73)

engagement in class and was doing well in most courses; however, she indicated that she struggled in Math and Science, for which her current grades were a C and D. Shelly did not partake in clubs or after-school activities, and when asked about her interests, she replied, "nothing." However, Shelly reported a strong sense of faith and attended church weekly.

Guiding Conception With Research Support

Perhaps the most vulnerable developmental stage for the onset of depression is adolescence, and not surprisingly, almost half of adolescents reporting at least subclinical depressive symptoms (Hankin & Abramson, 2002). One reason for this vulnerability is that adolescence is also categorized by an increase in social demands and stresses like negotiating friendships, the development of romantic relationships, and separation from caregivers. As such, a consistent finding in the literature is that an interpersonal life stressor often precedes adolescent depression. According to Davey, Yucel, and Allen (2008), almost half of adolescents experiencing their first episode of depression have had a relationship breakup in the previous year. Additionally, Mazza, et al. (2010) identified positive family and interpersonal relations as the strongest protective factors against depression. Given the central role of interpersonal functioning in the development of adolescent depression, an intervention, such as IPT-AST, which focuses on improving relationships and building interpersonal skills, is a valuable and appropriate model for preventing the onset of depression.

Also, IPT-AST is particularly appealing to adolescents because of the emphasis on interpersonal relationships and because it is short term, which may be more acceptable for adolescents resistant to intervention. The two pre-group sessions and eight group sessions involved can usually be conducted within a 3-month period, which is typically the time interval for school semesters. The group aspect of IPT-AST is a central component of the model because it provides an opportunity for adolescents experiencing similar difficulties to connect with each other and allows them to practice these interpersonal skills in a comfortable and natural context.

Assessment

Menorka – Positive-Outcome Case
Presenting problem and history. At her eligibility evaluation in ninth grade, Menorka endorsed four subthreshold symptoms of depression, including anhedonia, indecision, nonrestorative sleep, and worthlessness. Additionally, she reported experiencing clinical levels of depressed mood and fatigue. Menorka specified that on days when she feels sad, it is difficult to "get over the feeling." Her CGAS score was a 73, indicating mild impairment. Menorka acknowledged that while her current depressive symptoms have impacted her relationship with her

mother and friends, she does not feel that it interferes with her academic functioning. Menorka's score on the CES-D (Total = 29) during the initial screening and her score on the CDRS-R (t-score = 62) during the baseline evaluation were both elevated. Menorka endorsed several symptoms of depression, but based on the severity of her symptoms she does not currently meet criteria for a mood disorder.

During the evaluation, Menorka explained that she has been experiencing these symptoms for the past month and a half because "it feels like I don't have anyone." Menorka elaborated that she has been spending less time with her friends because they are reportedly very preoccupied with their boyfriends. She expressed jealousy and sadness for being the only one of her friends without a boyfriend. Similarly, she has been feeling increasingly lonely in the evenings because of recent changes to her mother's work schedule. Menorka used to spend evenings with her mother, but now she sees her for a few minutes after school and spends the remainder of the evening alone and bored.

Additionally, Menorka reported that she struggles with her body image. She frequently compares herself to others and thinks she is fat. Menorka shared that upon looking in the mirror, she often thinks, "I don't like what I see." Furthermore, she indicated that it is difficult for her to attend a school where most of the students have both parents to provide for them and are from more financially stable homes. Menorka explained, "I only have a mom at home, so sometimes it's hard not to feel inferior to the other students."

When assessed for past psychopathology, Menorka met criteria for depressive disorder not otherwise specified (DD NOS) due to a depressive episode in eighth grade. Specifically, Menorka was experiencing clinical levels of depressed mood, anhedonia, fatigue, worthlessness, and self-harm behavior and subthreshold levels of nonrestorative sleep, diurnal mood variation, and passive suicidal ideation. Menorka explained that eighth grade was particularly difficult for her because of peer pressures to engage in various self-emancipating behaviors (e.g., sex and drug and alcohol use). To cope with these negative feelings and pressures, Menorka cut her wrists with a scissor or razor 1–2 times per month throughout eighth grade. In the spring of eighth grade, Menorka disclosed these incidents to her mother and has since stopped engaging in self-harm behaviors. Menorka experienced reprieve from her DD NOS symptoms throughout the summer months between eighth and ninth grade, but her symptoms began to reemerge when she transitioned to ninth grade and started attending a new school.

During the eligibility evaluation, Menorka also reported some symptoms of generalized anxiety disorder (GAD), which is supported by her responses on the SCARED (Total = 20; GAD = 9). However, the frequency and intensity of Menorka's anxiety symptoms were not severe enough to meet criteria for an anxiety disorder. In addition to anxiety and depression, Menorka's evaluator assessed for mania, psychosis, eating disorders, disruptive behavior disorders, attentional problems, tic disorders, substance use, and trauma history. Menorka denied any concerns in these areas.

Vulnerabilities and strengths. Menorka has experienced several environmental stressors that may make her more vulnerable to developing depression, including past exposure to domestic violence, homelessness, economic hardship, and a single-parent home (Wolfe & Mash, 2006). She also has a reported history of substance abuse on her paternal side of the family and a history of depression on her maternal side of the family. During the baseline evaluation, Menorka's mother reported that Menorka had elevated symptoms of depression (CES-D = 20). In addition, Menorka's depressive episode in eighth grade increases her risk of experiencing a future episode. Moreover, Menorka's negative attributions about herself may also make her more vulnerable to depression (Cohen, Young, & Abela, 2012).

Nevertheless, Menorka exhibits several strengths that may have contributed to her positive response to the intervention. Self-report measures (reported in Table 4.5) indicate that, relative to the means of the other participants in the IPT-AST groups, Menorka experiences a high sense of self-efficacy in school (SES: self-efficacy: 13; School Work: 15) as well as a high level of behavioral and emotional engagement in school (SARAC: Behavioral Engagement: 40; SARAC: Emotional Engagement: 39). She is also involved in several social activities (e.g., dance team and church) and reports having some friendships. Furthermore, Menorka expressed that when she has a problem, she confides in her pastor and that her belief in God has helped her to overcome transient thoughts of death in the past. Research indicates that religion and spirituality may serve as protective factors against depression and other psychopathology (Hill & Pargament, 2003; Mazza et al., 2010).

SHELLY – NEGATIVE-OUTCOME CASE

Presenting problem and history. At her eligibility evaluation, Shelly endorsed three threshold symptoms of depression, including, fatigue, nonrestorative sleep, and excessive guilt. Additionally, she reported experiencing four subthreshold symptoms of depressed mood, worthlessness, decreased appetite, and rejection sensitivity. Her CGAS score was a 68, indicating mild to moderate impairment in her overall functioning. Shelly's reported elevated symptoms of depression and impairment are supported by results from supplemental measures, which ranged from scores indicating mild depressive symptoms (CES-D = 19) at the initial screening to moderate depressive symptoms (CDRS-R, t-score = 70) during her baseline evaluation. It is important to note that the baseline evaluation occurred 1 month after the initial screening, and this time interval may relate to the discrepancy in the severity of Shelly's symptoms on these depression measures. In line with this possibility, the interview and CDRS-R data suggest that Shelly's symptoms worsened during this time period. Although Shelly endorsed several current symptoms of depression, the severity and intensity of these symptoms do not warrant a depression diagnosis.

Shelly reported a long history of being bullied by her peers, but she indicated that her depressive symptoms worsened in seventh grade after two embarrassing situations during which she was excessively teased and rumors were spread about her. At this time, Shelly's stepfather also moved into her home, which

Table 4.5 QUANTITATIVE DATA OF CASES COMPARED TO MEANS OF IPT-AST PARTICIPANTS AT FIVE TIME POINTS

Scale	Pretreatment			Posttreatment			6-Month			12-Month			18-Month		
	Menorka	Shelly	IPT-AST	Menorka	Shelly	IPT-AST	Menorka	Shelly	IPT-AST	Menorka	Shelly	IPT-AST	Menorka	Shelly	IPT-AST
DEPRESSION SYMPTOMS															
CES-D	29*	19*	26.56*	7	16*	10.86	7	24*	12.5	3	29*	10.76	4	19*	9.53
CDRS-R	62	70*	51.75	60	62	44.24	37	62	40.1	30	64*	44.01	51	57	39.47
K-SADS Depressive Diagnosis	None	None	0	None	None	0	None	None	0	None	DD NOS	2	None	MDD	1
CGAS (Overall Functioning)	73	68	70.75	78	72	76.63	78	74	78.41	80	70	77.62	77	65	79.38
Parent CES-D	20*	21*	12.17	7	19*	11.15	30*		12.14		38*	12.58	15	9	8.81
ANXIETY SYMPTOMS (SCARED)															
Total	20	18	22.53	10	16	12.77	7	29*	13.03	5	19	9.15	3	19	8.16
Panic	2	3	4.22	1	2	1.91	1	8*	2.32	1	4	1.56	0	5	1.28
GAD	9	2	7.33	4	6	3.94	5	108	4.65	3	3	3.29	2	8	2.97
Social Phobia	1	9	5.56	1	7	4.54	0	8*	3.53	0	7	2.91	0	7	2.84
SOCIAL SUPPORTS															
PSS Family	13	17	13.94	19	19	15.11	19	19	14.55	20	15	15.82	20	17	16.22
PSS Friends	20	11	15.69	20	5	16.8	19	18	17.03	20	16	17.21	20	16	17.75
SOCIAL FUNCTIONING															
SAS School	1.33	1.67	1.81	1	1.17	1.65	1	1.67	1.58	1.17	1.67	1.64	1.33	1.33	1.47
SAS Friends	1.78	2.67	2.18	1.33	3	1.76	1.22	1.89	1.84	1.11	1.89	1.7	1.44	2.22	1.65
SAS Family	1.67	1.5	2.1	1.67	2.17	1.81	1.67	1.83	1.81	1.17	1.83	1.67	1.83	2	1.54

(continued)

Table 4.5 Continued

Scale	Pretreatment			Posttreatment			6-Month			12-Month			18-Month		
	Menorka	Shelly	IPT-AST	Menorka	Shelly	IPT-AST	Menorka	Shelly	IPT-AST	Menorka	Shelly	IPT-AST	Menorka	Shelly	IPT-AST
SAS Dating	3	3.5	3.33	3	3	2.66	3	3	2.75	3	1.5	2.59	2.5	2.5	2.5
SAS Total	1.74	2.17	2.16	1.48	2.3	1.82	1.43	1.91	1.84	1.3	1.78	1.75	1.61	1.96	1.66
FAMILY CONFLICT (CBQ)															
CBQ Mom (Child)	3	1	5.06	0	3	4.17	1	4	4.15	0	5	3.71	1	8	3.59
CBQ Dad (Child)		0	5.6	2	3	5.27	2	6	6.63	0	15	5.7		11	3.68
CBQ Parent	12	8	6.44	4	8	6.47	5		5.86		7	6	3	8	4.5
SCHOOL FACTORS															
SARAC Behavioral Engagement	40	36	30.58	37	35	31.14	40	31	30.94	40	29	30.97	37	36	32.63
SARAC Emotional Engagement	39	30	30.72	37	27	32.57	40	25	32.68	40	27	31.76	35	26	33
Self-Efficacy in School	13	11	11.25	13	10	11.46	15	11	11.68	15	12	11	12	12	12.48
School Work	15	9	11.06	14	12	11.4	15	13	11.5	15	10	10.8	12	10	11.62

*Clinically significant.

was initially a difficult transition for her. Shelly elaborated that she cried several times a week due to feeling ostracized by peers and admitted that she had passive suicidal thoughts on a few occasions. Shelly's depressive symptoms persisted throughout seventh and eighth grade, but they were not severe enough to warrant a diagnosis.

These symptoms lifted during the summer before ninth grade. When she started high school in September, however, her symptoms returned, although not as intensely. Shelly explained that her experience with bullying has been better in high school, but that she still has moments of wanting to cry and difficulty trusting others. Shelly also indicated that with the exception of one best friend with whom she had a falling out, she has never developed any close friendships. She reported being very self-conscious of how others perceive her and is hesitant to confide in others because of her long history of being rejected and betrayed by her friends and her father. Furthermore, Shelly elaborated that because she feels uncomfortable expressing her negative feelings to others, she copes by withdrawing to her room, "crying [her] eyes out," writing in her journal, and praying.

In addition to her depressive symptoms, Shelly met criteria for a current insect phobia and reported elevated levels of anxiety (e.g., excessive worry about how others will perceive her, reassurance-seeking behaviors, muscle tension, and shaking); Shelly's scores on a standardized measure of anxiety disorders indicate some social phobia symptoms (SCARED: Total = 18, Social Phobia = 9). However, these symptoms were not severe enough to merit an anxiety diagnosis. Shelly also reported experiencing various hallucinations since age 7. Nevertheless, the content of her hallucinations was either religious or juvenile in nature, and thus it did not suggest clear psychopathology. For example, Shelly stated that she occasionally thinks she sees her cat that passed away when she was young. She also indicated that on a few occasions after listening to gospel songs, Shelly believed that God was speaking to her. Shelly is influenced by her cousin, who is a devout Christian and who tells Shelly that she often "speaks with God." In addition to anxiety and depression, Shelly's evaluator assessed for mania, eating disorders, disruptive behavior disorders, attentional problems, tic disorders, substance use, and trauma history. Shelly denied any concerns in these areas.

Vulnerabilities and strengths. Shelly has experienced several interpersonal stressors that may contribute to her vulnerability to depression, including, minimal parental support from her biological father, excessive and persistent bullying, and a lack of stable peer relationships (Allen et al., 2006; Klomek, Marrocco, Kleinman, Schonfeld, & Gould, 2007). Shelly also has a history of anxiety and depression on her maternal side of the family, and her mother endorsed elevated levels of depression during her own initial evaluation (CES-D = 21). Yet Shelly's strong sense of faith and weekly involvement with her church may serve as protective factors (Hill & Pargament, 2003; Mazza et al., 2010). She also has a positive sense of self-efficacy in school (SES: Self-efficacy: 11) and reported behavioral and emotional engagement in class (SARAC: Behavioral Engagement: 36; Emotional Engagement: 30).

Formulation, Goals, and Treatment Plan

An IPT case formulation typically involves identification of a specific interpersonal problem area that is thought to play a central role in the development and maintenance of an individual's depression. Thus, the goal of treatment in IPT is to simultaneously decrease depression symptoms and interpersonal problems by improving the identified problem area through the use of communication and interpersonal problem-solving strategies (Mufson, Dorta, Moreau, & Weissman, 2004; Weissman, Markowitz, & Klerman, 2000). However, because IPT-AST is a group prevention model, the intervention teaches communication and interpersonal problem-solving skills that can be applied to multiple relationships, rather than focusing on a primary interpersonal problem area. Nevertheless, during their individual pre-group sessions, students are asked to identify one or two interpersonal goals that they would like to work on over the course of group. These goals are frequently, but not always, related to one of three interpersonal problem areas: interpersonal role transitions (e.g., new school, divorce, and new sibling); interpersonal role disputes (e.g., independence from parents, hierarchical friendships, and responsibility); and/or interpersonal deficits (e.g., social withdrawal and limited friendship).

Both Menorka and Shelly seem to be experiencing depression symptoms as they navigate the transition from middle school to the new responsibilities and pressures of high school. In addition to this transition, Menorka's symptoms of depression seem to have been exacerbated by recent changes in the amount of time spent with friends and family and the resulting distance she feels in these relationships. Menorka explained that she has been feeling increasingly lonely and down since her friends started spending more time with their boyfriends and since her mother began a new job that no longer permits them to spend evenings together. Because of this change in schedule, Menorka also visits less often with her godmother, with whom she is very close. Due to the irritability associated with her depressive symptoms, Menorka has felt annoyed even when she has the chance to spend time with friends and family. Thus, Menorka's specific intervention goals were to (1) figure out ways to feel closer to and spend more time with her family and friends, and (2) express her feelings of frustration to her friends and family rather than withdrawing or arguing with them.

On the other hand, Shelly's depressive symptoms seem to be related to long-standing interpersonal deficits. More specifically, she struggles to trust others at her school and has ongoing concerns about being judged and bullied by peers. Furthermore, Shelly reported that she does not feel that she can confide in her mother, nor does she feel adequately supported by her. These negative interpersonal experiences and lack of support have contributed to Shelly's sad mood and social withdrawal. Accordingly, Shelly's group goals were to identify people in whom she can confide at school and to communicate more effectively with her mother about needing support.

Course of Intervention

OVERVIEW OF PRE-GROUP SESSIONS

Prior to beginning the group, the members have two individual sessions with a group leader during which the leader acquires relevant interpersonal information and orients the group member to the group format. Session length varies depending on school logistics and scheduling, but is usually between 30 and 45 minutes. The sessions involve reviewing the group member's mood and symptoms over the past week educating her about depression, prevention, and the IPT model conducting an interpersonal inventory and identifying goals for group.

The interpersonal inventory is an essential component of the IPT-AST intervention because it provides the clinician with information about the characteristics of the important relationships in the adolescent's life. During the interpersonal inventory, the adolescent uses concentric circles to visually represent his or her world interpersonally. The group member puts her name at the center and places important people in the other circles depending on their level of closeness and emotional impact on the group member. After this closeness circle has been created, the clinician assesses the strengths and weaknesses of each relationship, any recent changes in the relationship, and interpersonal patterns to be addressed during group (Mufson et al., 2004). The group leader also uses the closeness circle to help demonstrate the connection between the adolescent's relationships and her mood. Finally, the closeness circle is used to collaboratively develop individual goals to work toward during group.

All five group members (Menorka, Shelly, Sasha, Emma, and Joy) attended two pre-group sessions with one of the group clinicians, who are both doctoral-level psychologists.

Menorka – Pre-group Sessions

Menorka's first pre-group session was not audio-recorded and is thus unavailable for qualitative analysis. However, according to the progress note for this session, Menorka endorsed six symptoms of depression, including irritability, anhedonia, fatigue, indecisiveness, low self-esteem, and headaches. She also reported an average mood of 4 on a scale of 1 to10 (1 being the happiest and 10 being the worst).

During the second pre-group session, which was recorded, Menorka reported that her mood over the past week was a 3 and endorsed four depressive symptoms: difficulty sleeping, fatigue, decreased appetite, and frequent stomachaches. Menorka elaborated that she typically felt these symptoms when she was alone at night and waiting for her mother to return home from work. Once again, Menorka expressed intense worry over her mother's safety coming home late at night.

Menorka spent the remainder of the session using the closeness circle to describe her relationships with her best friends, mother, and godmother. Menorka reported a history of strong and stable relationships with friends and family. However, she indicated that over the past few months, her relationships have been strained by changing circumstances (e.g., best friends spending more time with boyfriends and changes to mom's work schedule). Menorka elaborated that she used to speak to her two best friends weekly, but both have recently been spending more time with boys instead of with her. Menorka reported she often feels frustrated, sad, and "left out," which leads her to feel annoyed about other situations involving these friends. When the group clinician asked how Menorka handles these negative emotions, she indicated that she either sends angry text messages or completely avoids the problem, both of which Menorka admitted contribute to a worsening of mood.

After describing the recent changes in relationships with her friends, Menorka discussed how she is no longer able to have daily visits with her godmother because of her mother's new work schedule. Menorka explained that she feels particularly close to her godmother and confides in her about everything, even boys. Unfortunately, now she hardly sees her outside of church. Because Menorka expressed sadness about spending less time with her friends and family, she and the clinician established a primary goal of helping her to feel closer to her godmother and friends. The clinician also suggested that it might be helpful for Menorka to let people know when she feels irritated sooner so that she does not carry the negative emotions and engages in fewer arguments. When the clinician presented this second goal, Menorka expressed concern about offending her friends if she explicitly acknowledged her irritability. The clinician validated her concern and explained that using the communication strategies in group would help her to both express her feelings and monitor the reactions of her friends. Menorka seemed satisfied with this response.

Throughout the session, Menorka exhibited a quiet demeanor and used a soft-spoken tone; she was cooperative and responsive when prompted. Menorka seemed to be aware of her emotions in specific interpersonal situations and how these interactions negatively impacted her mood. Additionally, she clearly articulated specific elements of her relationships that she wanted to change. Furthermore, Menorka seemed sensitive to her friends' perspectives and felt guilty about the possibility of offending them. These qualities suggest that Menorka is interpersonally oriented and values her relationships. The clinician also developed excellent rapport with Menorka by explaining the group process, giving her a chance to ask questions, and allowing time to collaboratively develop goals. Menorka's interest in the group was reflected in her questions and her request to have a letter sent to her homeroom teacher so that he could remind her to attend the group after school.

Shelly – Pre-group Sessions
During both of her pre-group sessions, Shelly indicated that her average mood over the past week was a 7 on a scale of 1 to 10 (1 being the best and 10 being the worst). She also endorsed seven depression symptoms, including irritability, anhedonia, insomnia, fatigue, decreased appetite, excessive guilt, and worthlessness.

On Shelly's closeness circle, she included several family members (e.g., mother, grandmother, uncle, aunt, and cousin), a school friend, and God. Shelly expressed that she felt close to most members of her family and that she did not have a contentious relationship with any of them. However, Shelly emphasized that she keeps the majority of her thoughts and feelings to herself. Shelly added that when she is feeling down or annoyed about something, she usually withdraws to her bedroom and writes about it in her journal. She rarely shares her emotions or problems with anyone, except her cousin. When the clinician asked Shelly to elaborate, Shelly described several invalidating experiences during which she had shared a problem with either a family member or a friend and they had told her to "just get over it." Shelly explained, "I am afraid people will think my thoughts are stupid and tell me to get over it, so I don't say anything at all and let out my feelings when I am by myself."

Shelly also mentioned several past and current incidents when she expressed herself to a classmate and was either betrayed or bullied. Despite alluding to a lack of support from and mistrust of others, Shelly indicated that she wanted her relationships to stay the same. A few times during the session, the clinician encouraged Shelly to consider the possibility of change, but Shelly seemed satisfied with her relationships, despite the identified problems. Nevertheless, Shelly articulated that she wanted to spend more time outside of school with a certain classmate with whom she could joke and be herself.

Throughout the discussion of interpersonal relationships, Shelly alluded to a general discomfort and unhappiness at her new school. For example, Shelly preferred to schedule her pre-group sessions during her lunch period. Arguably, when a student requests to miss lunch, which is the only opportunity to socialize freely during the school day, it may be indicative of a student's feelings of social isolation in the school. This hypothesis is supported by the fact that during the second pre-group session, Shelly stated, "I have no one at this school; I am alone." Even though Shelly reported that she is getting bullied less at her current school than in the past, this transition has been difficult for her because she feels that she does not have the support of teachers. Shelly acknowledged that she misses having a teacher whom she can trust with her problems, like she had at her previous school. Despite these current challenges, Shelly spoke at length about how her faith in God keeps her strong and hopeful about the future. She indicated that she prays daily and "prays extra when I am feeling sad." She acknowledged that God has saved her multiple times and helps her to overcome her struggles with self-esteem.

Because of time constraints, Shelly and the clinician only had 20 seconds to discuss goals prior to her returning to class. The clinician very quickly informed Shelly of two goals to consider working toward in group: (1) find people whom she can trust and feel close with and (2) find ways to talk to her mother about how she wants her to be more supportive of her. Shelly responded, "Okay" and abruptly left for class. It is unclear how much Shelly internalized these goals and how motivated she was to work toward them. If the clinician had more time, it may have been helpful to have a more extensive discussion about creating goals so that Shelly could have felt ownership over the process and investment in achieving them. Furthermore, it may have been helpful to make the goals more specific and aligned with Shelly's interests. For example, Shelly's goals could have been (1) to spend more time outside of school with the classmate with whom she feels comfortable and (2) to identify a teacher or school staff member with whom she can develop a supportive relationship. Shelly and the clinician also did not have time to discuss the structure of the group and Shelly's possible concerns about participating in group.

Shelly's speech was monotone, had a slowed tempo, and conveyed a sense of distress and sadness. She paused before responding to questions and was very hesitant to share information with the clinician. For example, when Shelly was describing how she was unable to discuss certain topics with her mother, she told the clinician, "I don't want to say it to you either because it's really private." Shelly's responses were often vague and the clinician had to ask several follow-up questions to understand the details of her experience in the situation. Nevertheless, Shelly became more animated when talking about her relationship with her cousin and with God. She also shared more information as she became increasingly comfortable with the clinician and was forthcoming about her loneliness and low self-esteem.

INITIAL PHASE OF GROUP SESSIONS

The initial phase of IPT-AST is comprised of sessions 1–3. These sessions are focused on developing rapport among group members, educating them about depression, and introducing the interpersonal skills that will be used over the course of group. Because group members are just beginning to develop comfort in the group setting, they are not expected to disclose personal information during this phase of the intervention. As mentioned earlier, group members begin each session completing the Depression Checklist checklist of symptoms and rating their mood on a scale of 1 to 10 (1 being the best and 10 being the worst).

Group Session 1

Both group leaders and three group members (Emma, Menorka, and Shelly) attended the initial group. After playing a rapport-building game, group members established group rules aimed at creating a comfortable and safe environment. Notably, two of the girls expressed concern about the potential imbalance of participation among group members. For example, Emma expressed that in previous groups she has felt uncomfortable because she was the only one contributing to the discussion. The group discussed ways to increase participation and comfort level. Next, group members learned about the symptoms of depression and engaged in activities to practice distinguishing between individuals who are depressed and those who have symptoms of depression that are not severe enough to meet criteria for a diagnosis. The group concluded with a discussion of common challenges that teenagers typically experience. Group members seemed to connect over shared experiences with peer pressure, family expectations, finding trustworthy friends, and concerns about boys and body image. Group leaders assured the girls that the interpersonal skills they would learn during group could help them to navigate these issues effectively and improve their mood. Finally, the girls shared their preference not to meet in the library, as the open space did not feel private. Group leaders were receptive to these concerns, and the decision was made to meet the following week in a classroom.

Menorka. Menorka's mood rating over the past week was a 4. On her depression checklist, she indicated that she sometimes feels hopeless, irritable, wants to nap, and has difficulty making decisions. She also indicated that she is experiencing decreased appetite, stomachaches, and difficulty sleeping. Menorka was cooperative and actively participated in group activities and discussions.

Shelly. Shelly's mood rating over the past week was a 6. On her depression checklist, she indicated that she sometimes feels sad, irritable, worthless, and has less energy. She also marked experiencing guilt and difficulty making decisions. Shelly presented as shy and spoke in a soft, monotone voice, but participated in all group activities and some discussions.

Session 2

Both group leaders and three group members (Emma, Sasha, and Menorka) attended the second group. Unfortunately, Shelly forgot about group and went straight home after school. Because this was Sasha's first session, group rules were reviewed and the girls played an abbreviated rapport-building game to welcome Sasha. The session focused on educating group members about how interpersonal interactions relate to mood. Group members practiced saying phrases using different tones and words to demonstrate how both verbal and nonverbal cues convey different feelings.

Group members also learned how to conduct a communication analysis to assess the effect that these cues have on an individual's mood and on the outcome of a conversation. A communication analysis involves collecting detailed information about the conversation in terms of what people said, how and when they said it, and how they felt in the situation. Group members participated in role-plays to demonstrate these concepts. They all seemed to strongly identify with the hypothetical role-play situations, so much so that they each disclosed a personal example of a similar experience. Clinicians underscored these parallel experiences and praised students for their courage to share personal information with the group. Both clinicians also tried to use the language of group members and consulted them as "experts" on being a teenager. This unassuming and open stance was encouraging for the girls, as they seemed to enjoy "educating" the clinicians on typical teen responses and issues.

Menorka. Menorka's mood rating over the past week was a 3. On her depression checklist, she indicated that she sometimes feels worthless, has less energy, difficulty falling asleep, and wants to nap. She also marked that she is experiencing increased irritability, a change in appetite, stomachaches, and difficulty making decisions. Menorka was rather quiet, but participated when appropriate. She was empathic toward others and particularly adept at noticing when individuals were experiencing conflicting emotions simultaneously.

Shelly. Shelly's mood and symptoms of depression were not documented for the second group because she did not attend the session.

Session 3

One group leader and two group members (Menorka and Emma) participated in the third group. The other group leader was unable to attend because of conflicting child care responsibilities. Shelly notified group leaders in advance that she would not be attending because she was missing school for her birthday, and Sasha did not show up for the session.

Despite the small showing, session 3 was very productive. The group clinician introduced the interpersonal skills to Menorka and Emma. The remainder of the session involved generating examples of these skills and using roleplays to practice using them in relevant situations. After practicing with two hypothetical situations, Emma volunteered to use the skills to plan a conversation she wanted to have with her mother about dating boys. With the help of the group clinician and Menorka, Emma scripted the potential conversation and practiced the skills in a role-play. Menorka shared with the group that she already successfully implemented certain strategies, and as a result, she has been able to confide in and feel closer to her mother. Menorka explained that last week her mother was eavesdropping on a phone conversation with a boy, whom she liked. However, instead of exploding as she may have done in the past, Menorka remembered what she had learned in last group's session. She stated:

> I used to always have a tone with my mom. I thought about what I learned in here and tried to change my tone and attitude. I used a calm voice when I told her about the boy, and I apologized for being on the phone with him. It was the first time she responded well to me, and I could treat her like a friend. I felt like she understood me.

Throughout the session, the clinician was supportive and encouraging of group members. Instead of directly challenging faulty communication, she used Socratic questioning to facilitate their own discovery of the utility of a specific comment or idea. Furthermore, to set up the group for realistic success, she also emphasized that these skills take practice and may require multiple conversations. At the conclusion of the session, Emma expressed relief about having both a plan and skills to help her articulate her thoughts more effectively to her mother.

However, Emma shared that she was concerned about the dynamics of the group for two reasons. First, Emma explained that in an earlier conversation that day, Sasha had indicated that she was uncertain about continuing with group, especially given that it was after school. Second, Emma expressed frustration that she was participating more in group discussions compared to other group members, in particular, Sasha and Shelly. Emma elaborated that if Shelly and Sasha had been present, she would not have been as forthcoming with her personal problems during this session. Emma clarified that it was easy to share in front of Menorka because they were good friends, but that Sasha and Shelly's quiet demeanor made her more hesitant to disclose information. Menorka added that it was difficult to trust group members with her personal experiences if other group members did not reciprocate this exchange of information. The clinician validated both of their concerns and engaged the girls in problem solving about how to increase attendance as well as trust within the group.

Menorka. Menorka's mood rating over the past week was a 2. On her depression checklist, she indicated that she sometimes feels worthless and irritable, has a decreased appetite, has less energy, and has difficulty sleeping and making decisions. She also marked that she has been taking more naps and feels like sleeping all of the time.

During session 3, Menorka not only demonstrated excellent knowledge of the skills, but she also initiated using these skills to approach interpersonal situations differently in her own life. During the initial phase, group members are typically encouraged to notice how their mood and relationships influence each other in between sessions, but they are not usually assigned formal homework of practicing these interpersonal skills until the middle phase of the intervention. Early on in the intervention, Menorka started to test out these interpersonal techniques and use them to directly achieve one of her group goals: become closer to friends and family. Additionally, both the praise she received from the group leader for practicing the skills and the positive outcome of her conversation were encouraging and may have made Menorka more likely to use these skills moving forward.

Furthermore, Menorka's insightful comments throughout the session suggest that her skills comprehension exceeds that of other group members. Two specific examples depict Menorka's internalization of the skills, particularly the strategy of "putting herself in other people's shoes." The group was discussing how their mothers are strict about allowing them to date boys. When the group leader asked about possible reasons for their mothers' sternness, Emma replied, "they don't understand, they are too concerned, that's it," while Menorka offered the possibility that their mothers "grew up differently—they are from a different generation." Menorka put herself in her mother's shoes to consider plausible reasons for her behavior.

Likewise, when planning for Emma's conversation with her mother, the group leader inquired about how a mother might feel if her daughter approached her and stated, "Mom, I know you are worried about something happening to me and that you just want what's best . . ." Emma responded that she thought the mother would feel even more upset and annoyed. Menorka indicated that if she was the mother, the statement would probably make her feel "stress-free because it communicates to me that my daughter knows how I am feeling. I would probably be more likely to let her go." Menorka's response suggests that she fully grasps the concept of "putting herself in other's shoes," and also that she understands the positive impact this strategy can have on the outcome of a conversation.

Shelly. Shelly's mood and symptoms of depression were not documented for the third group because she did not attend the session.

MIDDLE PHASE

The middle phase of IPT-AST consists of sessions 4–6. During the middle phase, group members use the interpersonal techniques learned in the initial phase to work on recent interpersonal problems, often related to their goals from the pre-group sessions. Typically, a group member provides a short synopsis of her problem, which is followed by a communication analysis of her most recent interpersonal interaction. During the communication analysis, group leaders assess the impact of specific verbal and nonverbal communication on the individual's feelings and the outcome of the conversation. Next, group members problem-solve, discuss interpersonal techniques that might be useful in a future conversation, and script a new conversation, incorporating these specific skills. Once the group member has a plan for a new conversation, she usually participates in at least one role-play with other group members so that she has the opportunity to practice using the skills in a realistic context. Other group members either participate in the role-play (as friend, mother, etc.) or act as coaches who hold up cards with the communication strategies to help keep group members on track. During this phase, group members are encouraged to test out these techniques at home and to provide the group with feedback about their experiences.

Session 4

Both group leaders and two group members (Shelly and Menorka) attended session 4. It is important to note that session 4 was rescheduled, and because of the school testing schedule, the only possible time to hold session 4 was the day before session 5. Shelly and Menorka were the only two group members who were available to attend sessions 4 and 5 on consecutive days.

Because Shelly had been absent for sessions focused on the interpersonal techniques, session 4 started with a review of these skills. Group leaders encouraged Menorka to explain each skill to Shelly, a task at which she excelled. Menorka provided a comprehensive description of the skills, even for those that had multiple components. For example, when explaining "strike while the iron is cold," Menorka indicated, "when you want to bring up an issue with someone, you need to initiate when they are calm, not irritated or busy, and when you are cool and not angry/tense." Menorka accurately emphasized that when using this skill, an individual should be aware of her mood and that of the other person. After reviewing the skills, the remaining time was split between working on Menorka's and Shelly's recent interpersonal interactions.

Menorka discussed a situation in which her friend was mad at her because Menorka had borrowed her friend's gym uniform earlier in the day and lost it (as she had done with her own). Menorka told her that she had already ordered new shirts for both of them, but that the order takes several weeks to process and the school is very strict about wearing uniforms at all times.

The group leaders engaged in problem solving with Menorka to determine her options moving forward. Menorka decided to ask the dean for help with the situation as well as to have a follow-up conversation with her friend. The group discussed interpersonal techniques that would be helpful in both situations; Menorka planned to talk to her friend the next morning before school and to speak with the dean directly after school. Menorka decided to use "put yourself in the other person's shoes" for both situations. For example, she practiced saying to her friend, "I could understand if you are still mad at me because you trusted me enough to lend me your shirt. I know I am responsible, but I didn't mean to lose it." With the assistance of group leaders, she also generated a list of possible solutions to present to the dean (e.g., giving her friend a pass or letting both of them wear a white shirt). Once Menorka felt confident about the goals of each conversation and how she wanted to communicate her points, she practiced with Shelly.

Shelly discussed a problem she was having with a boy from church who liked her, explaining that he had asked her out twice, but she did not know how to decline the offer. Shelly elaborated that she enjoys being friendly with this person, but that she is not interested in him romantically. The group discussed interpersonal techniques that might be helpful for Shelly to use to explain her feelings to her friend. Shelly's goal was to "say in the nicest way possible that we should remain friends." Once this goal had been set, Shelly practiced "putting herself in her friend's shoes" and using "I feel" statements during a role-play with Menorka. Shelly incorporated advice from the planning stage, stating, "I really like you and I hope that we can stay friends. I know you might be angry at me, but I hope we can still talk because I will always be here." Even after the role-play, Shelly remained concerned and felt guilty about letting down her friend. The group discussed the importance of having the conversation and helpful behaviors in which she could engage afterward to feel better (e.g., talking with her cousin or making an effort to say hello to the boy).

Because there were only two group members, the session was structured more like two individual sessions, with group leaders both focusing efforts on the identified adolescent, rather than a session involving rich group discussion. This structure allowed group members to receive more individualized attention from leaders, but also may have detracted from the group dynamic.

Menorka. Menorka's mood rating over the past week was a 1. On her depression checklist, she indicated that she sometimes has less energy, headaches, and difficulty making decisions. She also marked a decrease in appetite and increase in her naps. As part of the mid-intervention assessment, Menorka completed the CES-D, for which her score was a 19, indicating elevated symptoms. Although higher than the mid-intervention mean of the IPT-AST condition (16.33, SD = 7.68), her score was in the normative range compared to other participants.

Menorka was cooperative and remained focused throughout the session. She listened to group leader suggestions and tried to incorporate them into the role-plays. However, Menorka expressed feeling very guilty about the situation and repeatedly stated that this problem was her responsibility. She ultimately agreed to approach the dean, but was initially hesitant to assert herself and expressed some doubt about being understood by the school administration. Additionally, Menorka reported a moderate level of anxiety. On a few occasions she made comments such as, "When I hurt others, it makes me really worried to the point where I can't focus on anything in school, I feel tense, and I don't sleep. I definitely won't be sleeping tonight." Group leaders validated her feelings and Shelly reassured her that if she were in her friend's position, Shelly would forgive Menorka. Furthermore, when the group leader inquired about how Menorka was feeling at the end of the role-plays, she replied, "I feel very relieved."

Shelly. Shelly's mood rating over the past week was a 7. On her depression checklist, she indicated that she sometimes feels sad and worthless and has difficulty sleeping and making decisions. She also marked that she feels more irritable and guilty and that she has been taking more naps. As part of the mid-intervention assessment, Shelly completed the CES-D, for which her score was a 24, indicating depression symptoms at the clinical level (this score is also one SD above the mean of IPT-AST participant scores at mid-intervention).

During the first portion of the session, Shelly spoke in a very soft, almost inaudible voice and responded to questioning with one-word answers. It is important to note that Shelly missed the last two groups during which group members were informed that the group would become more personal starting in session 4. Thus, she may have been a bit hesitant to participate because the structure of this group was very different from session 1, the last group she attended. In addition to being hesitant to share details of the situation with the group, Shelly seemed unlikely to carry through with the conversation. The group leaders worked with Shelly to specify a good time to talk with her friend, but Shelly joked and stated, "New Year's," "in 10 years," or gave a vague answer. Group leaders emphasized the importance of following through with the conversation and Shelly seemed receptive to these points, but continued to express doubt. Additionally, Shelly performed well while practicing in the role-play with Menorka. Yet, when the group leaders inquired about how she felt afterward, she responded, "I feel horrible about how I did." This negative reaction reflects Shelly's pervasive negative self-concept.

Session 5

Both group leaders and three group members (Shelly, Menorka, and Emma) attended session 5, which was held the day after session 4. After group members completed their depression checklists, group leaders checked in about their experiences with work at home. Emma indicated that she had not spoken to her mother about dating because her family has been busy preparing to move to a new house. On the other hand, Menorka reported that she spoke with both the dean and her friend, and that both conversations went really well. The dean gave them a pass for gym and her friend seemed to be more understanding. Group leaders encouraged Shelly to summarize the situation involving her male friend, but Shelly refused, so the group leaders provided an abbreviated synopsis.

Group leaders also took time to address a quiet tension that seemed to stifle participation at the beginning of the session. Shelly's shyness about sharing her work from group yesterday triggered an irritated feeling in Emma. Usually boisterous and talkative, Emma became equally resistant to participating. When group leaders asked Emma to elaborate on her planned conversation with her mother, she vaguely replied, "I wanted to talk to her about something."

When Shelly briefly left the room to take a phone call, Emma reflected on her own behavior, indicating that she was not talking because Shelly was not talking. Similarly, when Shelly returned and when group leaders asked who wanted to work on an issue, they were met with silence. They acknowledged that absences have made it more difficult to share issues and asked the group if there were certain ways to help people feel more comfortable and safe. Emma took charge of the discussion, stating, "I understand if you have a personal issue you don't want to share, but make it seem like you are part of this group. Don't act like you don't want to be here. We are all here for the same reason." This spurred a conversation about reciprocal sharing and ways to signal to others that you are listening and engaged. Group members seemed to feel an increased sense of comfort and willingness to participate after the discussion.

The remainder of the session was spent practicing how to implement the communication and problem-solving skills in both hypothetical and personal situations. Group leaders started the session with hypothetical situations because group members were initially reluctant to discuss personal situations. Based on these hypothetical situations, group members discussed their own interpersonal concerns. Menorka planned a conversation with her cousin, who has been teasing her. Shelly sought help about ways to make trustworthy friends, and Emma discussed her feelings about moving away from her friends and extended family. At the conclusion of group, members were encouraged to continue the interpersonal work from session over the next week and to report back to the group about their experiences.

Menorka. Menorka's mood rating over the past week was a 1. On her depression checklist, she indicated that she sometimes experiences anhedonia, decreased appetite, headaches, fatigue, difficulty falling asleep, and worthlessness.

Because of the strained group dynamic, Menorka was initially hesitant to raise an interpersonal issue with the group. However, the hypothetical situation that was selected for the group to practice using the skills resembled a recent experience with her cousin. With encouragement from the group, Menorka shared her story. She explained that her cousin has been bothering her and calling her fat. Menorka hypothesized that these insults were an attempt to get her attention because they have been spending less time together. Menorka added that these comments were very hurtful because she is self-conscious about her body image.

The group discussed how Menorka could use the interpersonal strategies to express how she is feeling to her cousin and present alternative ways to get her attention. It was suggested that Menorka bring up these concerns when they are at an arcade and in a relaxed mood over the weekend. Menorka and Emma role-played the conversation, which barely needed modification from group leaders. Menorka acknowledged her interpersonal strength of "putting herself in other people's shoes," but added that she needs to work on decreasing her frequency of using "always" and "never" in conversations. After the role-play, group leaders asked how she was feeling and Menorka responded, "I feel relieved. He understood what I was saying, and I could really say how I feel. I don't think he will do it anymore."

Shelly. Shelly's mood rating over the past week was a 6. On her depression checklist, she indicated that she sometimes feels irritable, worthless, and guilty; has difficulty sleeping and making decisions; and has been taking more naps.

Like Menorka, Shelly was also reluctant to share and needed prompting and encouragement from group leaders. As usual, she spoke in a low, soft tone and provided short answers absent of details. Nevertheless, the second hypothetical scenario resonated with Shelly's most difficult interpersonal challenge. The card described a situation in which a girl was feeling lonely but did not know how to make friends. After reading the card, Shelly immediately stated, "This is hard for me."

This disclosure led to a rich discussion of suggestions for initiating friendships, including giving compliments, offering to help, introducing oneself, or joining an activity. Shelly was open to introducing herself, but she was less interested in group activities. During the discussion, Menorka shared her initial thoughts about Shelly when meeting her last summer: "I really liked you and wanted to be friends with you; you were less quiet." This resulted in an embarrassed grin spreading across Shelly's face. She explained that the summer was easier because there were fewer people, so she felt less intimidated. Shelly added that she has a much easier time making friends at church than at school, where people are not trustworthy. She stated, "I don't tell many people my secrets. I want someone who will be truthful with me because most people are fake. Some girls are mean because I'm not in their category." Emma validated Shelly's experience of shyness by sharing a story about how her cousin used to be the same way but has learned to become more open. There was not time for a role-play, but group leaders asked Shelly to consider a few people with whom she wants to become closer and next session would focus on rehearsing this conversation. Shelly agreed to think of potential candidates. This conversation about making friends seemed to unite the group and increase empathy. However, interpersonal techniques were not explicitly referenced, and Shelly did not have the chance to practice the skills actively during the session.

Session 6
Both group leaders and four group members (Menorka, Shelly, Emma, and Sasha) attended session 6. Of note, Sasha had not been present since session 2, so not only was this group her first middle-phase session, but she was also unfamiliar with the interpersonal skills.

After group members completed their depression checklists, group leaders checked in about their experiences with work at home. Emma and Sasha both reported that they had conversations about dating with their parents. Emma indicated that in her conversation with her mom she used some of the strategies that she had practiced during group. Additionally, Menorka approached her cousin about his tendency to tease her. She reported that her cousin was very receptive to her suggestions, and they had made plans twice since her conversation. Shelly indicated that she tried to be friendlier toward people at school by saying "hi," but she did not have the chance to identify specific individuals with whom she wanted to become closer. The remainder of group was spent planning a follow-up conversation that Emma could have with her mom as well as discussing issues around parental trust. At the conclusion of group, leaders encouraged members to spend the upcoming week working on their goals. This instance was the first mention of interpersonal goals since pre-group sessions, and these goals were not reviewed. Thus, some group members may have been unclear about the nature of their homework.

Menorka. Menorka's mood rating over the past week was a 2. On her depression checklist, she indicated that she sometimes experiences less energy, decreased appetite, difficulty making decisions, and stomachaches. She also marked that she has been taking more naps.

Menorka's presence during session 6 was more passive, but she spoke freely when prompted. She also became quite animated when sharing her experience using the interpersonal strategies with her cousin. She stated:

> At first it felt scary because I didn't want to use the wrong words and hurt him. I was nervous about making a mistake. I tried to remember what we practiced and avoid using "always" and "never." It ended up being really good.

This excerpt illustrates Menorka's insight about the role of communication in the outcome of a conversation and the impact it has on both her feelings and those of the other person. Furthermore, although Menorka's worry about harming others seemed distressing, it is indicative of how much she values her relationships.

Shelly. Shelly's mood rating over the past week was a 5. On her depression checklist, she indicated that she sometimes experiences sadness, irritability, less energy, and difficulty making decisions. She also marked that she has been feeling guiltier.

Shelly was difficult to engage during this session and typically remained silent when asked questions. When group leaders inquired about whether she had identified potential friends at school or church, she responded curtly, "I have friends at church." Group leaders seemed to sense her hesitancy and did not push Shelly further, despite the plan for the session to practice how Shelly could engage with people to get to know them better. However, Shelly indicated that for the first time she followed through with part of her homework by trying to be friendlier to classmates. She explained, "I tried to get over my shyness and just come out. I said hi to them and they seemed a little shocked because usually I am really quiet." Shelly's upbeat tone suggested that she seemed relatively satisfied with the outcome of her efforts. Even though her social initiation was a critical feat, Shelly didn't practice using the specific interpersonal strategies outside of the group setting, which is the main goal of the middle phase.

TERMINATION PHASE

The termination phase consists of sessions 7 and 8 and involves celebrating progress, discussing helpful and difficult strategies and their applicability to future interpersonal situations, and identifying personal warning signs of depression and appropriate prevention steps. Group members also discuss characteristics of other members that make them supportive and the importance of choosing friends based on these qualities.

Session 7

Both group leaders and three group members (Shelly, Menorka, and Emma) attended session 7. Group members completed their depression checklists and discussed experiences with their homework. Menorka shared that she had another follow-up conversation with her cousin about the positive changes in their relationship, and that as a result of this ongoing communication, she feels like he "really cares and listens to me now." Group leaders suggested that to maintain these interpersonal gains, Menorka may consider initiating another conversation during which she uses "I feel" statements to express her positive feelings since he stopped teasing her. Menorka was in favor of this idea and agreed to engage in this conversation before the final group.

Next, members reviewed their mood ratings over the course of the group and shared notable changes. Most group members indicated that their mood improved as group progressed, but Shelly reported that her mood worsened. When reflecting on this pattern, she bravely expressed to the group, "It is hard to be happy." This comment led to a discussion of helpful coping strategies group members use when they feel down, such as talking to a friend or family member. Shelly responded to these suggestions, confessing that she neither knew whom to confide in nor how to approach people about her feelings. The next 30 minutes of the session were dedicated to supporting Shelly and helping her to problem-solve this challenge. Group members and leaders validated her feelings. Menorka shared that she has felt down in the past, and Emma reassured Shelly that she wanted to help her feel better. Group leaders guided Shelly to identify a trusted family member, her cousin, and collaboratively planned and role-played a conversation using the interpersonal skills.

The group also discussed how outward presentations might not always be consistent with internal feelings (e.g., Shelly's shyness was initially misinterpreted in group as disinterest and not wanting help) and the importance of being explicit in communications about needs. Group leaders also emphasized that interpersonal skills can be used to strengthen positive relationships in addition to problem-solving about negative interpersonal interactions. The group then identified helpful and challenging skills and processed feelings about the group ending.

Menorka. Menorka's mood rating over the past week was a 2. On her depression checklist, she indicated that she sometimes experiences decreased appetite, less energy, worthlessness, and headaches.

Menorka presented as cheerful and hopeful throughout the session. Her change in communication patterns over the course of group was evident in her commentary on how her improved mood is related to changes in her relationship with her mom. She explained:

> My mood is going up. I'm talking to my mom more, especially if I don't like something or I don't feel comfortable, and I use the techniques. The other night I put myself in her shoes after I broke a phone rule and we ended up joking with each other instead of yelling.

Despite her noted progress, Menorka indicated that it is still difficult for her to use the "be specific" strategy because she has a tendency to use "always" and "never."

Shelly. Shelly's mood rating over the past week was a 7. On her depression checklist, she indicated that she sometimes experiences sadness, irritability, less energy, and passive suicidal ideation. She also marked that she has been napping more and that it has been increasingly difficult for her to make decisions.

Session 7 seemed pivotal for Shelly because it was the first time she allowed herself to be vulnerable in front of the group by sharing her interpersonal difficulties and her internal struggle. Instead of giving one-word answers or being nonresponsive, Shelly seemed to accept her central role. She was less guarded with her feelings, more open about her concerns, and more outwardly engaged in the group activities. This change was evidenced by her more audible voice, relaxed demeanor, and the frequent commentary by other group members that it was nice to see her smile and be herself around them. Following is an excerpt from the session that illustrates how the tremendous support and validation from group members empowered Shelly to disclose her current challenges. The conversation begins after a group leader inquires about why Shelly believes her mood has worsened over the course of group.

SHELLY: I try to feel better, but sometimes I feel bad about myself. Sometimes I just cry. I write in my journal to express myself because I don't want to say it to anyone. I want to keep it to myself.

GROUP LEADER: What do you think keeps you from sharing it with others?

SHELLY: I don't want to say.

EMMA: It's ok, you can say it in here. We won't judge you.

SHELLY: I try to tell myself to get over it, but I feel ugly. I'm not sure I'm a good person. I don't trust people to help me.

EMMA: I wasn't sure if you wanted our help in the beginning. You didn't talk or smile. But now you are a blossoming flower. You are expressing how you feel and you don't have to be in that shell. It's nice.

MENORKA: Yeah, like it made me feel good when you asked me if I was coming to group today. I liked that you came to talk to me.

GROUP LEADER: How does it feel to hear that?

SHELLY: Good (smiling).

This dialogue demonstrates how the group serves as a social lab for leaders to gather data about members' real-life social interactions with peers and allows members to receive direct feedback about their interpersonal presence. For example, a group leader pointed out Shelly's tendency to have negative expectations of herself and others, which leads her to be more shy and reserved. The leader encouraged Shelly to accept the possibility that people generally want to help her, but often do not know she wants help because of her guarded presentation.

When discussing strategies, Shelly identified "strike while the iron is cold" as most difficult for her. Perhaps this challenge of knowing when to initiate conversation hindered Shelly in successfully practicing the skills outside of the group setting. Nonetheless, Shelly left the session with information about how others perceive her and how this is sometimes different from her internal experience of a situation. Most important, she seemed to have ended group more confident that her peers wanted to support and help her. This session seemed in many ways transformative for Shelly but might have been even more effective if these issues were addressed during the middle phase, so she could extend these lessons outside of group and specifically work on using interpersonal strategies to improve her friendships.

Session 8

Both group leaders and four group members (Shelly, Menorka, Emma, and Sasha) attended session 8. After completing depression checklists and checking in about homework, the group discussed individual improvements with relationships and how this resulted in people feeling better. Next, leaders helped members to identify warning signs and discussed appropriate steps to take if members begin to notice these symptoms in the future. The group also discussed the qualities of supportive group members and how these characteristics represented those of a good friend (e.g., loyalty, trust, and giving good advice). Finally, group leaders elicited general feedback about the group process and celebrated the completion of the intervention with food and certificates. Group members acknowledged that trust was a barrier to group progress. They suggested encouraging group members to share personal information earlier and felt that giving examples of things former group members disclosed might help. Group members also indicated that trust is an issue throughout the school, not only because of the frequent peer gossip, but also because they do not feel that they can trust the administration, especially the guidance counselor.

Menorka. Menorka's mood rating over the past week was a 1. On her depression checklist, she indicated that she sometimes experiences irritability, decreased appetite, less energy, and stomachaches/headaches. She also marked that she been taking more naps.

Menorka shared that she had another conversation with her cousin, informing him that she has enjoyed spending more time with him and appreciates that he is no longer teasing her. When considering her own accomplishments in group, she stated, "Before, I would let things bother me and not talk to people about it. Now, with the tips you have given us, it puts us in a better position to talk when we feel upset." Menorka identified the following personal warning signs of depression: decreased appetite, less energy, and difficulty sleeping when she is worried.

Shelly. Shelly's mood rating over the past week was a 3. On her depression checklist, she indicated that she sometimes experiences irritability, guilt, and feels like napping more often. She also marked that it has been increasingly difficult for her to make decisions.

Shelly's mood markedly improved after receiving critical feedback from the group during session 7. She shared that she was unable to have the conversation with her cousin, but that she spoke briefly to a girl in church (no details were provided). Shelly added that throughout the group she has been working on talking more to friends, trusting others, and being more open with how she feels. Shelly identified the following warning signs of depression: sadness, worthlessness, difficulty sleeping, and getting upset over little things.

Intervention Monitoring and Use of Feedback Information

Group leaders received ongoing weekly feedback about each group member via the Depression Checklist, the Mood Ratings, and the information from the standardized measures (see Table 4.2). They were also in weekly supervision with the PI (J.F.Y.). Supervision was based on the PI's review of session audio recordings and involved discussion of use of IPT-AST strategies and how to modify sessions accordingly. Additionally, group session content was adjusted based on group member compliance with homework and reported experiences using the interpersonal strategies. Group leaders also began each session by asking about current interpersonal problems, and this information was incorporated into the session agenda.

Concluding Evaluation of Intervention Process and Outcome

Quantitative Evaluation

The results on the standardized self-report measures completed by Menorka, Shelly, and their parents, as compared with the mean of the IPT-AST participants, are summarized in Table 4.5. The battery of assessments evaluated depression and anxiety symptoms as well as school, social, and family variables. Figures 4.2 through 4.7 illustrate the change in Menorka and Shelly's depression symptoms, anxiety symptoms, parent–child conflict, and overall functioning over the course of the study. The details and significance of these results are explained in the sections that follow. Overall, the quantitative data indicated a positive effect of intervention for Menorka that was maintained over the next 18 months, and slight improvement from Shelly during the intervention with significant difficulties emerging during the follow-up phase.

Menorka's Positive Outcome

Symptoms and overall functioning. Based on diagnostic interviews using the K-SADS, Menorka did not fulfill the criteria for any diagnosis at the post-intervention, 6-month, 12-month, or 18-month follow-up assessments. Menorka denied experiencing clinical symptoms of depression at the post-intervention and 12-month evaluations, but she endorsed sad mood and nonrestorative sleep at the 6-month follow-up and decreased appetite at the 18-month follow-up. Furthermore, Menorka consistently reported positive social relationships and good academic functioning throughout the follow-up phase of the study. In particular, she indicated that she continued to feel very close to her mother.

However, during the 6-month evaluation, Menorka reported some self-consciousness around peers due to body image concerns. As illustrated, in

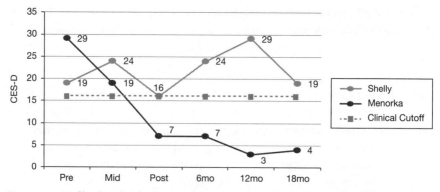

Figure 4.3 Profile Plots for the Center for Epidemiologic Studies-Depression Scale (CES-D).

Figures 4.3 through 4.5, Menorka's reported depressive symptoms (CES-D, CDRS-R) decreased and her overall functioning (CGAS) steadily improved at each time point. Furthermore, Menorka's scores on the CES-D were lower than the mean of IPT-AST participants at each time point after baseline (Table 4.5). According to her scores on the SCARED (Fig. 4.6), Menorka's subthreshold anxiety symptoms

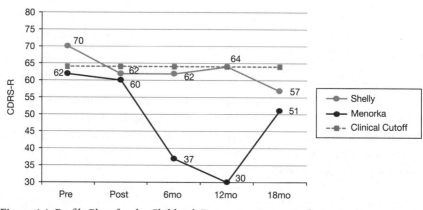

Figure 4.4 Profile Plots for the Children's Depression Rating Scale-Revised.

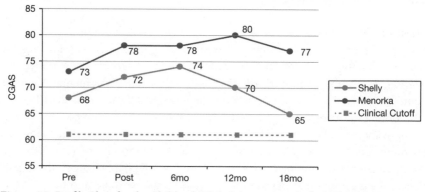

Figure 4.5 Profile Plots for the Children's Global Assessment Scale (CGAS).

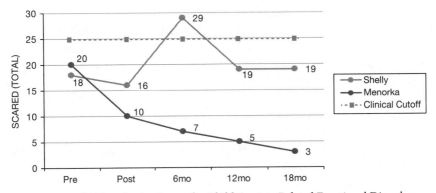

Figure 4.6 Profile Plots for the Screen for Child Anxiety Related Emotional Disorders.

also decreased over the course of the intervention, and these results were maintained at each time point.

Nevertheless, there is some discrepancy in the pattern of change of Menorka's reported depressive symptoms according to each measure. Figure 4.3 shows that she reported a large decrease in symptoms between pre-intervention and post-intervention on the self-report CES-D (29 to 7), which tapered during the follow-up phase (7, 3, 4). In contrast, Figure 4.4 shows that Menorka reported only a small decrease in symptoms between pre-intervention and post-intervention on the clinician-rated CDRS-R (62 to 60), although her score dropped more significantly during the follow-up phase (37, 30, 51).

In their review of rating scales for internalizing disorders, Myers and Winters (2002) recommend using both self-report and clinician-administered rating scales to provide the most accurate assessment of depressive symptoms. They also caution that rating scales, such as the CES-D and the CDRS-R, should not be used independently as diagnostic tools, but rather as a way to monitor symptoms over time. The CES-D assesses symptoms over a one-week period and the questions focus more on emotional domains of depression, while the CDRS-R captures symptoms over a two-week period and includes more physiological

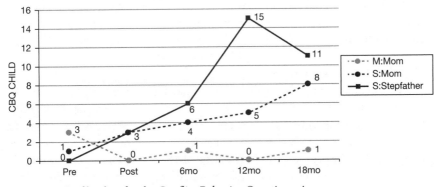

Figure 4.7 Profile Plots for the Conflict Behavior Questionnaire.

questions and items not specific to depressive symptoms (e.g., school functioning, social withdrawal) (Elmquist, Melton, Croarkin, & McClintock, 2010; Myers & Winters, 2002). Due to these instruments capturing slightly different time periods and information and their differing administration modalities (e.g., clinician administered vs. self-report), scores on these measures may vary. Yet, despite Menorka's discrepancy in scores, her score on both the CDRS-R and the CES-D reflect clinical symptoms in the normative range throughout the follow-up phase. Nonetheless, their inconsistency highlights the need to incorporate multiple forms of assessment when identifying the trajectory of a client's symptoms.

Social and school variable. According to scores on self-report measures (CBQ, PSS, SAS-SR, SES, SARAC), which are defined in Table 4.1 and presented in Table 4.5, Menorka's overall school and social functioning either remained consistent or improved. As shown in Figure 4.7, Menorka reported a decrease in parent–child conflict with her mother from pre-intervention to post-intervention (CBQ child: 3 to 0), which was maintained throughout the follow-up period. Likewise, her mother indicated a notable decrease in their negative communication and conflict from pre-intervention to post-intervention (CBQ parent: 12 to 4; see Table 4.5). Additionally, as shown in Table 4.5, Menorka's perceived support from family (PSS family) increased, and her perceived support from friends (PSS friends) remained high and stable. Her scores on these indices were also higher than mean scores of participants in the IPT-AST condition at all time points. With respect to school measures, Menorka reported a high sense of self-efficacy, schoolwork (SES), and school engagement throughout the study (SARAC), which was also greater than the mean for IPT-AST participants at all time points (see Table 4.5).

Attitude toward intervention. On the Attitude Toward Intervention Scale, Menorka reported that she found the intervention to be very helpful, and that she felt confident about the group ending. She was also reportedly satisfied with the length of the intervention and did not indicate a need for individual services. However, Menorka reported that she would have liked more opportunities for parent involvement in the intervention process. These post-intervention attitudes are consistent with Menorka's positive attitude toward the intervention during her pre-group sessions when she expressed excitement about group starting, and asked for the group leader to write her homeroom teacher a letter so that he could remind her to attend.

SHELLY'S NEGATIVE OUTCOME
Symptoms and overall functioning. Based on diagnostic interviews using the K-SADS, Shelly met criteria for a past episode of depressive disorder NOS at the 12-month evaluation as well as a past episode of major depressive disorder at the 18-month evaluation, both of which coincided with an interpersonal event that had occurred in the prior 6 months. Additionally, Shelly endorsed three threshold symptoms of depression (irritability, fatigue, and negative self-image) during the post-intervention assessment and depressed mood at the clinical level during the

6-month evaluation. This high level of depressive symptoms is reflected in the CES-D scores in Figure 4.3, which are all above the clinical cutoff. Shelly also consistently reported increased conflict with her mother and stepfather throughout the follow-up phase (see Fig. 4.7); and impaired academic functioning, romantic discord, and lack of peer support (see Table 4.5). For example, during the post-intervention assessment, Shelly indicated that she feels like an "outcast," and during the 6-month assessment, she reported having few friends and peer rejection.

Shelly explained that her depressive disorder NOS episode occurred 2 months prior to the 12-month follow-up and was triggered by an explosive argument she had had with her mother. After the argument, Shelly indicated that she had thoughts of wanting to "disappear" or "run away." According to her self-report during the 12-month follow-up, Shelly's mother also appeared to be experiencing depressive symptoms at the clinical level (CES-D = 38). Parental depression has been. indicated as a risk factor for adolescent depression (Mazza et al., 2010; Wolfe & Mash, 2006). In addition to Shelly's biological predisposition, her mother's depression may have impacted the parent–child interactions that preceded Shelly's depressive episode. During the 18-month follow-up, Shelly reported that she had a major depressive disorder episode over the summer months. At this time, she had a breakup with her girlfriend, and simultaneously, her mother found out she was bisexual and disclosed this information to her extended family.

As can be observed in Figures 4.3–4.5, Shelly's reported depressive symptoms (CES-D, CDRS-R) and overall functioning (CGAS) fluctuated and did not consistently improve. Similarly, as shown in Table 4.5, Shelly's scores on the SCARED indicate that her anxiety symptoms remained high throughout the study and reached the clinical level on several indices, including GAD, panic, and social phobia at the 6-month follow-up. Shelly's scores on self-report measures of anxiety and depression are consistent with her verbal reports during the diagnostic interviews at each time point, during which she reported subthreshold symptoms of social phobia and GAD. Both during the intervention and follow-up phases, Shelly's report of depressive symptoms, anxiety symptoms and overall functioning were more severe than the mean of participants in the IPT-AST condition (see Table 4, 5).

Social and school variables. As indicated during her diagnostic follow-up interviews, Shelly's social functioning seemed to deteriorate over the course of the study. Shelly's reported conflict with both her mother and stepfather (CBQ child) increased slightly during the intervention and continued to worsen throughout the follow-up phase (see Fig. 4.7). Additionally, Shelly's mother reported high parent–child conflict and negative communication (CBQ parent) both at pre-intervention and at all subsequent follow-ups. Conversely, Shelly's responses on the PSS and SAS reflect a stable level of perceived support from family. Yet her perceived support from friends decreased between pre-intervention and postintervention (PSS friends: 11 to 5; SAS Friends: 2.67 to 3; see Table 4.5) and fluctuated at subsequent time points. Finally, she reported a stable and adequate sense of self-efficacy and schoolwork (SES) that was consistent with reports of other IPT-AST participants throughout the study (see Table 4.5).

Attitude toward intervention. On the Attitude Toward Intervention Scale, Shelly reported that the intervention was very helpful and indicated that she felt neutral about the group ending. However, she reported that she felt the length of the intervention was too long, and she would have preferred more individual services.

QUALITATIVE EVALUATION: INDIVIDUAL FACTORS CONTRIBUTING TO INTERVENTION OUTCOMES

Attitude toward change. Menorka's positive attitude toward change was apparent from the outset of the intervention. When asked about possible changes in her relationships during pre-group sessions, she volunteered several, which made the task of developing her goals relatively straightforward. Additionally, Menorka showed initiative by practicing the new interpersonal strategies at home during the initial phase of the intervention, even though members were not yet expected to practice at home. These early attempts to modify her communication patterns may have been rewarding, and thus they increased the likelihood that she would continue to work on changing her interactions with others. Menorka also voluntarily identified IPT-AST strategies that were more difficult for her (being specific) and actively worked on improving her use of these strategies.

In contrast, Shelly exhibited resistance to change in the pre-group sessions that persisted throughout the intervention. Despite acknowledging dissatisfaction in her relationships, Shelly indicated that she wanted her relationships to stay the same. Additionally, even though Shelly participated in role-plays during group, she avoided selecting a specific time to have these actual conversations, which suggests some reluctance to change. This apparent contrast in Shelly and Menorka's attitude toward change parallels their divergent outcomes.

Worthlessness. Shelly and Menorka both endorsed feelings of worthlessness at baseline and at various points throughout the group. Yet Menorka's feelings of worthlessness seemed to be mostly related to her negative body image (i.e., her concern about being overweight compared to peers), whereas Shelly's negative self-concept appeared to be more pervasive.

Shelly expressed both during group and evaluations that it was difficult to be happy because she felt "ugly," disliked by others, and "not a good person." Given that Shelly disclosed that she was bisexual during the 18-month evaluation, it is also possible that she was questioning her sexual identity at the time of the group. Research has shown that at different stages of sexual identity development, individuals may be at greater risk of psychological distress and negative self-concept (Cochran, Sullivan, & Mays, 2003; Meyer, 2013). Furthermore, sexual minority individuals are vulnerable to internalizing the "sexual stigma" prevalent in society and, thus, may adopt society's negative attitudes about themselves and engage in negative self-evaluation (Glassgold, 2009). Because of the severity of Shelly's symptoms of worthlessness and her global negative self-concept, she may have been more suited to an individual intervention where she may have felt more comfortable addressing these sensitive issues. However, even in her individual sessions, she expressed discomfort sharing personal information with the group leader. This suggests that she may have been hesitant to disclose her feelings and concerns even within the context of an individual intervention.

Negative cognitive style. Shelly not only expressed negative beliefs about herself during group, but her statements also suggested that she tends to make negative attributions. For example, in her pre-group session, she described that her classmates are always giggling together, and she is certain that they are making fun of her. She also reported negative expectations of how others will respond to her. For example, Shelly explained that she is reluctant to confide in her mother or godmother because they would most likely respond, "Just get over it." Similarly, Shelly shared that her peers are fake and do not want to help her, so she does not confide in anyone and has difficulty trusting the intentions of others. Perhaps, Shelly was hesitant to confide in her group for fear that they too would hurt or embarrass her. This negative expectation may have inhibited her level of engagement and acceptance of other group members' support. On the other hand, Menorka welcomed support from the group and, although anxious, seemed hopeful that others would respond well to her attempts to use the interpersonal strategies.

Anxiety symptoms. Shelly and Menorka both reported subsyndromal anxiety at baseline, but Shelly reported more symptoms of social anxiety and Menorka reported more symptoms of generalized anxiety. Shelly's social anxiety symptoms seem to have stemmed in part from a specific episode in seventh grade during which she was repeatedly teased after forgetting words during a presentation. Her extensive history of bullying, betrayal, and social rejection has also contributed to Shelly's more reserved and anxious presentation. These qualities may have affected her ability to feel comfortable and develop rapport with the group. For example, Shelly refused to share certain information during both her pre-group and group sessions. Because Shelly was resistant to share, it made it more difficult for the group to give her targeted help earlier in the intervention. Furthermore, Shelly acknowledged that the most difficult IPT-AST skill for her to implement was "strike while the iron is cold." Shelly's apparent difficulty of knowing when and how to initiate conversations is demonstrative of her social anxiety symptoms, and it may have contributed to her difficulty completing group homework and her overall experience in the intervention. As a result, Shelly's anxiety symptoms seemed to worsen over the course of the study (Fig. 4.7) and may have interfered with intervention efficacy.

Conversely, as Menorka became more adept at using the IPT-AST skills in her conversations, she seemed to become less anxious about the possible negative outcomes of having these conversations. In her pre-group session, Menorka worried about how her friends would respond when she shared with them her feelings of frustration and hurt. However, she was able to express these negative emotions in conversations with her mother and her cousin during the intervention and to see others respond favorably. At times, Menorka's anxiety even seemed to impel her to complete the IPT-AST homework. For example, Menorka was so anxious about the situation with her friend and the gym shirt that she engaged in both conversations practiced in group the following day. Overall, the intervention seemed to have a positive impact on Menorka's anxiety, as illustrated by the notable decrease in reported symptoms throughout the intervention and follow-up period (Fig. 4.7).

Interpersonal history. Another important individual factor to consider in the differences in intervention effect is interpersonal histories. During the interpersonal inventory, Menorka reported a history of supportive relationships with friends and family, but indicated that she was experiencing a recent negative change in these relationships (i.e., feeling more distant from and arguing more with friends, godmother, and mother). Thus, Menorka's goals evolved based on a desire to regain this closeness that she had previously experienced in her relationships.

Conversely, Shelly reported a long history of invalidating social experiences, betrayal, and rejection from both peers and family, rather than a recent change in her relationships. It is certainly possible that because of its short duration, group structure, and educational framework, IPT-AST was not an appropriate modality to address Shelly's persistent and ingrained interpersonal problems and resulting interpersonal deficits and social withdrawal.

QUALITATIVE EVALUATION: INTERVENTION FACTORS AS POTENTIAL MECHANISMS OF CHANGE

Setting and accomplishing goals. Menorka's and Shelly's experiences with setting and working toward goals were considerably different during the group and may have impacted their divergent outcomes. Because of time constraints during the pre-group sessions, Shelly did not have the chance to develop her own goals. The clinician created goals that addressed directly Shelly's interpersonal problems (i.e., find people whom she can trust and get more support from her mother); yet they ran out of time to discuss the feasibility of these goals and Shelly's investment in them, and to modify them accordingly. Given Shelly's significant interpersonal deficits, these broad goals may have been too ambitious for her. Perhaps, something more manageable would have been to ask her classmate, with whom she already feels comfortable, to sit together at lunch or to hang out after school.

Conversely, during pre-group sessions Menorka had ample time to develop and modify her goals so that they felt doable for her. Menorka's work in group was also directly related to her goals of feeling closer to and communicating with others about her negative emotions. For example, Menorka communicated effectively with her cousin and mother about her negative emotions, which resulted in her feeling closer to both of them. Perhaps, because Menorka actively participated in the development of her goals, they were more salient to her than to other group members during the intervention (individual goals were not explicitly mentioned until session 6 and were not reviewed).

Shelly's interpersonal problems were also discussed during the intervention, but she did not effectively work on her goals outside of the group setting. Group members engaged in two rich discussions about Shelly's difficulties establishing friendships and trusting others. And Shelly took the important initial steps of acknowledging her difficulties and seeking support from group members, but she barely used the interpersonal skills to work directly on her goals. Individual booster sessions may have been an ideal opportunity for Shelly to work more actively and directly on her goals.

In a broader context, Shelly did not achieve the focal goal of each intervention phase. The main goals of the initial phase are to develop trust among group members and to learn the interpersonal strategies. The main goal of the middle phase is to improve relationships through practice of these strategies. Because Shelly was absent during sessions 2 and 3, the sessions during which the interpersonal strategies are taught, Shelly entered the middle phase of the intervention without knowledge of the skills. She also did not have a chance to develop trust with other group members during the initial phase, which may have been particularly important for Shelly, given her social anxiety symptoms and more guarded demeanor. As previously mentioned, Shelly engaged in productive discussions about her interpersonal difficulties, but she did not effectively work on improving a specific relationship through practice of the skills during the middle phase. In contrast, Menorka fulfilled the goals at each phase of the intervention.

Skills comprehension and practice. Not only was Menorka present during sessions 2 and 3 when the skills were taught, but she also personally taught Shelly the skills in session 4. By actively teaching the skills, Menorka may have extended her own understanding of these interpersonal concepts; it also allowed group leaders to check for any misunderstandings. Additionally, Menorka's insightful comments while problem-solving and planning conversations reflected a level of skills comprehension beyond that of other group members (see summary of session 3). Because Shelly missed the psychoeducation sessions and did not often contribute to planning conversations in group, it is unclear how much she internalized the IPT-AST skills.

Furthermore, Menorka successfully used the IPT-AST skills in five conversations outside of group, all of which had positive outcomes and impact on her mood (e.g., mother, dean, friend, cousin, and cousin follow-up). Additionally, Menorka actively participated in group role-plays to plan for these conversations and consistently reported at the end of each role-play that she felt either "relieved," "good," or "more understood." Thus, practicing the skills in session seemed to have an immediate positive impact on Menorka's mood.

Conversely, Shelly practiced being more outgoing with others outside of group (e.g., saying "Hi"), but she did not have extensive conversations where she employed the strategies to improve a specific relationship. Moreover, role-plays did not seem to have an immediate positive impact on her mood, as she indicated after one role-play that she still felt "horrible" and "guilty." The exception to this was during session 7, when Shelly opened up and practiced the skills in a role-play conversation about how she needed more support from her cousin. Subsequently, Shelly's reported mood rating improved for the first time between sessions.

QUALITATIVE EVALUATION: GROUP FACTORS
Group dynamics may have also contributed to the difference in intervention effects for Menorka and Shelly. It is possible that Menorka felt more comfortable in group given her history of friendship with Emma. Yet this friendship dyad

may have had the opposite effect on Shelly in terms of her comfort and sense of belonging within the group. Shelly's reserved demeanor was initially misinterpreted by Emma and Menorka as apathy and sometimes resulted in a stifled discussion. Once group leaders helped members to reframe their perception of Shelly as shy instead of disinterested, they became more outwardly supportive of her. As a result, Shelly was able to be more expressive and forthcoming; however, this shift in group dynamic did not occur until sessions 6 and 7. Furthermore, it seemed like Sasha's intermittent attendance detracted at times from the trust that was gradually evolving within the group.

Nevertheless, group leaders were sensitive and adept at directly addressing trust and comfort issues as they surfaced. It is important to note that this observed reluctance to trust may reflect the level of trust in the overall school environment. Group members all adamantly expressed that they could not trust the school guidance counselor with personal information, and at various points in group they discussed how teachers and staff were unapproachable when students had problems. Given Shelly's trying relationship history, she may have been more vulnerable to these trust issues than Menorka.

SYNTHESIS OF FINDINGS FROM RCT AND CASE STUDY APPROACHES

Case Study Findings That Support Young et al. (2010)

Many of these case study findings support and thus illustrate the results of Young et al. (2010) as well as the outcomes of previous studies and corollary analyses of IPT-AST (Young, Gallop, & Mufson, 2009; Young, Kranzler, Gallop, & Mufson, 2012; Young et al., 2012; Young, Mufson, & Davies, 2006). Menorka's consistent reduction in depressive symptoms and improvement in overall functioning, as noted on standardized measures and during her qualitative evaluations, is consistent with the significant decrease in depressive symptoms and improvement in overall functioning observed in the IPT-AST condition in Young et al. (2010) and in a prior study of IPT-AST (Young et al., 2006). Furthermore, Shelly's decline in functioning and onset of depression paralleled the trajectory of other nonresponders to IPT-AST who experienced depressive episodes 6 months or more after the intervention phase (Young et al., 2010). The reported improvements in Menorka's mother–child conflict and perceived interpersonal supports are also consistent with corollary findings of significant reductions in mother–child conflict (Young et al., 2009) and improved social functioning (Young et al., 2012) for adolescents in IPT-AST.

Similar to most participants in Young et al. (2010), Menorka and Shelly both reported subthreshold symptoms of anxiety at baseline, and the trajectory of their anxiety symptoms paralleled that of their depressive symptoms. Menorka's anxiety outcomes support findings from Young et al. (2012) in that her anxiety consistently decreased throughout the intervention and follow-up phase (see Fig. 4.6).

On the other hand, Shelly's anxiety symptoms decreased minimally during the active phase of the intervention and increased to the clinical level during the follow-up phase, paralleling the trajectory of her depressive symptoms. Notably, Menorka endorsed several GAD symptoms, whereas Shelly reported primarily social anxiety symptoms. Interventions that are interpersonally focused may be particularly beneficial for adolescents with comorbid symptoms of depression and GAD due to the common interpersonal nature of worries in the GAD population (Roemer, Molina, & Borkovec, 1997; Young et al., 2012). Conversely, Young et al. (2012) found minimal reductions in social anxiety during the intervention and follow-up phase, and other studies suggest that adolescents with comorbid social anxiety and depression have worse treatment outcomes (Young et al., 2012). The case study illustrated that Shelly's social anxiety interfered with her ability to participate in and benefit from the group and, as a result, may have also negatively impacted her depression outcome. Thus, the role of social anxiety as a predictor of change in depressive symptoms in IPT-AST should continue to be examined. Future studies should also investigate the efficacy of IPT-AST as a transdiagnostic preventative intervention for adolescents with comorbid subclinical symptoms of depression and GAD, as the communication and interpersonal problem-solving skills taught in IPT-AST may be particularly relevant for adolescents with this clinical profile (see Young, Mufson, & Benas, 2013, for a discussion of IPT as a transdiagnostic approach for youth depression and anxiety).

Case Study Findings That Extend Young et al. (2010)

Young et al. (2010) demonstrated that IPT-AST is an effective indicated prevention program for adolescents with subsyndromal depression. However, Shelly and Menorka possessed risk factors of depression beyond their subclinical depressive symptoms. It is important to consider the potential link between these additional risk factors and intervention outcomes. Both Shelly and Menorka reported a family history of depression and Menorka reported a previous episode of depressive disorder NOS. In addition, Menorka reported a history of environmental stressors (e.g., homelessness, exposure to domestic violence, single-parent household, and economic hardship), whereas Shelly reported a history of interpersonal dysfunction (e.g., bullying, peer rejection, lack of stable peer relationships, social withdrawal, and limited and inconsistent parental support).

Several research studies have linked environmental stressors, notably, low socioeconomic status (SES) and poverty, to family conflict and depression in children and adolescents (Mazza et al., 2010; McLeod & Nonnemaker, 2000; Wadsworth & Compas, 2002; Wolfe & Mash, 2006). The study sample in Young et al. (2010) and in previous IPT-AST and related efficacy research consisted primarily of adolescents from low-income households (e.g., Mufson et al., 2004; Young, Mufson, & Davies, 2006). The robust intervention effects from these studies along with Menorka's positive outcome indicate that youth who experience economic distress can benefit from IPT interventions. This may be particularly true for adolescents who are interpersonally oriented, such as Menorka. Her initiative in making interpersonal changes and concern for how her own behaviors affected her friends and family suggest a high degree of sociotropy, which has been identified as a possible moderator of IPT-AST (Horowitz et al., 2007). Menorka worked diligently to make positive changes in her interpersonal relationships, which, in turn, may have decreased her risk for depression despite these significant environmental stressors.

Research has also documented that social behavioral deficits, such as social helplessness and ineffective interpersonal problem solving, and low social support predict depression in youth (Abela & Hanken, 2008; Prinstein & Aikins, 2004). Although interpersonal interventions target interpersonal problems by teaching communication and problem-solving skills, patients identified as having "interpersonal deficits" are thought to fare worse in treatment. For instance, Sotsky et al. (1991) found that elevated social dysfunction was associated with poorer outcomes in IPT. However, a more recent efficacy study of IPT with depressed adults found that treatment outcomes were unrelated to patients' identified interpersonal problem areas, which included role disputes, role transitions, interpersonal deficits, and grief (Levenson et al., 2010).

The relative efficacy of IPT interventions with specific interpersonal goals or problem areas has not yet been examined in adolescents. Despite IPT-AST's explicit focus on bolstering interpersonal skills, it is possible that adolescents, like Shelly, who suffer from chronic interpersonal deficits and low social support, require a different intervention modality. It may be difficult for adolescents with a history of chronic interpersonal dysfunction not only to engage in the group but also to work on these pervasive interpersonal deficits, given the format and content of the sessions. Hypothetical scenarios used in the initial phase typically involve conflict with peers and/or family members, and middle-phase work is primarily focused on applying the skills to specific interpersonal events, such as approaching a teacher about a problem, sharing feelings with a friend, or negotiating responsibilities with caregivers. When there is an absence of a specific interpersonal event, and instead, the goal is to become closer with others (as with Shelly), it may be more challenging to incorporate this into group examples and to apply the skills. Future research should examine whether IPT-AST is more effective for youth who have specific interpersonal events to work on rather than a goal of increasing relationships and decreasing social withdrawal.

In addition to the potential significance of an adolescent's interpersonal history, qualitative analyses highlight the disparity in the extent to which Menorka and Shelly internalized and practiced the IPT-AST skills. Shelly was absent for sessions 2 and 3, which is when the skills are introduced and taught to group members. Group leaders reviewed the skills in session 4 with Shelly, but it is possible that missing these critical educational sessions affected her level of comprehension. In addition, Shelly practiced the skills much less than Menorka in and out of session. Menorka practiced using the IPT-AST skills to improve her communication in various interpersonal situations, including asserting herself with school staff, problem-solving peer conflict, strengthening her relationship with her cousin, and communicating more effectively with her mother about house rules. Perhaps because of the range of situations addressed and the frequency at which she practiced, Menorka's ability to implement the skills generalized to more situations, making her better equipped to cope with future interpersonal challenges.

On the other hand, Shelly's work during group was mostly focused on discussions about developing trustworthy friendships. Her subsequent depressive disorder NOS and major depressive disorder episodes were preceded by interpersonal events that involved parental conflict and a breakup, as opposed to issues around friendship, the context in which she discussed and minimally practiced skills during group. Both parent–child conflict and relationship breakups are associated with increased risk for depression (e.g., Allen et al., 2006; Davey, Yucel, & Allen, 2008; Eberhart & Hammen, 2006; Joyner & Udry, 2000; La Greca & Harrison, 2005; Sheeber, Davis, Leve, Hops, & Tildesley, 2007; Stice, Ragan, & Randall, 2004). It is possible that Shelly was ill equipped to handle these interpersonal events, given her lack of practice during the group, both generally and specifically related to interpersonal conflict. Additional case studies and group-level studies should further explore the generality of these findings with Shelly. This research would examine the interaction among the multiple components of skills practice to determine whether skills comprehension, frequency of practice, and/or the specific interpersonal scenarios practiced are associated with intervention outcomes. Relatedly, future studies should identify whether missing the educational component of the initial phase (sessions 2 and 3) affects skills comprehension and intervention outcomes.

Furthermore, the experiences of sexual-minority youth, like Shelly, in IPT-AST and other group interventions warrant further examination. During the follow-up phase, Shelly disclosed to her evaluator that she had been in romantic relationships with males as well as with a female. Shelly's sexual identity was never formally discussed during the intervention phase, but she reported that she spoke with family members about "boys" and briefly discussed an interpersonal issue regarding a male peer during group. Not enough information is known about the chronology of Shelly's stages of sexual identity development and the study timeline to understand the relationship between these respective experiences. However, if Shelly was questioning her sexual orientation during the intervention phase, this may have contributed to her visible discomfort confiding in a group focused primarily on heterosexual romantic relationships and composed of heterosexual females. Even in the first group when members were charged with the task of educating group leaders about common problems teens face, the topic of sexual orientation was not elicited. Adolescents who identify as sexual minorities may experience minority stress and are thus at greater risk for psychological distress, depression, negative self-concept, and peer victimization (Cochran et al., 2003; Meyer, 2013). The components of minority stress can certainly affect an adolescent's comfort level, self-perception, and interactions with others during groups like IPT-AST, particularly for individuals with low levels of peer trust and support like Shelly. Thus, the relationship between an adolescent's sexual orientation, qualitative experience in IPT-AST, and intervention outcomes should continue to be explored.

The case study findings also convey the relevance of cognitive mechanisms in intervention outcomes. Stable cognitive vulnerability factors, including a depressogenic inferential style, typically emerge by adolescence and have been indicated in the development of depression across the life span (Abela & Hanken, 2008; Cohen, Young, & Abela, 2012). Moreover, Prinstein and Aikins (2004) found that for adolescents with high levels of depressogenic attributions, peer rejection predicted depressive symptoms. Although not formally assessed during the intervention, Shelly's thoughts of worthlessness and negative expectations of interpersonal events, in particular related to peer rejection and victimization, reflect a depressogenic inferential style. Furthermore, Shelly's negative attitude toward change throughout the intervention conveyed a hopeless attitude that is consistent with a negative cognitive style.

It is possible that these pervasive depressogenic cognitions developed in part from Shelly's invalidating interpersonal history, and it is critical to acknowledge the potential influence of both of these factors on her ability to engage with other group members, participate in activities, and conduct work at home. For example, Shelly may have been reluctant to try out the communication skills outside of group because of her negative expectation that ultimately people will not like her. Similarly, she may have worried about confiding in group members if her assumption was that people will judge her and will not understand her challenges. On the other hand, Menorka's negative self-concept seemed to be limited to concerns about her body image. Even when Menorka acknowledged that it was hurtful for her cousin to call her "fat," she interpreted his behavior as an attempt to get attention from her rather than internalizing the insults. Menorka undoubtedly expressed worry about her relationships and acknowledged her own anxieties about using the skills, but this worry seemed to drive her efforts to modify her communication in her relationships. Further investigation of the relationship between cognitive and interpersonal vulnerabilities and intervention outcomes will help to distinguish the specific type of individual risk profiles that are well suited for IPT-AST and those that may benefit from an intervention that utilizes different processes.

Implications for Future Research and Implementation

The aforementioned mixed-methods analysis highlights the importance of repeated practice of IPT-AST skills in various, relevant interpersonal scenarios while receiving feedback from trusted peers. These findings raise the question of optimal dosage of the intervention with respect to three specific areas: (1) developing group trust, (2) providing sufficient opportunities for skills practice, and (3) modifying the intervention for adolescents with specific clinical profiles.

In schools, in particular, establishing and maintaining a safe and comfortable group setting is difficult due to several obstacles, including, peer interactions outside of group, the prevalence of gossip, potential school staff involvement, and the stigma commonly associated with receiving mental health services. One barrier to Shelly's ability to use the group to strengthen her communication skills was her guardedness and mistrust of other group members. However, toward the end of group, Shelly was the focus of some very powerful discussions during which she opened up to group members about her difficulties making friends and received pertinent feedback about how she comes across to others. Because this discussion did not occur until session 6, she was unable to incorporate the feedback into her skills practice during the middle phase. Likewise, several group members were reluctant to share because of expressed concerns about the climate of trust and support within the group and even within the school. Additional IPT-AST group sessions may have nurtured greater intimacy and trust, and subsequently, increased engagement from Shelly and other group members during middle-phase sessions. In their meta-analysis of school-based depression prevention programs, Calear and Christensen (2010) found that groups consisting of 8–12 sessions were an optimal duration for students to process and apply new skills. Extending the number of group meetings in the IPT-AST intervention by a few sessions may also permit interpersonal skill building with a wider range of interpersonal situations. For example, most of the hypothetical role-plays outlined in the manual as well as the student-generated discussions about interpersonal events are focused on specific problems that typically involve conflict (perhaps because these are easier to identify and share). Additional sessions may allow for more opportunities to discuss application of the skills to other interpersonal goals, such as making friends and increasing interpersonal supports. This added opportunity for practice could increase the likelihood of generalization and, thus, the potential preventative effect of the intervention.

Moreover, supplementing the IPT-AST groups with individual sessions during or after the intervention might also allow for more personalized work on interpersonal goals, especially for more sensitive topics (e.g., sexual orientation, divorce, or abuse). We are currently investigating the efficacy of a modified version of IPT-AST that includes an individual mid-group session and four monthly individual booster sessions following the group intervention. Individual mid-group and booster sessions allow group leaders the opportunity to re-evaluate interpersonal goals, continuously assess skills comprehension, and address additional relevant interpersonal issues. However, it is important to account for logistical factors that impact implementation. Extending the intervention with additional group and/or individual sessions increases cost, school space needs, and time commitment from staff and students. Thus, the identified potential benefits of a longer intervention warrant further empirical investigation and should involve evaluation of these other implementation factors.

Finally, it is important to consider the variables previously discussed and how these may be used to inform intervention suitability and options for levels of care. Shelly's social anxiety, depressogenic inferential style, chronic interpersonal deficits, and resistance to change were all identified as influential factors in her negative intervention outcome. Her case study illustrates how these variables worked together to affect Shelly's negative experience in the IPT-AST group and in the eventual development of her depression. Statistical investigation of these potential moderators in group-level studies can help quantitatively identify adolescents who may be better suited for a different modality or intervention as well as those, like Menorka, who will greatly benefit from IPT-AST. Furthermore, as an indicated prevention intervention, IPT-AST could be considered within an individualized stepped-care approach to depression prevention in adolescents. Continuous assessment of these variables can help differentiate adolescents who are likely to acquire the tools to prevent depression after the IPT-AST intervention and those who may require a higher level of care, such as subsequent individual booster sessions or adjunct individual therapy.

Conclusion

Menorka's case study underscores how, despite her economic stressors and history of depression, her positive attitude toward change, eagerness to utilize the skills, sociotropy, and history of positive interpersonal relationships facilitated her engagement with the intervention and subsequent mastery of the skills. As a result, the positive intervention effect was apparent not just in the reduction of her depressive and anxiety symptoms but also in the notable improvements in her interpersonal relationships, self-concept, and overall functioning. Conversely, Shelly's absences, interpersonal deficits, social anxiety, and negative cognitive style made it difficult for her to fully engage and practice skills with the group to increase her relationships. Shelly's challenges with trust were also apparent in the group as a whole and even extended to group members' feelings of support and trust within the school. Hopefully, the individual, intervention, and setting characteristics identified and discussed in these systematic case studies will inform future research and implementation so that we can better understand who benefits from IPT-AST and how the intervention can be tailored to generate more long-term effects in preventing adolescent depression.

REFERENCES

Abela, J. R. Z., & Hankin, B. L. (2008). *Handbook of depression in children and adolescents*. New York, NY: The Guilford Press.

Allen, J. P., Insabella, G., Porter, M. R., Smith, F. D., Land, D., & Phillips, N. (2006). A social-interactional model of the development of depressive symptoms in adolescence. *Journal of Consulting and Clinical Psychology, 74*, 55–65.

Barrett, P. M., Farrell, L. J., Ollendick, T. H., & Dadds, M. (2006). Long-term outcomes of an Australian universal prevention trial of anxiety and depression symptoms in children and youth: An evaluation of the FRIENDS Program. *Journal of Clinical Child and Adolescent Psychology, 35*, 403–411.

Birmaher, B., Brent, D. A., Chiappetta, L., Bridge, J., Monga, S., & Baugher, M. (1999). Psychometric properties of the Screen for Child Anxiety Related Emotional Disorders (SCARED): A replication study. *Journal of the American Academy of Child and Adolescent Psychiatry, 38*, 1230–1236.

Brent, D. A., Holder, D., Kolko, D., Birmaher, B., Baugher, M., Roth, C., Iyengar, S., & Johnson, B. A. (1997). A clinical psychotherapy trial for adolescent depression comparing cognitive, family and supportive therapy. *Archives of General Psychiatry, 54*, 877–885.

Calear, A. L., & Christensen, H. (2010). Systematic review of school-based prevention and early intervention programs for depression. *Journal of Adolescence, 33*, 429–438.

Clarke, G., Rohde, P., Lewinsohn, P., Hops, H., & Seeley, M. S. (1999). Cognitive-behavioral treatment of adolescent depression: Efficacy of acute group treatment and booster sessions. *Journal of the American Academy of Child and Adolescent Psychiatry, 38*, 272–279.

Clarke, G. N., Debar, L., Lynch, F., Powell, J., Gale., J., O'Connor, E., . . . Hertert, S. (2005). A randomized effectiveness trial of brief cognitive–behavioral therapy for depressed adolescents receiving antidepressant medication. *Journal of the American Academy of Child and Adolescent Psychiatry, 44*, 888–898.

Cochran, S. D., Sullivan, J. G., & Mays, V. M. (2003). Prevalence of mental disorders, psychological distress, and mental services use among lesbian, gay, and bisexual adults in the United States. *Journal of Consulting and Clinical Psychology, 71*, 53–61.

Cohen, J. R., Young, J. F., & Abela, J. R. Z. (2012). Cognitive vulnerability to depression in children: An idiographic, longitudinal examination of inferential styles. *Cognitive Therapy Research, 36*, 643–654.

Connor-Smith, J. K., Compas, B. E., Wadsworth, M. E., Thomsen, A. H., & Saltzman, H. (2000). Responses to stress in adolescence: Measurement of coping and involuntary stress responses. *Journal of Consulting and Clinical Psychology, 68*, 976–992.

Coyne, J. C. (1976). Depression and the response of others. *Journal of Abnormal Psychology, 85*, 186–193.

Davey, C. G., Yucel, M., & Allen, N. B. (2008). The emergence of depression in adolescence: Development of the prefrontal cortex and the representation of reward. *Neuroscience and Behavioral Reviews, 32*, 1–19.

Eberhart, N. K., & Hammen, C. L. (2006). Interpersonal predictors of onset of depression during the transition to adulthood. *Personal Relationships, 13*, 195–206.

Emslie, G. J., Rush, A. J., Weinburg, W. A., Kowatch, R. A., Hughes, C. W., Carmody, T., & Rintelmann, J. (1997). A double-blind randomized, placebo-controlled trial of fluoxetine in children and adolescents with depression. *Archives of General Psychiatry, 54*, 1031–1037.

Elkin, I., Shea, M. T., Watkins, J. T., Imber, S. D., & Sotsky, S. M., Collins, J. F., . . . Docherty, J. P. (1989). National Institute of Mental Health Treatment of Depression Collaborative Research Program: General effectiveness of treatments. *Archives of General Psychiatry, 46*, 971–983.

Elmquist, J. M., Melton, T. K., Croarkin, P., & McClintock, S. M. (2010). A systematic overview of measurement-based care in the treatment of childhood and adolescent depression. *Journal of Psychiatric Practice, 16*(4), 217–234.

Fergusson, D. M., Horwood, L. J., Ridder, E. M., & Beautrais, A. L. (2005). Subthreshold depression in adolescence and mental health outcomes in adulthood. *Archives of General Psychiatry, 62*, 66–72.

Fergusson, D. M., & Woodward, L. J. (2002) Mental health, educational and social role outcomes of adolescents with depression. *Archives of General Psychiatry, 59*, 225–231.

Frank, E., Kupfer, D.J., Buysse, D. J., Swartz, H. A., Pilkonis, P. A., Houck, P. R., Rucci, P., Novick, D. M., Grochocinski, V. J., & Stapf, D. M. (2007). Randomized trial of weekly, twice-monthly, and monthly interpersonal psychotherapy as maintenance treatment for women with recurrent depression. *American Journal of Psychiatry, 164*, 761–767.

Frank, E., Kupfer, D. J., Wagner, E. F., MacEachran, A. B., & Comes, C. (1991). Efficacy of interpersonal psychotherapy as a maintenance treatment of recurrent depression: Contributing factors. *Archives of General Psychiatry, 48*, 1053–1059.

Garrison, C. Z., Jackson, K. B., Marsteller, F., McKeown, R., & Addy, C. (1990). A longitudinal study of depressive symptomatology in young adolescents. *Journal of the American Academy of Child & Adolescent Psychiatry, 29*(4), 581–585.

Garrison, C. Z., Addy, C. L., Jackson, K. L., McKeown, R. E., & Waller, J. L. (1991). The CES-D as a screen for depression and other psychiatric disorders in adolescents. *Journal of the American Academy of Child and Adolescent Psychiatry, 30*, 636–641.

Gillham J. E., Reivich K. J., Freres D. R., Chaplin, T. M., Shatte, A. J., Samuels, B., ...Seligman, M. E. (2006). School-based prevention of depression and anxiety symptoms in early adolescence: A pilot of a parent intervention component. *School Psychology Quarterly, 21*, 323–348.

Glassgold, J. M. (2009). The case of Felix: An example of gay-affirmative, cognitive-behavioral therapy. *Pragmatic Case Studies in Psychotherapy, 5*(4), 1–21. Available at: http://pcsp.libraries.rutgers.edu/. doi: http://dx.doi.org/10.14713/pcsp.v5i4.995

Gordon, R. S. (1983). An operational classification of disease prevention. *Public Health Reports, 98*, 107–109.

Gotlib, I. H., Lewinsohn, P. M., & Seeley, J. R. (1995). Symptoms versus a diagnosis of depression: Differences in psychosocial functioning. *Journal of Consulting and Clinical Psychology, 63*, 90–100.

Hammen C. (1992). Cognition, life stress, and interpersonal approaches to a developmental psychopathology model of depression. *Development and Psychopathology, 4*, 189–206.

Hill, P. C., & Pargament, K. I. (2003). Advances in the conceptualization and measurement of religion and spirituality. *American Psychologist, 58*, 64–74.

Hoagwood, K., & Olin, S. S. (2002). The NIMH blueprint for change report: Research priorities in child and adolescent mental health. *Journal of the American Academy of Child and Adolescent Psychiatry, 41*, 760–767.

Hollon, S. D., Thase, M. E., & Markowitz, J. C. (2002). Treatment and prevention of depression. *Psychological Science in the Public Interest, 3*(2), 39–77.

Horowitz, J. L., & Garber, J. (2006). The prevention of depressive symptoms in children and adolescents. A meta-analytic review. *Journal of Consulting and Clinical Psychology, 74*(3), 401–415.

Horowitz, J. L., Garber, J., Ciesla, J. A., Young, J. F., & Mufson, L. (2007). Prevention of depressive symptoms in adolescents: A randomized trial of cognitive-behavioral and interpersonal prevention programs. *Journal of Consulting and Clinical Psychology, 75*(5), 693–706.

Horwath, E., Johnson, J., Klerman, G. L., & Weissman, M. M. (1992). Depressive symptoms as relative and attributable risk factors for first-onset major depression. *Archives of General Psychiatry, 49*, 817–823.

Institute of Medicine (2009). *Preventing mental, emotional, and behavioral disorders among young people: Progress and possibilities.* Washington, DC: The National Academies Press.

Joiner, T. E.Jr., & Coyne, J. C. (Eds., 1999). *The interactional nature of depression.* Washington, DC: American Psychological Association.

Joyner, K., & Udry, J. R. (2000). You don't bring me anything but down: Adolescent romance and depression. *Journal of Health and Social Behavior, 41,* 369–391.

Judd, L. L., Paulus, M. P., Wells, K. B., & Rapaport, M. H. (1996). Socioeconomic burden of subsyndromal depressive symptoms and major depression in a sample of the general population. *American Journal of Psychiatry, 153,* 1411–1417.

Kaufman, J., Birmaher, B., Brent, D., & Rao, U. (1997). Schedule for affective disorders and schizophrenia for school-age children—Present and lifetime version (K-SADS-PL): Initial reliability and validity data. *Journal of the American Academy of Child and Adolescent Psychiatry, 36,* 980–988.

Keller, M. B., Lavori, P. W., Friedman, B., Nielson, E., Endicott, J., McDonald-Scott, P., & Andreasen, N. C. (1987). The longitudinal interval follow-up evaluation: A comprehensive method for assessing outcome in prospective longitudinal studies. *Archives of General Psychiatry, 44,* 540–548.

Kennard, B., Silva, S., Vitiello, B., Curry, J., Kratochvil, C., Simons, A., ...March, J. (2006). Remission and residual symptoms after short-term treatment in the treatment of adolescents with depression study (TADS). *Journal of the American Academy of Child and Adolescent Psychiatry, 45,* 1404–1411.

Kessler, R. C., & Walters, E. E. (1998). Epidemiology of DSM-III-R major depression and minor depression among adolescents and young adults in the National Comorbidity Survey. *Depression and Anxiety, 7,* 3–14.

Klomek, A. B., Marrocco, F., Kleinman, M., Schonfeld, I. S., & Gould, M. S. (2007). Bullying, depression, and suicidality in adolescents. *Journal of the American Academy of Child and Adolescent Psychiatry, 46,* 40–49.

La Greca, A. M., & Harrison, H. M. (2005). Adolescent peer relations, friendships, and romantic relationships: Do they predict social anxiety and depression? *Journal of Clinical Child and Adolescent Psychology, 34,* 49–61.

Levenson, J. C., Frank, E., Cheng, Y., Rucci, P., Janney, C. A., Houck, P., & Forgione, R. N., Swartz, H. A., Cyranowski, J. M., & Fagiolini, A. (2010). Comparative outcomes among the problem areas of interpersonal psychotherapy for depression. *Depression and Anxiety, 27,* 434–440.

Lewinsohn, P. M., Clarke, G. N., Hops, H., & Andrews, J. A. (1990). Cognitive-behavioral treatment for depressed adolescents. *Behavior Therapy, 21,* 385–401.

Lewinsohn, P. M., & Clarke, G. N. (1999). Psychosocial treatments for adolescent depression. *Clinical Psychology Review, 19,* 329–342.

Lewinsohn, P. M., Roberts, R. E., Seeley, J. R., Rohde, P, Gotlib, I. H., & Hops, H. (1994). Adolescent psychopathology: II. Psychosocial risk factors for depression. *Journal of Abnormal Psychology, 103,* 302–315.

Lewinsohn, P. M., Rohde, P., Klein, D., & Seely, J. R. (1999). Natural course of adolescent major depressive disorder: 1. Continuity into young adulthood. *Journal of the American Academy of Child and Adolescent Psychiatry, 38,* 56–63.

Lewinsohn, P. M., Solomon, A., Seeley, J. R., & Zeiss, A. (2000). Clinical implications of "subthreshold" depressive symptoms. *Journal of Abnormal Psychology, 109,* 345–351.

Lock, S., & Barrett, P. M. (2003). A longitudinal study of developmental differences in universal preventive intervention for child anxiety. *Behaviour Change, 20*(4), 183–199.

Lowry-Webster, H., Barrett, P. M., & Dadds, M. R. (2001). A universal prevention trial of anxiety and depressive symptomatology in childhood: Preliminary data from an Australian study. *Behaviour Change, 18*, 36–50.

Lowry-Webster, H., Barrett, P., & Lock, S. (2003). A universal prevention trial of anxiety symptomatology during childhood: Results at one year follow-up. *Behaviour Change, 20*(1), 25–43.

Luty, S. E., Carter, J. D., McKenzie, J. M., Rae, A. M., Frampton, C. M. A., Mulder, R. T., & Joyce, P. R. (2007). Randomised controlled trial of interpersonal psychotherapy and cognitive-behavioural therapy for depression. *The British Journal of Psychiatry, 190*, 496–502.

Mazza, J., Fleming, C. B., Abbott, R. D., Haggerty, K. P., & Catalano, R. F. (2010). Identifying trajectories of adolescents' depressive phenomena: An examination of early risk factors. *Journal of Youth and Adolescence, 39*, 579–593.

McLeod, J. D., & Nonnemaker, J. M. (2000). Poverty and child emotional and behavioral problems: Racial/ethnic differences in processes and effects. *Journal of Health and Social Behavior, 41*, 137–161.

Meyer, I. H. (2013). Prejudice, social stress, and mental health in lesbian, gay, and bisexual populations: Conceptual issues and research evidence. *Psychology of Sexual Orientation and Gender Diversity, 1*(S), 3–26.

Mrazek, P. J., & Haggerty, R. J., eds (1994). *Reducing risks for mental disorders: Frontiers for preventive intervention research.* Washington, DC: National Academy Press.

Myers, K., & Winters, N. C. (2002). Ten-year review of rating scales. II: Scales for internalizing disorders. *Journal of the American Academy of Child and Adolescent Psychiatry, 41*(6), 634–658.

Mufson, L., Dorta, K. P., Moreau, D., & Weissman, M. M. (2004). *Interpersonal psychotherapy for depressed adolescents* (2nd ed,). New York, NY: Guilford Press.

Mufson, L., Dorta, K. P., Wickermaratne, P., Nomura, Y., Olfson, M., & Weissman, M. M. (2004). A randomized effectiveness trial of interpersonal psychotherapy for depressed adolescents. *Archives of General Psychiatry, 63*, 577–584.

Mufson, L., Gallagher, T., Dorta, K. P., & Young, J. F. (2004). Interpersonal psychotherapy for adolescent depression: Adaptation for group therapy. *American Journal of Psychotherapy, 58*, 220–237.

Mufson, L., Weissman, M. M., Moreau, D., & Garfinkel, R. (1999). Efficacy of interpersonal psychotherapy for depressed adolescents. *Archives of General Psychiatry, 56*, 573–579.

New Freedom Commission on Mental Health (2003). *Achieving the promise: Transforming mental health care in America.* Final report. Rockville, MD: Department of Health and Human Services.

Pine, D. S., Cohen, E., Cohen P., & Brook, J. (1999). Adolescent depressive symptoms as predictors of adult depression: Moodiness or mood disorder? *American Journal of Psychiatry, 156*, 133–135.

Poznanski, E. O., & Mokros, H. B. (1996). *Children's Depression Rating Scale, Revised (CDRS-R).* Los Angeles, CA: Western Psychological Services.

Prinstein, M. J., & Aikins, J. W. (2004). Cognitive moderators of the longitudinal association between peer rejection and adolescent depressive symptoms. *Journal of Abnormal Child Psychology, 32*(2), 147–158.

Puig-Antich, J., Kaufman, J., Ryan, N. D., Willamson, D. E., Dahl, R. E., Lukens, E., . . . Nelson, B. (1993). The psychosocial functioning and family environment of depressed adolescents. *Journal of the American Academy of Child and Adolescent Psychiatry, 32,* 244–253.

Radloff, L. S. (1977). The CES-D scale: A self-report depression scale for research in the general population. *Applied Psychology Measures, 1,* 385–401.

Roberts, C., Kane, R., Thomson, H., Bishop, B., & Hart, B. (2003). The prevention of depressive symptoms in rural school children: A randomized controlled trial. *Journal of Consulting and Clinical Psychology, 71,* 622–628.

Roemer, L., Molina, S., & Borkovec, T. D. (1997). An investigation of worry content among generally anxious individuals. *The Journal of Nervous and Mental Disease, 185,* 314–319.

Rudolph, K. D., Flynn, M., & Abaied, J. L. (2008). A developmental perspective on interpersonal theories of youth depression. In J. R. Z. Abela & B. L. Hankin, (Eds.), *Handbook of depression in children and adolescents* (pp. 79–102). New York, NY: Guilford Press.

Rudolph, K. D., Hammen, C., & Burge, D. (1994). Interpersonal functioning and depressive symptoms in childhood: Addressing the issues of specificity and comorbidity. *Journal of Abnormal Child Psychology, 22,* 355–371.

Shaffer, D., Gould, M. S., Bird, H., & Fisher, P. (1983). A Children's Global Assessment Scale (CGAS). *Archives of General Psychiatry, 40,* 1228–1231.

Sheeber, L. B., Davis, B. Leve, C., Hops, H., & Tildesley, E. (2007). Adolescents' relationships with their mothers and fathers: Associations with depressive disorder and subdiagnostic symptomatology. *Journal of Abnormal Psychology, 116,* 144–154.

Sloane, R. B., Staples, F. R., & Schneider, L. S. (1985). Interpersonal therapy versus nortriptyline for depression in the elderly. In G. D. Burrow, T. R. Normal, & L. Dennerstein (Eds.), *Clinical and pharmacological studies in psychiatric disorders* (pp. 344–346). London, UK: Libbey.

Sotsky, S. M., Glass, D. R., Shea, M. T., Pilkonis, P. A., Collins, J. F., Elkin, I., . . . & Oliveri, M. E. (1991). Patient predictors of response to psychotherapy and pharmacotherapy: Findings in the NIMH Treatment of Depression Collaborative Research Program. *American Journal of Psychiatry, 148*(8), 997–1008.

Stice, E., Shaw, H., Bohon, C., Marti, C. N., & Rohde, P. (2009). A meta-analytic review of depression prevention programs for children and adolescents: Factors that predict magnitude of intervention effects. *Journal of Consulting and Clinical Psychology, 77*(3), 486–503.

Stice, E., Ragan, J., & Randall, P. (2004). Prospective relations between social support and depression: Differential direction of effects for parent and peer support? *Journal of Abnormal Psychology, 113,* 255–259.

Sweeting, H., Young, R., West, P., & Der, G. (2006). Peer victimization and depression in early-mid adolescence: A longitudinal study. *British Journal of Educational Psychology, 76,* 577–594.

US Public Health Service (2000). *Report of the Surgeon General's Conference on Children's Mental Health: A natural action agenda.* Washington, DC: U.S. Public Health Service.

Wadsworth, M. E., & Compas, B. E. (2002). Coping with family conflict and economic strain: The adolescent perspective. *Journal of Research on Adolescence, 12*(2), 243–274.

Weissman, M. M., & Bothwell, S. (1976). Assessment of social adjustment by patient self-report. *Archives of General Psychiatry, 33,* 1111–1115.

Weissman, M. M., Markowitz, J. C., & Klerman, G. L. (2000). *Comprehensive guide to interpersonal psychotherapy.* New York, NY: Basic Books.

Weissman, M. M., Prusoff, B. A., Di Mascio, A., Neu, C., Goklaney, M., & Klerman, G. L. (1979). The efficacy of drugs and psychotherapy in the treatment of acute depressive episodes. *American Journal of Psychiatry, 136,* 555–558.

Weist, M. D., & Paternite, C. E. (2006). Building an interconnected policy-training-practice-research agenda to advance school mental health. *Education and Treatment of Children, 29,* 173–196.

Weisz, J. R., McCarty, C. A., & Valeri, S. M. (2006). Effects of psycho-therapy for depression in children and adolescents: A meta-analysis. *Psychological Bulletin, 132,* 132–149.

Wolfe, D. A., & Mash, E. J. (2006). *Behavioral and emotional disorders in adolescents: Nature, assessment, and treatment.* New York, NY: The Guilford Press.

Young, J. F., Gallop, R., & Mufson, L. (2009). Mother-child conflict and its moderating effects on depression outcomes in a preventive intervention for adolescent depression. *Journal of Clinical Child and Adolescent Psychology, 38,* 696–704.

Young, J. F., Kranzler, A., Gallop, R., & Mufson, L. (2012). Interpersonal Psychotherapy-Adolescent Skills Training: Effects on school and social functioning. *School Mental Health, 4*(4), 254–264.

Young, J. F., Makover, H. B., Cohen, J. R., Mufson, L., Gallop, R., & Benas, J. S. (2012). Interpersonal Psychotherapy-Adolescent Skills Training: Anxiety outcomes and impact of comorbidity. *Journal of Clinical Child and Adolescent Psychology, 41*(5), 640–653.

Young, J. F., & Mufson, L. (2003). *Manual for Interpersonal Psychotherapy-Adolescent Skills Training (IPT-AST).* Unpublished manual.

Young, J. F., Mufson, L., & Benas, J. S. (2013). Interpersonal psychotherapy as a transdiagnostic approach. In J. Ehrenreich-May & B. Chu (Eds.), *Transdiagnostic mechanisms and treatment for youth psychopathology* (pp. 183–202). New York, NY: Guilford.

Young, J. F., Mufson, L., & Davies, M. (2006). Efficacy of interpersonal psychotherapy-adolescent skills training: An indicated preventative intervention for depression. *Journal of Child Psychology and Psychiatry, 47*(12), 1254–1262.

Young, J. F., Mufson, L., & Gallop, R. (2010). Preventing depression: A randomized trial of interpersonal psychotherapy-adolescent skills training. *Depression and Anxiety, 27,* 426–433.

Young, J. F., Mufson, L., & Schueler, C. M. (2016). *Preventing adolescent depression: Interpersonal psychotherapy – adolescent skills training.* New York, NY: Oxford University Press.

COMMENTARY
Identifying Moderators of Change From Both RCTs and Case Studies

Laura J. Dietz

As a clinical researcher and practitioner with a specialty interest in preadolescent and adolescent depression and structured treatments for it, I was particularly interested in Kerner and Young's excellent and engaging chapter (this volume) that focuses on and adds importantly to the research knowledge base on this topic. As these authors point out, depression, like other mental disorders, often begins early in life and has a recurrent course. Early-onset depression (i.e., depression occurring before the age of 18) has a more debilitating and severe course of disorder as compared to that of adult-onset depression marked by greater functional impairment, increased likelihood of depression recurrence, and higher risk of suicidality (Geller et al., 2001; Kovacs et al., 1984; Puig-Antich et al., 1985; Zisook et al., 2007). Moreover, depression remains a leading cause of disability worldwide (Murray & Lopez, 1996). All this highlights the urgency of efforts for the early detection and prevention of youth depression and efforts to reduce risk for recurrent courses of disorder.

Universal prevention efforts to decrease depression onset in youth have produced inconsistent findings. The Penn Resiliency Program (PRP; Positive Psychology Center, University of Pennsylvania), a cognitive-behavioral depression prevention program, is among prevention intervention programs that have been extensively tested and have the best evidence base for reviewing the program's effectiveness. Although PRP has demonstrated lower ratings of depressive symptoms relative to a no-treatment control across a 3-year period, it was not more effective than an attention-control intervention that provided psychoeducation about improving communication, family conflict, friendships, self-esteem, and body image in decreasing mean levels of depressive symptoms or preventing the onset of elevated depressive symptoms over the follow-up period (Gillham et al., 2007). Cognitive-behavioral models of intervention like PRP focus primarily on *intrapersonal* skills, like thought/ feeling identification, cognitive restructuring, problem solving, behavioral activation, and relaxation. The limited success of these programs suggests that it would be worthwhile to try out programs that focus on the interpersonal context of depression, and on how disruptions in relationships may affect depression onset and symptom maintenance, that is, on programs that emphasize improving *interpersonal* skills and *interpersonal* relationships. This is the type of therapeutic program that Kerner and Young describe in their chapter.

THE RCT STUDY

The RCT study Kerner and Young present focuses on the efficacy of Interpersonal Psychotherapy—Adolescent Skills Training (IPT-AST), a school-based prevention intervention for adolescents with elevated depressive symptoms.

In its structure and themes, IPT-AST actually delivers aspects of both individual and group intervention. Two individual, pre-group sessions with each adolescent allows the group leader to provide psychoeducation about depression and a brief orientation to the group intervention. Most important, these individual pre-group sessions help establish the conceptualization of the adolescent's interpersonal context and identified problem area through the Closeness Circle and the Interpersonal Inventory, as described in the Kerner and Young chapter.

As also described by Kerner and Young, the eight group sessions follow three phases of treatment. The initial phase (sessions 1–3) focuses on establishing rapport and guidelines for group members, providing psychoeducation about depression, and introducing communication analysis as a method of demonstrating how interactions with family members and peers affect adolescents' mood.

In the middle phase (sessions 4–6) adolescents discuss with the group examples of current difficulties they experience in interpersonal relationships and engage in problem solving and role-play with group members utilizing different communication skills in response to stressful interpersonal situations. Group leaders encourage adolescents to practice interpersonal skills outside of group, in "real-world" contexts with family members or peers.

IPT-AST's termination phase (sessions 7–8) balances celebrating the group members' progress and completion of the program with individualizing a plan for each member should he or she experience depression in the future. This phase of treatment also allows for processing the termination of relationships between group members, while encouraging the members to use the supportive qualities of the group as examples of interpersonal relationships that sustain normal mood.

Throughout the phases, and as illustrated in Kerner and Young's qualitative case studies of Shelly and Menorka, IPT-AST also incorporates aspects of group therapy process whereby group members provide support and validation, as well as challenges to and feedback regarding the maladaptive interpersonal patterns exhibited by the members that may complicate relationships with others.

Taken together, the IPT-AST sessions are designed to improve upon models of depression prevention that rely solely on group psychoeducation and the didactic presentation of skills. In keeping with a focus on interpersonal contexts, IPT-AST uses the interpersonal context of the group to illustrate the affective experience of using interpersonal skills and the reciprocal process of experiencing more positive responses from others.

In their chapter, Kerner and Young review the evidence base for IPT-AST and highlight the open questions regarding the intervention's long-term efficacy, treatment moderators, and the potential for personalization of treatment. The RCT they describe (based on Young, Mufson, & Gallop, 2010) shows that IPT-AST demonstrates significant decreases in at-risk adolescents' depressive symptoms, social impairment, and parent–child conflict across the acute intervention period (pre- to posttreatment) as compared to the control condition of usual school counseling.

However, the protective effects of this intervention were not sustained beyond a 6-month follow-up period, and in their chapter Kerner and Young describe additional planned research to investigate methods, including booster sessions for IPT-AST participants, to increase the long-term efficacy of this intervention. On the other hand, it is very important to underscore the importance of IPT-AST to maintain reductions in depressive symptoms and to prevent onset of depressive disorders in at-risk adolescents in the 6 months following a brief psychosocial intervention. Given the high degree of self-reported depressive symptoms in their research participants, IPT-AST can be viewed as an effective intervention for reducing the onset of emergent depression in youths.

MODERATOR VARIABLES

On average, Kerner and Young's group results show that for up to 6 months—but not for more than 6 months—the adolescents in their IPT-AST groups showed significantly more reductions in their self-reported depressive symptoms, social impairment, and parent–child conflict than a matched usual school counseling control group. However, a look at the results by individual participants, as exemplified by the case studies, reveals that some individuals, as shown in the case study of Menorka, did extremely well and sustained their gains through the 18-month follow-up, while others, as shown in the case study of Shelly, made little progress over the course of the group. What moderator variables account for these individual differences?

There are two approaches to answer this question. One is to search for the moderator variables through group research, assessing which particular variables correlate with individual differences in response to the IPT-AST program. Using this approach, Kerner and Young report secondary analyses of past group research on the efficacy of IPT-AST that suggest some aspects of parent–child conflict and affiliative behavior that act as moderators of treatment outcomes: at-risk adolescents with high pretreatment indices of parent–child conflict and sociotropy (high investment in interpersonal relationships) have better treatment outcomes in IPT-AST than do adolescents experiencing less interpersonal conflict and/or who ascribe less importance to interpersonal relationships.

These moderator findings inform the ability to personalize IPT-AST as a preventive treatment option by considering both adolescents' characteristics and the putative treatment mechanisms of IPT-AST. To begin with, it would stand to reason that adolescents experiencing mood disturbance and distress related to interpersonal conflict and/or who value relationships with family members and peers would benefit from a psychosocial intervention that focuses on both the interpersonal context of depression *and* strategies for improving interpersonal communication and problem solving. Next, the ability to maximize the effectiveness of prevention interventions for at-risk adolescents based on pretreatment characteristics may substantially decrease the likelihood of developing a depressive disorder and improve estimates of effect sizes for IPT-AST.

Lastly, findings that IPT-AST were more effective in adolescents reporting high parent–child conflict and/or affiliative behavior may also provide circumstantial support for the mechanisms of action of this treatment. IPT hypothesizes that onset of depressive symptoms is correlated with increased interpersonal difficulties and posits that reductions in depressive symptoms result from improving interpersonal relationships by reducing conflict, improving communication, and increasing social support (Lipsitz & Markowitz, 2013). In adolescents with high levels of parent–child conflict, IPT-AST may reduce their interpersonal conflict, which may in turn decrease depressive symptoms. Likewise, in adolescents with high affiliative behavior, IPT-AST may increase their interpersonal effectiveness in relationships, which in turn may decrease depressive symptoms. Although future studies further examining mediators of IPT-AST must be conducted, the RCT findings Kerner and Young report support the idea that decreases in parent–child conflict and increases in affiliative behaviors act as mechanisms for reducing depression.

THE CASE STUDIES

A second approach to explain individual differences in response to the IPT-AST groups is to look for moderator variables within individual cases. In Kerner and Young's chapter, the case studies describing a successful case and less successful case, Menorka and Shelly, respectively, highlight the strengths and limitations of IPT-AST. The case studies point to specific moderators in each client that seemed to be associated with the client's outcome. Specifically, although both adolescents were characterized as having elevated depressive symptoms temporally related to the transition from middle to high school, there appeared to be significant differences in their psychosocial and interpersonal histories that accounted for their treatment outcomes.

Menorka

Menorka presented with a clear elevation in depressive symptoms that she attributed to changes in her close interpersonal relationships and subsequent experiences of loneliness. These changes included her mother and godmother's work schedules that allowed for less time with Menorka, and friends initiating dating relationships and being less available for social activities. Although Menorka's depressive symptoms were clinically significant, they did not appear to impair her school performance or her social involvement with peers during the school day.

Also, despite a history of psychosocial risk (i.e., low socioeconomic status, parental divorce, paternal incarceration, and early exposure to domestic violence),

Menorka did not experience chronic or ongoing exposure to parental psychopathology, marital conflict, or other early childhood adversities that are linked to developmental trajectories of mental disorder or impaired functioning. Menorka appeared to benefit from a secure attachment relationship with her mother that may have contributed to her overall resilience, as evidenced by her social competence, such as in her perspective taking and lack of anxiety about social initiation with family members and peers.

IPT-AST appeared to be a good intervention for Menorka because of the interpersonal nature of her concerns, her high degree of affiliative behavior and social competence, and the absence of social anxiety in disclosing feelings and initiating interpersonal interactions. Her success with IPT-AST can also be attributed to a lack of extenuating conditions that are associated with poor treatment response across clinical modalities, such as parental depression, comorbid psychiatric disorders, abuse or maltreatment, and/or a history of poor school performance. Menorka attended all the individual pretreatment sessions and the group sessions, set and achieved personal goals, and appeared to benefit from the support given by group leaders and members, one of whom was an established friend before the IPT-AST group. Menorka's treatment response was evidenced in the first phase of treatment, as she reported a decrease in depressive symptoms after 3 weeks, and a complete remission in symptoms by end of the intervention, which was continued through the 18-month follow-up period.

Shelly

In contrast, Shelly presented with a significant history of psychosocial risk factors, chronic stressors, and few protective factors. Much of this may have influenced her emergent depressive symptoms as she transitioned to high school and likely contributed to her unsuccessful treatment response to IPT-AST. As with Menorka, Shelly experienced the divorce of her parents at an early age along with an estranged relationship with her father. However, Shelly may not have had the experience of a secure attachment relationship with her mother, given the characterization of their ongoing relationship as distant and conflictual. Although little detail is provided about her stepfather, it is possible that Shelly's experience of her mother as being emotionally unavailable intensified during this family transition.

Unlike Menorka, who experienced competence in school and with peers, Shelly had a chronic history of poor school performance and peer victimization. It is likely the high levels of fear of evaluation, rejection sensitivity, and interpersonal avoidance resulting from peer maltreatment intensified Shelly's social anxiety at school and contributed to low affiliative behavior and difficulties initiating with others.

Shelly's sexual identity issues and her emerging bisexuality also appear to be significant contributors to her social anxiety and her interpersonal avoidance. Sexual minority youth (SMY) report higher rates of peer victimization compared to heterosexual youth (see Freidman et al., 2011), and peer victimization has been hypothesized to mediate the relationship between SMY and poor mental health outcomes (Safren & Heimberg, 1999). Specifically, SMY are at higher risk for depression and suicidality than their heterosexual peers, and bisexual youth have the *highest rates* of depression and suicidal behavior compared to youth identifying singly as either gay or lesbian (Marshal et al., 2011).

Taken together, Shelly's reluctance to disclose personal information in the IPT-AST group, to initiate conversations with family members or peers, and to actively participate in group discussions regarding dating issues may reflect her discomfort with identifying as bisexual and/or disclosing her questions about sexual orientation.

Lastly, aspects of group treatment and the dynamics between members may have also contributed to Shelly's poor treatment response to IPT-AST. Group treatment has the potential to be helpful for at-risk adolescents with social anxiety, interpersonal avoidance, and a history of peer maltreatment, offering them a supportive and corrective interpersonal experience with peers and adults. However, as with any type of exposure treatment, group therapy also has the potential to increase anxious adolescents' distress at a point in treatment when they have no new strategies for regulating negative emotions.

Unlike Menorka, who experienced little increase in distress in the group setting, Shelly's social anxiety and fear of evaluation may have contributed to her missing two out of three sessions in the initial phase of IPT-AST. Shelly's fear of self-disclosure and negative evaluation may have also been intensified in the group setting. This intensification could have provided a barrier to Shelly's setting goals and identifying and discussing relevant issues related to her depression, all reducing the likelihood that Shelly could productively process outcomes of interpersonal experiments conducted outside of the IPT-AST group. The present group format of IPT-AST may be a less effective intervention for adolescents with significant social anxiety, and future iterations of this treatment should test the effectiveness of a sequenced model of IPT-AST that involves an increased number of individual therapy sessions and a graded transition to group treatment.

The preexisting friendship between Menorka and Emma may have also increased Shelly's apprehension and negative predictions about being accepted into the group. Shelly's expectations of interpersonal relationships may have been confirmed by Emma's criticism about her reserved presentation and criticisms of her lack of participation during group. Although the group experience is often perceived to be a means of creating increased social support, the group dynamics Shelly experienced may have contributed to her not feeling supported and to having a poor response to IPT-AST. An individual model of treatment may have been more effective in providing support and increasing strategies for initiating social interactions with peers and family members. In addition, it should be noted that Shelly started to show positive movement late in the therapy, in sessions 7 and 8 of the group, suggesting that a longer group experience could have been particularly helpful for her.

THE DEVELOPMENTAL PERIOD FOR PREVENTIVE INTERVENTION

The qualitative case studies of Menorka and Shelly describing successful and non-successful courses of IPT-AST highlight an important issue in the prevention science literature: the appropriate developmental period for targeting the prevention of depression in youths at risk for depression. Through the case descriptions, Kerner and Young present individual qualitative evidence that converges with an existing quantitative, group literature that support prevention of depression interventions to begin during the *preadolescent* years, ages 8–12 (Keenan et al., 2008). Although studies approximate that 0.4% to 2.5% of preadolescent children experience depression, they underestimate the number of preadolescents who do not meet full diagnostic criteria for major depressive disorder (MDD) but present for outpatient treatment with clinically significant depressive symptoms and functional impairment (Angold, Costello, Farmer, Burns, & Erkanli, 1999). As such, preadolescents with depressive disorders may be underdiagnosed and go untreated.

In both case examples drawn from the IPT-AST RCT study, Menorka and Shelly first evidenced impairing symptoms of depression in middle school, while between ages of 11 and 13. Both girls attributed the onset of preadolescent depressive symptoms to stress in peer relationships: with Menorka feeling pressured to engage in risk-taking behaviors by peers, and Shelly experiencing peer victimization (i.e., bullying, teasing, and rumor spreading). As pubertal onset is beginning at earlier chronological ages (Worthman, 1999), developmental changes in the salience attributed to interpersonal relationships once attributed to adolescents only are evident in preadolescent children.

Clinical studies suggest a strong association between depression in preadolescents and adverse family environments marked by high levels of discord, conflict, and disengagement (Fendrich, Warner, & Weissman, 1990; Nomura, Wickramaratne, Warner, Mufson, & Weissman, 2002; Puig-Antich et al., 1985). Offspring of depressed parents often present with manifestations of depression in the preadolescent period, as they may have genetic loading for mood disorders and/or may be exposed to stressful parent–child interactions; while in a parallel way, positive parent–child relationships may buffer preadolescents from the stress from peer relationships and, in doing so, may decrease their risk for depression in adolescence (Young, Berenson, Cohen, & Garcia, 2005). Psychosocial intervention with depressed preadolescents presents an opportunity to reduce family and interpersonal risk factors that may increase the likelihood of recurrent depression in adolescence. Future investigations of IPT-AST may consider adapting this group intervention to preadolescents at risk for depression.

FURTHERING THE STUDY OF MODERATORS

In sum, Kerner and Young's case study findings complement their RCT findings by providing an alternative way to generate moderators of the success or failure of the

IPT-AST group program, along with a method to examine the interactions among these moderators. For example, Kerner and Young conclude that Menorka's success was moderated by factors like "her positive attitude toward change, eagerness to utilize the skills, sociotropy, and history of positive interpersonal relationships" (p. 174), whereas Shelly's lack of success was moderated by her "absences [from the group], interpersonal deficits, social anxiety, . . . [a] negative cognitive style [that] made it difficult for her to fully engage and practice skills with the group to increase her relationships, [and] challenges with trust [that] were also apparent in the group" (p. 174). These multiple and interacting moderators demonstrate the real-world complexity of applying manualized treatment and the need to adapt a program such as IPT-AST to the individual needs, vulnerabilities, and strengths of different types of young adolescents at risk for full-blown depression. Kerner and Young's work shows the power of triangulating both group research and case study research methods to discover and explore these moderating variables and to incorporate them into future research and treatment planning.

REFERENCES

Angold, A., Costello, E. J., Farmer, E. M., Burns, B. J., & Erkanli, A. (1999). Impaired but undiagnosed. *Journal of the American Academy of Child and Adolescent Psychiatry*, 38, 129–137.

Friedman, M. S., Marshal, M. P., Guadamuz, T. E., Wei, C., Wong, C. F., Saewyc, E. M., & Stall, R. (2011) A meta-analysis of disparities in childhood sexual abuse, parental physical abuse, and peer victimization among sexual minority and sexual nonminority individuals. *American Journal of Public Health, 101*, 1481–1494.

Fendrich, M., Warner, V., & Weissman, M. M. (1990). Family risk factors, parental depression, and psychopathology in offspring. *Developmental Psychology, 26*, 40–50.

Geller, B., Zimerman, B., Williams, M., Bolhofner, K., & Craney, J. L. (2001). Adult psychosocial outcome of prepubertal major depressive disorder. *Journal of the American Academy of Child and Adolescent Psychiatry, 40*(6), 673–677.

Gillham, J. E., Reivich, K. J., Freres, D. R., Chaplin, T. M., Shatte, A. J., Samuels, B., . . . Seligman, M. E. (2007). School-based prevention of depressive symptoms: A randomized controlled study of the effectiveness and specificity of the Penn Resiliency Program. *Journal of Consulting and Clinical Psychology, 75*, 9–19.

Keenan, K., Hipwell, A., Feng, X., Babinski, D., Hinze, A., Rischall, M., & Henneberger, A. (2008). Subthreshold symptoms of depression in preadolescent girls are stable and predictive of depressive disorders. *Journal of the American Academy of Child & Adolescent Psychiatry, 47*, 1433–1442.

Kovacs, M., Feinberg, T. L., Crouse-Novak, M., Paulauskas, S. L., Pollock, M., & Finkelstein, R. (1984). Depressive disorders in childhood. II. A longitudinal study of the risk for a subsequent major depression. *Archives of General Psychiatry, 41*(7), 643–649.

Lipsitz, J. D., & Markowitz, J. C. (2013). Mechanisms of change in interpersonal therapy (IPT). *Clinical Psychology Review, 33*, 1134–1147.

Marshal, M. P., Dietz, L. J., Friedman, M. S., Stall, R., Smith, H. A., McGinley, J., . . . Brent, D. A. (2011). Suicidality and depression disparities between sexual minority and heterosexual youth: A meta-analytic review. *The Journal of Adolescent Health, 49*, 115–123.

Murray, C., & Lopez, A. (1996).*The global burden of disease.* Cambridge, MA: Harvard School of Public Health, WHO, and World Bank.

Nomura, Y., Wickramaratne, P. J., Warner, V., Mufson, L., & Weissman, M. M. (2002). Family discord, parental depression, and psychopathology in offspring: Ten-year follow-up. *Journal of the American Academy of Child & Adolescent Psychiatry, 41*, 402–409.

Puig-Antich, J., Lukens, E., Davies, M., Goetz, D., Brennan-Quattrock, J., & Todak, G. (1985). Psychosocial functioning in prepubertal major depressive disorders. II. Interpersonal relationships after sustained recovery from affective episode. *Archives of General Psychiatry, 42*, 511–517.

Safren, S. A., & Heimberg, R. G. (1999). Depression, hopelessness, suicidality and related factors in sexual minority and heterosexual adolescents. *Journal of Consulting and Clinical Psychology, 67*, 859–866.

Worthman, C. M. (1999). Epidemiology of human development. (1999). In C. W. Panter-Brick (Ed.), *Hormones, health and behavior: A socio-ecological and lifespan perspective* (pp. 47–104). Cambridge, England: Cambridge University Press.

Young, J. F., Berenson, K., Cohen, P., & Garcia, J. (2005). The role of parent and peer support in predicting adolescent depression: A longitudinal community study. *Journal of Research on Adolescence, 15*, 407–423.

Zisook, S., Rush, A. J., Lesser, I., Wisniewski, S. R., Trivedi, M., Husain, M. M., . . . Fava, M. (2007). Preadult onset vs. adult onset of major depressive disorder: A replication study. *Acta Psychiatrica Scandinavica, 115*(3), 196–205.

5

Transference-Focused Psychotherapy for Adult Borderline Personality Disorder

KENNETH N. LEVY, KEVIN B. MEEHAN, TRACY L. CLOUTHIER,
FRANK E. YEOMANS, MARK F. LENZENWEGER,
JOHN F. CLARKIN, AND OTTO F. KERNBERG ■

Commentary by William E. Piper
and Carlos A. Sierra Hernandez

THE RCT STUDY

Introduction

Borderline personality disorder (BPD) is a chronic and debilitating mental health problem characterized by a pattern of chaotic interpersonal relationships, emotional lability, impulsivity, angry outbursts, suicidality, and self-mutilation (APA, 2000, 2013; Skodol et al., 2002). It is a highly prevalent disorder; its prevalence is estimated at approximately 1%–6% of the general population (Grant et al., 2008; Lenzenweger, Lane, Loranger, & Kessler 2007; Torgersen, Kringlen, & Cramer, 2001; Zanarini et al., 2011), 10%–23% of psychiatric outpatients (Korzekwa, Dell, Links, Thabane, & Webb, 2008; Magnavita, Levy, Critchfield, & Lebow, 2010; Zimmerman, Rothschild, & Chelminski, 2005), 20%–25% of inpatients (Oldham et al., 1995; Zanarini et al., 2004), and 6% of primary care patients (Gross et al., 2002). The majority of individuals diagnosed with BPD are women (APA, 2013).

Individuals with BPD often suffer from significant behavioral problems. An estimated 69%–75% of individuals diagnosed with BPD have engaged in self-injurious behaviors (Kjellander, Bongar, & King, 1998). Alcohol and drug abuse, high-risk sexual behavior, and disordered eating are also common in this population. The completed suicide rate among BPD patients is also high, estimated as being between 3% and 9.5% (McGlashan, 1986; Paris, 1999; Stone, 1983).

Additionally, BPD is frequently comorbid both with other personality disorders and with other more episodic disorders that were formerly included on Axis I in previous editions of the *DSM* such as mood, anxiety, and substance use disorders (Zanarini et al., 1999). While patients with BPD utilize higher levels of mental health services, they often do so in chaotic ways; patterns of erratic attendance and repeated dropout, refusal to take psychiatric medications as prescribed, and pervasive noncompliance are common in this population (Bongar, Peterson, Golann, &, Hardiman, 1990; Zanarini & Frankenburg, 2001). Patients with borderline personality disorder are notoriously difficult to treat. Given its prevalence, comorbidity, and significant risks of distress and behavioral dysfunction, BPD represents a major public health problem.

GOAL 1 OF THE RESEARCH: COMPARING THE EFFECTIVENESS OF DIFFERENT MODELS FOR TREATING BPD

The rationale behind the current RCT was twofold. First, the researchers wished to conduct a trial that would assess the efficacy of transference-focused psychotherapy (TFP; Clarkin, Yeomans, & Kernberg, 2006), a manualized psychodynamic psychotherapy for BPD. TFP had already shown evidence of effectiveness using patients as their own controls (Clarkin et al., 2001) and in comparison to a treatment-as-usual group (Levy, Clarkin, Foelsch, & Kernberg, in review), but it had not yet been tested in the context of an RCT. The researchers also wanted to avoid some of the weaknesses of previous RCTs for BPD, such as small sample sizes (Clarkin et al., 2004), and comparison with a treatment-as-usual (TAU) condition, rather than with another active treatment for BPD (e.g., Bateman & Fonagy, 1999; Linehan et al., 1991). The campus at Cornell Medical College presented a unique opportunity in that there were three distinct long-standing programs of treatment for BPD that were well represented by active faculty, all with a presence on campus. The three approaches were transference-focused psychotherapy, which had been represented on campus since the mid 1970s when Otto Kernberg arrived as medical director. In the early 1980s, along with John Clarkin and Frank Yeomans and other colleagues, he developed TFP, which evolved out of expressive psychodynamic psychotherapy as practiced in the Menninger Project (Kernberg et al., 1972). Dialectical behavioral therapy (DBT) was also well represented on campus. In the mid-1980s Marsha Linehan spent a sabbatical semester at Cornell Medical College where she brought DBT to the campus. Along with Charles Swenson and other colleagues (Cynthia Sanderson and Perry Hoffman among others), the first DBT program outside of Seattle was established. Swenson, Sanderson, Hoffman, and others at Cornell were personally trained by Linehan and have become leaders in the training and implementation of DBT.

Before DBT was brought to campus, a central debate among the Cornell psychiatry and psychology faculty concerned the emphasis on expressive versus supportive psychotherapy techniques in the treatment of borderline and narcissistic patients. The debate was represented internationally between Kernberg and Kohut with regard to narcissism and Kernberg and Adler with regard to BPD. On campus, the discussions centered on the work of Rockland (1992) and colleagues (e.g., Appelbaum, 2005) on supportive therapy versus those of Kernberg and TFP (e.g., Clarkin, Yeomans, & Kernberg, 1998). Thus, the campus was flush with excitement and discussion of these various approaches.

All three approaches found interested constituents and subsequently flourished. Each program was able to adhere to its core principles, yet also interacted collegially and in the spirit of scholarship. In line with this, by having each of the three therapy models conducted by strong adherents of that model, we avoided the problem of bias due to researcher allegiance (Munder, Flückiger, Gerger, Wampold, & Barth, 2012). Thus, in developing the RCT reported in this chapter, the aim was to take advantage of this unique situation on campus and to compare the efficacy of TFP for treating BPD against that of DBT, an active alternative treatment for BPD whose efficacy had been previously established in a seminal clinical trial (e.g., Linehan et al., 1991). DBT was also being evaluated in several other clinical trials at the time (Linehan et al., 1999, 2002, 2006). Our RCT design allowed for the comparison of two theoretically contrasting approaches to the treatment of BPD: the psychodynamic model of TFP, and the CBT model using DBT. In taking advantage of the expertise on campus, rather than a treatment-as-usual comparison, a third active intervention, a supportive psychodynamic treatment, was adapted (Appelbaum, 2005) from Rockland's model for treating BPD (SPT; Rockland, 1992). This approach was also included as a component control for attention and support, as this modality does not utilize transference interpretation, an intervention considered to be one of the "active ingredients" of TFP; nor does it include skills training as does DBT. This design allowed for the comparison of TFP with another treatment based on a psychodynamic model (SPT), but one that explicitly avoids the process of transference and countertransference interpretations considered central to TFP.

GOAL 2 OF THE RESEARCH: INVESTIGATING PATIENT CHARACTERISTICS AND MECHANISMS

A second goal of the study was to examine patient characteristics and underlying mechanisms of BPD that might predict treatment response (Clarkin et al., 2004). In a series of manuscripts we have examined deficits in effortful control, amygdala and prefrontal cortex functioning, impulsivity, attention, executive functioning, aggression, positive and negative emotion, and mentalizing capacity (Critchfield et al., 2004; Fertuck, Lenzenweger, & Clarkin, 2005; Hoerman et al., 2005; Lenzenweger et al., 2004; Levy et al., 2005, 2006; Posner et al., 2002; Silbersweig et al., 2007). These studies have shown basic deficits in core aspects of neurocognitive and psychological functioning that are consistent with theories regarding the developmental psychopathology in BPD (Levy, 2005). For instance, Posner et al. (2002) found, relative to temperamentally matched controls, that those subjects with BPD tended to experience difficulty in resolving a nonaffective cognitive conflict task during the course of an attention task. Fertuck et al. further found that this attentional problem was related to the severity of BPD pathology. Likewise, Lenzenweger et al. (2004) found that BPD patients, as compared to normal controls, displayed deficits in sustained attention, working memory, and executive functioning. Levy et al. (2005) found that these deficits in attention and executive functioning were related to impairments in mentalizing as measured by reflective function on the Adult Attachment Interview. These deficits in the conflict aspect of attention tasks were related to alliance in psychotherapy but were mediated by mentalizing (Levy et al., 2010). Importantly, although BPD patients showed difficulty with mentalizing, they were amenable to treatment in TFP (Levy et al., 2006).

HYPOTHESES TESTED

The RCT was designed to examine three questions. The first was whether TFP is as efficacious or more so than DBT, a treatment whose efficacy had already been well established in clinical trials. The second was whether TFP is more efficacious than a psychodynamic model that does not address transference-based phenomena. If this is the case, it would provide evidence of the clinical utility of addressing these phenomena through transference interpretation. The third was whether TFP would result in a different pattern of results on a range of outcome measures than would DBT or SPT, which could provide information about the impact on BPT psychopathology and dynamics of the different theories and approaches underlying the three treatments. Within the context of this hypotheses, this chapter is focused primarily on TFP, rather than on the three treatments equally.

INCLUSION OF ELEMENTS FROM BOTH EFFICACY
AND EFFECTIVENESS DESIGNS

The design of the study incorporated characteristics of both efficacy and effectiveness studies. Similar to efficacy studies, the design of this RCT incorporated random assignment of patients to treatments, as well as the use of manualized treatments, blind raters, therapists blind to all baseline assessments, and specific and reliably measured outcome variables. Similar to effectiveness studies, a range of BPD patients were included in the study based on inclusion/exclusion criteria used in clinical practice; therapists provided treatment in their private offices in the community rather than in a university or hospital setting; and psychopharmacological treatment was decided on an individual case basis (see later). Finally, as mentioned earlier, the study was also designed to avoid some of the weaknesses of previous RCTs for BPD by including large sample sizes and comparison with other, active treatments.

Method

CASE-FINDING PROCEDURES, INCLUDING DIAGNOSTIC EVALUATION
PROCEDURES AND AN INTENT-TO-TREAT ANALYSIS FLOW CHART

Patients were recruited within a 50 mile radius of New York City. The vast majority of patients (97%) were referred by mental health professionals. Others were self-referred or referred by family members. Potential participants were initially screened for age and location with telephone interviews; those who were deemed

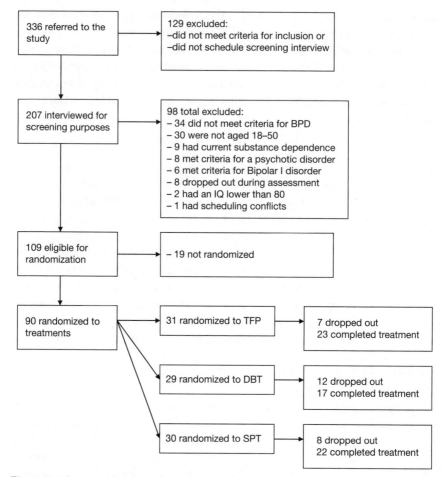

Figure 5.1 Intent-to-Treat Analysis Flow Chart.

suitable at this stage were then assessed in face-to-face interviews with trained evaluators, as described next, prior to being randomized to treatment. Written informed consent was obtained after all study procedures had been explained to participants.

As shown in the intent-to-treat flow chart presented in Figure 5.1, between 1998 and 2003, 336 patients were referred to the project. Of these, 129 either did not meet criteria for inclusion or decided not to schedule an intake interview. A total of 207 individuals were interviewed. Ninety-eight of these were excluded due to not meeting criteria for BPD ($n = 34$); age outside the 18–50 range ($n = 30$); meeting criteria for current substance dependence ($n = 9$), a psychotic disorder ($n = 8$), or bipolar I disorder ($n = 6$); dropouts during assessment ($n = 8$); having an IQ below 80 ($n = 2$); and prohibitive scheduling conflicts ($n = 1$). Of the 109 who were eligible for randomization, 90 were randomly chosen for treatment. These 90 participants so chosen did not differ from the 19 who were not chosen for treatment in terms of demographics, diagnostic data, or severity of psychopathology. Further details about participant referral and selection, rater and participant characteristics, and reliability of assessments are available elsewhere (Critchfield, Levy, & Clarkin, 2007).

Diagnostic evaluation procedures The Structured Clinical Interview for *DSM-IV*-Research Version (SCID-I; First, Gibbon, Spitzer, & Williams, 1997) was used to assess *DSM-IV* Axis I diagnoses, including exclusion diagnoses such as psychotic disorders. The SCID-I is a structured clinical interview used for making *DSM-IV* Axis I diagnoses in adults.

The International Personality Disorder Examination (IPDE; Loranger, Sartorius, Andreoli, & Berger, 1994) was used to assess personality pathology in potential participants. The IPDE is a semistructured diagnostic interview used for diagnosing personality disorders. It consists of 99 items, each of which is designed to assess a *DSM-IV* personality disorder criterion, arranged according to six themes (e.g., Self, Work), along with a detailed scoring manual (Loranger et al., 1994). Items are rated on a three-point scale: 0 = *absent or normal*, 1 = *exaggerated or accentuated*, 2 = *meets criteria or pathological*. Items consist of one or more primary and follow-up questions; all positive responses are followed by requests for supporting examples. After the questions are exhausted, the interviewer is free to inquire further in order to be able to score the item to completion. The IPDE generates probable (when an individual meets a subthreshold number of diagnostic criteria) and definite diagnoses for each of the *DSM-IV* personality disorder diagnoses, as well as dimensional scores for each diagnosis.

Interrater reliability of assessment interviews was good to excellent for all Axis I and Axis II disorders, with kappas ranging from .59 for anxiety disorders to 1.00 for alcohol or substance dependence. The kappa for BPD was .64, and the ICC for dimensional criteria ratings was .86. All kappa and ICC coefficients were in the good-to-excellent range (Fleiss, 1971). More information about diagnostic interviewers, interviewer training, and reliability procedures is available elsewhere (Critchfield, Levy, & Clarkin, 2005).

RANDOMIZATION PROCESS

Following an initial assessment to determine whether they met criteria for participation in the trial, patients were randomized to one of three year-long outpatient treatment conditions, using a simple randomization procedure administered by a person independent of the study in order to protect against unseen threats to validity and to minimize bias in assignment to treatment conditions.

This randomization process resulted in 31 patients being assigned to TFP, 29 patients to DBT, and 30 patients to SPT. Of these, one patient assigned to TFP was removed early in the study, when it became apparent that this individual had a psychotic disorder that had not been detected during the assessment. Additionally, one patient assigned to DBT withdrew from the study following randomization but prior to attending the first session.

PARTICIPANTS, INCLUDING THEIR BACKGROUND DEMOGRAPHIC CHARACTERISTICS

Patients included 90 adults (83 women; 92.2%) who were between the ages of 18 and 50. Patient demographics are presented in Table 5.1.

PRIMARY AND SECONDARY OUTCOME MEASURES

Suicidality, aggression, and impulsivity were selected as primary symptom outcome domains—because of their direct and specific connection to the psychopathology associated with BPD. They were measured as follows:

Table 5.1 PARTICIPANT CHARACTERISTICS

Characteristic	N	%
Gender		
Women	83	92.2
Men	7	7.8
Marital status		
Married	7	7.7
Divorced	40	44.4
Living with partner	11	12.2
In a relationship	21	23.3
Education		
Less than high school	3	3.3
High school graduate	7	7.8
Some college	28	31.1
Associate's degree	6	6.7
College degree	29	32.2
Graduate training	17	18.9
Employment		
Full-time	30	33.3
Part-time	23	25.6
Ethnicity		
Caucasian	61	67.8
African American	9	10.0
Hispanic	8	8.9
Asian	5	5.6
Other	7	7.8
Lifetime Axis I disorders		
Any mood disorder	69	76.7
Any anxiety disorder	43	47.8
Any eating disorder	30	33.3
Drug/alcohol abuse/dependence	34	37.8
Suicidal behavior		
Prior suicidal behavior	51	56.7
Prior parasuicidal behavior	56	62.2
No history of suicidal/parasuicidal behavior	15	16.7

Suicidality. The suicidality subscale of the Overt Aggression Scale—Modified (OAS-M; Coccaro, Harvey, Kupsaw-Lawrence, Herbert, & Bernstein, 1991) was used to assess patients' suicidality. The OAS-M is a 25-item clinician administered semistructured interview covering the areas of aggression, irritability, and suicidality.

Aggression. Patients' aggression was assessed using the Anger, Irritability, and Assault Questionnaire (AIAQ; Coccaro & Kavoussi, 1997). The AIAQ is a 28-item self-report version of the OAS-M designed to measure impulsive aggressive behaviors and attitudes. It generates four scales: anger, irritability, verbal assault, and direct assault. It covers the past week, past month, in addition to past behaviors extending to childhood.

Impulsivity. The Barratt Impulsiveness Scale–II (BIS-II; Patton, Stanford, & Barratt, 1995) was used to assess impulsivity. The BIS-II is a 34-item self-report measure, with items rated on a 4-point Likert scale (from "Rarely/Never" to "Almost Always/Always"). The BIS-II consists of three factors: attention, motor/acting without thinking, and nonplanning. It is the most widely known and used measure of impulsivity. These factors are also referred to as Factor 1, 2, and 3, respectively.

Anxiety, depression, and social adjustment were considered secondary-outcome domains because they are associated with a range of psychological disorders, including BPD. These were measured as follows:

Anxiety. The anxiety subscale of the Brief Symptom Inventory (BSI; Derogatis, 1993) was used to assess anxiety. The BSI is the 53-item short form of the Symptom Checklist-90-R (SCL-90-R) and measures nine domains of distress and symptomatology, including measures of depression, anxiety, hostility, somatization, and psychosis.

Depression. The Beck Depression Inventory-II (BDI-II; Beck, Steer, & Brown, 1996) was used to assess depressive symptoms. The BDI-II is a 21-item self-report questionnaire, which measures cognitive, somatic, and behavioral indices of current depression; each item is rated on a scale from 0 to 3.

Social adjustment. The patients' SCID-I interview, using both interviewer ratings, was used to derive a social adjustment scale using the Global Assessment of Function (GAF) scale, called the "GAF Social Adjustment" measure (First et al., 1997). A second measure of social adjustment was derived from the Social Adjustment Scale ("SAS Social Adjustment"; Weissman & Bothwell, 1976). The SAS is a semistructured interview that assesses social functioning and adjustment in five domains: work (employment, housewife, student), social and leisure activity, relationships with extended family, marital role and parental role, as well as an overall global adjustment score, which comprises the SAS Social Adjustment score. This instrument has high test-retest reliability (.80). The primary and secondary outcome variables were assessed at four time points: baseline, 4 months, 8 months, and 12 months (end of the treatment period). Each patient in the RCT was measured on these variables at roughly the same intervals.

TFP-Specific, Structural Measures

A distinctive aspect of the TFP model (but not the DBT or SPT models) is the incorporation of two major concepts of psychoanalytic theory—attachment organization and reflective functioning (RF), or mentalization. We therefore predicted that TFP would have a more positive impact on these two variables than would DBT or SPT. These variables, which were assessed prior to the beginning of treatment and after treatment had ended, were measured by means of the Adult Attachment Interview (AAI; George, Kaplan, & Main, 1985). This semistructured interview consists of questions concerning the interviewee's experiences with childhood caregivers and the influence of these experiences on his or her adult personality. It is transcribed verbatim.

Attachment organization. Attachment organization was considered to be an important outcome domain given that the vast majority of BPD patients exhibit an insecure attachment organization, and given the predominance of interpersonal dysfunction associated with BPD (Levy, 2005). It was measured in two ways, derived from Main and Goldwyn's (1984) coding system: a Coherence of Narrative score and an attachment classification: secure, preoccupied, dismissing, unresolved, or "cannot classify" (Main et al., 2008).

Attachment organization is assessed based on the manner in which people discuss their childhood memories. There are five main AAI classifications: *Secure* individuals can discuss both positive and negative childhood memories coherently and openly, and appear to reflect on their thinking as they speak. *Preoccupied* individuals discuss childhood memories in an incoherent manner that suggests a lack of distance or perspective. *Dismissing* individuals discuss attachment relationships in either a devaluing or an idealized manner, with little use of concrete examples to support their view. The *Unresolved* classification represents a lack of resolution of experiences related to loss or trauma; unresolved individuals exhibit lapses in the monitoring of speech or reasoning in talking about traumatic experiences. The *Cannot Classify* category represents individuals who demonstrate contradictory or competing attachment patterns, or who fail to demonstrate a single state of mind with respect to attachment. AAI classifications do not appear to be influenced by social desirability, intelligence, or autobiographical memory not related to attachment experiences (Bakermans-Kranenburg & van IJzendoorn, 1993).

Reflective functioning (RF). This is an aspect of mentalization, defined as the ability to make inferences about the intent underlying behavior in oneself and others by evoking and reflecting on one's own experience (Fonagy, Gergely, Jurist, & Target, 2002; Fonagy & Target, 1996). Fonagy, Steele, Steele, and Target (1998) have developed an RF score that can be derived from the AAI. Given that there is some association between low RF and a diagnosis of BPD (Fonagy et al., 1996), change in RF was considered to be a potentially relevant outcome variable. As with attachment organization, RF was assessed before and after treatment.

Intervention, Including Guiding Conception and Procedures

Transference-focused psychotherapy (TFP; Clarkin, Yeomans, Kernberg, 1999, 2006; Kernberg, Selzer, Koenigsberg, Carr, & Appelbaum, 1989; Yeomans,

Clarkin, & Kernberg, 2015). TFP is a highly structured, manualized, twice-weekly modified psychodynamic treatment based on Kernberg's (1984) object relations model of BPD. The primary goal of TFP is to reduce symptomatology and self-destructive behavior by modifying disparate and split representations of self and others characteristic of BPD (Levy et al., 2006). TFP begins with explicit setting of the frame or contract-setting to clarify the conditions of therapy, the method of treatment, the hierarchy of behaviors to be addressed during sessions, the roles of patient and therapist in treatment, and the management of suicidal urges and behavior. The setting of the frame is a collaborative process that involves a diagnostic assessment using Kernberg's structural interview (Kernberg, 1984). The interviewing phase typically takes between 2–3 sessions and involves acquiring a complete symptom picture as well as information about the patient's relationship and work functioning. A central aspect of this assessment involves assessing the patient's descriptions of self and important others in order to understand the patient's level of differentiation and integration of self and other representations.

The information gathered during the structural interview is then used to set the treatment frame with the patient, which is established before beginning therapy. The process is a collaborative one in which the therapist presents the rationale for elements of the therapy, and the patient discusses any concerns he or she may have. The therapist combines flexibility and openness to discussion with adherence to essential aspects of the treatment. In addition to defining the responsibilities of patient and therapist, the structure provided by the contract protects the therapist's ability to think clearly and reflect, provides a safe place for the patient's dynamics to unfold, and sets the stage for exploring and interpreting the meaning of deviations from the frame such as missing or coming late to sessions or withholding details about suicidality. When there are deviations from the frame, referring back to the contract supports the patient's capacity to step outside of the moment and to view his or her behavior from alternate perspectives. An implicit message in the establishment of the contract is that all feelings can be experienced and reflected upon, in contrast to the patient's felt need to manage threatening aspects of affective experience through acting out and projection. The establishment of an agreed-upon frame can take another 2–5 sessions. It is important that the patient has the chance to express any concerns and conversely that the therapist explore any superficial acquiescence on the patient's part.

Once the contract is set, the primary focus of TFP in session is on the affect-laden themes that emerge in the relationship between BPD patients and their therapists. During the first year of treatment, TFP focuses on containing acting-out behaviors, as well as identifying and recapitulating the patient's predominant relational patterns as they are experienced and expressed in the here and now of the relationship with the therapist. To effect change, the therapist uses the techniques of clarification, confrontation, interpretation, and transference interpretation (interpretation of patient–therapist interactions in session that demonstrate the patient's split perceptions of self and other).

In TFP, interpretation is viewed as the route to integrating the disparate perceptions and representations of self and other that are characteristic of BPD. As the split representations of self and other and dysfunctional relational patterns typical in this population are likely to arise in the relationship with the therapist, transference interpretation is viewed as one of the primary ways to effect change. TFP consists of two weekly individual sessions, typically of 45 or 50 minutes depending on what is the therapist's typical "therapy hour." Phone contact with the therapist between sessions is discouraged except to reschedule or, in the case of an emergency (understood to mean a significant and unexpected life event such as the death of a loved one, and not emotional upset or suicidal ideation, which is frequent and not unexpected in this population), in order to ensure that the action takes place within the twice-weekly sessions.

Sessions typically occur twice weekly, but the length of the treatment may vary. Unlike typical short-term structured manuals, the TFP manual is not written for a specific time frame nor is it highly structured. Rather it is principle-based, like that of Linehan's manual. Similar to Linehan, who conceptualizes treatment of BPD as being a multiyear process, TFP is a long-term treatment; however, for the purpose of the RCT treatment, length has been artificially constrained to a year for all treatments. Similar to studies of DBT (Linehan et al., 1993, 1994), patients in our RCT had the option of continuing in treatment past the initial year that the study assessed for purposes of testing its efficacy. In the TFP manual, treatment is conceptualized as having four phases: (1) the assessment phase; (2) the early treatment phase characterized by tests to the frame such as lateness or purposeful withholding and containment of impulsive behavior, such as suicidality; (3) the midphase characterized by movement toward integration and identity consolidation but with continued episodes of regression; and (4) the advanced treatment and termination phase. Phases 3 and 4 correspond to Howard and colleagues' (1996) conception of remediation and rehabilitation, with remediation being characterized by symptom improvement and rehabilitation characterized as personality change.

Dialectical behavior therapy (DBT). DBT is a manualized cognitive-behavioral treatment for BPD with two components: (1) individual therapy and (2) group skills training (Linehan, 1993). There is a weekly session of each. One of the guiding principles of this form of treatment is finding a balance between encouraging the patient to change and accepting the patient as he or she is. As such, the treatment integrates change-focused strategies such as problem solving with acceptance and validation of the patient's experience.

The individual therapy component focuses on an identified hierarchy of target behaviors, with suicidal and parasuicidal behaviors at the top, which the patient tracks using daily diary cards. "Behavioral chain analysis," which identifies the functional pattern and sequence of events, cognitions, and emotions resulting in these target behaviors is used in order to help the patient identify what triggers the behavior and alternative strategies for coping.

The group component consists of skills training intended to help patients develop more adaptive means of coping with seemingly intolerable emotions, instead of resorting to behaviors that may be destructive to the patient and to his or her relationships. Skills training sessions consist of teaching new skills to patients and providing homework for patients to attempt between sessions in order to practice and reinforce these skills. Skills taught in DBT include mindfulness, interpersonal effectiveness, emotion regulation, and distress tolerance. Skills are integrated into individual treatment when problematic situations, such as suicidal or parasuicidal urges, present themselves. Therapists help patients identify appropriate skills to use in place of maladaptive coping strategies, with the hope that patients can eventually apply the skills on their own in order to function in a more adaptive manner.

Therapists are available via pager between sessions for brief coaching to help patients fight parasuicidal urges and engage in appropriate means of coping with intense emotions and stressful life events.

Supportive psychotherapy (SPT). SPT is a manualized, psychoanalytically oriented treatment for BPD (Appelbaum, 2005) adapted from a commonly used psychodynamic supportive psychotherapy (Rockland, 1989, 1992). Sessions are once or twice weekly. The primary goal of SPT is to bring about changes through the development of a healthy, collaborative relationship with the therapist, and to replace self-destructive enactments with verbal expression of conflicts. Instead of using interpretation to achieve these goals, as in TFP, in SPT, change is thought to occur through the patient's identification with the reflective capacities of the therapist.

As in the other two treatments, SPT begins with a contract-setting phase, and the initial stages of therapy focus on behaviors that threaten the patient's safety, interfere with therapy, and disrupt psychosocial functioning, as priorities for treatment. Another focus of the initial stages of SPT is fostering an atmosphere of safety and security, as well as a sense of collaboration between patient and therapist. Therapists are attuned to the type of transference the patient experiences, as well as the dominant affect associated with it; they accept and use any positive transference the patient may experience, but they refrain from interpreting transference.

SPT also utilizes supportive techniques, such as describing significant aspects of the patient's self in order to encourage greater identity consolidation, fostering the patient's sense of agency and mastery of impulses and emotions, and encouraging socially acceptable ways of expressing impulses (such as exercise or creative expression). Emotional support, advice, and direct environmental intervention may also be provided. Therapists foster the alliance and encourage mentalization and identification of defensive processes, but they also provide reassurance and advice in a manner consistent with other psychodynamic supportive psychotherapies (Adler, 1985, Wallerstein, 1986).

Comparison among treatments. In relation to TFP, the SPT treatment was conceptualized as a component control condition, with the proposed active ingredient of TFP (transference interpretation) being proscribed in this modality.

In relation to TFP, the DBT treatment was particularly different concerning the frame of the therapy. To avoid the secondary gain that can be experienced by extra contact with the therapist and to encourage the development of autonomy (Yeomans, 1993), the TFP therapist is considered unavailable between sessions except in the case of emergencies, whereas in DBT the patient is encouraged to phone the individual therapist between sessions. Another difference is the emphasis in TFP on technical neutrality (not siding with any part of the patient's internal conflicts but rather helping the patient see and resolve the conflicting parts within himself) versus strategies used in DBT, including validation, coaching, and cheerleading, that may temporarily suppress, but not integrate negative internal forces. Still another difference between TFP and DBT is that while both deal with emotionally laden thoughts, in DBT these thoughts are examined in relation to specific behavioral situations in the patient's life, whereas the cognitions in TFP tend to be related to internal representations of important people and relationships in the patient's life.

Despite these differences, both TFP and DBT have in common a firm, explicit contract; a focus on a hierarchy of acting-out behaviors; a highly engaged therapeutic relationship; a structured, disciplined approach; and utilization of supervision groups as essential for therapists.

THERAPISTS

Therapists were selected on the basis of having previously established competence in their respective treatment modality (TFP, DBT, or SPT). All possessed advanced degrees in social work, psychology, or psychiatry, and had at least 2 years of experience treating BPD patients. The TFP therapists were eight experienced individuals with postdoctoral training. Their experience level ranged from faculty/staff psychiatrists with at least 10 years of experience to faculty/staff psychologists with at least 2 years of experience treating BPD patients and specific training in TFP.

The DBT therapists were five experienced individuals with postdoctoral training. Their experience level ranged from faculty/staff psychologists with 10 years of experience to faculty/staff psychologists with at least 2 years of experience treating BPD patients. Importantly, all the DBT therapists had specific training in DBT (all therapists having attended multiple intensive trainings with Linehan or other certified trainers) and were therapists within the Cornell and Columbia medical school day-hospital DBT programs.

The SPT therapists were seven experienced individuals with postdoctoral training. Their experience level ranged from faculty/staff psychiatrists with at least 15 years of experience to faculty/staff psychologists and social workers with at least 2 years of experience treating BPD patients and specific training in SPT.

PROCESS OF IMPLEMENTING THE RCT

Each of the three treatment groups was administered and supervised by a recognized expert in that treatment modality; TFP was supervised by Frank Yeomans, DBT was supervised by Barbara Stanley, and SPT was supervised by Ann Appelbaum. These treatment condition leaders selected a total of 19 therapists based on their previously established competence in their respective modality. Therapist characteristics are described earlier. All therapists were monitored and supervised weekly by the treatment condition leaders, who were available to observe videotapes of sessions, provide feedback, and who rated therapists on their adherence and competence within their respective modality.

In addition to being assigned to a year-long therapy condition, all patients were evaluated for pharmacotherapy at entry into the study. Study psychiatrists were blind to treatment group assignments. To reduce subjectivity in deciding on medication, a medication algorithm was used to guide psychopharmacological treatment (Soloff, 2000).

Results

The present analyses are based on the patients who completed at least three assessments, which includes $n = 23$ in TFP, $n = 17$ in DBT, and $n = 22$ in SPT. These patients were deemed to have received a sufficient "dose" of treatment, having completed at least 9 months of the year-long treatment.

Medication Treatment at the Start of Treatment

Based on the medication algorithm mention earlier, at the start of treatment, 52% of TFP patients, 70% of DBT patients, and 65% of SPT patients were prescribed medication, and the percentage of patients on medication remained relatively constant during the treatment period. Given that there were no differences between the three groups of patients on symptom domains assessed at the start of treatment, differences in the percentage of patients prescribed medication could not be attributed to differences in severity across the treatment groups.

Primary and Secondary Outcome Measures

Individual growth-curve analysis. The individual growth-curve approach hypothesizes that for each individual, the outcome variable is a specified function of time called the individual growth trajectory (comprised of two unknown individual growth parameters—an intercept and a slope—that determine the shape of individual true growth over time), plus error. The individual intercept parameter represents the net "elevation" of the trajectory over time. The individual slope parameter represents the rate of change over time and in this study is the within-person rate of change in the dependent variable over time. Individual growth trajectories were specified at level 1 and capture individual change over time. A level two model was then used to investigate the way that the individual growth parameters at level one are related to between-subjects factors. More information about the analytic procedures used is available elsewhere (Clarkin et al., 2007; Levy et al., 2006).

We used an unconditional growth model, which revealed that for all the domain dimensions, the average elevation for all three groups of patients differed significantly from zero ($p < .001$). These findings indicate significant levels of distress and impairment was present in our sample. This was expected, since borderline personality disorder patients are substantially impaired.

We also found that the estimated average rates of change (i.e., slopes) also differed significantly from zero for all of the domain dimensions except for the Barratt Factor 3 impulsivity and anxiety dimensions, indicating that much change over time was evident in the data (all $p \leq .05$).

First we examined whether the age at which a participant entered the study was related to change on the various domain variables. Age at entry into the study was not associated with the initial level of symptoms, or with change in most symptom domains; and age at entry was not included in further analyses.

The next second set conditional analyses we investigated were the impact of the three treatments on the level and rate of change (slope). The results of these level 2 conditional analyses are presented in Table 5.2. The prediction of slope (change) at level 2 by each of the three treatments was significant for depression, anxiety, global functioning, and social adjustment (all $p < 0.05$). The direction of effects was toward symptom improvement. Both transference-focused psychotherapy and dialectical behavior therapy were significantly associated with improvement in suicidality over time, and both transference-focused psychotherapy and supportive treatment were significantly associated with improvement in anger over time. Only transference-focused psychotherapy was significantly predictive of symptom improvement in Barratt Factor 2 impulsivity, irritability, verbal assault, and direct assault. Supportive treatment alone was predictive of improvement in Barratt Factor 3 Impulsivity. None of the three treatments was associated with improvement in Barratt Factor I impulsivity.

Thus, transference-focused psychotherapy predicted significant improvement in 10 of the 12 variables, dialectical behavior therapy in 5 of the 12 variables, and supportive treatment in 6 of the 12 variables.

Contrast analyses and intent-to-treat analysis. Contrast analyses (Rosenthal, Rosnow, & Rubin, 2000) were used to statistically test specific predictions about primary outcome symptom differences across the three treatments based on previous research and content focus in the treatment manuals. Two of the main ones included the prediction that DBT would lead to significantly lower levels of suicidality, and TFP, to significantly lower levels of anger. Although the latter prediction was not confirmed, the former yielded a contrast that approached significance ($p < .07$; Clarkin et al., 2007): TFP and DBT were associated with a greater improvement in suicidality than SPT, and there was no difference between TFP and DBT on this variable.

An intent-to-treat analysis (Clarkin et al., 2006) was also conducted in order to determine whether patients dropping out of treatment groups impacted the pattern of findings across treatments compared to when analyses were restricted to patients who completed the treatment. The results indicated that patient attrition did not change the pattern of results.

CHANGE IN TFP-SPECIFIC OUTCOME DOMAINS
Attachment. Because patients were administered the AAI only before and after treatment, only those patients who completed treatment could be included in these analyses.

Table 5.2 RESULTS OF CLARKIN ET AL. (2007) RANDOMIZED CLINICAL TRIAL

Symptom-Based Measures	Significance of Change		
	TFP	DBT	SPT
PRIMARY			
Suicidality[a]	<.05	<.05	ns
Anger[a]	<.05	ns	<.05
Irritability[a]	<.05	ns	ns
Verbal Assault[a]	<.05	ns	ns
Direct Assault[a]	<.05	ns	ns
Barratt Factor 1 Impulsivity: Attention[b]	ns	ns	ns
Barratt Factor 2 Impulsivity: Motor/Acting Without Thinking[b]	<.05	ns	ns
Barratt Factor 3 Impulsivity: Nonplanning[b]	ns	ns	<.05
SECONDARY			
Anxiety[c]	<.05	<.05	<.05
Depression[d]	<.05	<.05	<.05
GAF Social Adjustment[e]	<.05	<.05	<.05
SAS Social Adjustment[f]	<.05	<.05	<.05

NOTE: All significant change was in the direction of less impairment.
[a]Suicidality, Anger, Irritability, Verbal Assault, and Direct Assault were assessed with the Overt Aggression Scale—Modified version (OAS-M; Coccaro, Harvey, Kupsaw-Lawerence, Herbert, & Bernstein, 1991) and the Anger, Irritability, and Assault Questionnaire (AIAQ; Coccaro & Kavoussi, 1997).
[b]Barratt Factors are from the Barratt Impulsivity Scale (Patton, Stanford, & Barratt, 1995).
[c]Anxiety was assessed with the Brief Symptom Inventory (BSI; Derogatis, 1993).
[d]Depression was assessed with the Beck Depression Inventory (Beck, Steer, & Brown, 1996).
[e]GAF represents the DSM-III Global Assessment of Functioning scale score (First et al., 1997).
[f]SAS represents the Social Adjustment Scale (Weissman & Bothwell, 1976).

Prior to the start of treatment, patients' attachment classifications were as follows:

- 3 (5%) were classified as securely attached,
- 9 (15%) were classified as preoccupied,
- 18 (28.3%) were classified as dismissing,
- 19 (33.3%) were classified as unresolved, and
- 11 (18.3%) were coded as "cannot classify."

Following the treatment process, a total of 9 patients (15%) were classified as securely attached across the entire sample, which represented a significant change

Table 5.3 RESULTS OF LEVY, MEEHAN, KELLY, ET AL. (2006)
RANDOMIZED CLINICAL TRIAL

Structural Measures	Clinical Cutoff Point	TFP		DBT		SPT		Contrast
		Pre-Tx	Post-Tx	Pre-Tx	Post-Tx	Pre-Tx	Post-Tx	
Reflective Functioning[a]	5	2.86	4.11	3.31	3.38	2.8	2.86	TFP> DBT = SPT
Coherence of Narrative[a]	5	2.93	4.02	3.00	3.25	3.25	3.16	TFP> DBT = SPT

NOTE: Higher scores indicate healthier functioning.
[a]Both measures were based on content from the Adult Attachment Interview (AAI). Reflective Functioning was scored using Fonagy et al.'s (1997) manual, and Coherence of Narrative was assessed based on the AAI's coding system (Main & Goldwyn, 1984).
DBT, dialectical behavior therapy; SPT, supportive psychodynamic treatment; TFP, transference-focused psychotherapy.

from the initial number of 3 (5%). There was also a nonsignificant decrease in the number of patients classified as unresolved, with 13 patients (21.7%) in this category after treatment compared with 19 (33.3%) at the beginning of treatment. When the treatment group was taken into account, the change in number of patients classified as secure was significant only in TFP, not in DBT or SPT, thus confirming our hypothesis that changes in attachment were a particular focus in TFP compared to the other two treatments.

Reflective functioning and coherence of narrative. On both of these variables, contrast analysis revealed that TFP participants experienced greater improvement than did those in DBT or SPT (see Table 5.3). This confirms our hypothesis that TFP would have a greater impact on these two variables because of their particular relevance in TFP's theory of BPD psychopathology and methods for combating it.

DIFFERENTIAL EFFECT OF MEDICATION ON TREATMENT GROUPS
We investigated whether medication interacted differentially with any of the three treatments to increase change for patients in one or more of the treatments. To examine this possibility, we conducted a parallel set of growth-curve analyses on only those subjects who had been medicated at the study entry and through at least the third assessment. In sum, the pattern of findings (direction of effects, effect sizes) across the 12 dependent variables for the three treatments in this restricted cohort where medication was held constant was highly similar to those found for the cohort as a whole, indicating a lack of differential impact of medication status on the three treatment groups.

Discussion

The primary finding of this RCT is that all three treatments studied—TFP, DBT, and SPT—showed statistically significant improvement in multiple, primary and secondary symptom domains relevant to BPD over the course of a year of outpatient treatment. This suggests that these three structured treatments for BPD patients are generally equivalent with respect to broad positive change (Roth & Fonagy, 2005). Because in terms of past RCTs, DBT is considered the "gold standard" of treatment for BPD, the fact that TFP and SPT were found to be generally equivalent to the DBT benchmark constitutes important empirical support for these latter two treatments. In this regard, note that medication was part of the design so as to mirror naturalistic practice. Because differences in the percentage of patients prescribed medication could not be attributed to differences in initial severity across the treatment groups, we conclude that the outcomes comparing the three psychosocial treatments were independent of the impact of medication.

Two other RCTs evaluating the TFP treatment of BPD were conducted at about the same time as our RCT, including one by Giesen-Bloo et al. (2006) and one by Doering et al. (2010). Consistent with our findings, Doering et al. (2010) found that TFP was superior to treatment offered by an experienced community psychiatrist; and Giesen-Bloo et al. (2006) found that both TFP and schema-focused therapy (SFT) yielded statistically and clinically significant improvements on a variety of measures after 1-, 2-, and 3-year treatment periods. In some analyses, SFT showed greater efficacy than did TFP.

In our analysis of the Giesen-Bloo et al. study (Levy et al., 2012; Yeomans, 2007), we argue that a number of issues with the study design could account for the researchers having found lesser efficacy for TFP. First, the randomization failed, as indicated by the fact that the TFP condition included twice as many (76% vs. 38%) recently suicidal patients as the SFT group. This could contribute to differences in outcome across treatment groups, given that suicidality has previously been found to significantly impact treatment outcome (Arntz, 2004). Second, significant differences between the two treatment groups were only present in the intent-to-treat analyses, but not in the completer analyses (Arntz, 2004; Kellogg & Young, 2006), suggesting a loss of validity due to nonrandom dropout. Third, therapist adherence ratings for the TFP group were much lower than for the SFT group, suggesting that TFP was not as well delivered in this study. Fourth, there are concerns about the integrity of the treatments in the study. For example, therapist supervision was provided by peers ("intervision") rather than by experts in the treatment modality, which, given the lower adherence among TFP therapists, likely resulted in therapists in that treatment group also receiving lower quality intervision than therapists in the SFT group. Further, an expert consultant reported that he had expressed concern about therapist adherence to the research team, but that no action was taken to address this issue (Yeomans, 2007). Finally, therapists and assessors were not blind to ongoing outcome measures. This could have contributed to demoralization among the TFP therapists, while potentially enhancing the motivation of the therapists in the Schema-Focused Therapy group (Chalmers et al., 1981). In light of these issues, it would be premature and irresponsible to conclude that TFP is less efficacious than SFT on the basis of this one rather flawed study.

Because the different models are based on different theories of change, our overall finding of the equivalence of TFP, DBT, and SPT suggests that there may be different routes to improvement. In DBT, there is a focus on direct, behavioral skills training to help patients regulate emotions and reduce symptoms; in TFP, there is a focus on developing greater self-control through integrating representations of self and others as they become active in the therapeutic relationship, with a particular use of transference interpretation; and in SPT, the focus is on a supportive relationship and using the therapist as a model of reflection, without the use of transference interpretation. Both future group studies and future case studies like the ones described later in this chapter will be helpful in comparing and contrasting these different theoretically based routes to improvement in patients with DBT.

As summarized in Table 5.2, the fact that of the eight primary symptom variables, TFP was statistically significantly associated with improvement in six; DBT, with improvement in one; and SPT, with improvement in two suggests that TFP has a particularly efficacious impact on the primary symptom variables.

Future research will need to examine (a) whether the overall improvements in primary outcome symptoms across the three therapies are maintained over time; and (b) whether the improvement differences in the outcome measures we found hold up with larger samples and, if so, how these improvement differences are related to the differences in the theories behind the TFP, DBT, and SPT treatments (Clarkin & Levy, 2006).

Finally, our hypotheses about the greater ability of TFP to effect structural personality changes in patients with BPD were confirmed, indicating the statistically significant superiority of TFP in effecting improvements in healthy attachment, in reflective functioning, and in narrative coherence. This confirmation provides additional evidence of the theoretical promise of TFP and its ability as a treatment to effect the positive personality changes that underlie and sustain symptomatic change.

THE CASE STUDIES

The Nature and Rationale for the Specific Cases Selected for the Case Studies

Of the 30 patients randomized to TFP, we have chosen two patients who are illustrative of the process of treatment in TFP, and yet each experienced and responded to like interventions in distinct ways that were reflected in differential outcomes. The two patients, Ms. J and Ms. V, were both women in their early 30s who presented for treatment after having little benefit from prior psychotherapies and pharmacotherapies as well as little success in past work environments. Both women were diagnosed with BPD and randomized to the same therapist in TFP. The therapist was male and an experienced clinician who had practiced and supervised TFP for many years. Each patient was treated twice-weekly in his private practice office in close proximity to the affiliated medical center sponsoring the RCT. As part of the RCT, each patient agreed to be treated in 1 year of TFP. However, at the end of that year each patient was offered the option of continuing treatment in the therapist's private practice. Although the primary focus of the summaries of these cases will be on the year when the RCT was conducted, changes and developments subsequent to the RCT will be discussed as well.

Despite similarities, these two women also differed in a number of respects that shall be elaborated on in their respective summaries. The cases differ in the trajectory of change observed—however, it is important to note that in assessing change we are not limiting ourselves to symptomatic change on self- and clinician-report measures. In fact, one of the explicit goals of TFP is to take the patient beyond symptom change and strive toward structural change—a process of integration of disparate aspects of personality functioning. It has been observed empirically that although many patients with BPD become less symptomatic over time when evaluated longitudinally, impairments in work and relationship functioning tend to persist (Zanarini, Frankenburg, Reich, & Fitzmaurice, 2010a, 2010b). By enacting change at the level of personality organization, TFP seeks not only to decrease impulsive and aggressive behaviors but also to increase the capacity to create, enjoy life, develop intimacy, and invest in goals and relationships. Though both women were less symptomatic in terms of the primary outcome measures after 1 year, they differed considerably in terms of the degree of structural change that was accomplished.

The Clients

Ms. J, a Client With a Positive Outcome
Ms. J was a single, unemployed Asian woman who started TFP at age 32 after having been in psychotherapeutic and psychiatric treatments since age 17 with no demonstrable change. In fact, her condition had worsened to the point where she spent the 6 months prior to beginning TFP isolated in her apartment, watching television, eating and gaining weight, and only rarely bathing. She presented for treatment because of depressed mood with chronic suicidal ideation, occasional self-destructive behavior, anger and irritability, and very poor interpersonal and work functioning.

Ms. V, a Client With a Negative Outcome
Ms. V, a 33-year-old single Caucasian woman, was referred for TFP by staff at the hospital where she had been receiving outpatient psychotherapy. V was unemployed and depended on medical disability benefits to pay her expenses. V, who had a history of abusing alcohol, led a very limited life. She lived in a subsidized

apartment and had no regular activities outside of the treatments she had participated in and AA meetings two or three times a week. She had not worked or studied in many years. She had limited social involvements, having coffee with friends from AA and having an intermittent and stormy relationship with a boyfriend with no plans for settling down in a permanent relationship or establishing a family. She had been treated in just about every inpatient, partial, and outpatient program in the hospital associated with the RCT for the previous 10 years with little benefit.

Guiding Conception With Research Support

The guiding conception as well as relevant research that informs this case study is presented in "Intervention, Including Guiding Conception," in the Method section in the description of the RCT Study earlier.

Ms. J's Positive-Outcome Therapy: Assessment, Formulation, and Course

Assessment of Ms. J's Problems, Goals, Strengths, and History Presenting Problems

J was a 32-year-old woman who had immigrated to the United States from Asia as a young child with her parents. She had been referred by a psychiatrist psychoanalyst she consulted with after reading about borderline personality. She was concerned that she had experienced little benefit from a number of psychotherapies and pharmacotherapies over the last 15 years that had considered her diagnosis to be bipolar disorder. While she presented with self-destructive, angry, and irritable behaviors that led to the destruction of many relationships and jobs, in the 6 months prior to treatment she had withdrawn from social and occupational functioning altogether and had rarely left her apartment.

In terms of relational functioning, a striking feature of J's presentation was her attribution of hostile intentions to others, and a tendency to locate her own anger as residing within others rather than herself (i.e., projection). For example, her first words on entering her therapist's office for the first time were: "The woman on the bus was staring at me. I could tell she hated me, so I stared right back!" J did not have insight into the fact that she may be eliciting, and not just subject to, hostile interactions. Aside from past stormy interactions with coworkers, J had no friends. She dated occasionally but had no history of sexual relations.

History

J was the middle daughter in a highly educated family and her father was a successful professional. J's education ended when she dropped out of school at age 25 after 1 year of postcollege training in a technical field. After that she held a series of semiskilled jobs but was repeatedly fired from these jobs because of her difficulty getting along with others. She stopped working when she began to get rejected from every job to which she applied. She attributed this to an irrational prejudice against her, denying that her behavior and attitudes had any role in her interpersonal difficulties.

BPD Features

J's scores on the standardized measures, both at intake and at 1 year, are shown in Table 5.4. To put these scores in context, the clinical cutoff point for each measure is presented where available, along with the means of Ms. V, the other patient described here, and the TFP group means at both those time points. As can be seen, relative to other patients in the TFP group, J's scores were more impaired in a variety of areas. Specifically, on the primary aggression symptom scores, J presented with higher levels on the irritability score (J = 1.91; TFP M = 1.79); verbal assault score (J = 2.44; TFP M = 1.58); the direct assault score (J = 1.00; TFP M = .68); and the nonplanning component of the Barratt Factor 3 impulsivity score (J = 23.00; TFP M = 21.38).

On the secondary symptom scores, J was more impaired in social functioning, as reflected in her two social adjustment scores (on the GAF scale [J = 40.00; TFP M = 51.82] and on the SAS scale[1] [J = 7.00; TFP M = 4.53]). Also J was more depressed (J = 55.00; TFP M = 42.17).

Consistent with these scores, J evidenced many of the clinical features characteristic of patients with BPD: emotional instability, behavioral instability, relational instability, and identity instability (or identity diffusion). In fact, on a structured diagnostic interview for personality disorders (IPDE; Loranger, 1999) the clinician confirmed the presence of all nine of the *DSM-IV* criteria for BPD. She additionally met criteria for narcissistic personality disorder (NPD; 7 of 9 symptoms endorsed) and for avoidant personality disorder (APD; 4 of 7 symptoms endorsed).

In terms of primary outcome domains, J had a history of episodes in which she would self-injure in the context of chronic suicidal ideation that included a combination of despair and anger. Although J did not present with active suicidal behavior in the month prior to the initial assessment on the OAS-M, she did present with some self-injurious behaviors in the form of superficially cutting her arms. J's elevated aggression scores in Table 5.4 were reflected in instances of verbal anger and irritability toward strangers (e.g., angrily accusing people she encountered such as salespeople, bus drivers, and security officers of being rude to her, sometimes filing complaints that seemed to be based on very little). Moreover, given that the time period evaluated was over the prior month, during which she had been shut in her apartment, her aggression measures were thought to underestimate her capacity for verbal aggression.

In terms of measures of attachment organization, which are thought to be specifically targeted in TFP (Levy et al., 2006), J presented on the Adult Attachment

---

1. On this measure, higher scores reflect more impairment.

Table 5.4 Comparison of the Scores of the TFP Group and Ms. V and Ms. J

Measure	Clinical Cutoff Point	TFP Mean at Intake	TFP Mean at 1 Year	Ms. J at Intake	Ms. J at 1 Year	Ms. V at Intake	Ms. V at 1 Year
			PRIMARY OUTCOME				
Suicidality	na	week: 1.07 month: 2.15	week: 0.64 month: 1.00	week: 2.00 month: 2.00	week: 0.00 month: 3.00	week: 0 month: 1.00	week: 0 month: 0.00
Anger	na	week: 12.43 month: 54.19	week: 9.41 month: 26.50	week: 9.00 month: 42.00	week: 1.00 month: 13.00	week: 0.00 month: 12.00	week: 6.00 month: 18.00
Irritability	na	1.79	1.57	1.91	1.36	0.91	1.55
Verbal Assault	na	1.58	1.31	2.44	1.11	2.22	2.11
Direct Assault	na	0.68	0.69	1.00	0.80	0.60	0.60
Barratt Factor 1 Impulsivity: Attention	na	29.65	28.82	24.00	25.00	21.00	25.00
Barratt Factor 2 Impulsivity: Motor/Acting Without Thinking	na	13.76	12.04	8.00	8.00	14.00	12.00
Barratt Factor 3 Impulsivity: Non-Planning	na	21.38	20.22	23.00	18.00	20.00	10.00

Table 5.4 CONTINUED

Measure	Clinical Cutoff Point	TFP Mean at Intake	TFP Mean at 1 Year	Ms. J at Intake	Ms. J at 1 Year	Ms. V at Intake	Ms. V at 1 Year
			SECONDARY OUTCOME				
Anxiety	1.5	1.64	1.16	1.33	0.67	2.83	0.50
Depression	14	42.17	35.27	55.00	26.00	54.00	27.00
GAF Social Adjustment	70	51.82	60.38	40.00	45.00	50.00	60.00
SAS Social Adjustment	na	4.53	4.04	7.00	5.00	5.00	3.00
			STRUCTURAL MEASURES				
Reflective Functioning	5	2.81	4.11	-1.00	6.00	3.00	3.00
Coherence of Narrative	5	2.93	4.02	1.50	4.00	2.50	3.00

NOTE: Lower scores indicate less impairment, except for GAF Social Adjustment, Reflective Functioning, and Narrative Coherence, which are the reverse. For citations on the scales, see Tables 5.2 and 5.3.

Interview (AAI) with the attachment style labeled "Cannot Classify" (CC). The name of the CC category is deceptive, in that it implies a style that could not otherwise be specified, when in fact the CC style is distinctive in its vacillations between contradictory or competing attachment patterns. In the context of her narrative of attachment relationships, J was observed to swing between a preoccupied style of angry and entangled descriptions that suggested a lack of distance from these early experiences, and a dismissive style in which attachment relationships were discussed in devaluing and derogatory terms. These were often not supported by examples that might flesh out the reasons for her contempt. The dramatic swings in the narrative—from needy and overinvolved to distant and unconcerned—resulted in little coherence overall (as reflected in her narrative coherence score of 1.5).

The AAI was also evaluated for the level of reflective functioning (RF; Fonagy et al., 1998), which assesses the capacity for mentalization with regard to attachment relationships. As shown in Table 5.4, J's interview was rated a –1, which is the lowest score allowable on the interview. When the measure was initially developed, +1 was the lowest score allowable and reflected a disavowal of reflection on relationships (e.g., "I have absolutely no idea why my mother would do that, not a clue"). However, Fonagy and colleagues found that when seeking to apply the scale to a forensic sample they observed an even more dramatic type of disavowal of reflection in which the very act of being asked to reflect on the mental states of attachment figures was experienced as a hostile affront (e.g., "How dare you ask me why my mother would do that, only a monster parading around like a psychologist would ask such a thing"). J evidenced many instances of these kinds of antireflective statements in which the very act of clarifying attachment experiences on the part of the interviewer was experienced as an intrusive aggression.

The initial stages of TFP involve not only diagnostic and attachment interviews but also a structural interview (Kernberg, 1985) that evaluates the level of integration of the patient's internal representations of self affectively related to others. J said at one point in the structural interview that she had never had sexual relations, and at another point that she considered herself promiscuous. While clarification led to understanding that she considered herself promiscuous in her fantasy life, it was clear that J's sense of self was characterized by identity diffusion—her self-perception fluctuated according to how she felt about herself internally at a given moment, rather than a stable sense of self anchored in the realities of her external life. This assessment by the therapist, although not coded or categorized by a rating scale by the therapist, was consistent with the ratings shown in Table 5.4 made by independent coders based on a separate independent assessment, including the aforementioned reflective functioning score (Clinical Norm = 5; TFP = 2.81; J = –1.50) and narrative coherence score (Clinical Norm = 5; TFP = 2.93; J = –1.50).

In terms of treatment history, J had three brief psychiatric hospitalizations. J's past outpatient therapists and pharmacologists most often diagnosed her as bipolar, and she had had many trials of neuroleptics, antidepressants, anxiolytics, and mood stabilizers; she was on a mood stabilizer with questionable efficacy when she began TFP. A diagnostic assessment indicated that her affective instability was characterized by dramatic shifts in mood that were short lived and context driven, with no indication of persistent mood episodes, necessitating a change of diagnosis from bipolar to borderline personality disorder.

Despite these challenges, J also evidenced a number of strengths. J was clearly intelligent and articulate; her interpersonal difficulties in occupational and academic settings seemed to be in spite of her possessing genuine skills. Furthermore, J was also motivated for treatment; despite reticence about her therapist's capacity and intention to help her, she clearly wanted to improve her mood, relationships, and work functioning.

Ms. J's Formulation and Treatment Plan

J presented with a combination of labile emotions, intense negative affects, identity diffusion, and primitive defenses (e.g., projection) that indicated both a diagnosis of BPD and a poor level of integration in the patient's internal representational world. Narcissistic features were also present in a chronic devaluing and contemptuous stance toward others despite the patient's failure to succeed in the very same areas in life that were the focus of her criticism (e.g., calling others "losers" for not achieving more occupationally).

In formulating a treatment plan, TFP utilizes a hierarchy of priorities that first emphasizes the safety of the patient and, secondly, emphasizes the stability of the continuing treatment. Despite a past history of self-injury in the context of suicidal ideation, at the start of treatment her suicidal ideation, although chronic, was passive and of low intensity.

While vigilant for changes in her mental status that might put her safety at risk, the therapist planned to focus primarily on aspects of the patient's presentation that were most likely to impede her utilization of the treatment and her achieving higher levels of occupational and relational functioning. In this regard the therapist was most impressed with the level of aggressive affect that J consistently attributed to others. Her hostile attributions led to accusatory and inflammatory behaviors that had toxic effects in all past work, academic, and relationship contexts. Furthermore, aggressive affect was observed to be manifesting in the treatment almost immediately, with responses of condescension and contempt to relatively benign questions by the therapist. Whereas her emerging anger and mistrust toward the therapist presented a risk to the continuity of the treatment, from a TFP perspective it also created an important opportunity in that the patient's core dynamic was activated in the immediate experience of the therapist, and therefore subject to reflection and modification.

Furthermore, the therapist's formulation of J's aggressive affect also included its potential protective function—her pervasive anger precluded experiencing and metabolizing other emotional experiences that may have been too painful to experience. With so many lost relationships and squandered opportunities in her past, J had much to mourn; however, her pervasive anger seemed to keep potential sadness, regret, and shame at bay, with periodic but intense surges of despair in the form of suicidality. That is, her unrelenting anger created an obstacle to her understanding and effectively acting on a wider repertoire of emotions.

The therapist hoped that working with the patient's narratives of her experiences of herself in relation to others, in combination with her way of experiencing the relationship with him, would help her become more aware of the full range of her affects and more able to incorporate them into an integrated and harmonious identity.

The treatment plan was for twice-weekly TFP for 1 year. After the diagnostic assessment, the therapist provided the patient with a layman's description of his diagnostic impression and then went on to discuss the treatment contract. The therapist's discussion of the diagnosis with the patient represents a psychoeducational element of TFP. It is considered necessary to have some common ground in the therapist's and patient's understanding of the latter's difficulties in order to have a meaningful discussion of the rationale for the treatment that will be recommended. The therapist first explained that we can think of personality in general as the spontaneous ways a person thinks and feels about himself/herself and others and the ways he/she spontaneously reacts to events in life. The therapist further described personalities as encompassing a broad range of personality traits and styles (e.g., introverted versus extraverted). He went on to explain that we think of a personality disorder when an individual's personality traits are (1) extreme and (2) inflexible in a way that does not permit successful adaptation to different life circumstances. With this broad concept of personality disorder in mind, he specified that the diagnosis that he felt best characterized her—borderline personality disorder (BPD)—involved difficulties in four areas: (1) emotions, which are experienced intensely and are rapidly shifting, (2) relationships, which tend to be characterized by confusion and conflicts, (3) behaviors, such as cutting in her case, that are an attempt to discharge distressing affects states, and (4) an underlying confusion and lack of clarity about her sense of self. He explained that this last characteristic of BPD is often the central problem in that the lack of a coherent identity can lead to a desperate sense of emptiness, difficulty in contextualizing and modulating affects, and confusion in a person's position in life and in relation to others. This discussion of diagnosis is essential to see if the patient will join the therapist in considering that her problems have a significant psychological component (in contrast, for example, with the view that the problem is exclusively biologically determined). J said that this understanding of her difficulties made sense to her.

With regard to the contract, in addition to the general requirements of treatment regarding attendance and participation in therapy, the therapist discussed parameters around self-destructive behaviors, which includes clear communications about the patient's responsibility for her own behaviors, as well as expectations of limiting the use of hospital visits to only the most acute crises. Another one of the first conditions of treatment was to become involved in a regularly scheduled activity. Although providing specific directives around participating in work or other structured activities is not usually associated with psychodynamic treatments, in our experience many patients with BPD often function below their occupational capacity, and this is often motivated by fear of interpersonal conflicts in such settings and/or the shame of working in a diminished role as evidence of their having not thrived in life. At the time of assessment, J was avoiding life as a way of avoiding her shame, and this left her so socially isolated that addressing her experience of self in relation to others in the treatment would be of limited value. Therefore, part of the treatment-planning process involved coming to an agreement about what structured activities would be appropriate to increase the patient's level of functioning. The therapist explained to her that attending therapy sessions without any active engagement with others (the patient had been living a very isolated life) would likely be a sterile endeavor. J's initial response was that she could not work with others because they were prejudiced toward her and always rejected her. The therapist explained that he understood the interactions would be difficult but that one of the functions of the therapy sessions would be to explore and understand the difficulties she experienced interacting with others. J then found a part-time volunteer position tutoring high school students.

Ms. J's Course of Therapy
Early Phase of TFP Therapy, Sessions 1 to 24: From 1 to 3 Months
In the early stages of TFP, the therapist works to clarify the patient's experience of the self in relation to others and the accompanying affect (or the object relational dyad), both in external relationships and inside sessions with the therapist. From the first session, J's interactions with her therapist were characterized by a nonstop monologue that overrode any attempt he might make to speak. His initial attempts at intervention were to try to clarify the role of the patient in relation to the therapist in such moments. That is, her verbal domination had the effect of putting her in control, in response to which the therapist found himself feeling helpless. Thus, the dominant affects for each of them were frustration and muted anger. After being immersed in this experience for over a month, he began to direct her attention to this behavior, offered a description of it, and wondered with her what might motivate this controlling way of interacting. This interchange comes from the twelfth session.

T: It might help to look at the style of communication that's developed in these sessions.

J: I don't know what you're talking about.

T: You're telling me a lot of things, but there's a particular style you have of talking here.

J: So what?

T: It might help us understand something about how you feel about yourself and about others.

J: What do you mean?

T: Would you agree that you tend to talk nonstop here without leaving me much room to participate?

J: You told me to say everything on my mind—are you contradicting yourself now?

T: It's true that you're doing what I suggested, but there might be something to learn about how you're doing it.

J: What do you mean?

T: Would it surprise you to hear that the way you talk so rapidly and without stopping leaves me feeling a little "pinned down"?

J: "Pinned down"?

T: Yes, like it's hard for me to participate, like I'm under a kind of control of yours.

J: That sounds like your problem.

T: It could be, but it involves you. I just wonder what would lead to your talking in a way that leads to this feeling of control . . .

J: (bursting into tears) If I didn't control you, you'd leave me . . . like everyone else!

In this way, J began to reflect on the interaction she was displaying with her therapist. Such interventions brought into focus two object relational patterns. The first was what was visible on the surface: the patient rigidly controlling her therapist. The second was deeper—that of the abandoner and the abandonee. After describing J's controlling behavior in a way that brought it to her awareness, the therapist began to become more aware of a subtle level of the interaction suggesting the longing for a relationship—a positive connection with desire for connection of a still unspecified nature (partly parental, partly friendly, partly romantic) that emerged at times in the tone of the interaction between them and that had been largely kept from view because of her controlling behavior. J's anxiety about this possibility (feeling attached) seemed to motivate the controlling behavior since it was connected with the assumption of rejection. Starting in the third month of therapy, the therapist began a process of repeated clarification of this dynamic in the context of the therapeutic relationship. He would point out the hidden longing for connection, which J tentatively agreed with, and her pattern of responding to it by a controlling or rejecting gesture toward him. In the third to sixth month of therapy, J was able to access the longing for attachment and fear of abandonment that fueled her angry and controlling behavior, and she was able to begin to take a reflective stance in relation to her view of the therapist.

As a TFP treatment progresses, the therapist slowly works toward confronting discrepancies within the patient's experience of self, as well as disparities between how the patient views himself or herself and acts in the world (including with the therapist). As previously noted, although J experienced herself as victim to the hostility and prejudices of others, she struggled to see and acknowledge how aggressive her condemnations of others could be. In sessions, this could take the form of her refrain that therapy was not helping and she may as well jump out the window. Outside of therapy it was reflected in actions such as threatening to report a security guard to her apartment building's administration, and thus endangering his job, because she felt he had been rude to her. As the treatment progressed and J became more aware of her need to control the therapist out of fear of his abandoning her, the therapist began to gently confront J with the fact that it was she—not the therapist—who was placing distance between them as they worked to form an alliance; that of the two of them she appeared to be the one who was on the verge of becoming fed up and leaving.

Although discrepant with her self-experience and its accompanying anxiety, she was intrigued by such observations and began occasionally to notice that while she often complained of others treating her harshly and rejecting her, she could treat others, including her therapist, in a similar way. In TFP terms, she became aware of oscillations within a dyad involving a critical abandoning person and the abandoned object of criticism. For example: "I guess I see now that when I say you're useless and that I may as well jump out the window, that I'm being hard on you and threatening to end the relation. Before I thought it was just telling you how bad I felt." Thus, in the initial months of therapy, J began to consider not only that her attributions regarding the therapist might not be accurate, but also that she could behave in the rejecting way she had experienced him behaving toward her. This was the beginning of her understanding of how she may project aggressive affects within her onto others; that experiences of anger that she felt to be happening in the external world may, in fact, be driven by her own internal world.

Middle Phase of TFP Therapy, Sessions 25 to 72: From 3 Months to 9 Months; and End Phase, Sessions 73 to 100, From 9 Months and Beyond
The phases of TFP overlap to some degree. Early-phase issues might still recur at points after middle-phase issues, like exploring oscillations of internal dyads, has begun. In the middle phase of TFP, the therapist begins to actively interpret the function of oscillations between dyads as experienced in the relationship with the therapist. The therapist begins to evaluate the motivation for the patient's rigid adherence to pathological patterns despite the damage caused to relationships and life goals. In a session 6 months into the treatment, J started as she often had by talking in a challenging and controlling way. However, building on the work they had done up to that point, her therapist was able to help her more quickly get to the point of reflecting on the interaction and considering emotional aspects of the situation against which she had been defending. She began by stating that she had been feeling suicidal and had taken "a lot of pills." After conducting an assessment and feeling assured that her safety was not at risk, the therapist tried to understand the affective and relational context of her suicidal gesture. In response, J said, "My wanting to kill myself has nothing to do with your going away." (The therapist was about to leave for 10 days.) The therapist pointed out that J's critical and controlling discourse might be related to a sense of humiliation if she was convinced he did not care about her, while there was indirect evidence that he and the therapy were important to her.

J: You say the same thing to every one of your patients! I'm not like all of them!

T: That's a powerful statement. It seems that you feel here like you're an object on an assembly line.

J: [with sudden change from anger to sadness]: I don't feel that I deserve to be here . . . [covering her face with her hands]. I just feel badly that I have to walk around with other human beings. . . .

T: I think you don't want me to see you in the longing that you feel. You don't mind if I see you in your anger and your rejection of me. You don't want me to see the longing, because you think I'll just use that to humiliate you, by rejecting, by turning away from you.(The therapist then suggested that her fear of rejection could explain the off-putting way in which she interacted—she might induce rejection to feel she controlled it.)

J: You mean because I think that rejection is inevitable I try to confirm it, like by dressing this way [she typically dressed in an unkempt way]? I just feel like the tragedy of everything, of all of this, is that I have help available. . . . You're actually working with me . . .

An essential element of TFP is picking up on evidence of emotions that appear either at separate moments in time from the more predominant emotions, or that are communicated through the nonverbal or countertransference channels of communication in contrast to direct verbal communication. For example, despite her hostile and rejecting verbalizations, J communicated her deep commitment to the treatment through consistently and punctually attending appointments, giving significant thought to what the therapist said between sessions, and displaying apparent upset at his impending departure for a vacation.

In terms of the therapist's countertransference, his internal emotional experience of her, despite J's hostility, was a warm and a genuine interest in working with her and a feeling of commitment to and concern about her struggles. From this vantage point, the disparity between what she said with words and what she conveyed in behavior and evoked within the therapist became a meaningful point of intervention.

Interpretation of the motivations for the split between the idealized and persecutory segments of her mind helped to resolve her identity diffusion and bring about a coherent sense of self. J came to the understanding that she harbored an intense longing for the perfect caretaker/companion in life (the idealized segment) and that any failure in others' responses to her was perceived by her as harsh rejection and attack (the persecutory segment). She further came to understand that the attack she saw as coming from others corresponded to the aggressive response she experienced (but consciously denied) toward others when they disappointed her. As J shifted from talking about wanting to kill herself to what she was feeling toward her therapist, she moved from a dyadic interaction imbued with negative affect that served defensive purposes (an internalized critical other rejecting an unworthy abandoned self) to a dyad imbued with care and dependency. She was beginning to become aware of the part of her internal world that consisted of a harsh angry voice and was a condensation of aspects of her fiery temperament and internalized experiences of criticism and rejection as she was growing up. She was also becoming aware of a part of her internal world that longed for an ideal loving connection. She continued, "I guess there's a longing in a way, 'cause I did come on time, I didn't really want to come, but I do long to come here, in a way, I guess I do.... I remember this boy in high school. I never thought he'd speak to me. One day ..."

J's relinquishing her chronic, defensive, belligerent stance can be understood in relation to her having begun to reflect on negative affects she had consistently projected onto others. This process of reflection helped her see that the negative affects in relation to others—affects that had dominated her life for years—were not the whole story. Her therapist helped her understand that, in addition to existing in their own right, these negative affects protected her from an even more distressing prospect: the hopeless experience of having and then losing positive affects through rejection. J came to understand and acknowledge that, in fact, she very badly wanted to experience closeness and connection with others, but the fear of having and then losing intimacy led her to rage at the forgone conclusion of its loss. This awareness, in turn, allowed her to experience other, more positive and nuanced states of mind with regard to her therapist. In place of her extreme reactions based on the projection of the image of a powerful but indifferent and rejecting other, she could begin to see that he had genuine concern for her even if it did not correspond to her wish for a perfect caretaker who could perceive and take care of her every need.

En route to integration of the positive and negative mental representations of self and others, the TFP therapist is often alert to shifts in these representations, which may manifest as idealization of previously devalued others (and vice versa). With regard to intimate and sexual relations, while J had previously eschewed relationships with men, whom she expected to be predatory and rejecting, she began an early period of being attracted to narcissistic, unavailable men. She would initially idealize these men, as they idealized themselves, which precluded the development of deeper and more intimate relationships.

A subtle parallel process also began to emerge in the treatment, with J's erotic transference to the therapist suggested in moments of seductive posture toward him, although only rarely verbalized. When acknowledged, J's mention of sexual feelings toward the therapist alternated between an initial excitement followed by shame and a sense of danger. The therapist helped her to appreciate the multiple meanings and functions of her sexual feelings: On the one hand, she was beginning to allow herself to experience feelings of intimacy and vulnerability with the therapist that she had previously denied, while, on the other hand, she was doing this yet again with an unavailable man (the therapist) who could not respond to her wishes on that level. This awareness allowed her to begin to appreciate experiences of intimacy between herself and others in more nuanced and realistic terms.

The termination process with Ms. J is described later in this chapter in the section on her therapy outcome.

Ms. V's Negative-Outcome Therapy: Assessment, Formulation, and Course

ASSESSMENT OF MS. V'S PROBLEMS, GOALS, STRENGTHS, AND HISTORY PRESENTING PROBLEMS

V was a 33-year-old single Caucasian woman who presented for TFP by her outpatient psychotherapist. V had been unemployed for some time and depended on medical disability benefits. V led a very limited life. She lived in a subsidized apartment, spent time reading, and occasionally writing poetry. She had a history of alcohol abuse and attended two AA meetings each week. She had a boyfriend but reported regular conflicts with him. She was alienated from her family of origin. For 10 years, since the age of 23, the patient's activities centered on the hospital associated with the RCT. She was always in some form of treatment there, moving from inpatient stays for suicidal ideation, to the partial hospital program, to every form of individual and group therapy that the hospital offered. She also had trials of every type of antidepressant and antianxiety medication with little benefit.

In the first evaluation session, V responded to the therapist's question about why she was seeking treatment by calmly responding that she had "refractory depression." This surprised the therapist, because the outpatient staff had referred her to TFP for treatment because of their impression that she had a severe personality disorder.

History

V was the product of a volatile marriage that ended in divorce when she was 15 years old. Her parents were both physically aggressive with her as well as with each other, and at a young age she was exposed to their sexual improprieties that eventually led to the marriage dissolving. She also reported instances of physical abuse from her older brother, to which her parents turned a blind eye. As a result, she described often feeling in a heightened state of vigilance and terror, a feeling she began to numb with alcohol in her late teens. However, at the start of treatment she had maintained abstinence from alcohol for a number of years.

BPD Features

At intake, there appeared to be a discrepancy between V's self-report on the standardized measures and the clinician's assessment of V's functioning. Upon initial evaluation on a structured diagnostic interview for personality disorders (IPDE; Loranger, 1999), the clinician diagnosed V with BPD (six of nine symptoms endorsed). She additionally met criteria for antisocial personality disorder (ASPD; seven of seven symptoms plus two conduct specifiers endorsed) and for avoidant personality disorder (APD; five of seven symptoms endorsed).

In contrast, on the standardized measures shown in Table 5.4 and relative to the TFP mean, V presented with a lower level on the suicidality measure (for the past week, $V = 0$; TFP $M = 1.07$; for the past month, $V = 1.00$; TFP $M = 2.15$); a lower score on anger (V = 12; TFP M = 54.9); a lower score on irritability (V = .91, TFP M = 1.79); and a lower score on direct assaultive behavior (V = .60; TFP M = .68).

On the other hand, V did have a higher score on verbal assault (V = 2.22; TFP M = 1.58), presenting instances in her clinical interview of verbal anger and irritability, primarily toward her boyfriend (e.g., yelling at him in public places or storming out of restaurants in the course of a meal).

In terms of impulsivity on the Barratt factors, V endorsed difficulties on a par with the TFP average in the areas of motor/acting without thinking and nonplanning. Overall, it should be noted that the vast majority of her social contacts in the period prior to treatment were either with her outpatient providers or her boyfriend—V's functioning was otherwise too impoverished to be having interactions because of the potential for conflict.

In terms of measures of attachment organization, V presented on the AAI with a Dismissive attachment style. She tended to discuss attachment relationships with a sparseness that left attributions of herself and others, including vaguely positive and negative statements, without substantiation. Of note, despite being both exposed to and the victim of terrifying violence throughout her childhood, she discussed these events with a cool detachment that excluded any sense of her affective experience.

The AAI was also evaluated for the level of reflective functioning (see Table 5.4) and V scored a 3 (on a scale of –1 to 9, with a clinical cutoff of 5), which represents concrete or canned attributions of mental states. For example, after reporting her parents being physically abusive toward each other, and turning a blind eye to her brother's physical abuse toward her, when asked to reflect on why her "parents acted as they did when you were a child" she responded, "It was the people they were, they were doing the best they could as they were. Um, it was the forces that shaped their lives . . . " Unlike the antireflective refusals to consider mental states seen at the lowest points of the reflective functioning scale, in this naïve/simplistic type of reflective functioning, broad generalities of what motivates all people (and therefore not these parents in particular) are the focus of attributions. For V this seemed to function to disavow knowledge of how her parents could have been capable of enacting cruelty on each other and not protected her from the same.

In the initial assessment, despite her low level of occupational and relational functioning, V also evidenced a number of strengths. Her commitment to abstinence and regularly attending AA suggested an ability to set and carry through on treatment goals. Furthermore, V was a bright woman who appeared to have genuine artistic talents in both writing and music, and derived enjoyment from practicing her art. She expressed frustration at not having been able to actualize her artistic dreams, and she appeared motivated to find ways to bring her musical and literary goals to fruition.

Ms. V's Formulation and Treatment Plan

In formulating the case, it was notable that V's mood did not appear depressed, and after a thorough evaluation the therapist concluded that she had BPD as well as comorbid narcissistic personality disorder (NPD) with antisocial traits. This diagnosis was based, among other things, on the therapist's observation that the patient's history of depression seemed related to a discrepancy between her image of what her life should be like (a famous musician) and her lack of success in life—a state that she attributed to depression but that actually was more a cause of her depressed state.

Furthermore, the therapist observed that there seemed to be no medically valid barrier to V working and thus no indication that her disability status was valid. Whereas her borderline and narcissistic personality traits created anxiety and tension in her interactions with others, our experience in TFP is that a patient's "real-time" experience of interactions provides important material for the therapy sessions and that, in turn, working on this material in therapy can help the patient change the anxious and conflicted responses to others that he or she traditionally experienced.

A significant impediment to V's working was her narcissistic attitude that she should not have to participate in work that she considered "average," which she was told her job was. Notably, while V was reluctant to concur explicitly with this assessment, she communicated in many ways that she felt entitled to her disability benefit not because she saw herself as an incapacitated person but because she had felt severely wronged in her life and deserving of compensation. She did not view her benefits as transitional income while attempting to "get back on her feet," but rather, given that she had for many years supported herself with these benefits and would continue to do so for the foreseeable future, viewed them as her right. She evidenced no remorse for past exploitative use of social welfare and treatment systems.

V was randomly assigned to the TFP condition. In accordance with the TFP model, the therapist discussed his diagnostic impressions with the patient. Clinicians are commonly reluctant to share personality disorder diagnoses with patients (and this is especially so with BPD, NPD, and ASPD), often out of fear that the patient will experience the diagnosis as invalidating or inflammatory. However, from a TFP perspective not only is it important to come to a shared understanding of the nature of the pathology, but also in our experience patients often feel validated by a clear explication of their internal processes. The therapist explained to V that while he did not question that she experienced depressed moods, such moods can stem from different sources. He shared his impression that she experienced a gap in her mind between the person she would like to be, that she felt she deserved to be, and the realities of her life.

V's depressed moods and difficulty functioning were contextualized in terms of moments in which she felt too in touch with having fallen short of aspirations and recognitions of which she felt deserving. V was willing to consider the new personality disorder diagnoses; though wary, she felt it better captured her experience and sounded less hopeless than "refractory depression." In a similar way, the therapist described the elements of BPD in her clinical picture as manifestations of an underlying lack of clarity about her identity and sense of self, which left her subject to anxiety and depression about the course of her life. Furthermore, her difficulty internally processing and modulating painful affects led to them often being acted out behaviorally, which resulted in instability in her relationships.

An essential early intervention in TFP is the contract-setting process, during which the general conditions of treatment are articulated and agreed upon. Because the manner in which the terms of the treatment plan are negotiated often become emblematic of the relational patterns of focus in the treatment, the treatment contracting process in TFP is often longer than other treatments (usually 2–5 sessions). In addition to discussing expectations within sessions (consistently attending, arriving on time, speaking without censoring, etc.), expectations about the ways in which the patient will work toward increasing his or her level of functioning outside of sessions were also discussed. What was striking about V, as with many patients with BPD, was the degree to which she seemed to be underfunctioning relative to her intelligence and capabilities. Essentially, she had been functioning as a professional patient for the past decade, despite being an artistically talented woman who was clearly capable of more. However, when the therapist discussed the need for her to engage in some form of work or study in conjunction with treatment, V vehemently responded that any such activity would lead to relapsing into a depressed state that would destroy any progress she had made and could threaten her life.

During the contract-setting process the TFP therapist does not necessarily have the expectation that the requirements of treatment will be immediately agreed upon and subsequently adhered to. In fact, the patient's ambivalence about agreeing to or complying with treatment expectations often provides an essential window into the patient's experience of the self as affectively related to others (i.e., the "object relational" dyad). In response to the expectation of structured activity, V saw herself as potentially harmed, and in fact the therapist's initial countertransferential reaction to her was to feel guilty for proposing a condition of treatment that could harm her. However, after internally reviewing the basis for his diagnostic impressions and assessment of her capacity to work, he felt confident that structured activity was necessary to increase her level of functioning: something like a part-time job or volunteer job or enrolling in college classes. From that vantage point, he could see that a pattern seemed to be emerging, in which the patient saw herself as victim to the therapist's harmful behaviors and attitudes. However, the therapist was also aware that when V vehemently rejected the notion of structured activity that he brought up in the contract-setting sessions, she did it in a menacing way, and the therapist was afraid that she would leave treatment. Yet, for V, the notion of herself as aggressor, as opposed to victim, appeared to be outside of her immediate awareness.

Another major goal of the contract-setting process in TFP is to address any areas of secondary gain, that is, benefits that the patient derives from symptoms that may serve to undermine treatment goals. In discussions of increasing her level of structured activity, not only did it become clear that V feared that her increased functioning might threaten the stability of her medical disability benefits and subsidized housing, but also that she felt entitled to this support and saw others (e.g., the therapist, the government) as trying to steal what was rightfully hers. A dyadic interaction seemed to be emerging in which V saw the world along the lines of predator and prey, leading to an attitude that you need to take what you must to survive; "don't let what's yours be stolen from you."

Accordingly, the therapist proceeded with the discussion of the need for her to work, now very attentive to V's attempt to safeguard the secondary gains of her illness. As he continued to discuss active engagement in a structured activity, he reminded her that the decision to enter into this treatment was up to her, and that alternately he could refer her to a less intensive maintenance therapy for people with chronic conditions who did not have the potential to get better in significant ways, as she had received at the hospital in the past (to no benefit). He reminded her that the treatment they were discussing was an intensive treatment geared to people who had the potential for significant change, including increased autonomy and better functioning. This discussion seemed to appeal to the part of the patient that wished to have a more productive life and not to give in to the passive dependency wishes that went along with her narcissistic disappointment in life. The therapist's reasons for recommending this RCT included the fact that these treatments have been shown to help people with severe personality disorders, and TFP in particular has been shown to help patients change from a borderline to a more integrated personality structure, with a corresponding improvement in the ability to function and find some measure of satisfaction in work and love. His reasons also included the fact that V appeared to be intelligent and articulate.

Even so, the nature of V's goals remained unclear. Therefore, the therapist continued the discussion of the treatment contract, which included coming to an agreement about treatment goals. As the discussion continued, V stated that she would like to become autonomous. However, the therapist was not sure if this was a sincere wish or if she was stating it in order to have treatment. Deciding to take the patient at her word, he continued with the discussion of what kind of engagement in an activity would be in line with the patient's interest and serve a therapeutic purpose. The notion of finding an activity that corresponds to an interest of the patient can be a step in addressing and working on the identity diffusion that characterizes patients organized at a borderline level. In the treatment contract-setting phase of the therapy, after a discussion that lasted two sessions, in which the patient began by proposing unsubstantial activities such as helping out at the neighborhood girls' basketball practice on Saturday afternoon, the patient and therapist came to an agreement that the patient would enroll in two classes at the local community college to improve her computer skills.

Ms. V's Course of Therapy

The early phase of therapy was characterized by difficulty engaging the patient in observing and reflecting on her interpersonal patterns and on her experience of self as affectively related to others, including aspects of the interaction with the therapist. In one of the first sessions after the treatment moved from the contracting phase to the therapy itself, the therapist tried to bring the patient's attention to how reactions she may be having to him might have an influence on her feelings, thoughts, and behaviors. The therapist, having just returned from a week's absence, suggested: "Although you say the session before my going away 'just slipped your mind,' I wonder if the fact that I was going to be away may have had an impact on how you were feeling." V responded very defensively: "I don't want to go there. I had an earlier therapist who thought that everything I thought and did was related to her and it got very messy. I started thinking about her too much and everything got worse. We had to end that therapy." The therapist was disappointed to encounter this level of resistance to working within the transference and kept in mind that any references to issues and feelings that emerged between them would have to be proposed with utmost tact.

In TFP, the therapist remains continually attentive to threats to a continued and productive treatment, which may include enactments in the transference that make the experience of the treatment either unproductive or intolerable for the patient. It was unclear what got "messy" for V in her last treatment, and she made clear her intentions not to elaborate, but the therapist wondered if a relationship reflecting intolerably painful attachment experiences in the past came to be replicated in the relationship with the prior therapist. The current therapist was eager to discuss that prior therapist's experience with the patient, in order not to replicate interventions or ways of relating to V that had previously been unsuccessful. However, after obtaining V's consent to contact the previous therapist, that therapist never returned his calls. Although it remained unclear what happened in the therapeutic relationship in her past treatment, what was striking was the degree to which V denied any emerging attachment relationship in the present treatment. V displayed a generally dismissive and devaluing attitude toward the therapist. When he tried to draw the patient's attention and curiosity to this, she responded regularly: "You're a means to an end. You're like my dentist. I go to him for specific help and I'm coming here for specific help. What I feel isn't the issue, and I don't feel much about you anyway."

The therapist believed that understanding these dismissive and distancing reactions to him was crucial to understanding V's relational problems in external relationships. V often vacillated between volatility and avoidance in relationships, but she externalized all responsibility for these difficulties to others, whom she saw as unfairly critical and manipulative of her. For example, she often felt exploited by the people in her AA group because they gave her too many tasks and responsibilities. The therapist heard echoes of their therapeutic relationship in these concerns, because he also imposed on her tasks and responsibilities that were likely evoking similarly negative affects, but she was adamant in wanting to keep the focus on her life outside the therapy. Although there is value in noting patterns in external relationships, the most progress in understanding, according to TFP, generally comes from experiencing, observing, and reflecting on the patterns as they emerge "live" in the treatment. However, V shut down that process of exploration in ways that precluded the type of "here-and-now" examination that is the core of TFP and is believed to lead to change and growth. Instead, V kept the focus on "extra-transferential" relations and issues, expressing the concern that she was barely able to manage somewhat superficial relationships in AA meetings and her classes.

In hindsight, this too paralleled her relationship to the therapist, which she kept superficial and hanging by a thread. V completed the 1 year of the RCT. Despite her experience in her classes that others did not like her and were unfair to her, she completed her course work and was able to start a clerical job in which she could use the computer skills she had learned. However, her therapist continued to have the impression that she was holding onto this job "by a thread," both because in this setting she again felt exploited, and because her commitment to her occupational development seemed tenuous. V was dismissive of the therapist's efforts to understand this pervasive feeling of exploitation. He noted that perhaps this feeling seemed to show up in every context because she carried it within her, and that if they could address the feeling of exploitation inside the therapy, she would be able to function better in outside settings. V was also dismissive of successfully completing her coursework and getting a job, which were viewed not as personal or professional accomplishments but rather as demands imposed upon her with which she resentfully complied. The gap between her significant, creative talents and her minimal functioning at work was again discussed, but met with frustration that she had "checked the box" asked of her by the therapist in getting a job, and therefore she could not understand why he was pushing her on her functioning at work.

The termination process with Ms. V is described later in the chapter in the section on her therapy outcome.

Therapy Monitoring and Use of Feedback Information

The therapists attended weekly supervision group meetings. Traditional clinical supervision was augmented by the use of the TFP Rating of the Therapist Adherence and Competence Instrument. This instrument rates the therapist's adherence to the basic principles and techniques of TFP, such as setting up and maintaining the treatment contract and appropriate use of the techniques of clarification, confrontation, interpretation, technical neutrality, and the use of countertransference.

Therapists took turns presenting video recordings of sessions to the cell leader, Otto Kernberg, as well as to peers. Kernberg and other therapists commented on material presented in the videotapes, and all participants completed the adherence instrument forms. These forms were used both to monitor therapist compliance and to aid in providing supervision, especially by Kernberg and other senior therapists (e.g., Frank Yeomans). Therapists were alerted if they deviated from adherence to the treatment model. Additional individual supervision was available if the therapist appeared to deviate from the treatment model for more than two sessions.

Concluding Evaluation of the Therapy's Process and Outcome

Ms. J's Positive Outcome and Therapy Process

On the standardized measures, J showed improvement—dramatic in some instances—in almost all her primary- and secondary-outcome standardized scores. Specifically, as shown in Table 5.4, she had improved from intake to 1 year on suicidality, the four aggression scores, on one of the three impulsivity scores (with basically no change on the other two), and on all four of the secondary-outcome scores.

From the therapist's point of view, he independently observed that J had made substantial changes in 1 year of TFP, in some areas much more than was reflected in her standardized measures. As has been previously noted, while in the month prior to beginning treatment J endorsed some self-injurious behaviors on the Overt Aggression Scale-Modified (OAS-M) and verbally aggressive behaviors on the AIAQ subscale of the OAS-M, she had been so isolated in her apartment that she struggled to produce recent examples of the fiery and explosive behaviors that she had struggled with for some time. At the end of 1 year of TFP she had a markedly richer social life and was actively dating. Therefore, she was exposed to a far greater repertoire of social opportunities that included both positive and pleasurable experiences as well as some angry and irritable ones. Furthermore, the ruptures with these somewhat narcissistic men did at times bring about feelings of shame and subsequent suicidal ideation (that she had previously avoided through never dating at all). Thus, J's improvement at 1 year was all the more impressive.

After 1 year of treatment the changes in J's attachment organization and reflective functioning were more dramatic and consistent with the therapist's perception of the changes she made. J had shifted to a Preoccupied attachment style. The fact that this is not a "Secure" attachment style may belie the improvement observed. Whereas before her Cannot Classify (CC) attachment pattern described earlier led to marked vacillations between a Preoccupied style of angry and entangled descriptions and a Dismissive style of devaluing and derogatory descriptions, over the course of the year she organized around a consistent style. Unlike CC, the Preoccupied style is thought to represent an intact (albeit not secure) strategy for getting one's attachment needs met, and thus serves an adaptive function. The same cannot be said for the incoherent and disorganizing effect of vacillating between two opposing styles, and therefore this stabilization is understood to be a sign of progress on the path toward security of attachment for such patients (Diamond et al., 2014).

J evidenced a dramatic improvement in her capacity to reflect on mental states with herself and within others on the reflective functioning (RF) scale, As shown in Table 5.4, prior to treatment J's interview was rated as a –1, which is considered "negative" RF and indicative of resistance and/or bizarre responses to an opportunity to reflect. At the end of treatment, J's interview was rated as a 6, which is between "ordinary" and "marked" RF. Whereas clinical samples tend to display RF around 3, healthy control samples display RF at 5 or higher, and thus this aligns J's capacity for mentalization with nonpatient samples. Not only did she no longer experience being asked to reflect on the mental states of attachment figures as a hostile affront, but now she was actually curious about her mind and the minds of others, and displayed genuine insights into others' motivations.

As part of this same growth in J's structural functioning, her related, narrative coherence score went from 1.50 at intake to 4.00 at 1 year, just below the clinical cutoff of 5.00.

Of note, there is often the assumption that psychodynamic treatments focus a great deal on early childhood experiences, which would make gain in the capacity to reflect on those relationships not particularly impressive. However, TFP does not place particular emphasis on childhood relationships, but rather focuses on relational dynamics in the here and now. This is consistent with the therapist's own impression of this treatment, which spent relatively little time on early experiences with parents except to contextualize her relational assumptions in her current life.

At the end of 1 year in the RCT, J was offered the option of continuing TFP in the therapist's private practice, to which she agreed and during which time she continued to make substantial gains. J's complaints of mistreatment gradually decreased; she reported less anxiety and more positive interactions in her volunteer work setting, where she was offered a paid position after a year. After 3 years of therapy, she started a relationship with and eventually married a man whose empathy she appreciated, in contrast to the illusion of an ideal she was attracted to in the earlier objects of her desire. By the end of 5 years of therapy, J had achieved stability in her work life, having obtained a master's degree and become steadily employed in a full-time position, got married, and developed friendships and meaningful interests in the arts.

Ms. V's Negative Outcome and Therapy Process

V was noted to evidence improvement on her standardized, primary- and secondary-outcome measures after 1 year of TFP. As shown in Table 5.4, she showed modest improvement on the primary measures of suicidality, verbal assault, and motor/acting without thinking, and on the four secondary-outcome measures. On the other hand, she showed worsening on measures of anger, irritability, and attention. Notably, in V's case as well there was a discrepancy between changes observed on the measures as compared to the therapist's report, but this time in the other direction; despite her self-reported changes, the therapist continued to have concerns that core aspects of her pathology remained intact.

As has been previously noted, in the month prior to beginning treatment, V presented with instances of verbal anger and irritability on the AIAQ and impulsivity on the BIS-II, and the vast majority of her social contacts were limited to therapists or her boyfriend, otherwise being too impoverished to be having interactions with the potential for conflict. After 1 year of TFP her irritable and impulsive behaviors had slightly reduced on some of these measures, but the therapist had the impression that this was despite never having really challenged herself in the relational contexts most likely to elicit the very feelings that she sought to address. She kept her contacts with people at her AA meeting, her classes, and eventually her clerical job to a minimum, and was in a stable pattern of conflict with her on-again/off-again boyfriend.

In terms of measures of attachment organization and reflective functioning, V continued to demonstrate a Dismissive attachment style, as well as low levels of reflective functioning (scores of 3 at both intake and 1 year) and narrative coherence (scores of 2.50 at intake and 3.00 at 1 year). V continued to discuss attachment relationships with a cool detachment, although qualitatively it was observed that she was more derogatory and overtly angry and negative in her descriptions of attachment relationships than the year prior. For example, the 1-year score of 3 on reflective function was associated with numerous instances of broad generalities regarding mental states that provided little specificity for what her parents may have thought, felt, or wanted in particular (e.g., they are merely "screwed up" people who alternately "tried their best"). By contrast, the TFP group mean scores increased significantly after 1 year of treatment on both reflective functioning (intake = 2.81, 1 year = 4.11) and narrative coherence (intake = 2.93, 1 year = 4.02).

At the end of 1 year in the RCT, V was offered the option of continuing TFP in the therapist's private practice. Although she accepted this offer, a few months later V stated that she had decided to end the therapy. Her therapist was concerned because she had not addressed the overwhelming feeling of being exploited in relationships, which not only put her job at risk but was also reflected in ongoing conflicts with the men she dated and the few friends she had. Despite her therapist's strong recommendation to continue with treatment, the patient thanked him for his help in a perfunctory way and ended the therapy. The therapist had no way to be sure of V's reasons for ending therapy, but in hindsight the therapist wondered whether the toxic effect of V's overwhelming feeling of exploitation, in combination with her tendency to "turn the tables" and find ways to exploit others and the social system, made the therapy relationship intolerable, as it had in so many other relationships, and also undesirable, insofar as it called on her to take responsibility for her life.

Regarding these feelings of exploitation, in V's early attachment relationships, such as those with her parents and older brother, she was treated in violent and manipulative ways, which led her to view dependent relationships in terms of predator and prey. V may have feared the answers to the therapist's questions about what she thought motivated the expectations he placed on her, perhaps not wanting to even consider the possibility that she had again found herself being exploited by someone on whom she had begun to depend. Keeping the therapeutic relationship superficial functioned temporarily to keep that fear at bay. However, despite some modest gains in her work functioning, keeping affect at a distance also precluded a deeper understanding of the nature of her fear, and as a result little changed in her relational functioning. As the treatment plodded along, the therapist likely felt an urgency for her to want more out of her life and began to increase the pressure, which may have played into her fear of exploitation as she felt manipulated by the therapist's changing expectations. Perhaps, rather than confront the predator she imagined but had been working hard not to see in her therapist—which would have brought that element of her internal world into the therapeutic dialogue—she evasively ran for the door.

COMPARISON OF THE MS. J AND MS. V CASES

Both J and V presented with BPD and avoidant personality disorder (AVPD), although they differed in terms of J further presenting with narcissistic personality disorder (NPD), and V, with antisocial personality disorder (ASPD). At the end of 1 year of TFP, both J and V evidenced modest improvements in their angry, irritable, and impulsive behaviors (note the improvements on the OAS-M, AIAQ, and Barratt Impulsivity Factors in Table 5.4; for instance, over the course of treatment, J's reported verbal assault score dropped from 2.44 to 1.11, while V's verbal assault score dropped from 2.22 to 2.11). Furthermore, after 1 year of treatment both women were gainfully employed, although they each had a different subjective experience of working (muted pride in J, resentment in V).

Regarding social adjustment, even though V was functioning at a higher absolute level than J at 1 year (60 versus 45, respectively), qualitatively J had made substantial changes in her willingness to risk feeling vulnerable in order to work toward creating the kinds of relational experiences she sought for herself. In contrast, V continued to privilege protecting herself from experiences of vulnerability, even at the expense of working toward richer relationships. Furthermore, J grew considerably in her capacity to mentalize thoughts, feelings, and motivations within herself and others (with a 1-year reflective functioning score of 6). Her capacity to provide a coherent narrative to her attachment experiences, while still somewhat angry and entangled, stabilized around an organized pattern of seeking out her attachment needs. In contrast, with a 1-year reflective functioning score of 3, V showed no change in these domains, continuing to approach her mental state and that of others with a cool detachment and clichéd understandings that also likely served to protect her from experiences of vulnerability.

The discrepancies in both their attachment organization and comorbid personality pathology shed light on why J and V may have differentially benefitted from TFP. What became clear both in J's attachment narratives and her approach to relationships was that underneath it all she desperately wanted to relate to others. While her desire to be loved and respected was revealed to be considerable during the course of treatment, she went to great lengths in the early phases of treatment to deny this longing for connection, both to others as well as to herself. Her derogation of relationships served as a defense against her longing; J would have surely put a twist on Tennyson and asserted that it is "better to never have loved at all, than to have loved and lost."

J was so sure of her inevitable disappointment that she lashed out at those whom she believed would surely abandon her in a matter of time, if they had not done so already, and therefore at the start of treatment J had stopped bothering to relate to anyone. She would narcissistically denigrate others as a preemptive strike against the denigrations that were surely going to be directed at her. However, that longing for connection was still there, acting as a quiet but powerful motivation. The therapist's capacity to endure and contain her derogation long enough to see and give voice to her underlying needs for intimacy and connection in the form of transference interpretations paved the way for powerful change in the way she oriented herself toward relationships. This is most clearly reflected in her attachment status after 1 year of treatment, which was organized around her preoccupation with the degree to which her relational needs were being met, whereas the need to disavow attachment longings had receded into the background.

In contrast, any desire for longing or connection experienced by V was consistently muted by representations of relationships organized in terms of predator and prey, as is often the case in patients with comorbid antisocial personality disorder. Any desire she may have had to connect (with the therapist, her classmates, her coworkers, a more stable boyfriend) was likely equated in her mind with the kind of vulnerability and letting down of one's guard that occurs in the moment before an attack begins. Whereas deep down J wanted (and yet feared) her underlying needs for intimacy and connection to be seen, V's experience of similar transference interpretations may have been experienced as the actualization of the vulnerable experience she had organized her life around avoiding. Furthermore, the therapist's efforts to move her toward higher levels of occupational functioning were likely perceived as seeking to deny her the very benefits that were rightfully hers.

From what seemed to be V's vantage point of the therapy dyad being organized around predator-prey, why would the therapist ask V to relinquish her disability status and return to work? At best he was naïve (as predators often are), blindly giving her bad advice, unintentionally hurting her in the process, and in doing so revealing his incompetence as a therapist. This possibility—therapist-as-naïve—also left him open to the possibility of being V's prey, in that she might be able to use him to get benefits for which she might not genuinely qualify. At worst he was out to steal from her (as predators often do), tricking her into giving up what she needed to survive and leaving her with nothing. While we can only speculate as to how she may have perceived the therapist, either (or, likely, both) of these perceptions of the therapist would have contributed to maintaining a cool detachment both within her relationships and within her own mind, as reflected in no change in attachment or reflective functioning scores.

This raises the question of whether or not V might have responded better to a different kind of treatment. For example, V may have been more receptive to a supportive treatment that would likely have done more to meet her where she was, rather than nudge her toward life changes she clearly did not want to make. The TFP therapist was concerned that V had spent a large portion of her adult years supported by hospital staff and government assistance, despite being clearly capable of more. However, it became apparent over time that the therapist felt more urgently about changing V's life circumstances than V did. This raises a question with important clinical (and ethical) implications—should the therapist have kept the focus on the more modest changes V was willing to make—or fought even harder for V to feel a sense of urgency and work to reach her potential?

In terms of the treatments in this RCT, supportive psychotherapy (SPT) would likely have done more to understand V's "refractory depression" as a reality of her subjective experience and worked to help her understand her experience of being abused and manipulated by others. Another BPD therapy not included in the present RCT, mentalization-based therapy (MBT; Bateman & Fonagy, 1999), would similarly have focused on V adopting a mentalizing stance by becoming curious about her thoughts, intentions, beliefs, and especially the awareness of manifest affects about herself and others. Rather than challenging self-attributions as involving distortions, as would be done in TFP, SBT and MBT would be more likely to accept V's subjective experience of being exploited and manipulated as "real" and "accurate" to her. Such interventions may have bolstered the therapeutic alliance, which was felt by V's therapist to be often strained in TFP. While it is quite likely V would have preferred these other therapeutic approaches, it should be noted that during the course of V's many previous hospital-based outpatient treatments she had received a number of supportive psychotherapies, with little change noted, leading those supportive therapists to recommend her to this RCT in the hope of her receiving TFP.

In terms of the other treatment in this RCT, dialectical behavior therapy (DBT; Linehan, 1993) likely would have approached the aforementioned question regarding acceptance of V's more modest goals versus substantial change in her level of functioning not as a dichotomy, but as a dialectic within which both needs could be respected and understood. The DBT therapist would likely have sought to validate V in her current experience of feeling abused and exploited, while also questioning whether she was working toward "a life worth living." A DBT therapist would maintain that V's abused and exploited self-image stems from countless painful invalidating experiences, and these real experiences need to be acknowledged as such. Not to validate this aspect of V's experience, a DBT therapist might say, would be to provide the patient with one more version of an invalidating environment. More akin to mentalization-based therapy, a DBT therapist would accept the patient's subjective experience as "real" and "accurate" to her, and therefore respond to it as such.

By contrast, the TFP therapist actively challenged the notion of V as always the one being exploited by examining this perception of self in relation to others in all the forms it took, including situations in which V was the one to exploit others. The TFP therapist aimed to observe the totality of V's experience, with the hope this would allow her to achieve a more integrated, balanced view of herself, others, and relationships. The therapist worried that to validate V's self-perception as being victimized and manipulated would be to affirm a distorted view of herself. Furthermore, this would leave a crucial underlying motivation of this self-perception unaddressed—namely, the secondary gain derived from her benefits. In that light, it could be argued that the TFP therapist might have utilized *more* transference interpretations. For example, these would have included interpretations that highlighted V's efforts to keep the focus outside of the transference so as to maintain V's view of herself as exploited, including by the therapist.

However, this "doubling down" on transference interpretations may not be supported by data indicating high rates of dropout when therapists overinterpret (or when CBT therapists continue with their techniques) in the face of a patient's non-responsiveness (Piper et al., 1999). Perhaps most fruitful for V may have been a more integrative approach that combined elements of DBT, such as joining a skills group, to supplement her work in TFP. Recent research suggests that DBT skills groups may successfully augment non-DBT treatments (Harely, Baity, Blais, & Jacobo, 2007).

SYNTHESIS OF THE FINDINGS FROM THE RCT AND CASE STUDY APPROACHES

What We Learned From the RCT Study

In this section we discuss what we have learned from our study. We focus on issues related to efficacy and effectiveness of TFP, the nature of improvement, the role of structural variables, personal qualities that promote and hinder change, structural and change processes, and the matching different treatment theories to different patients.

THE EFFICACY AND EFFECTIVENESS OF TFP AS ANOTHER APPROACH TO BPD

Historically, BPD has been thought to be difficult to treat, with patients frequently not adhering to treatment recommendations, using services chaotically, and repeatedly dropping out of treatment. They also happen to be harder on therapists than any other disorder. Many clinicians are intimidated by the prospect of treating BPD patients and are pessimistic about the outcome of treatment, with good reason. Therapists have displayed high levels of burnout and have been known to be prone to enactments and even engagement in iatrogenic behaviors. Beginning with Linehan's seminal 1991 RCT showing that DBT was efficacious in comparison to treatment as usual, and the increasing number of studies finding efficacy for treatments based on both cognitive-behavioral therapy and psychodynamic therapy, we now know that BPD can be a treatable condition. These RCT studies and their follow-ups, like the one we described earlier, consistently find that 50%–60% of BPD patients improve during the course of year-long treatments.

With this in mind, the findings in the present RCT of equivalence between TFP and DBT provide important evidence to specifically support TFP's efficacy against the benchmark of DBT. This finding is strengthened by a number of methodological elements in the study design. First, the possibility of bias from therapist research allegiance was controlled by having each therapy model administered by a team highly knowledgeable in and committed to it. Second, the design included essential efficacy elements to ensure internal validity, such as random assignment of patients to treatments, manualized treatments, blind raters, therapists blind to all baseline assessments, and specific and reliably measured outcome variables. Third, the design also built in the external validity associated with effectiveness studies by including in the study a range of BPD patients based on inclusion/exclusion criteria used in clinical practice; therapists who provided treatment in their private offices in the community rather than in a university or hospital setting; and psychopharmacological treatment decided on an individual basis so that the use of medication was not standardized, but on the basis of a clinical algo-rithm, so as to be independent of assignment to treatment group.

Because the different models—TFP, DBT, and SPT—are based on different the-ories of change, the overall finding of their equivalence suggests that there may be different theoretically based routes to improvement in the treatment of BPD as gauged by symptoms. In DBT, there is a focus on direct, behavioral skills training to help patients regulate emotions and reduce symptoms; in TFP, there is a focus on developing greater self-control through integrating representations of self and others as they become active in the therapeutic relationship, with a particular use of transference interpretation; and in SPT, the focus is on a supportive relation-ship and using the therapist as a model of reflection, without the use of trans-ference interpretation. Both future group studies and future case studies like the ones described here will be helpful in comparing and contrasting these different theoretically based routes to improvement in patients with DBT.

In addition to the general equivalence among the three treatment models, in one of the contrast analyses, TFP and DBT approached statistical significance in their association with decreased suicidality compared with SPT, and they were not statistically significant from each other. In addition, the TFP group showed statistically significant improvement in 10 of 12 primary- and secondary-outcome variables, compared with the DBT group being associated with statistically signif-icant improvement in 5 of 12 variables, and the SPT group, with statistically sig-nificant improvement in 6 of 12 variables. Overall, while these differences among the three groups were not statistically significant, they suggest the possibility of certain advantages in TFP over the other two treatments that merit further study.

THE NATURE OF IMPROVEMENT

The improvements documented in Tables 5.2 and 5.3 are statistically significant and, while often much less than we desire for our patients, do indeed represent clinically significant improvement. By clinically significant improvement, we do not necessarily mean that these patients are functioning at levels consistent with non-BPD patients but that the level of improvement shown represents a change in clinical functioning. For example, many patients treated in our RCT were no longer engaging in self-injury on a regular basis or at all by the end of treatment (often within 4–6 months of beginning treatment). The reduction in this beha-vior frequently would lead to fewer emergency room visits, hospitalizations, and days hospitalized. For example, after one year the GAF Social Adjustment scores increased from 40–50 to 60–70.

However, despite these changes, many of these patients were still frequently unhappy, experienced shifts in their perception of themselves and others that interfered with intimacy, and were still unable to decide and commit to produc-tive work in a way consistent with their interests and capacities. Along these lines, Linehan et al. (1994) themselves noted in their early naturalistic follow-up that although the "subjects in the dialectical behavior therapy group acted better . . . *they were still miserable*," experiencing "moderate symptoms" and/or "generally functioning with some difficulty" and living lives of quiet desperation (p. 1775).

Similarly in our study, many patients in all three treatment conditions made important improvements. However, those symptom improvements were not always associated with sufficient change. Clearly, more improvement was needed. A GAF score of 65 represents a clinically significant improvement when compared to functioning at a 45; however, a GAF score of 65 is far from that to which most people would aspire. Nonetheless, we would contend that this improvement is clinically significant. A BPD patient who is not self-injuring and therefore needing to be taken to the emergency room and possibly hospitalized is typically able to relate better with significant others.

The "successful" case of J underlines the aforementioned points in a dramatic way. Although, as we documented, she made considerable progress in her first year, she had only made a gain in her GAF Social Functioning score from 40 to 45. She achieved a full recovery (a GAF of around 70) only after 4 additional years of therapy.

THE ROLE OF STRUCTURAL VARIABLES

TFP's theory of BPD psychopathology and its associated treatment model are organized in part around the variables of attachment, mentalization/reflective functioning, and narrative coherence, and thus the treatment targets these variables. Our findings support the unique role that TFP has in facilitating improvement in these areas. Specifically, for attachment, only in the TFP group was there a significant increase in the number of patients who moved from an insecure to a secure attachment by the end of the 1-year therapy. And for reflective functioning and narrative coherence, TFP patients experienced a statistically significantly greater improvement in both these variables than did those in DBT or SPT.

The greater improvement in the attachment, reflective functioning, and narrative coherence measures for the TFP group confirms our hypothesis that TFP would have a bigger impact on these two variables because of their particular relevance in TFP's theory of BPD psychopathology and methods for combating it.

What We Learned From the Case Studies

The findings from the RCT are important for establishing the efficacy and effectiveness of TFP in treating the average BPD patient, and the findings are useful in the study of mechanisms of change, such as the findings concerning the structural variables. However, by necessity, RCT knowledge has to simplify the clinical complexity of a year of psychotherapy with an individual with severe BPD psychopathology. This simplification limits the value of RCT knowledge in providing practitioners a rich picture of the patient and pragmatic guidance in the therapeutic process. In contrast, and in a complementary way, case studies are designed to capture this clinical complexity, with the resultant advantages for the practitioner. In addition, by revealing and exploring in rich context the nature of BPD psychopathology and the effects of treatment on it, case studies provide an alternative route for uncovering mechanisms of change.

The comparison of client characteristics and the therapeutic process embedded in the cases of J and V are instructive. In many ways, J and V and their therapies were quite similar. They were both women in their early 30s who presented for treatment after deriving little benefit from prior psychotherapies and pharmacotherapies as well as little success in past work environments. Both women were diagnosed with BPD and avoidant personality disorder and were randomized to the same therapist in TFP. The therapist was male and an experienced clinician who had practiced and supervised TFP for many years. Each patient was treated twice-weekly in his private practice office in close proximity to the affiliated medical center sponsoring the RCT. As part of the RCT, each patient agreed to be treated in 1 year of TFP. At the end of that year each patient was offered the option of continuing treatment in the therapist's private practice.

And yet J and V had such different outcomes. For example, the therapist perceived J as a strong success, who showed dramatic movement over the 1-year therapy in connecting to the therapist and acknowledging and processing her vulnerabilities, and who enthusiastically continued in therapy for 4 more years to make more pervasive structural personality and social functioning improvements.

In contrast, the therapist viewed V as making no movement in her highly defensive stance to the world over the 1 year of therapy, and then refusing to continue in the therapy. Some of this difference is reflected in the pre-post standardized measures. For example, at the end of therapy, both J and V had substantial decreases in the secondary symptoms. However, on the anger-during-the-previous-month measure, J had a substantial decrease (from 42 to 13), while V had an actual increase over the same period (from 12 to 18). Also, J showed dramatic increases in her attachment, reflective functioning, and narrative coherence measures, while V showed essentially no change.

PERSONAL CAPACITIES PROMOTING OR HINDERING CHANGE

In examining the personal qualities of the two clients, the contrast between J and V highlights the importance of a patient's capacity to respond and overcome layers of resistance and defensiveness (as in the case of J) and a patient's lack of this capacity (as in the case of V). Another mechanism of change frequently missed involves the role of secondary gain. It seemed clear from V's case study that the secondary gain associated with her illness was a strong force in her resisting openness to the pain and distress associated with change. Specifically, for the 10 years before the RCT, V had been treated in just about every inpatient, partial hospitalization, and outpatient program in the hospital associated with the RCT. Although this did not result in change, it did legitimize her disability payments and subsidized housing, creating an equilibrium she did not seem motivated to change.

UNDERSTANDING STRUCTURAL OR PROCESS CHANGES

J's case study also helps to elaborate on the way in which TFP impacts on reflective functioning and narrative coherence, revealing a process in which J moved from the lowest score on reflective functioning of −1.00 to a 6.00 at 1 year, above the clinical cutoff of 5.00; and from 2.50 to 4.00 on narrative coherence. From the detailed data about J's therapeutic process, it seems clear that the structural changes she made in the first year of treatment, for example, in her reflective functioning, provided the tools she was able to use in the next 4 years of therapy to move beyond symptomatic change to completely transform her life such that she established a healthy, mutually compatible marriage; obtained a master's degree; became steadily employed in a full-time position; and developed genuine friendships and meaningful interests in the arts.

The cases suggest that structural changes in attachment, reflective functioning, and narrative coherence brought about through the therapeutic process are predictors of the maintenance of improvement and continued improvement. For example, J's great improvement in these variables after 1 year seemed to be core in facilitating her great success in the next 4 years of therapy, and V's lack of improvement in these variables was associated with very little change and dropping out of the therapy after 1 year.

To understand when these variables come into play in the change process, Howard et al. (1996) suggested a three-phase dose–response model of psychotherapy in which patients initially experience remoralization (the initial boost experienced from the feeling that help is there), followed by remediation (symptom reduction), and finally by rehabilitation (establishing adaptive ways of living, also conceived of as personality change). Remoralization is usually accomplished quickly, whereas remediation is more gradual and typically occurs between 3 and 8 months. Rehabilitation is quite gradual and can take years. Each phase may have different treatment goals, measurable by different outcome variables, and require different interventions.

We would suggest that the pattern of changes we observed in our two patients, J and V, illustrates quite nicely the process articulated by Howard and colleagues. Whereas both patients showed remoralization and remediation, with statistically significant increases on the four secondary variables (see Table 5.4), we would contend that only J achieved rehabilitation. While it was clear by the end of the first year that J had made important strides, many of her most substantial changes occurred a number of years after the completion of the study. We believe that these improvements were set in motion, at least in part, by the structural and process changes indicated by healthier attachment, more reflective functioning, and better narrative coherence. We would contend that J's continued symptomatic improvement over the subsequent 4 years is highly suggestive of rehabilitative change. Interestingly, despite obvious changes in her life as reflected in the standardized secondary-outcome measures at 1 year as shown in Table 5.4, in the therapy V continued to present herself as quite distressed and in fact much more so than J, who had similar symptom scores after 1 year of therapy (see Table 5.4).

MATCHING DIFFERENT TREATMENT THEORIES TO DIFFERENT PATIENTS

Because the different models—TFP, DBT, and SPT—are based on different theories of change, the overall finding of their equivalence suggests that there may be different theoretically based routes to improvement in the treatment of BPD as gauged by symptoms. As we mentioned earlier, "in DBT, there is a focus on direct, behavioral skills training to help patients regulate emotions and reduce symptoms; in TFP, there is a focus on developing greater self-control through integrating representations of self and others as they become active in the therapeutic relationship, with a particular use of transference interpretation; and in SPT, the focus is on a supportive relationship and using the therapist as a model of reflection, without the use of transference interpretation." Both future group studies and future case studies like the ones described herein will be helpful in comparing and contrasting these different theoretically based routes to improvement in patients with DBT.

Typically, 40%–50% of DBT patients in RCTs do not get better. Based on the design of an RCT, there is no way to know if those who are not successful in a particular treatment model would have done better in a different treatment model. It is possible that the reason why the different treatment models all significantly work on average is that they are working for *different types* of clients, not necessarily that a particular change mechanism works in the same way on all clients. For example, TFP seemed particularly well suited to J, as reflected in her very positive gains in healthy attachment and reflective functioning, which in turn anchored her in long-term therapy and led to a positive transformation in her relational and work life.

On the other hand, we speculated as to whether V's poor response to TFP was due to a poor fit between what V and what TFP requires of patients, as opposed to the more supportive modes of therapy within DBT and SPT. By focusing on the individual patient, case studies provide an excellent method for looking at the match between the complexities of the patient and the "demands" and "potential payoffs" associated with a particular treatment model.

In this regard, we could learn a great deal about matching by comparing a successful patient, "A," and an unsuccessful patient, "B," in, say, the DBT treatment condition. Comparing the differences between A and B versus J and V could enable us to start to better understand the common processes across TFP and DBT that lead to success, along with the treatment-model-specific processes that are differentially related to the patients, such that TFP would not have worked well with A, and DBT would not have worked well with J. Similar comparisons are suggested by bringing in SPT, which, to remind the reader, was psychodynamic like TFP, but unlike TFP, did not use transference interpretations.

Moreover, the example of patients J, V, A, and B include only four of the 62 patients who completed the TFP, DBT or SPT therapies. Conducting case studies on larger numbers of patients would allow for more methodologically powerful comparisons and "replications" of different patient-therapist-therapy matches and different patterns of therapeutic process and outcome.

In sum, the change variables found in our RCT were quantitatively observable and qualitatively and quantitatively elaborated in the close examination of the cases of J and V using systematic case study methods articulated by Fishman, Messer, and their colleagues (Dattillo, Edwards, & Fishman, 2010; Fishman, 2005; Fishman & Messer, 2013; Messer, 2007). The case studies not only provide in-depth illustrations of the RCT findings that resonate with the experience of clinicians but also are an excellent source of hypotheses about the patient capacities and processes of structural change that help or hinder transference-focused psychotherapy.

ACKNOWLEDGMENTS BY LEVY ET AL.

This research was supported by grants from the National Institute of Mental Health, International Psychoanalytic Association, American Psychoanalytic Association and the Kohler Fund of Munich awarded to Kenneth N. Levy, and a grant from the Borderline Personality Disorder Research Foundation (BPDRF) awarded to Otto F. Kernberg and John F. Clarkin. We wish to acknowledge the assistance of Catherine Eubanks Carter, PhD, Kenneth L. Critchfield, PhD, Jill C. Delaney, MSW, Pamela E. Foelsch, PhD, Simone Hoermann, PhD, Maya Kirschner, PhD, and Joel McClough, PhD, for their assistance in conducting interview assessments. We also acknowledge the consultation of Armand Loranger, PhD, for assistance with training in the administration and scoring of the IPDE. Finally, we would like to thank the patients for their participation in the study.

REFERENCES

Adler, G. (1985). *Borderline psychopathology and its treatment*. New York, NY: Jason Aronson.

American Psychiatric Association (2000). *Diagnostic and statistical manual of mental disorders* (4th ed., text revision). Washington, DC: Author.

American Psychiatric Association. (2013). *Diagnostic and statistical manual of mental disorders* (5th ed.). Arlington, VA: Author.

Appelbaum, A. H. (2005). Supportive psychotherapy. In J. Oldham, A. Skodol, & D. Bender (Eds.), *Textbook of personality disorders* (pp. 311–326). Arlington, VA: American Psychiatric Publishing.

Arntz, A. (2004). Borderline personality disorder. In T. A. Beck, A. Freeman, & D. D. Davis (Eds.), *Cognitive therapy of personality disorders* (2nd ed., pp. 87–215). New York, NY: Guilford Press.

Bakermans-Kranenburg, M. J. & Van IJzendoorn, M. H. (1993). A psychometric study of the Adult Attachment Interview: Reliability and discriminant validity. *Developmental Psychology, 29*(5), 870–879.

Bateman, A. & Fonagy, P. (1999). Effectiveness of partial hospitalization in the treatment of borderline personality disorder: a randomized controlled trial. *American Journal of Psychiatry, 156*(10), 1563–1569.

Beck, A. T., Steer, R. A., & Brown, G. K. (1996). *Manual for the Beck Depression Inventory* (2nd ed.). San Antonio, TX: The Psychological Corporation.

Bongar, B., Peterson, L. G., Golann, S., & Hardiman, J. J. (1990). Self-mutilation and the chronically "suicidal" emergency room patient. *Annals of Clinical Psychiatry, 2*, 217–22.

Chalmers, T. C., Smith, H., Blackburn, B., Silverman, B., Schroeder, B., Reitman, D., & Ambroz, A. (1981). A method for assessing the quality of a randomized control trial. *Controlled Clinical Trials, 2*(1), 31–49.

Clarkin, J. F., Foelsch, P. A., Levy, K. N., Hull, J. W., Delaney, J. C., & Kernberg, O. F. (2001). The development of a psychodynamic treatment for patients with borderline personality disorders: A preliminary study of behavioral change. *Journal of Personality Disorders, 15*(6), 487–495.

Clarkin, J. F. & Levy, K. N. (2006). Psychotherapy for patients with borderline personality disorder: Focusing on the mechanisms of change. *Journal of Clinical Psychology, 62*, 405–410.

Clarkin, J. F., Levy, K. N., Lenzenweger, M. F., & Kernberg, O. F. (2004). The Personality Disorders Institute/Borderline Personality Disorder Research Foundation randomized control trial for borderline personality disorder: Rationale, methods, and patient characteristics. *Journal of Personality Disorders, 18*, 52–72.

Clarkin, J. F., Levy, K. N., Lenzenweger, M. F., & Kernberg, O. F. (2007). Evaluating three treatments for borderline personality disorder: A multiwave study. *American Journal of Psychiatry, 164*, 922–928.

Clarkin, J. F., Yeomans, F., E., & Kernberg, O. F. (1998). *Psychotherapy for borderline personality.* New York, NY: Wiley.

Clarkin, J. F., Yeomans, F. E., & Kernberg, O. F. (2006). *Psychotherapy of borderline personality.* Washington, DC: American Psychiatric Press.

Coccaro, E. F. & Kavoussi, R. J. (1997). Fluoxetine and impulsive-aggressive behavior in personality disordered subjects. *Archives of General Psychiatry, 54*, 1081–1088.

Coccaro, E. F., Harvey, P. D., Kupsaw-Lawrence, E., Herbert, J. L., & Bernstein, D.P. (1991). Development of neuropharmacologically based behavioral assessments of impulsive aggressive behavior. *The Journal of Neuropsychiatry & Clinical Neurosciences, 3*, s44–s51.

Critchfield, K. L., Levy, K. N., & Clarkin, J. F. (2005). The relationship between impulsivity, aggression, and impulsive-aggression in borderline personality disorder: An empirical analysis of self-report measures. *Journal of Personality Disorders, 18*(6), 555–570.

Critchfield, K. L., Levy, K. N., & Clarkin, J. F. (2007). The Personality Disorders Institute/ Borderline Personality Disorder Research Foundation randomized control trial for borderline personality disorder: Reliability of axis I and II diagnoses. *Psychiatric Quarterly, 78*(1), 15–24.

Dattilio, F. M., Edwards, D. J. A., & Fishman, D. B. (2010). Case studies within a mixed methods paradigm: Toward a resolution of the alienation between researcher and practitioner in psychotherapy research. *Psychotherapy Theory, Research, Practice, Training, 47*, 427–441.

Derogatis, L.R. (1993). *Brief Symptom Inventory (BSI): Administration, scoring, and procedures manual* (3rd ed.). Minneapolis, MN: National Computer Systems.

Fertuck, E. A., Lenzenweger, M. F., & Clarkin, J. F. (2005). The association between attentional and executive controls in the expression of borderline personality disorder features: A preliminary study. *Psychopathology, 38*(2), 75–81.

First, M. B., Gibbon, M., Spitzer, R. L., & Williams, J. B. W. (1997). *Structured clinical Interview for Axis I DSM-IV disorders (SCID-I), clinical version.* New York, NY: Biometrics Research Department, New York State Psychiatric Institute.

Fishman, D. B. (2005.) Editor's introduction to PCSP—From single case to database. *Pragmatic Case Studies in Psychotherapy, 1*(1), 1–50. Available at http://pcsp.libraries. rutgers.edu/. doi: http://dx.doi.org/10.14713/pcsp.v1i1.855

Fishman, D. B. & Messer, S. B. (2013). Pragmatic case studies as a source of unity in applied psychology. *Review of General Psychology, 17*, 156–161.

Fleiss, J. L. (1971). Measuring nominal scale agreement among many raters. *Psychological Bulletin, 76*, 378–381.

Fonagy, P., Gergely, G., Jurist, E., & Target, M. (2002). *Affect regulation, mentalization, and the development of the self.* New York, NY: Other Press.

Fonagy, P., Leigh, T., Steele, M., Steele, H., Kennedy, R., Mattoon, G., Target, M., & Gerber, A. (1996). The relation of attachment status, psychiatric classification, and response to psychotherapy. *Journal of Consulting and Clinical Psychology, 64*(1), 22–31.

Fonagy, P., Steele, M., Steele, H., & Target, M. (1998). *Reflexive-function manual: Version 5.0 for application to the adult attachment interview.* Unpublished manual, University College, London.

Fonagy, P. & Target, M. (1996). Playing with reality: I. Theory of mind and the normal development of psychic reality. *International Journal of Psychoanalysis, 77*, 217–234.

George, C., Kaplan, N., & Main, M. (1985). *The adult attachment interview.* Unpublished manuscript, University of California at Berkeley.

Grant, B. F., Chou, S. P., Goldstein, R. B., Huang, B., Stinson, F. S., Saha, T. D., ..., & Ruan, W. J. (2008). Prevalence, correlates, disability and comorbidity of DSM-IV borderline personality disorder: Results from the Wave 2 National Epidemiologic Survey on alcohol and related conditions. *Journal of Clinical Psychiatry, 69*(4), 533–545.

Gross, R., Olfson, M., Gameroff, M., Shea, S., Feder, A., Fuentes, M., ... & Weissman, M. M. (2002). Borderline personality disorder in primary care. *Archives of Internal Medicine, 162*(1), 53–60.

Howard, K. I., Cornille, T. A., Lyons, J. S., Vessey, J. T., Lueger, R. J., & Saunders, S. M. (1996). Patterns of mental health service utilization. *Archives of General Psychiatry, 53*, 696–703.

Kellogg, S. H. & Young, J. E. (2006). Schema therapy for borderline personality disorder. *Journal of Clinical Psychology, 62*(4), 445–458.

Kernberg, O. F., Burnstein, E. D., Coyne, L., Appelbaum, A., Horwitz, L., & Voth, H. M. (1972). Psychotherapy and psychoanalysis: Final report of the Menninger Foundation's psychotherapy research project. *Bulletin of the Menninger Clinic, 36*(1), 1–275.

Kernberg, O. F. (1984). *Severe personality disorders: Psychotherapeutic strategies.* New Haven, CT: Yale University Press.

Kernberg, O. F., Selzer, M., Koenigsberg, H. W., Carr, A., & Appelbaum, A. (1989). *Psychodynamic psychotherapy of borderline patients.* New York, NY: Basic Books.

Kjellander, C., Bongar, B., & King, A. (1998). Suicidality in borderline personality disorder. *Crisis, 19*(3), 125–135.

Korzekwa, M. I., Dell, P. F., Links, P. S., Thabane, L., & Webb, S. P. (2008). Estimating the prevalence of borderline personality disorder in psychiatric outpatients using a two-phase procedure. *Comprehensive Psychiatry, 49*(4), 380–386.

Lenzenweger, M. F., Lane, M. C., Loranger, A. W., & Kessler, R. C. (2007). DSM-IV personality disorders in the national comorbidity survey replication. *Biological Psychiatry, 62*(6), 553–564.

Levy, K. N. (2005). The implications of attachment theory and research for understanding borderline personality disorder. *Development and Psychopathology, 17*, 959–986.

Levy, K. N., Clarkin, J. F., Foelsch, P. A., & Kernberg, O. F. (in review). Transference focused psychotherapy for patients diagnosed with borderline personality disorder: A comparison with a treatment-as-usual cohort. *Manuscript submitted for publication.*

Levy, K. N., Edell, W. S., & McGlashan, T. H. (2007). Depressive experiences in inpatients with borderline personality disorder. *Psychiatric Quarterly, 78*(2), 129–143.

Levy, K. N., Meehan, K. B., Kelly, K. M., Reynoso, J. S., Weber, M., Clarkin, J. F., & Kernberg, O. F. (2006). Change in attachment patterns and reflective function in a randomized control trial of transference focused psychotherapy for borderline personality disorder. *Journal of Consulting and Clinical Psychology, 74*(6), 1027–1040.

Levy, K. N., Meehan, K. B., & Yeomans, F. E. (2012). An update and overview of the empirical evidence for transference-focused psychotherapy and other psychotherapies for borderline personality disorder. In R. A. Levy, J. S. Ablon, & H. Kächele (Eds.), *Psychodynamic psychotherapy research* (pp. 139–167). New York, NY: Springer.

Linehan, M. M., Tutek, D. A., Heard, H. L., & Armstrong, H. E. (1994). Interpersonal outcome of cognitive behavioral treatment for chronically suicidal borderline patients. *American Journal of Psychiatry, 151*, 1771–1776

Linehan, M. M. (1993). *Cognitive-behavioral treatment of borderline personality disorder.* New York, NY: Guilford Press.

Linehan, M. M., Armstrong, H. E., Suarez, A., Allmon, D., & Heard, H. (1991). Cognitive-behavioral treatment of chronically parasuicidal borderline patients. *Archives of General Psychiatry, 48*, 1060–1064.

Loranger, A. (1999). *International Personality Disorder Examination (IPDE) manual.* Odessa, FL: Psychological Assessment Resources, Inc.

Loranger, A. W., Sartorius, N., Andreoli, A., & Berger, P. (1994). The international personality disorder examination: The World Health Organization/alcohol, drug abuse, and mental health administration international pilot study of personality disorders. *Archives of General Psychiatry, 51*(3), 215.

Magnavita, J. J., Levy, K. N., Critchfield, K. L., & Lebow, J. L. (2010). Ethical considerations in treatment of personality dysfunction: Using evidence, principles, and clinical judgment. *Professional Psychology: Research and Practice, 41*(1), 64–74.

McGlashan, T. H. (1986). The Chestnut Lodge follow-up study: III. Long-term outcome of borderline personalities. *Archives of General Psychiatry, 43*, 20–30.

Messer, S. B. (2007). Psychoanalytic case studies and the pragmatic case study method. *Pragmatic Case Studies in Psychotherapy, 3*(1), 55–58. Available at http://pcsp.libraries.rutgers.edu/. doi: http://dx.doi.org/10.14713/pcsp.v3i1.894

Munder, T. F., Flückiger, C., Gerger, H., Wampold, B. E., & Barth, J. (2012). Is the allegiance effect an epiphenomenon of true efficacy differences between treatments? A meta-analysis. *Journal of Counseling Psychology, 59*(4), 631–637.

Oldham, J. M., Skodol, A. E., Kellman, H. D., Hyler, S. E., Doidge, N., Rosnick, L., & Gallahar, P. E. (1995). Comorbidity of Axis I and Axis II disorders. *American Journal of Psychiatry, 152*(4), 571–578.

Paris, J. (1999). Borderline personality disorder. In T. Millon, P. H. Blaney, & R. D. Davis (Eds.), *Oxford textbook of psychopathology* (pp. 625–652). New York, NY: Oxford University Press.

Patton, J. H., Stanford, M. S., & Barratt, E. S. (1995). Factor structure of the Barratt Impulsiveness Scale. *Journal of Clinical Psychology, 51*, 768–774.

Piper, W. E., Ogrodniczuk, J. S., Joyce, A. S., McCallum, M., Rosie, J. S., O'Kelly, J. G., & Steinberg, P. I. (1999). Prediction of dropping out in time-limited, interpretive individual psychotherapy. *Psychotherapy, 36*(2), 114–122.

Posner, M. I., Rothbart, M. K., Vizueta, N, Levy, K. N., Evans, D. E., Thomas, K. M., & Clarkin, J. F. (2002). Attentional mechanisms of borderline personality disorder. *Proceedings of the National Academy of Sciences, 99*(25), 16366–16370.

Rockland, L. H. (1989). *Supportive therapy: A psychodynamic approach.* New York, NY: Basic Books.

Rockland, L. H. (1992). *Supportive therapy for borderline patients: A psychodynamic approach.* New York, NY: Guilford Press.

Roth, A. & Fonagy, P. (2005). *What works for whom? A critical review of psychotherapy research* (2nd ed.). New York, NY: Guilford Press.

Rosenthal, R. & Rosnow, R. L. (1991). *Essentials of behavioral research: Methods and data analysis* (2nd ed.). New York, NY: McGraw-Hill.

Rosenthal, R., Rosnow, R. L., & Rubin, D. B. (2000). *Contrasts and effect sizes in behavioral research: A correlational approach.* New York, NY: Cambridge University Press.

Roth, A. & Fonagy, P. (2005). *What works for whom? A critical review of psychotherapy research* (2nd ed.). New York, NY: Guilford Press.

Skodol, A. E., Gunderson, J. G., Pfohl, B., Widiger, T. A., Livesley, W. J., & Siever, L. J. (2002). The borderline diagnosis I: Psychopathology, comorbidity, and personality structure. *Biological Psychiatry, 51*(12), 936–950.

Soloff, P. H. (2000). Psychopharmacology of borderline personality disorder. *Psychiatric Clinics of North America, 23*(1), 169–192.

Stone, M. H. (1983). Long-term outcome in personality disorders. *British Journal of Psychiatry, 162,* 299–313.

Torgersen, S., Kringlen, E., & Cramer, V. (2001). The prevalence of personality disorders in a community sample. *Archives of General Psychiatry, 58,* 590–596.

Wallerstein, R. (1986). *Forty-two lives in treatment.* New York, NY: Guilford Press.

Weissman, M. M. & Bothwell, S. (1976). Assessment of social adjustment by patient self-report. *Archives of General Psychiatry, 33,* 1111–1115.

Yeomans, F. E. (2007). Questions concerning the randomized trial of schema-focused therapy vs. transference-focused therapy. *Archives of General Psychiatry, 64*(5), 609–610.

Yeomans, F. E., Clarkin, J. F., & Kernberg, O. F. (2015). *Transference-focused psychotherapy borderline personality disorder: A clinical guide.* Washington, DC: American Psychiatric Publishing.

Yeomans, F. E. (1993). Treatment planning: When a therapist overindulges a demanding borderline patient. *Hospital and Community Psychiatry, 44*(4), 334–336.

Zanarini, M. C. & Frankenburg, F. R. (2001). Olanzapine treatment of female borderline personality disorder patients: A double-blind, placebo-controlled pilot study. *Journal of Clinical Psychiatry, 62*(11), 849–854.

Zanarini, M. C., Frankenburg, F. R., Hennen, J., & Silk, K. R. (2004). Mental health service utilization of borderline patients and Axis II comparison subjects followed prospectively for six years. *Journal of Clinical Psychiatry, 65*(1), 28–36.

Zanarini, M. C., Frankenburg, F. R., Reich, D. B., & Fitzmaurice, G. (2010a). The 10-year course of psychosocial functioning among patients with borderline personality disorder and axis II comparison subjects. *Acta Psychiatrica Scandinavica, 122*(2), 103–109.

Zanarini, M. C., Frankenburg, F. R., Reich, D. B., & Fitzmaurice, G. (2010b). Time-to-attainment of recovery from borderline personality disorder and its stability: A 10-year prospective follow-up study. *American Journal of Psychiatry, 167*(7), 663–667.

Zanarini, M. C., Frankenburg, F. R., Reich, D., Marino, M. F., Haynes, M. C., & Gunderson, J. G. (1999). Violence in the lives of adult borderline patients. *Journal of Nervous and Mental Disease, 187,* 65–71.

Zanarini, M. C., Horwood, J., Wolke, D., Waylen, A., Fitzmaurice, G., & Grant, B. F. (2011). Prevalence of DSM-IV borderline personality disorder in two community samples: 6,330 English 11-year-olds and 34,653 American adults. *Journal of Personality Disorders, 25*(5), 607–619.

Zimmerman, M., Rothschild, L., & Chelminski, I. (2005). The prevalence of DSM-IV personality disorders in psychiatric outpatients. *American Journal of Psychiatry, 162*(10), 1911–1918.

COMMENTARY
Complementarity and Clinical Implications in Using a Mixed-Methods Approach

William E. Piper and Carlos A. Sierra Hernandez

When I (the first author, W. E. P.) read the chapter by Levy, Meehan, Clouthier, Yeomans, Lenzenweger, Clarkin, and Kernberg (2016), my immediate reaction was a flashback to the initial RCT that I conducted in the mid-1970s. This included a comparison of psychodynamic group therapy by psychiatric residents in their first year of training with a treatment-as-usual condition for young adults suffering from neurotic or mild characterological problems, using a battery of 10 sociometric measures taken prior to and after 3 months of treatment (Piper et al., 1977).

The design we used was heavily influenced by the "thin" prototype of the RCT at the time, which emphasizes experimental control in contrast to clinical richness and relevance to naturalistic practice. As I have written, this thin type of RCT

> only focuses on pre-therapy to post-therapy efficacy in averaged form, only reports results in terms of statistical significance and effect size, and only studies atypical patients [e.g., those with only a single diagnosis], therapists [e.g., those who are inexperienced and in training], and therapies [e.g., those that use highly structured manuals involving sequentially specific procedures]. (Piper, 2000, p. 6)

The two following group therapy trials that my research team conducted provided findings that were more complex and more clinically valuable. They included

> (1) ways of preparing patients for group therapy (Piper, Debbane, Garant, & Bienvenu, 1979), (2) ways of coordinating the interventions of co-therapists in groups (Piper, Doan, Edwards, & Jones, 1979), ... (3) ways of composing groups to enhance remaining, working, and benefiting (Connelly & Piper, 1989), ... [and] detailed process analysis work using a modification of the Hill Interaction Matrix. (Piper, 2000, p. 6).

Our next clinical trial was even more ambitious (Piper, Debbane, Bienvenu, & Garant, 1984). It compared four forms of psychodynamic therapy (short-term individual, short-term group, long-term individual, and long-term group), that is, four types of bona fide treatments. In contrast to the earlier thin RCT designs, this RCT was a rather hefty, "thick" trial that involved detailed process analyses of therapist interventions, outcome assessments during treatment, a focus on patient characteristics as predictor variables, and reasons for dropping out of therapy. We developed a process measure to assess therapist interpretations, and we also developed two interview-based measures of the patient's quality of object relations (Piper & Duncan, 1999) and psychological mindedness (McCallum & Piper, 1997). It should be noted that these two measures are similar to Levy et al.'s variables of attachment organization and reflective functioning, respectively. That my research team and Levy's research team should be drawn independently to these variables seems clearly rooted in their importance in psychodynamic theory.

In sum, I began my RCT research with a narrow focus on testing one bona fide treatment against treatment as usual and isolating just a few discrete variables while experimentally controlling for everything else by random assignment. The research then evolved to a broader focus by adding to my RCT designs the systematic study of a variety of client, process, therapy modality, and other contextual variables, all of which can serve as mechanisms of change in their roles as moderators or mediators (Comer & Kendall, 2013; Kazdin, 2009). This evolution occurred for two main reasons: The first was my increasing recognition of the complexity of human relationships and of the treatments aimed at ameliorating intrapsychic and interpersonal difficulties. The more I studied the clinical cases that comprised my RCT therapy groups, the more I became aware of how multidimensional and situationally specific the clinical therapy processes were. The second was the need to reduce the gap between, on the one hand, the results of laboratory-like RCTs as they relate to questions of "efficacy" (that is, the rigor of the results within the study itself, termed "internal validity"), and, on the other hand, questions of effectiveness (that is, the application of the results to naturalistic settings, termed "external validity"). Thus, I became more and more aware that in order for knowledge from RCTs to be applicable to therapy as routinely practiced, the RCTs had to capture the conditions under which routine practice takes place. In fact, as I read the Levy et al. chapter, I became more persuaded that the next step in deepening the investigation of complex therapy phenomena is to add systematic case studies to the process.

ALIENATION BETWEEN RESEARCHERS AND CLINICIANS

Based on this, it is no surprise to learn that the two of us (W. E. P. and C. A. S. H.) enthusiastically agree with a 2010 article by Dattilio, Edwards, and Fishman— three of this book's coeditors—that provides an in-depth exploration of the alienation between researchers and practitioners in psychotherapy research. In their exploration of this alienation, Dattilio et al. suggest that to use group-based, quantitative empirical evidence to substantiate clinical decision making can potentially ignore important sources of individual case variation. This can include a client's own personality style, its interaction with the treatment under study, and the implication of this interaction for treatment outcomes. This limitation led Dattilio et al., along with other researchers and clinicians, to propose a mixed-method paradigm as one possible solution of this alienation. As further developed in this book, these authors suggest that a viable intersection between group-based quantitative psychotherapy data and individually based qualitative psychotherapy data lies in the complementarity of knowledge derived from a randomized clinical trial (RCT) and knowledge derived from case studies drawn from the RCT. This "mixed-method" approach is particularly well suited to guiding the case conceptualization and treatment of serious mental health conditions and disorders, such as the one under focus in the Levy et al. chapter, namely, borderline personality disorder (BPD).

BPD is typically characterized by affective instability, marked impulsivity, suicidal ideation and/or behavior, and severe deficits in occupational and interpersonal functioning (e.g., Oldham, 2006). Due to its complex presentation, high rates of comorbidity with other disorders, and challenges associated with its treatment, many borderline individuals do not receive effective therapy (Bender et al., 2001). This reality persists despite current heightened research interest in BPD and its treatment. As described later, the research described in Levy et al.'s chapter—both the RCT and the case studies—very importantly adds to our knowledge of effective interventions for BPD, hence narrowing the researcher–clinician divide.

DESIGN STRENGTHS IN LEVY ET AL.'S RCT

Effectiveness Features

In light of the previous discussion, we were particularly interested in design features in the research described in Levy et al.'s chapter that contributed to conclusions about transference-focused psychotherapy's effectiveness, that is, ways in which the therapy in the RCT incorporated many of the characteristics of routine practice and thus increased generalization of the findings to normative practice. These characteristics included using the types of inclusion/exclusion criteria employed in clinical practice; having therapists provide TFP at the usual clinical frequency—twice a week; having therapists provide treatment in their private offices in the community rather than in a university or hospital setting; deciding on psychopharmacological treatment based on the individual case (while reducing subjectivity by employing a medication algorithm); and providing patients the opportunity to continue therapy after the research treatment period of 1 year, since TFP is frequently a multiyear therapy in routine practice. Importantly, Levy et al. were aware of the trade-off between adherence to efficacy logic and to effectiveness logic, and the authors statistically checked that their deviations from strict efficacy procedures did not result in any quantitative differences in their results.

Eliminating Researcher Allegiance Effects

A rather persuasive problem in the RCT literature is that of the existence of "researcher allegiance" [RA], that is, a researcher's "belief in the superiority of a treatment [and] . . . the superior validity of the theory of change that is associated with the treatment" (Leykin & DeRubeis, 2009, p. 55), leading to a bias in results in accordance with those beliefs. For example, in a recent mega-analysis of all available meta-analytic estimates (N = 30) of the association between RA and psychotherapy outcome, Munder et al. (2013) found a correlation of .262 ($p = .002$), which corresponds to a moderate effect size.

As a protection against allegiance effect, in the RCT described in the Levy et al. chapter, the three treatments involved—transference-focused psychotherapy, dialectical behavior therapy, and supportive psychotherapy—were conducted by teams that had a high allegiance to their respective model. In the words of Levy et al., "The campus at Cornell Medical College [where the RCT was conducted] presented a unique opportunity in that there were three distinct long-standing programs of treatment for BPD that were well represented by active faculty, all with a presence on campus" (p. 191).

Theoretical Yield

The RCT was designed not only to evaluate whether TFP in itself was efficacious but also to evaluate whether the therapy worked in the manner described by the transference-focused, psychoanalytic theory underlying the therapy. One approach to doing this was to compare TFP with SPT, with the latter differing from TFP specifically by SPT's lack of the use of transference interpretation. Another approach was to study the impact of two variables, which tap into some of the core mechanisms that TFP theory hypothesizes are crucial to therapeutic change. Both of these variables relate to the hypothesized difficulties underlying BPD, particularly including disparate and split representations of the self and others, and the inability to think openly and constructively about these representations.

One of the relevant variables was Attachment Organization, assessed by how openly and coherently a patient is able to discuss and think about his or her positive and negative childhood memories. The other, a related variable, was Reflective Functioning, which Levy et al. define as "the ability to make inferences about the intent underlying behavior in oneself and others by evoking and reflecting on one's own experience" (p. 198). The findings in the RCT that both Attachment Organization and Reflective Functioning were associated with therapeutic change in the TFP condition but not in the other two conditions provides confirming evidence for the hypotheses about the distinctive role each of these two variables plays in the processes underlying TFP.

THE CONTRIBUTION OF CASE STUDIES

As mentioned earlier, case studies provide an additional way of enriching the yield of RCT research for understanding in more depth the processes leading to successful versus unsuccessful therapy. This point is cogently illustrated in the two patients—Ms. J and Ms. V—described in Levy et al.'s chapter, who were both drawn from the TFP group. At intake both patients appeared to be quite similar.

> Both women [were] in their early 30s . . . [and] presented for treatment after having little benefit from prior psychotherapies and pharmacotherapies as well as little success in past work environments. Both women were diagnosed with BPD and randomized to the same therapist in TFP. The therapist was male and an experienced clinician who had practiced and supervised TFP for many years. Each patient was treated twice-weekly [using the same TFP manual] in his private practice office in close proximity to the affiliated medical center sponsoring the RCT. As part of the RCT, each patient agreed to be treated in 1 year of TFP. (pp. 208–209)

However, in contrast to their apparent similarities and having received very similar therapy, after 1 year they had dramatically different outcomes, both quantitatively and qualitatively. For example,

> qualitatively J had made substantial changes in her willingness to risk feeling vulnerable in order to work toward creating the kinds of relational experiences she sought for herself. In contrast, V continued to privilege protecting herself from experiences of vulnerability, even at the expense of working toward richer relationships. (p. 232)

The therapy process descriptions of the cases provide rich examples of J and V's different reactions to the therapy. Although both were initially angry and defensive and distanced themselves from the therapist, J became more open to reflecting on her behavior, especially within the therapy room, and thus more open to transference interpretations, the heart of the TFP method. For example, in the twelfth session, in response to the therapist's observation about J's defensive, nonstop dialogue, J burst into tears and said, "If I didn't control you, you'd leave me . . . like everyone else!" (p. 218). J's growth in her ability for self-awareness was indicated by the move from her initial Reflective Functioning score of −1.00 to a 1-year score of 6.00, above the clinical cutoff of 5.00. As another example, J made major improvement over the course of 1 year in her Attachment Organization score.

In contrast, Ms. V showed no growth in her ability over the year of TFP therapy to become more reflective. For example, her score on the Reflective Functioning measure was 3.00, both at the beginning and end of therapy, and her score on the Attachment Organization measure did not change. Throughout the therapy, she was intensely defensive and not at all open to the transference-interpretation potential of TFP. Of particular note in V's case was the issue of secondary gain. For example,

> . . . in discussions of increasing her level of structured activity, not only did it become clear that V feared that her increased functioning might

threaten the stability of her medical disability benefits and subsidized housing, but also that she felt entitled to this support and saw others (e.g., the therapist, the government) as trying to steal what was rightfully hers. A dyadic interaction seemed to be emerging in which V saw the world along the lines of predator and prey, leading to an attitude that you need to take what you must to survive; "don't let what's yours be stolen from you." (pp. 225–226)

Finally, as mentioned earlier, at the end of the 1 year of therapy called for in the treatment protocol, each of the patients was offered additional therapy in the therapist's private office, as a clinical opportunity beyond the formal RCT treatment. The differing reactions of the patients indicate confirming evidence of their different degree of progress. J enthusiastically agreed and

continued to make substantial gains. J's complaints of mistreatment gradually decreased; she reported less anxiety and more positive interactions in her volunteer work setting, where she was offered a paid position after a year. After 3 years of therapy, she started a relationship with and eventually married a man whose empathy she appreciated, in contrast to the illusion of an ideal she was attracted to in the earlier objects of her desire. By the end of 5 years of therapy, J had achieved stability in her work life, having obtained a master's degree and become steadily employed in a full-time position, got married, and developed friendships and meaningful interests in the arts. (p. 230)

In contrast, whereas V initially accepted the offer of additional treatment,

a few months later V stated that she had decided to end the therapy. Her therapist was concerned because she had not addressed the overwhelming feeling of being exploited in relationships, which not only put her job at risk but was also reflected in ongoing conflicts with the men she dated and the few friends she had. Despite her therapist's strong recommendation to continue with treatment, the patient thanked him for his help in a perfunctory way and ended the therapy. (p. 231)

IMPLICATIONS FOR CLINICIANS

Meehl's (1957) assertion of there being a disconnect between clinical practice and research findings stills applies today. As discussed earlier, many clinicians have turned away from RCT-based psychotherapy research as a guide to practice because of the lack of generalization of the findings to their particular cases. The project described in Levy et al.'s chapter goes a long way toward addressing this disconnect because the efficacy-oriented design features in the RCT component and the case studies help to make the results of the project very relevant to routine practice. Two points are noteworthy in this regard.

To begin with, the Levy et al. project is the first to investigate the efficacy and effectiveness of TFP compared to two alternative and well-established treatments for BPD. The results provide persuasive evidence indicating that all three treatments under study (i.e., TFP, DBT, and SPT) yielded clinically and statistically significant changes in the BPD clients randomized to each treatment. For clinicians treating clients with BPD, this result provides a broader field of action when choosing an efficacious treatment for their BPD clients, knowing that there are different theory-based options in selecting how to treat a particular client. Of course, it is important to note that the efficacy of these three treatments was achieved under controlled and specific conditions chosen by Levy and colleagues. These include the availability of expert (or at least very knowledgeable) therapists to treat clients, the availability of supervision by senior clinical experts, a close adherence to treatment manuals, and the use of blind raters. Most clinicians in the community cannot afford some, if not all, of these controlled conditions. As such, although it is advantageous for clinicians to recognize the availability of efficacious treatments for the treatment of BPD, research also has to be conducted on the generalizability of their results, that is, how broadly their findings apply when these specific conditions are not met.

Secondly, the case studies in Levy et al.'s project can help clinicians by documenting the particular processes by which change takes place, as in the case of J, or does not, as in the case of V. Even within a successful patient like J, there are many barriers and resistances that were documented that are very helpful for practitioners to learn about. Also, the successful case of J makes it clear that the kind of success at 1 year that the RCT documented was limited compared to a nonclinical population; and that it took 4 more years of continued TFP therapy for J to be a full success. In fact, J's success in the first year consisted in good part in the creation of openness to and motivation for the next 4 years of therapy, characteristics that were not generated in the unsuccessful case of V.

Finally, the presentation of variability of outcomes within the TFP group of the RCT, a group of participants who achieved significant positive change overall, shows that, as expected for most treatments, TFP—at least as delivered by the manualized version used in the RCT—is not effective for every client. This suggests that individual differences among clients receiving the same treatment can and do affect treatment outcome. This knowledge, not previously available for TFP with BPD clients, encourages clinicians to think about their clients' personality, congruency with the treatment and readiness for psychotherapy.

In a similar way, the knowledge stemming from this investigation also underscores the need for clinicians to be attentive to the responsiveness of their BPD clients regarding the treatment being provided. If clients are not being responsive to the treatment, it is important for the clinician to evaluate why this is happening and to explore new avenues. As explained by Levy et al., Ms. V., the poor-outcome client, perhaps could have benefitted from an integrative approach that allowed for the incorporation of DBT skills into the treatment being provided. Although this integration would have not been possible within an RCT, clinicians in the community are encouraged to think about the interaction between his or her client's personality and other individual characteristics, on the one hand, and the treatment being provided, on the other.

IMPLICATIONS FOR RESEARCHERS

The use of an RCT and associated case studies, that is, a mixed method to understand the efficacy and effectiveness of TFP as well as its mechanisms of change also has a number of important implications for researchers. First, as was the case for clinicians, researchers benefit from knowing the mechanisms of change in TFP beyond the differential effectiveness of TFP, DBT, and SPT. This involves uncovering the theoretical route by which TFP effects change and, above all, the degree to which clinical change parallels theory-based ideas of change in TFP. In Levy et al.'s study the structural variables theoretically proposed to underlie change in BPD clients receiving TFP were hypothesized to be attachment style, reflective functioning, and narrative coherence. Their results support this hypothesis and, therefore, suggest that BPD clients who would generally benefit from receiving TFP would experience positive changes in these domains. The case studies further elaborate the role of these theoretically important variables and add specifics as to how they function within diverse patients and how patients are differentially responsive to attempts to positively impact these variables in therapy.

Also of interest is the general issue of matching. The cases of J and V dramatically show how TFP can be an excellent match for one client, and a poor one for another client, respectively.

Finally, there has been a movement in psychotherapy research from work that focuses solely on the effectiveness and efficacy of a treatment program to work that focuses on the experiences of the therapist and the client in conjunction with understanding the clinical effect of the treatment (Miller, Hubble, Chow, & Seidel, 2013). This movement suggests that it is only from a bottom-up perspective that researchers can accurately capture individual-level effects of treatments. Case studies have typically been employed as a first step to theory building from the ground up, for example, the work of Freud, Rogers, Wolpe, and Beck. The inclusion of case examples by Levy et al. provides researchers with a clear indication of what it is like for the client and the therapist to be sitting across from each other, how transference interpretations affect the client–therapist therapeutic relationship, and how the client experiences the process of addressing her BPD while participating in TFP. It is only through this kind of groundwork that the researcher can advance our knowledge of TFP and its applicability to BPD clients.

CONCLUSIONS

The aim of this commentary was to highlight how the incorporation of a mixed-method design in the study of the effectiveness and efficacy of TFP for BPD clients is beneficial for both the researchers interested in these investigations but also, and as importantly, for clinicians who are eager to apply this scientific knowledge. The use of mixed-methods designs affords both clinicians and researchers not only a deeper understanding of the process of therapy vis-à-vis the theory underlying it but also guidelines and examples for how to apply the results of the study to community practice.

In sum, Levy et al's study serves as an exemplar of methodological innovation. In it the authors were not only able to cement the reputation of TFP as an effective treatment for BPD, but they also found TFP to be at least as efficacious as other well-established treatments for this disorder. Furthermore, through the use of a mixture of a "rich" RCT and systematic case studies drawn from the RCT, the authors were also able to identify theoretically based mechanisms of change of TFP for BPD and to provide insight into the possible interaction between individual client characteristics and these mechanisms. As a whole, thanks in large part to Levy et al's methodological design and the complementarity of an RCT and case studies, the amount and quality of scientific knowledge resulting from this empirical investigation is sizable and sophisticated.

REFERENCES

Bender, D. S., Dolan, R. T., Skodol, A. E., Sanislow, C. A., Dyck, I. R., McGlashan, T. H., . . . Gunderson, J. G. (2001). Treatment utilization by patients with personality disorders. *American Journal of Psychiatry, 158*, 295–302.

Comer, J. S., & Kendall, P. C. (2013). Methodology, design, and evaluation in psychotherapy research. In M. J. Lambert (Ed.)., *Bergin and Garfield's handbook of psychotherapy and behavior change* (6th ed.). New York, NY: John Wiley.

Connelly, J. L., & Piper, W. E. (1989). An analysis of pretraining work behavior as a comparison variable in group therapy. *International Journal of Group Therapy, 39*, 173–189.

Dattilio, F. M., Edwards, D. J., & Fishman, D. B. (2010). Case studies within a mixed methods paradigm: Toward a resolution of the alienation between researcher and practitioner in psychotherapy research. *Psychotherapy, 47*, 427–441.

Kazdin, A. E. (2009). Understanding how and why psychotherapy leads to change. *Psychotherapy Research, 19*, 418–428.

Levy, K. N., Meehan, K. B., Clouthier, T. L., & Yeomans, F. E., Lenzenweger, M. F., Clarkin, J. F., & Kernberg, O. F. (2016). Transference-focused psychotherapy for adult borderline personality disorder. In D. B. Fishman, S. B. Messer, J. A. Edwards & F. M. Dattilio (Eds.), *Case studies within psychotherapy trials: Integrating qualitative and quantitative methods*. New York, NY: Oxford University Press.

Leykin, Y., & DeRubeis, R. J. (2009). Allegiance in psychotherapy outcome research: Separating association from bias. *Clinical Psychology: Science and Practice, 16*, 54–65.

McCallum, L., & Piper, W. E. (1997). *Psychological mindedness: A contemporary understanding*. Mahwah, NJ: Lawrence Erlbaum Associates.

Meehl, P. E. (1957). When shall we use our heads instead of the formula? *Journal of Counseling Psychology, 4*, 268–273.

Miller, S. D., Hubble, M. A., Chow, D. L., & Seidel, J. A. (2013). The outcome of psychotherapy: Yesterday, today, and tomorrow. *Psychotherapy, 50,* 88–97.

Munder, T., Brütsch, O., Leonhart, R., Gerger, H., & Barth, J. (2013). Researcher allegiance in psychotherapy outcome research: An overview of reviews. *Clinical Psychology Review, 33,* 501–511.

Oldham, J. M. (2006). Borderline personality disorder and suicidality. *American Journal of Psychiatry, 163,* 20–26.

Piper, W. E., (2000). Collaboration in a new millennium. *Psychotherapy Research, 11,* 1–11.

Piper, W. E., Debbane, E. G., Bienvenu, J. P., & Garant, J. (1984). A comparative study of four forms of psychotherapy. *Journal of Consulting and Clinical Psychology, 52,* 268–279.

Piper, W. E., Debbane, E. G., & Garant, J. (1977). An outcome study of group therapy. *Archives of General Psychiatry, 34,* 1027–1032.

Piper, W. E., Debbane, E. G., & Garant, J., & Bienvenu, J. P. (1979). Pretraining for group psychotherapy: A cognitive-experiential approach. *Archives of General Psychiatry, 36,* 1250–1256.

Piper, W. E., Doan, B. D., Edwards, E. M., & Jones, B. D. (1979). Cotherapy behavior, group therapy process and treatment outcome. *Journal of Consulting and Clinical Psychology, 47,* 1081–1089.

Piper, W. E., & Duncan, S. C. (1999). Object relations theory and short-term dynamic psychotherapy: Findings from the Quality of Object Relations Scale. *Clinical Psychology Review, 19,* 668–686.

6

Motivational Enhancement Therapy for Increasing Antidepressant Medication Adherence and Decreasing Clinical Depression Among Adult Latinos

ALEJANDRO INTERIAN, ARIANA PRAWDA,
DANIEL B. FISHMAN, AND WILLIAM M. BUERGER ■

Commentary by John C. Norcross

THE RCT STUDY

Introduction

Major depressive disorder is a significant public health problem, with nearly 15 million Americans (6.6% of the population) experiencing symptoms of depression each year, making it the leading cause of disability for people ages 15–44 (Kessler et al., 2003; NIMH, 2008).

Although this public health problem impacts the entirety of the United States, Latinos have unfortunately been reported to face a number of challenges in meeting their depression treatment needs. Latinos with depression are more likely to underutilize services, have limited access to culturally and linguistically appropriate treatment, and have high rates of attrition during the first and second stages of antidepressant treatment (Atdjian & Vega, 2005; Rios-Ellis, 2005; Warden et al., 2007, 2009). This pattern of low engagement and adherence has also manifested in the form of low rates of psychotropic medication adherence among Latinos

(Lanouette et al., 2009; Olfson, Marcus, Tedeshi, & Wan, 2006; Sleath, Rubin, & Hustin, 2003), which one study of monolingual Latinos living in New York City found to be lower than 20% (Opler et al., 2004).

These findings are particularly disconcerting because nonadherence with antidepressant medication has been shown to be associated with a decreased reduction of depressive symptoms and an increased risk of relapse among clients with depression (Melartin et al., 2005; Melfi et al., 1998). In addition, antidepressant medication is the most frequently used mental health intervention in the United States (Olfson, Marcus, & Druss, et al., 2002), a fact that draws attention to the widespread impact of this pattern of lower adherence. Thus, the reasoning behind our RCT study was that improving adherence to antidepressant medication has the potential to significantly improve depression outcomes among Latinos.

There are several factors that may contribute to the lower adherence among Latinos. These may not be soley due to treatment access or costs, as antidepressant adherence in this group remains lower, even after studies adjust for these variables (Olfson, Marcus, Tedeshi, & Wan, 2006; Sleath, Rubin, & Hustin, 2009). Findings such as these points to the role of other factors. Among them, evidence reveals that Latinos, compared to non-Latino Caucasians, manifest a lower preference for antidepressant medication and lower expectations about its effectiveness (Cooper et al., 2003; Givens, Houston, Van Voorhees, Ford, & Cooper, 2007). In addition, in terms of social context, Latinos are more likely to encounter views that are unaccepting and stigmatizing toward antidepressants (Anglin, Link, & Phelan, 2006; Schnittker, Freese, & Powell, 2000; Whaley, 1997).

Altogether, this combined set of findings illustrates the challenges Latinos with depression face when embarking on treatment, challenges which ultimately impact the cost–benefit analysis of antidepressant use. Thus, addressing adherence in this population requires an understanding of these experiences, so that a therapeutic discussion can occur on the potential benefit of medication treatment in relation to the challenges. In the "Method" section, we describe how these issues were incorporated into an intervention for addressing antidepressant adherence among the Latino population with depression.

We began by choosing an intervention that did not simply provide psychoeducation or correct misconceptions about medication, but rather sought to empathize with and acknowledge the concerns that our clients faced regarding antidepressants. With this in mind, we selected a motivational interviewing (MI)–based intervention (Hettema, Steele, & Miller, 2005; Miller & Rollnick, 2002), given its empirically demonstrated ability to address ambivalence in its many forms and thus to constructively discuss with clients many of the barriers to medication adherence listed earlier. Our version of it is called "motivational enhancement therapy for antidepressants" (META).

In addition to selecting an MI-based procedure because of its responsiveness to a client's particular experiential world, we employed focus groups to adapt the content of META to be relevant to the group of Latinos served by the local clinic. The procedures for doing this are described under the "Interventions" section.

The subsequent RCT examined the extent to which, compared to usual care, culturally adapted MI would improve antidepressant adherence among Latino outpatients receiving treatment for depression at a community mental health center (CMHC), and whether this in turn led to decreased depression symptom levels and to improved rates of symptom remission. (For details not included in this chapter about the RCT, see Interian, Lewis-Fernández, Gara, & Escobar, 2013.)

Method

CASE-FINDING PROCEDURES
All participants were recruited between July of 2007 and December of 2009 from a CMHC located in central New Jersey. Three participants were recruited through flyers, and the rest ($n = 47$) were referred by their treating psychiatrist. To be considered eligible for the study, participants were required to be (a) Latino; (b) between the ages of 18 and 25; (c) prescribed antidepressant medication; and (d) diagnosed with either major depressive disorder (including psychotic features) or dysthmia, using the Structured Clinical Interview for DSM-IV (SCID; First, Spitzer, Gibbon, & Williams, 2005).

Note that low antidepressant adherence was not an explicit criterion of selection. Rather, the research team assumed, based on the fact that antidepressant adherence tends to be low in general and even lower among underserved populations, that the present sample would generally have low adherence. And in reality, the control group reported, on average, only taking their antidepressant 41% of days, which was very similar to low rates of adherence reported previously (Olfson et al., 2006).

Participants were excluded from the study if they were (a) pregnant or nursing, (b) medically unstable, or (c) diagnosed with bipolar disorder or a substance use disorder within the last year. The Institutional Review Board of Robert Wood Johnson Medical School (now part of Rutgers University) approved all study procedures and consents.

PARTICIPANTS
A total of 50 participants who met the inclusion and exclusion criteria were recruited for this study. Participants were randomly assigned to either the usual care (UC) condition or the enhanced treatment condition (UC + Motivational Enhancement Therapy for Antidepressants ["META"]). The interested reader is referred to Interian et al. (2013) Table 1 for a detailed presentation of the sample's baseline characteristics, including demographic and usual care treatment (i.e., psychopharmacology, psychotherapy attendance) features. Briefly, it will be noted that most participants were female, predominantly Spanish-speaking, and born outside of the United States. Most of the sample had considerable experience with depression and antidepressant medications. Participants received an average of 5 to 7 years of antidepressant treatment, prescribed for depression that had been

diagnosed an average of 5 to 8 years prior. Also, most participants had access to at least one CMHC psychotherapy appointment. Finally, 96% of the participants (*n* = 48) remained engaged in the study through time 2. By time 3, this number had reduced to 88% of the participants (*n* = 44).

ASSESSMENTS

Times of assessment. Upon being determined to be eligible for the study, participants were scheduled for a baseline session held 1–2 weeks after the referral. During the baseline session, participants were asked to complete a baseline evaluation (time 1), which consisted of a demographic form, the SCID, and a prescription assessment, as well as measures of depression and antidepressant medication adherence. Participants' antidepressant medication was then transferred to a container with an electronic cap (Medication Event Monitoring System, or "MEMS"®), and participants were instructed only to take medication from the provided container.

Follow-up assessments were also carried out 5 weeks (time 2) and 5 months (time 3) after the baseline evaluation. Research assistants blind to the treatment condition readministered the depression, medication adherence, and prescription measures, and adherence data were collected from the participants' MEMS® containers.

The MEMS® measure. Data from the MEMS® cap yielded the primary adherence measure. MEMS® caps were provided to participants at time 1 and scanned at times 2 and 3. The MEMS® recorded daily openings on their medication container for their primary antidepressant. The number of days a MEMS® bottle was opened divided by the total number of days in a time period was defined as the adherence number during that time period.

The Self-Reported Medication Taking Scale (SMTS; George, Peveler, Heileger, & Thompson, 2000). The SMTS, which was also used to assess adherence, contains four items, from 0 (least difficulties) to 4 (most difficulties). Previously, using the MEMS adherence number as a criterion, we found that a Spanish-language version of the SMTS had acceptable reliability and validity (Interian, 2010). We employed the SMTS to adjust for the MEMS numbers for baseline adherence.

The Beck Depression Inventory-IID (BDI-II; Beck, Steer, & Brown, 1996). This measure was developed in English to assess depressive symptoms, and since then it has been successfully applied to Spanish-speaking populations (Penly, Wiebe, & Nwosu, 2003; Wiebe & Penley, 2005). Scores on the BDI-II range from 0 to 63, with a score of 0–13 indicating minimal depression; 14–19, mild depression; 20–28, moderate depression; and 29–63, severe depression.

The BDI-II and the SMTS were administered in English or Spanish, depending on the client's preference.

Prescription data. Given that participants were receiving individualized psychopharmacological treatment, data about this treatment were collected from each participant. Specifically, each participant was asked to list his or her psychotropic prescriptions, and the information he or she provided was subsequently transformed into variables on the individual's psychopharmacology regimen (for specific variables, see Interian et al. [2013]).

Visit attendance data. Data from the CMHC's scheduling database were used to derive information about whether a participant had attended at least one psychotherapy visit during the course of the study and, if so, the total number of psychotherapy visits occurring while participating in the study.

COORDINATION WITH THE CMHC CLINICIANS

While carrying out this study, the META research team integrated itself with the treatment team of the CMHC. The principal investigator (A. I.) often attended treatment meetings at the CMHC so that the research and usual care activites could be coordinated, when necessary. In terms of the motivational interviewing, no issues of conflict arose. This is probably due to the fact that the MI operates with principles and procedures—like empathy, support, and confidence building—that are common factors in most therapy models, and thus are consistent with these models. Further ensuring compatibility with the treatment team is that one inclusion criterion required that an antidepressant—a focus of the RCT—was part of their treatment plan. Finally, the intervention developed motivation for overall treatment engagement, including both the clients' medication adherence and their reliance on the CMHC therapy. As a result, META functioned as an adjunctive treatment to usual mental health care.

INTERVENTIONS

All interventions were conducted in the participants' language of choice, which was usually Spanish. The CMHC clinicians were not informed of the participants' study condition, but it is possible that they were informed by the participants themselves.

Usual care (UC). Participants in the usual care (UC) condition were treated in the bilingual division of the CMHC by agency psychiatrists and therapists who were not involved with the META study. Treatment consisted of both psychotherapy and pharmacotherapy, and it was not influenced by researchers involved in the META study.

As context, it is important to point out that the quality of services offered by the CMHC is better than the average CMHC. A specific example, relevant to the present study, is that the CMHC has a Latino-focused treatment program with bilingual providers available.

META. Participants in the META condition received three sessions of motivational interviewing in addition to UC. Two 60-minute META sessions were provided between the time 1 and time 2 assessments, and an additional 60-minute booster session was provided between the time 2 and time 3 assessments. The META intervention sought to increase motivation for antidepressant medication adherence, while also providing nonjudgmental and empathic feedback regarding the client's concerns. The intervention focused on identifying and exploring barriers to medication adherence, both in the past and in the present (as measured using the MEMS® container). Participants were also asked to engage in problem-solving potential future barriers to adherence, which included sending a written adherence plan by mail. The META intervention also included psychoeducation regarding antidepressant medication, when appropriate.

MI-based interventions like META have accumulated a large evidence base across a span of years and have been examined for a wide variety of clinical problems (e.g., adherence, substance use, diet and exercise, HIV risk reduction, and smoking; Hettema et al. 2005; Miller & Rollnick, 2002). Besides being an adjunct to therapy, MI has also been shown to be an evidence-based therapy in itself, for example, in the well-known MATCH study of alcohol dependence (Project MATCH Research Group, 1997), and as a component in an evidence-based therapy, for example, in the COMBINE study of alcohol dependence (Anton et al., 2006). It is also included in the list of "Research-Support Psychological Treatments" on the Web site of the Society for Clinical Psychology (Division 12 of the American Psychological Association; http://www.div12.org/psychological-treatments/treatments/metmetcbt-for-mixed-substance-abuse/). More detail about MI is reviewed in the Case Studies section under the heading "Guiding Conception."

Cultural adaptation of META. We focused on identifying antidepressant adherence issues and reasons for nonadherence that were relevant to Latino patients of this particular CMHC, and adapting the META intervention to actively respond to these. Our main source of information in doing this was a series of focus groups conducted prior to the study. These focus groups identified cultural values that acted as sources of motivation for the clients, such as *trabajando dura* (working hard) and *luchar* or *luchando* (surviving difficult times). For example, *luchar* emphasized the value of struggling or confronting the frequent psychosocial stressors often experienced by low-income Latinos. Although this value provided many participants with feelings of pride, resiliency, and strength, it also acted as a barrier to treatment and medication adherence, fueling attitudes such as "You can't solve your problems by just taking a pill." Being aware of this value allowed clinicians to identify the concept of *luchar* when it arose and to reframe the taking of antidepressant medication as an act of strength and durability rather than resignation.

Cultural considerations unrelated to motivation were also illuminated during the focus groups, such as *familismo* (the importance of family) and *personalismo* (the expectancy of personalized relationships with providers). These values were then used to inform how motivational interviewing was adapted for this population, such as through the use of multiple phone and letter reminders (in line with the value of *personalismo*), and the use of cultural sayings or *dichos* that were in line with the central tenets of motivational interviewing (e.g. "*Para nadar hay que tirarse en el agua*" or "To swim, one must jump in the water").

The focus groups also drew attention to the stigmatization of antidepressant use, as well as the fear that taking pills may lead to adverse physical reactions (Interian, Martinez, Guarnaccia, Vega, & Escobar, 2007). Awareness of this concern again allowed clinicians to empathize with participants' concerns but to reframe the use of antidepressant medication as something that contributes to (rather than detracts from) one's physical health. The concerns identified during this focus group, as well as the adaptations made to account for them, have been described in a separate paper (Interian, Martinez, Rios, Krejci, & Guarnaccia, 2010).

Outreach efforts. Because treatment retention rates can be low among Latino clients with depression (Miranda, Nakamura, & Bernal, 2003), the clinicians, in a MI "spirited" way, engaged in considerable outreach efforts. As a result, an emphasis in applying MI with this population included attempts at multiple phone contacts, the use of confirmation phone calls, and appointment reminder letters. The META clinicians encouraged the clients' to be actively engaged in their treatment by empowering them to make their own decision about taking the medication. This was compatible with the cultural expectation of *personalismo*, where relationships with providers are personalized and involve trust (*confianza*).

Monitoring the fidelity of treatment. The META intervention was conducted by a clinical psychologist who holds a state license and three psychology doctoral students. The Motivational Interviewing Treatment Integrity scales were utilized to assess the fidelity of the treatment (MITI; Moyers, Martin, Manual, Hendrickson, & Miller, 2005). Average MITI scores for the first two sessions of treatment (provided by an independent rater) indicated that "competency" was achieved on four of six indicators (empathy, spirit, reflection:question ratio, MI adherent), and "proficiency" was achieved for the remaining two indicators (complex reflections, open-ended questions).

Results

Baseline Characteristics

The baseline characteristics of the META and UC conditions were compared with respect to demographics, number of psychotherapy appointments at the CMHC, and on a variety of baseline psychopharmacology regimen characteristics, such as type of antidepressant employed, dosage changes over time, medication switches over time, usage of an augmentive psychotropic, length of antidepressant use at baseline, and daily dose for the primary antidepressant. The results showed that there were no statistically significant differences between the META and UC conditions on any of the appointments and psychopharmacological variables.

Outcomes on Antidepressant Adherence

Results showed significant intervention effects on antidepressant adherence. META participants showed statistically significantly higher adherence to their antidepressants than UC at time 2 (5 weeks after baseline) and at time 3 (5 months after baseline). Specifically, the mean adherence rate was 71.94% in the META condition and 41.72% in the UC group. Similarly, at time 3, the META adherence rate was 59.81% and the UC condition adherence rate was 33.57%. Both of these differences were statistically significant at the $p < .01$ level in analyses that adjusted for baseline on the Self-Reported Medication Taking Scale (SMTS) and for having attended at least one psychotherapy session.

OUTCOMES ON DEPRESSION

Depression outcomes were evaluated with the BDI-II. Participants in both study conditions had a mean BDI-II score above 29 at time 1, which is indicative of severe depression. Repeated-measures ANOVAs, adjusted for having attended at least a psychotherapy appointment, showed that the groups did not significantly differ over time on depression symptom severity levels.

All the initial scores on the BDI-II were above 14, which is the clinical cutoff point between minimal and mild depression. Depression symptom remission at a later point in time is defined as a BDI-II score that is below this clinical cutoff point. At time 2 (5 weeks after baseline), the remission rates of the META and UC groups were 35% and 30%, respectively, which was nonsignificant (Fisher's Exact Test, $p = .765$). At time 3 (5 months after baseline) the respective rates were 50% for META and 20.8% for UC, which was significant (Fisher's Exact Test, $p = .042$). A logistic regression adjusting for baseline depression severity and having attended at least one psychotherapy appointment was conducted. This analysis showed that META participants had nearly six times the odds of achieving symptom remission. A subsequent model added participants' total antidepressant adherence during the 5-month period as a predictor and found that META participants remained significantly more likely to achieve symptom remission. On the other hand, the analysis showed that antidepresssant adherence was not significantly related to depression remission. (For more details on the logistic regression analysis, see Interian et al., 2013.)

Discussion

This RCT study performed an initial examination of an intervention (META) that was tailored, based on clients' perspectives, to address antidepressant adherence in a primarily Spanish-speaking Latino population. The data suggest that META was largely successful in this regard, having contributed to statistically significant and clinically meaningful increases in antidepressant medication adherence at both time 2 and time 3, with rates of medication adherence for participants in the META condition in time 3 almost doubling those of participants in the UC condition (59.81% versus 33.57%). META also displayed high rates of engagement and treatment retention, and was delivered with reasonable fidelity to MI principles.

Findings drawn from the depression outcomes are more complex. Whereas no significant differences in the sheer amount of depressive symptom reductions on the BDI-II were found between the two groups, META participants were six times more likely to have experienced a remission of their depressive symptoms at time 3, that is, a final score on the BDI-II of less than 14. This seemingly counterintuitive finding is the result of the differences between group-level versus individual-level analyses, and it will be explored in greater detail in the "Synthesis" section. Finally, no significant relationship was found to exist between antidepressant adherence and rates of depression remission.

THE CASE STUDIES

Nature and Rationale for Specific Cases Selected for the Case Studies

The cases of "Lupe," "Maria," and "Ana" were chosen for study because, respectively, they represented good examples of a positive outcome, negative outcome, and mixed outcome for the application of motivational interviewing to increase or sustain adherence to antidepressant medication. These cases were distinctive for several reasons. First, they showed different patterns of depression levels (as measured by the BDI) while participating in the research study. Specifically, as shown in Table 6.1, Lupe's scores significantly subsided, Maria's scores at first substantially decreased and then to some extent increased, and Ana's scores did not significantly change.

Table 6.1 BECK DEPRESSION INVENTORY (BDI)–II SCORES
ACROSS ASSESSMENT PERIODS

Time of Administration	BDI-II for Lupe	BDI-II for Maria	BDI-II for Ana	Mean BDI-II for All Patients in the META Treatment Group
Prior to MI intervention (T1)	43	48	26	31.1
Post MI intervention (T2)	9**	27*	35	21.1
4-month follow-up to MI intervention (T3)	3**	33*	23	18.1

NOTE: 0–13, minimal or no depression; 14–19, mild depression; 20–28, moderate depression; 29–63, severe depression.

* *Reliable improvement* on Jacobsen and Truax's (1991) Reliable Change Index; that is, (a) statistically significant change occurred between admission and the subsequent assessment, but (b) the participant did not achieve a move from the clinical to normal range on her scores.

** *Reliable change* on Jacobsen and Truax's (1991) Reliable Change Index; that is, (a) statistically significant change occurred between admission and the subsequent assessment, and (b) the participant achieved a move from the clinical to normal range on her scores.

MI, motivational interviewing.

SOURCE: Cutoff scores from Beck, A. T., Steer, R. A., & Brown, G. K. (1996). *Manual for the Beck Depression Inventory-II*. San Antonio, TX: Psychological Corporation.

Table 6.2 Percentage of Adherent Days for All Three Cases

Time of Administration	Lupe	Maria	Ana	Mean for All Patients in the META Treatment Group
First 10 days	80%	10%	100%	
Post MI Intervention (T2)	93.5%	78.8%	93.5%	75.8%
4-month follow-up to MI intervention (T3)	89%	37.1%	72%	65.7%
Total adherence	89.5%	49.1%	78.7%	69.6%

MI, motivational interviewing.

Second, each case's level of adherence to the antidepressant medication was noteworthy (see Table 6.2). Lupe's scores were high at the beginning of the study and remained high, Maria's adherence scores fluctuated and lacked sustainability, and Ana's adherence scores started high and diminished toward the end.

The data used in the case studies included audiotapes of the three META sessions, the quantitative data about each case, and an exit interview conducted by one of the clinical research team with each participant at the 5-month follow-up assessment session. (All these data were available on each of the META participants.) The purpose of the exit interview was to obtain a detailed, phenomenological "picture" of what it was like for the subject to participate in the study and to learn what kind of impact the treatment had on the participant's life.

Finally, note that the case studies that follow are based on a doctoral dissertation by the second author (A.P.). For more details on META intervention and the case studies, see the dissertation (Prawda, 2010).

The Clients

LUPE, A CLIENT WITH A POSITIVE OUTCOME

At the time of the study, Lupe was a 46-year-old, married, monolingual, Spanish-speaking Ecuadorian woman with two children ages 13 and 23. Lupe's first experience of depression occurred during her adolescent years but was left untreated. Her depression emerged for the second time 20 years later, at the age of 35, after immigrating to the United States from Ecuador. At the intake phase of the study, Lupe met the *DSM-IV* diagnostic criteria for a major depressive episode with subthreshold psychotic features (i.e., hearing her name being called, hearing doors open, hearing people talk when nobody was present).

MARIA, A CLIENT WITH A NEGATIVE OUTCOME

At the time of the study, Maria was a 30-year-old, monolingual, Spanish-speaking Venezuelan woman. She had immigrated to the United States 2.5 months prior to becoming a participant in the study. After learning that her husband had been having an extramarital affair and that he had fathered a child with another woman, she fell into a depressive episode. Maria met the *DSM-IV* criteria for a major depressive disorder, recurrent with psychotic features.

ANA, A CLIENT WITH A MIXED OUTCOME
At the time of the study, Ana was a 27-year-old, monolingual, Spanish-speaking Guatemalan woman who was living with her partner and their two children, ages 5 and 3. She had immigrated to the United States 8 years prior to her participation in the study. At intake, Ana met criteria for a diagnosis of chronic major depressive disorder.

QUANTITATIVE DATA ON INITIAL FUNCTIONING AND CHANGE OVER TIME
Quantitative data for the three clients at three points throughout the study on the BDI measure of depression and on adherence to medication can be found in Tables 6.1 and 6.2, respectively.

Guiding Conception With Research Support

LOGIC MODEL
In the original application for the funding of the META project, the focus was on employing MI to motivate depressed Latino clients to increase their adherence to antidepressant medication. We did not plan for the META to have an independent therapeutic function in itself. However, during the study, the clinical experiences of the META team led them to start suspecting that such a result of the MI intervention was happening; that is, clients seemed to be getting benefits from the intervention beyond what it was originally designed for. The results of the RCT further raised this possibility for the principal investigator (A. I.). The case studies allowed us to take a closer look at the details of how this might be happening. This closer look stimulated us to develop a "logic model" (Yin, 2014) that would encompass and conceptualize both the original focus of the project—to increase medication adherence—and the findings that the META intervention had therapeutic results in and of itself.

The resulting logic model is presented in Figure 6.1. The model is a broad one, comprehensively encompassing the multiple mechanisms and other factors that can cause a mental disorder like depression, along with possible comorbid psychopathology and other life difficulties.

As shown in Figure 6.1, the model has 10 components. The core of the model is the individualized case formulation approach of Jacqueline Persons (2008, 2013), in which a client's *origins* (box 1) lead to causal *mechanisms* (boxes 2–5), which are activated by *precipitating factors* (box 6) to create *symptoms and other problems* (box 7) like depression. The forces leading to such symptoms and other problems are represented in Figure 6.1 by solid arrows. There are also the client's individual

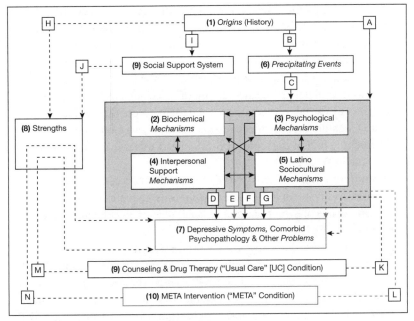

Figure 6.1 Logic Model for the META Study.
Note re words in italics: These words indicate the key concepts in Persons' (2008, 2013) case formulation model, including boxes 1-7.
Note re the light versus dark lines for the boxes and arrows. The components and processes involved in the initial main focus of the RCT study have light lines. These include the goal of META (box 10) to impact (arrow L) on hypothesized biological mechanisms underlying depression (see box 2, arrow E, and box 7).
Note re the solid and dashed arrows. The solid arrows lead to depressive symptoms and other problems, and the dashed arrows lead to the amelioration of these.
*Note re the Latino Sociocultural Mechanisms: Note that in the context of the figure, "sociocultural" includes both social factors, such as immigration status and economic disadvantage, along with cultural factors, such as language preference, cultural identity and values, and degree of assimilation. Note also that sociocultural factors can act both (a) as mechanisms of illness (box 5), e.g., by impacting on the way depressive symptoms are viewed by a client and the client's countervailing values for overcoming them, and also (b) as influences on the other boxes in Figure 6.1, e.g., migration can be a precipitating event (box 6) by placing an enormous strain an individual's social support system (box 9). Thus in the logic model, sociocultural factors can be seen as not only a particular type of mechanism, but also as a type of back drop that colors the entire model.

strengths and social support system that can be mobilized as forces for positive change; and these are represented in the figure by dashed arrows. This model functions as follows:

- A client's history, or *Origins* (box 1 in the figure) leads (arrow A in the figure) to the development of underlying *Mechanisms* (boxes 2-5), which are fundamental processes that cause the development of psychopathological *Symptoms*, such as depressive disorder (the focus in the META study), and other psychological *Problems*, such as marital conflict (box 7). In the model, four types of mechanisms are differentiated: Biochemical (box 2), Psychological (box 3), Interpersonal (box 4), and Sociocultural (box 5), which in the META study involves Latino cultural issues. Arrows among the mechanisms indicate the reciprocally causal interactions among them. (Note that sociocultural factors include not only mechanisms but also have a much more overarching role in the logic model. Some of this role is outlined in the footnote in Figure 6.1).

- Recent *Precipitating Events* (box 6) from a client's recent history (arrow B) activate (arrow C) the *Mechanisms*, causing (arrows D–G) the emergence of *Symptoms and Other Problems*, like the depressive symptoms targeted in the META study (box 7).
- At the same time, there are positive processes and components in a client's life that provide protective factors against the development and/ or intensity of *Symptoms* and *Other Problems*. These are captured in a client's Strengths (box 8), which emerge from an individual's *Origins* (arrow H). In addition, a client's *Origins* (box 1) help to create (arrow I) his or her present Social Support System (box 9), which adds to (arrow J) his or her Strengths (box 8).

There are two types of therapeutic interventions in the META project. One is a usual care (UC) condition, called in Figure 6.1 "Counseling and Drug Therapy" (box 9), provided to all the clients in the study through their local CMHC. The other is the META intervention condition (box 10), provided by the META project staff to the clients in the RCT treatment condition. These two types of therapy are designed to reduce symptoms and other problems by reversing and/or mitigating the effects of the mechanisms, as reflected in arrows K and L. In this process, each type of therapy draws on the client's Strengths (box 8) in positively impacting (arrows M and N) on the *Symptoms and Other Problems* (box 7).

Regarding the effect of therapeutic interventions on mechanisms, it should be noted that the ability of therapy to mitigate or reverse the effects of mechanisms means that the mechanisms can actually function in a positive way. For instance, one possible psychological mechanism, my belief that I am a particular type of person, can cause problems if my belief is that I am a bad person based on negative scanning of my behaviors and others' reactions to them, but it can also cause positive results if my belief is that I am a good person based on realistic scanning of my behaviors and others' reactions to them.

Table 6.3 provides some examples of how the clinical details of the case studies, presented below, fall into the categories of the logic model in Figure 6.1. The larger meaning of Table 6.3 is discussed later in the Synthesis section.

Component	Lupe	Maria	Ana
1. Origins	• 46, married, monolingual, two children • Graduated high school in Ecuador • Immigrated to the United States at 34 • Raped at 15 • Degree in nursing, practiced in Ecuador • Multiple jobs before treatment • Unemployed for 3 years • $1,200 monthly disability benefits • Previous periods when independent and stable	• 30, monolingual Spanish, Venezuelan, High school education • Immigrated to United States • Recently married • Living with friends • Unemployed • 2–3 sessions of psychotherapy in Venezuela after attempted suicide	• 27, monolingual Spanish, Guatemalan • Living with partner and two children • Fifth grade education level • Pulled out of school in fifth grade to work • Immigrated to United States • Unemployed • Caring for children full time • Saw a psychiatrist on two occasions prior to treatment • No history of hospitalization • Drank heavily from 15 to 17
2. Biological Mechanisms	• Zoloft after attempted suicide • Lexapro after husband's surgeries • Discontinued Lexapro after insurance stopped covering • Citalopram (40 mg) at intake • Took medication inconsistently • 4 additional medications for medical concerns	• Lexapro (10 mg) and Abilify (15 mg) • Discontinued Lexapro after 2 days of bad side effects (e.g., nausea, dizziness, and stomach pain) • Took medication inconsistently • Positive response to Cymbalta; felt more relaxed, ruminated less on betrayal, sleeping better	• Prescribed Lexapro (10 mg) and Seroquel (25 mg) • Medication effective in reducing rumination, and the frequency and intensity of intrusive nightmares • Would occasionally forget to take her medication • Sleeping pills allowed her to escape intrusive thoughts, but also caused drowsiness

(continued)

Table 6.3 Continued

Component	Lupe	Maria	Ana
3. *Psychological Mechanisms*	• Concerns about medication side effects (e.g. weight gain) • Belief that medication was not effective • Concerned that medication could be addictive, dangerous • Belief that medication was not the answer to life's problems • Viewed medication as important, but had ambivalence about taking it	• Desire to take medications to help her sleep • Concerns about medication side effects (e.g. weight gain, addiction) • Belief that medication was not effective • Low confidence in taking medication (3.5/10 on scale) • Ambivalence about taking medications • Tendency to externalize successes • Belief that others would criticize her for being "too dramatic"	• Difficulty remembering to take medications • Concern about becoming addicted to medications • High sensitivity for retraumatization due to PTSD • Tendency to make external attributions for her success • Ambivalence about taking sleeping medication, due to drowsiness • Fear of relapsing into a depressive state • Shame that "strangers" (i.e., treatment team) cared about her more than her own family • Feelings of anger toward her father; history of sexual abuse • Fear of other men
4. *Interpersonal Support Mechanisms*	• Trying to parent young children • Left behind support system in Ecuador • Initially, only social support in the United States was her husband • Husband described as possessive and abusive • Family, therapist, doctor encouraged her to take medication	• Client's family unsupportive of pharmacotherapy • Husband distant and less affectionate • Heartbroken, humiliated, and hopeless after finding out about husband's affair • Lack of social support upon moving to United States • Reluctant to confide in others or ask for help	• Lived with sister, brother-in-law • Doctor, therapist encouraged to take medication • Socially isolated • No resistance from family regarding pharmacotherapy • Belief that medication would not interfere with her ability to work • Improved relationship with her son after initial MI session

Table 6.3 Continued

Component	Lupe	Maria	Ana
	• Strong working alliance	• Friends provide motivation for treatment	• After behavioral changes, son began to express his love for her, leading to increased feelings of competence
	• Improved relationships and a more relaxed home environment at the conclusion of therapy	• Appreciated treatment team's concern for her	• Reluctant to turn to others for support
	• Supportive relatives increased her motivation for pharmacotherapy	• Referred to MI clinician as *"more than just a doctor"*	• Belief that she will be seen as "crazy"
			• Unable to identify social supports
			• Appreciative of staff outreach
5. *Latino Cultural Mechanisms*	• Values included: work, independence, spirituality, children, family	• Values included spirituality, self-reliance	• Shame and stigma over mental illness
	• Belief that *"God helps he who rises to the occasion"*	• Belief that *"God squeezes but does not choke."*	• Religious beliefs acted as a protective factor
	• Belief that *"Grain by grain, the hen gets a mouthful"*	• Recently lost faith in God, due to her continued suffering	• Value of *"putting forth effort"* and *"moving forward"*
	• Desire to feel close to her "home country" as part of her relapse prevention plan	• Still, identified religion as a protective factor	
6. *Precipitating Events*	• First depressive event episode occurred after rape at 15	• Found out husband had been having affair and fathered other child	• First depressive episode after incest by father at 12
	• Suicide attempt after immigration to United States	• Sent to stay with husband's friends in Illinois	• Also sexually abused by two different men during adolescence
	• Depression worsened 2 years later, after husband underwent open-heart surgery	• Breaking up with boyfriend (initial depression at 14)	• Retraumatized after finding a male in the woman's bathroom at the factory where she worked
	• Five-year depressive episode after ending Lexapro and treatment	• Distressed by another woman who treated her poorly and said bad things about her (at 17)	• Tendency to become retraumatized after speaking about her sexual abuse

(continued)

Table 6.3 CONTINUED

Component	Lupe	Maria	Ana
7. Depressive Symptoms, Comorbid Psychopathology, & Other Problems	• Attempted to burn self after rape • Attempted suicide by putting acid on wrists • At intake, fit *DSM-IV* criteria for MDD with subthreshold psychotic features • Anxiety and isolation increased after husband's medical issues • At intake, reported feeling very depressed, tired, sad, increasingly aggressive, difficulty taking care of herself, anhedonia, changes in appetite, unable to get out of bed for days at a time, cried all day in front of others, difficulty staying focused, forgetful and indecisive, passive suicidal ideation • Auditory hallucinations • History of medical issues, several health problems at intake • BDI of 43 (Severe Depression)	• Met *DSM* criteria for MDD, recurrent with psychotic features • Anhedonia, rumination, hopelessness, suicidal ideation, worthlessness, apathy, feelings of guilt, blame, low self-esteem, low energy and fatigue, indecisiveness, and changes in her sleep and appetite • Psychotic symptoms: auditory and visual hallucinations • Presence of homicidal ideation • Attempted suicide at 14 by drinking bleach (after a breakup with her boyfriend) • Second suicide attempt at 17, by overdosing on Tylenol • Suicidal ideation while in Illinois with husband's friends • Third hospitalization after suicidal ideation and plan	• Chronic MDD and PTSD • Depressed mood, anhedonia, changes in sleep and appetite, fatigue, psychomotor retardation, feelings of guilt and worthlessness, trouble concentrating, suicidal ideation • Neglecting children • Auditory hallucinations, paranoid ideation • Chronic passive suicidal and homicidal ideation • Reexperiencing traumatic events • Visions of her children being sexually abused • Afraid of losing grip on reality • While depressed, often felt *"too old to pursue life"* • Avoided work after becoming traumatized by finding a male in the woman's bathroom
	• Suicidal ideation usually occurred during fights with her husband • Son got married and relocated to another state		• Suicidal ideation and depression accompany traumatic nightmares

Table 6.3 CONTINUED

Component	Lupe	Maria	Ana
8. *Strengths*	• Eager to regain emotional and occupational stability • Belief that medication was important and helpful • Confident in ability to take medication • Immediately fostered a strong working alliance • Positive expectations • High readiness to change • High self-efficacy • Recognized that relapse would be temporary	• High importance of taking antidepressant medication (10/10 on ratings scale) • Motivated to overcome depressive symptoms, gain employment, and establish a sense of independence • Cooperative with the clinician	• Motivated for treatment • Goals of no longer feeling afraid, enjoying her children, and gaining employment • Rated the importance of medication as a 10/10 • Rated her confidence in her ability to take her medication as a 10/10 • High readiness for change • Felt connected and grateful for clinic

BDI, Beck Depression Inventory; MDD, major depressive disorder; MI, motivational interviewing; PTSD, posttraumatic stress disorder.

The META Model

As mentioned under "Interventions" in the RCT section earlier, the META therapeutic model employed in this case was an adaptation of MI (Miller & Rollnick, 2002). In reviewing the literature, Hettma, Steele, and Miller (2005) describe MI as follows:

> Motivational interviewing (MI) was developed as a way to help people work through ambivalence and commit to change (Miller, 1983). An evolution of client-centered therapy, MI combines a supportive and empathic counseling style (Rogers, 1959) with a consciously directive method for resolving ambivalence in the direction of change. Drawing on Bem's self-perception theory (Bem, 1972) that people tend to become more committed to that which they hear themselves defend, MI explores the client's own arguments for change. The interviewer seeks to evoke this "change talk"—expressions of the client's desire, ability, reasons, and need for change—and responds with reflective listening. Clients thus hear themselves explaining their own motivations for change, and hear them reflected again by the counselor. Furthermore, the counselor offers periodic summaries of change talk that the client has offered, a kind of bouquet composed of the client's own self-motivational statements. (p. 92)

Thus, in line with DiClemente, McConnaughy, Norcross, and Prochaska's (1986) transtheoretical model, MI rests on an assumption that ambivalence is normal, viewing all clients as having reasons for *and* against wanting a particular behavior change. It is the role of the clinician to identify the various sources and forms of ambivalence, and to work empathically and collaboratively with the client to help identify and reinforce motivation for behavior change. In addition, motivation for behavior change is not a dichotomous or linear process. It is a dynamic process in which individuals fluctuate through various stages of readiness for change (e.g., precontemplation, contemplation, preparation, action, and maintenance).

Our cultural adaptation of MI within META to tailor it to Latino clients is described earlier in the RCT section under the heading of "Interventions."

Guiding Principles of Motivational Interviewing

Collaboration, respect for the autonomy of the individual, and compassion are all important factors that contribute to the "spirit" of MI. MI recognizes that the resources of change reside within the individual and strives to create a counseling atmosphere where clients are apt to express their intrinsic motivation for change and be the ones to generate the solutions. Miller and Rollnick (2002) argue that what people say about change predicts subsequent behavior. Therefore, the ultimate goal of MI is to elicit "change talk" so that the client can move closer to achieving his or her personal goals.

In general, MI rests on four basic principles. The first is *empathy*, which involves relating to the clients' experiences from the client's perspective, in contrast to relating to their experience from outside their perspective (judgment). Empathy can be achieved by respecting and understanding the client's position. Once empathy is established and communicated, it is believed that the client will open up to the possibility of change. Miller and Rollnick (2002) advise that counseling in a reflective and supportive manner decreases resistance, allowing for an increase in change talk.

The second principle, *developing discrepancy*, refers to the belief that motivation for change emerges when clients feel dissonance between their current behavior and their goals, beliefs, or values.

The third principle, *rolling with resistance*, offers a way of avoiding the arguing or confrontation that can result when one considers change. If a client becomes resistant in the face of potential behavior change, MI interventions would aim to reduce the resistance, not by confronting it, but by shifting the focus, reframing the issue, agreeing with the client in a way that changes the direction of the conversation, or emphasizing personal choice and control.

Finally, the fourth principle, *supporting self-efficacy*, refers to the confidence that is needed for a client to make a change. Self-efficacy can be supported through an honest belief that the client is capable of behavioral change if he or she chooses and commits to doing so. (For specific motivational techniques that were used throughout the sessions, see Appendix A in Prawda, 2010, pp. 89–91).

How META was adapted to the particular Latino population in the RCT, including Lupe, Maria, and Ana, was described in the "Interventions" section earlier.

Addressing Comorbidity Within META

The criteria for inclusion in the META study involved major depressive disorder (including psychotic features) or dysthmia, with exclusion criteria involving a diagnosis of bipolar disorder or a substance use disorder within the last year. As will be seen later from clients like Lupe, Maria, and Ana, a number of the clients in the META study appeared to have additional, comorbid diagnoses, like posttraumatic stress disorder (PTSD). The META treatment did not formally assess for and address such comorbid diagnoses, since META was designed to be adjunctive to existing CMHC treatment. That being said, the comorbidities made each person's experience unique. No two META cases were alike and all involved discussing treatment motivation within each person's unique narrative. For example, one person had a somatoform disorder that made her especially sensitive to and fearful of potential side effects. The META therapist wound up supporting her decision to not take the medication.

Nuts and Bolts of Each Session

Understanding the procedural details of META provides a framework for following the case studies. The time frame of the META intervention included assessment at entry (Time 1 [T1]); the two META interviews 1 and 2 weeks later, respectively; the second Time 2 (T2) assessment session 3 weeks after the second META session, by 5 weeks; the META Booster Session at 3 months; and the final

Time 3 (T3) assessment and Exit Interview session at 5 months into the study. Throughout the course of the study, participants continued to receive their "treatment as usual," which for all participants included medication management. Some participants were also in concurrent individual therapy, with variation in the frequency and modality of the individual therapy. (For the details of the participant flow in the study, see Interian et al., 2013.)

The META intervention was delivered through two phases, the motivational enhancement phase (session 1); and the commitment strengthening phase (sessions 2 and 3). In the motivational enhancement phase, the primary focus was on enhancing the client's motivation, getting the client to argue for change, and helping shift his or her decisional balance toward change. During this phase of treatment, there was very little discussion on specific action; rather, the emphasis was on helping the client resolve his or her ambivalence. The clinician was instructed to meet the client at his or her stage of change and gradually work toward eliciting and reinforcing change talk.

General tasks accomplished in session 1 included the following:

(a) informing the client of what was going to be done in the session and providing him or her with the opportunity to choose how to proceed (agenda setting);
(b) learning more about the client's depression;
(c) establishing the importance of solving the problem (i.e., reducing depressive symptoms);
(d) determining the source of motivation for the client by understanding his or her values and goals;
(e) assessing motivation for use of antidepressant medication. This was accomplished by using Miller and Rollnik's (2002) "ICF ruler" method of completing "Importance," "Confidence," and "Readiness" Scales, rated from "1–not at all important/confident/ready," to "10–extremely important/very confident/very ready");
(f) exploring reasons for and against adherence by means of a decisional balance;
(g) collecting data on use of antidepressant medication (scanning the MEMS container);
(h) providing feedback (i.e., reinforcement for days that medication was taken or exploration of reasons for days medication was not taken); and
(i) eliciting a preference to meet for a second META session.

The work of strengthening commitment to improve adherence for antidepressant medication occurred once the client was ready to take action (typically in session 2). If the client was not ready to change, however, the META clinician was instructed to remain in Phase 1, continue to meet him or her at his or her stage of change, and work toward helping the client develop more reasons for change. If the client was ready to take action, session 2 proceeded toward strengthening the client's commitment. In this case, session 2 focused on exchanging antidepressant information by:

(a) informally listening for/assessing antidepressant knowledge,
(b) reinforcing what participants already knew, and
(c) imparting information if necessary.

Additional tasks included:

(d) exploring experiences of nonadherence and relating those experiences to client's current plan (use of ICR ruler);
(e) framing adherence to medication as one way of achieving the client's goal;
(f) reflecting the other ways the client manages depression (i.e., attending therapy, accessing support network, positive thinking, exercise, behavioral activation, etc.);
(g) eliciting self-efficacy for adherence;
(h) anticipating barriers to adherence and providing the client with a menu of options for addressing those barriers so that he or she can maintain the desired level of adherence;
(i) arriving at an adherence plan; and
(j) eliciting the client's commitment toward the plan.

Finally, clients were offered a booster session (session 3) which provided the opportunity for them to continue to strengthen their commitment, review progress toward their adherence plan, support follow-through with change, and problem-solve any barriers to adherence that may have developed in the interim. If/when the client chose not to commit to taking the medication, the booster session shifted to reviewing his or her decision not to do so, considerations for taking medication in the future, providing information on relapse as a result of premature discontinuation, and exploring other ways of progressing toward achieving his or her goals.

GENERAL FORMULATION FOR ALL THREE CLIENTS

All three participants met symptom criteria for major depressive disorder at the time of the first assessment. Although none of the participants had manic symptoms or comorbid substance or alcohol abuse disorders, each one had other comorbid psychiatric symptoms like those associated with PTSD or mood-congruent psychosis. The depressive symptoms were long-standing for each participant, with symptoms dating back as early as childhood or adolescence. In addition, each participant faced significant psychosocial stressors, including immigration, acculturation, language difficulties, financial strain, and a limited social support network. The stressors combined with the depressive symptoms resulted in considerable difficulty with occupational and social functioning for each participant.

Goals for the participants generally included "feeling better" and returning to a previous state of adaptive functioning. Nonetheless, they all had struggled with ambivalent feelings about the role of antidepressant medication as part of their treatment. The source of the ambivalence often ranged from unpleasant side effects to lack of resources or information about the medication to fear of becoming addicted or dependent on the medication.

Lupe's Positive-Outcome Therapy: Assessment, Formulation, and Course

Assessment of the Lupe's Problems, Goals, Strengths, and History Background

Lupe was a 46-year-old, monolingual, Spanish-speaking Ecuadorian woman who immigrated to the United States at the age of 34. Lupe was married and had two children, ages 13 and 23 years. She was a high school graduate and had a degree in nursing. While living in Ecuador, Lupe practiced nursing for 4 years. When Lupe moved to the United States, she worked in a window factory for a few years, a pen factory for 6 months, and also part-time as a babysitter for 6 years. At the time of the first intake appointment for the research study, Lupe had been unemployed for 3 years. She and her husband depended on the $1,200 they receive a month from his disability benefits.

History

Lupe first experienced depression during her adolescence, at the age of 15, when she was raped. Shortly after this trauma, she attempted to burn herself by pouring alcohol on her body, but she was found uninjured by her sister. Her depression went untreated for 20 years. At the age of 35, it emerged again when she immigrated to the United States from Ecuador. Lupe's immigration triggered her depression because she left behind resources like her support system and family at a time in which she was trying to parent young children. She found herself facing new stressors and only had the support of her husband, someone whom she described as possessive and abusive. She recalled him calling her "crazy," "bipolar," telling her that she was worthless, and keeping her closed off to others.

Shortly after arriving in the United States, Lupe attempted suicide for the second time by putting acid on her hands and wrists. After this event, she was treated with medication (Zoloft). However, her depression worsened 2 years later when Lupe and her husband underwent a series of medical issues and surgeries. Her anxiety increased, and she withdrew from others. It was at this time that she presented to the outpatient mental health center, where she was officially diagnosed with depression and prescribed Lexapro. She continued with her course of medication for a few months but discontinued it once her insurance company stopped covering it. For the next 5 years, Lupe continued to battle depression with and without treatment. In January 2008, when the symptoms were no longer bearable, Lupe returned to the outpatient CMHC and was referred to the research study.

At the time of intake for the RCT, Lupe complained of feeling very depressed, tired, and sad. She had become increasingly aggressive, it was difficult for her to take care of herself (she would go 2–3 days without bathing), and she had lost pleasure in activities she had previously enjoyed (like babysitting children, regularly attending church, and having a sexual relationship with her husband). She had experienced changes in appetite (including significant weight gain of more than 100 lb) and changes in sleep patterns. She was also unable to get out of bed for days at a time, cried all day in front of others, felt irritable, blamed herself, and had difficulty staying focused. In addition, she was forgetful, indecisive, and was feeling worthless, "like garbage."

In fact, 4 weeks prior to her initial appointment, she experienced suicidal ideation, which consisted of "wanting to die," thoughts of cutting her veins, and the desire to "get rid of everything." For Lupe, her suicidal ideation usually occurred in the context of fights with her husband or when she felt "low." Additionally, Lupe was experiencing auditory hallucinations, which included hearing her name being called, doors being opened, and voices in the absence of people being present. She worried that she was "going crazy." Aside from feeling anxious and depressed, Lupe complained of several health problems, including gastric pain, constipation, chest pain, liver problems, headaches, and arthritis. Lupe was diagnosed with major depressive disorder and treated with 40 mg of Citalopram by her psychiatrist prior to being referred to the research study.

Status at Intake

Lupe met the *DSM-IV* diagnostic criteria for a major depressive episode with subthreshold psychotic features. She did not meet criteria for mania or alcohol/ substance abuse disorders and thus qualified to participate in the study. On the Beck Depression Inventory-II, Lupe obtained a score of 43, which is in the "severe depression" range (see Table 6.1). Specifically, she endorsed having the most difficulty with self-blame, appetite ("I feel like eating all the time"), irritability, feeling like a failure, difficulty with decision making, and lack of interest. Her subthreshold psychotic features consisted of hearing her name being called, hearing doors open, and hearing people talk when nobody is there.

Lupe's stated goal for taking antidepressant medication was "so that it can try to help me a little bit with my depression." Nonetheless, she faced the decision to take the medication (Citalopram 40 mg) with great ambivalence. On the one hand, she felt as though it was very important to take it and rated it a 10/10 on the Importance Scale. On the other hand, she had relatively low confidence in her ability to take the medication (4/10 on the Confidence Scale) and noted that she was not quite ready to take the medication (4/10 on the Readiness Scale). Most of Lupe's ambivalence was attributed to concerns over weight gain, other side effects like the experience of boredom in response to the medication, and feeling as though it was not very effective. In fact, Lupe reported that she was taking her medication inconsistently, at times stopping when she felt better as well as stopping when she felt worse.

The initial assessment also revealed specific attitudes and concerns that Lupe had about the medication. She wondered whether she really needed the medication and felt as though antidepressant medication was not the answer to one's problems in life. She was concerned that it could be dangerous and that she could become addicted to the medication. The most influential reason for her to take the medication was that her doctor, therapist, and family believed that she needed it.

Though Lupe had a significant history of depression, she also remembered periods of her life when she had adequate emotional and occupational functioning. During these periods, Lupe described herself as independent person who laughed all the time and sang songs at church. Aside from mental health problems, Lupe reported a history of medical problems, including gastric pain, obesity, constipation, asthma, chest pain, liver problems, headaches, and arthritis. For these medical problems, Lupe took an additional four medications on a daily basis.

LUPE'S FORMULATION AND TREATMENT PLAN
Lupe's main motivation to treat her depression and adhere to her antidepressant medication was to feel more energetic and to be able to engage in her life goals. She wanted to return to the person that she used to be, which for Lupe meant gaining independence, working, socializing more, and becoming a role model to her children. The main barriers that had prevented her from treating her depression were lack of insurance, limited financial resources, a feeling of boredom in response to taking to the medication, and concern about other medication side effects (particularly weight gain). In addition, Lupe had recently faced psychosocial stressors, which included her son getting married and relocating to another state as well as her husband undergoing open-heart surgery.

LUPE'S COURSE OF THERAPY
First Session
It was not surprising that Lupe was responsive to the META therapy. To start, Lupe immediately fostered a strong working alliance with the treatment team. Even prior to meeting with the META clinician, it appeared as though Lupe carried positive expectations into the experience. The research assistant had made extensive outreach efforts to recruit and engage Lupe in the study, which made her feel as though someone cared about her. This, in turn, became a motivating factor for improving her adherence to her treatment. In her own words, Lupe stated:

Pues me sentí un poquito mejor porque ella [the research assistant] me dio animo. Yo siento que es bien, bueno, yo siento que estas terapias son buenas, ayudan bastante . . .

Well, I feel a little better because she [the research assistant] gave me strength and I feel that it is good, I feel like these therapies are good, they help a lot . . .

Not only was the strong therapeutic alliance evident from Lupe's statements, but a careful review of the transcript from the first session also revealed that Lupe and the clinician were well attuned to each other. In fact, they often finished each other's sentences. This type of attunement demonstrates that META was effectively working. The following excerpt was taken from the first 2 minutes of the session:

> LUPE: . . . pero por lo menos me siento, mucho menos (mal) de lo que estaba antes, amm, pues me da un poquito de animo en el día pa'trabajar, con, con unas (medicinas) que me mando para dormir, duermo mejor, y, y así, no te voy a decir que me siento "alegre alegre", pero estoy comenzando a tomarla
>
> META CLINICIAN: Poquito a poquito
>
> LUPE: Poquito a poquito . . . porque por lo menos antes estaba bien triste, ahora me siento un poquito mas contenta . . .
>
> LUPE: . . . but at least I am feeling less worse than before, amm, I have a little bit more energy to work during the day with some of the medicines that the doctor gave me to sleep. I'm not going to say that I feel "happy happy", but I'm starting to take them
>
> META CLINICIAN: Little by little
>
> LUPE: Little by little . . . at least before I was sad, but now, I am a little bit happier.

Lupe appeared to present to the initial session with a high level or "readiness" for change. Lupe easily recognized that depression had "changed her as a person" and she was eager to return to the type of person she had been "before." The dissonance that this created for Lupe served to fuel her motivation to return to a "healthier" self.

The clinician also spent much of the first session guiding Lupe in talking about and identifying her values so that they could be woven into the META and produce more meaningful interventions. Lupe's values included being able to work, independence, belief in God, and being a strong example for her children. Once these values were identified, the clinician linked them to her goals: returning to her former self, obtaining her driver's license so that she could achieve independence, gaining employment so that she could be in charge of her own finances, and practicing assertiveness with others, particularly with her husband.

One of the most striking aspects of the first session with Lupe was the extent to which she was engaging in "change talk," a phase of META that usually takes time to develop. Lupe stated,

> Saber que yo puedo, si yo siempre he podido. ¿Porque no ahora? Caí en este trato, pero yo pienso que voy a salir.
>
> I know that I can, if I have always been able to. Why not now? I fell into this, but I think that I'll get out.

In addition to engaging in change talk, she spoke with confidence and a sense of self-efficacy. She began remembering instances where she succeeded, people who believed in her, and moments in which reducing her depressive symptoms had given her good results. Ultimately, she was fueling her motivation to keep her depressive symptoms at bay and "work" her treatment for the sake of her future, her children, and her family.

The first session concluded with an analysis of the role that medication had on her symptoms. Lupe was able to identify that the medication helped her feel more lively, and it reactivated her desire to engage in activities that she found pleasurable, like going to church and grooming herself. Lupe also acknowledged that medication was just one part of her overall treatment. In essence, it reduced her symptoms just enough to allow her to do the things that she wanted to do, leading to a surge in positive reinforcement and an improved sense of self. Lupe rated medication with high importance, and talking about its importance prompted her to remember her routine of taking it every morning. In addition, she asserted great confidence that she could take it as prescribed. She cited that the only barrier to taking the medication would be if her insurance changed, in which case she would ask for the medication to be changed. When Lupe received feedback from the MEMS® monitor, she was able to praise herself for doing a good job. Taken together, her ability to identify the components that helped her "fight" the depression, coupled with her high ratings, at the end of the first session, of importance and confidence regarding taking her medication, served to fuel her motivation and adherence to treatment.

Second Session

At the time of the second session, Lupe continued relishing in self-confidence and motivation to rid herself of the depression. The META clinician managed to deepen Lupe's motivation by linking it to religion, culture, and eventually her own self-efficacy (i.e., her belief that through her own effort she could take care of herself and evolve into the person she would like to become). Lupe began the session by immediately launching into her progress toward becoming healthy, which in this case included returning to being an active member of the church. This prompted a discussion about the role of God and prayer (one of Lupe's values) in helping her *seguir adelante* (move forward).

To sustain Lupe's gains, the META therapist also added Lupe's efforts or *poniendo de su parte* as a critical factor from which her motivation was rooted. The therapist noted that much of Lupe's success was due to the decisions she had made and the effort she had put forth in seeking help, albeit an uncomfortable process. Lupe confessed that at one point in her treatment, even though she had been taking the medication, she had been inconsistent, and she "didn't care about returning to the doctor." She recognized that these types of decisions prevented her from moving forward. The clinician highlighted her positive efforts through an MI technique called "reflection with a twist," and stated,

> Uno diría bueno, el medicamento ayudo pero, usted, usted fue la que tuvo que salir a buscar el medicamento.

One would say the medication helped, but you, you were the one who had to go out and look for the medication.

This type of internal attribution helped build Lupe's confidence and sense of self-efficacy.

During this session, the META clinician also touched on culture by incorporating the use of *dichos*, ultimately making the interventions more meaningful for Lupe. The two *dichos* that he introduced were "*A quien madruga, Dios le ayuda*" ("God helps he who rises to the occasion") and "*Grano a grano, la gallina llena el buche*" ("Grain by grain, the hen gets a mouthful"). Lupe's efforts, her "can do" attitude, and her belief in God were infused in a way that was culturally and religiously consonant. She responded positively to the use of *dichos* and even added one of her own, "*Todo lo puede Cristo como lo fortalece*" ("All that Christ can, he strengthens"). This demonstrated that the clinician and the client continued to be well attuned to each other, and that they were moving at the same pace and in the same direction.

Aside from reinforcing Lupe's gains, the second META session focused on identifying the work that was "left to be done" and Lupe's concerns about experiencing a relapse of depression. Again, Lupe was in an action-oriented stage of change, where she was ready to problem-solve and was full of change talk. Lupe made assertions like "My attitude toward life is changing," and "I'm doing the things I have to do, and I am feeling differently." She recognized that if she were to relapse, it would probably be temporary, and it would not mean that she would lose all the gains she had made.

Lupe articulated a relapse prevention plan that included continuing with her medication until she regained enough strength. Lupe also stipulated a plan to seek out therapy if she were to experience worsening depressive symptoms. Lupe addressed her experiences of discontinuing medication prematurely in the past and acknowledged that it quickly led to an increase in depression. Finally, she included the need to have support from her family, be connected to treatment providers, and feel close to her "home country" as part of her relapse prevention plan. Lupe and the META clinician determined that her move to Miami would serve as a protective factor as she would have the support from her son and be immersed in the Latino culture. This type of discussion worked to solidify her motivation by empowering her to handle any backslides or relapses.

The topic of premature discontinuation of medication was given special attention in the second session, especially because Lupe felt some ambivalence about this topic. On the one hand, she wanted to have a trial period of not using medication to see what would happen. On the other hand, she was afraid that discontinuing prematurely would lead to a surge in symptoms, and she did not want to return to that state of suffering. Ultimately, she recognized the "danger" that could occur from stopping her medication prematurely, stating that it was a risk she did not want to take. Furthermore, she reconfirmed a willingness to "put forth her part," which in this case meant taking her medication as indicated or for at least 6 months after her symptoms remitted.

The META clinician continued to engage in MI by anticipating potential barriers that would keep Lupe from taking her medication. They began by addressing previous barriers, which in Lupe's case included not having medical insurance to pay for the medication. Instead of offering Lupe solutions to these problems, the clinician built her sense of self-efficacy by eliciting what information she knew about programs that help people who lack prescription coverage. She remembered hearing about a discount program at Walmart and was able to ask the clinician more questions about how the program worked. She left feeling more confident and more informed about how to manage this type of barrier, should it present itself in the future. Furthermore, she was prompted to think about how she could find a psychiatrist and a psychologist once she moved. This way, she could ensure continuation of care and work toward preventing a relapse of depressive symptoms.

Another potential barrier that Lupe identified was the anticipated adjustment of moving to Miami. After all, it was Lupe's move to the United States that ostensibly triggered her depressive episode. Nonetheless, Lupe was able to problem-solve this barrier by recognizing that she was resilient and had experience adapting to new environments. She was excited to be surrounded by more family and cultural comforts. The move to Miami signified a return to feeling connected to others, which for Lupe had the potential to improve her quality of life.

Lupe also revealed her concerns about side effects from the medication, in particular, her weight gain. The META clinician noted the ambivalence about not wanting to gain weight (she was already 300 lb) but also not wanting to relapse into a deeper depression. Instead of advising Lupe, the clinician solicited her thoughts on the issue. She was able to come up with sensible solutions (exercise, eliminating sweets, and reducing caloric intake) to alleviate her concerns about weight gain without having to discontinue the medication. Together they also explored the option of asking the doctor to adjust her medication should the weight gain continue.

The second session concluded by scanning Lupe's MEMS® bottle. Again, she received the feedback that she was taking the medication with 93.5% adherence. This compares to the mean of the treatment group of 75.8% (see Table 6.2). She confirmed the *importance* and *confidence* that she placed on taking the medication as a 10/10, stating that she "will continue to fight to have the medication no matter where she is."

Unfortunately, due to Lupe's relocation out of state, she was unable to participate in the third META booster session.

Maria's Negative-Outcome Therapy: Assessment, Formulation, and Course

ASSESSMENT OF MARIA'S PROBLEMS, GOALS, STRENGTHS, AND HISTORY BACKGROUND

As mentioned earlier, Maria was a 30-year-old, monolingual, Spanish-speaking Venezuelan woman who had immigrated to the United States 2.5 months prior to becoming a participant in the study. She had a high school education and had worked in Venezuela as a seamstress for 8 years, earning about $1,300 to $1,400 Venezuelan bolivares per week. She was recently married and came to the United States to be with her husband, who was American. However, upon arriving in the United States, she learned that her husband had been having an affair and that he fathered another child.

History

Although Maria's depression was not officially diagnosed until a few months prior to her participation in the research study, it appeared that her depression dated back to her adolescence. Maria disclosed that she first felt depressive symptoms at age 14 when she broke up with a boyfriend. Shortly after this event, she attempted suicide by drinking from a bottle of bleach. She received 2–3 sessions of treatment in her home country of Venezuela. A few years later, at the age of 17, she again felt distressed by "another woman who treated her poorly and said bad things about her." She attempted suicide for the second time by overdosing on Tylenol.

Learning that her husband of 3 years was carrying on an affair with someone in the United States, and that he had fathered another child, precipitated Maria's depressive episode at the time of the research study. Maria explained that she had married an American citizen and had maintained a long-distance relationship with him with the intention of eventually immigrating to the United States to live with him. About 2 years into the relationship, Maria noticed that her husband started changing. He was ignoring her phone calls, was distant, less affectionate, and not providing as much financial support. She became suspicious that he was having an affair and began having nightmares. Around the time her visa was going to expire, she decided to come to California (unbeknownst to her husband) to confirm or disconfirm her suspicion. Shortly after, she discovered his infidelity. According to Maria, all of her dreams about a future with him were destroyed; she was heartbroken and humiliated.

Because she had nowhere to turn, she stayed with her husband and his mistress for 2 weeks in their home until she could gather enough money to return to Venezuela. This experience was incredibly difficult and uncomfortable for Maria because she witnessed the way her husband doted on his mistress and their child, all the while ignoring her needs and her pain. In addition, he was hurtful toward Maria, telling her that he no longer loved her, and that she "never knew how to make love anyway." Maria felt alone, sad, and angry. She was hopeless about her future and wondered whether she would ever forget what he had done to her, be able to heal from this experience, and be able to trust again.

Eventually, her husband made arrangements for Maria to stay with friends of his in Illinois. Maria's depression worsened while she was staying with her husband's friends. She began feeling suicidal and ended up being psychiatrically hospitalized. Even while hospitalized, she attempted to reach out to her husband, hoping that he would respond to her distress. Her outreach efforts failed: He hung up the telephone when she called. She asked him to pay for her antidepressant medications, but he refused. After being discharged from the hospital, Maria moved to New Jersey to be with another set of friends. She continued to be depressed, unable to eat and unable to attend to her activities of daily living (i.e., bathing and dressing). She was hospitalized for a second time, and upon her discharge, was connected with outpatient treatment at the CMHC where the research study was taking place. The psychiatrist diagnosed her with major depressive disorder and prescribed Lexapro (10 mg) and Abilify (15 mg).

Status at Intake

Maria met *DSM-IV* criteria for a major depressive disorder, recurrent with psychotic features. The psychotic features consisted of auditory hallucinations (voices telling her to kill herself) and visual hallucinations (black spots that appeared when she was sad and having suicidal ideation). She stated that she received special messages or premonitions from God telling her why her husband was not calling her and that he was being unfaithful. She also endorsed some homicidal ideation ("bad thoughts of killing someone or choking someone"), but she denied intent and plan. Maria noted that these psychotic symptoms had only been present for the last 2 months in the context of her depression.

Maria presented with ambivalence about whether or not to take antidepressant medication. On the Importance, Confidence, and Readiness Scales she rated the importance of taking antidepressants as a 10/10. She had moderate confidence in her ability to take the medication (8/10), but she was slightly less ready to take the medication (7/10). She had a history of two prior discontinuations, the most recent having been due to bad side effects after 2 days of taking the Lexapro. She also admitted that in the last month, she tended to forget the medication, she would discontinue the medicine when she began feeling better, and also discontinue the medicine when was feeling worse.

Her main reason for taking the antidepressant was to help her sleep. She was also somewhat motivated by having the doctor tell her that she needed to take the medication and by a fear of being rehospitalized. However, she had serious concerns about the kinds of effects that the medication could have on her body. She had already experienced some side effects such as nausea, dizziness, and stomach pain. In addition, she was concerned about whether or not the medication would cause lasting damage and whether she could become addicted to it. She had little faith that the medication would help her feel better and actually felt as though the medication would interfere in her ability to reach certain goals. She also lacked support from her family; they did not want her to be on medications. Finally, Maria faced additional obstacles to obtaining the medication, including lack of insurance and limited income.

Maria's ambivalence about taking antidepressant medication was evident in her adherence behavior. At the time of the first evaluation, she admitted that in the last month, she tended to forget the medication, at times was not careful in taking the medication, discontinued when she began feeling better, and also discontinued when feeling worse.

MARIA'S FORMULATION AND TREATMENT PLAN

At the time of the study, Maria's depression was most influenced by a recent betrayal from her husband. She wanted to move past her depressive symptoms (i.e., anhedonia, rumination, hopelessness, and suicidal ideation) and to stabilize sufficiently so that she could gain employment and establish a sense of independence. Her main reason for taking the antidepressant was to help her sleep. She was also somewhat motivated by having the doctor tell her that she needed to take the medication and by a fear of being rehospitalized. Maria's long-term goals included marrying, having children, and traveling. Her ability to "move forward" was guided by values like religion, faith, and a strong belief in taking care of herself. Obstacles to treatment included lack of insurance and financial resources; sensitivity to medication side effects like nausea, sleepiness, and stomach pain; lack of faith in the effectiveness of the medication; and lack of social support. In addition, her depressed mood, in and of itself, presented as an obstacle to treatment.

Maria's Course of Therapy
First Session

In her META sessions, Maria presented with some difficulty in forming a rapid therapeutic alliance. Although she was very cooperative with the clinician, she appeared somewhat indifferent, deferential, slower than Lupe to warm up, and frequently offered one-word responses to the clinician's questions. The clinician attempted to engage Maria in brief chitchat at the beginning of the META session as a way of building rapport. In addition, the clinician attempted to empower Maria to take the lead in the session by offering her a menu of options and asking her how she would like to proceed with the session. Despite these interventions, Maria depended on the clinician to guide the session.

Maria was most open when talking about the events that led to her recent bout of depression. She spent much of the first part of the session providing the details and the chronology of her husband's affair. She explained that while they were in a long-distance relationship, he would visit her frequently and tell her that he wanted her to come to the United States so that they could buy a house, have children, and build a future together. She noted that he treated her well throughout the course of their relationship; he was attentive and generously sent her money. Maria then described how she became suspicious of her husband once she noticed his behavior changing. According to Maria, he started calling her less, stopped sending her money, and responded evasively to the idea of her coming to the United States once her visa was expiring. She shared her reaction to learning about the betrayal and the feelings of humiliation, sense of worthlessness, disappointment, and hopelessness that followed.

Throughout Maria's account of the affair, the META clinician asked clarifying questions and validated her experience by providing reflective statements and being empathic. The use of "complex reflections," which are meant to validate and amplify the client's experience, proved to be fruitful in broadening the scope of the discussion. Maria realized that beyond being affected by her husband's betrayal, she was questioning whether she would ever be able to heal from this event and learn to love and trust again.

> MARIA: Y pienso que esto como que nunca lo voy a olvidar. Me va costar. Lo que me paso, lo que el me hizo. Porque yo creía en el plenamente. Lo mas lejos que yo tuviera es lo que el llego hacer.

CLINICIAN: Entonces tienes ese temor de que ha sido como, una herida tan, tan grave y tan profunda que, nunca vas a sanar.

MARIA: Pienso eso. ¿Como voy a estar? Con ese dolor y pensando, en todo lo que el me hizo. Porque yo confiaba en el y de la manera en que el me trataba. Pienso que si el, que decía que me quería mucho, me hizo eso, que no me hará otra persona que no me quiera.

MARIA: And I think that I may never forget this. It will be very hard. What happened to me, what he did to me. I unequivocally believed in him. It was the furthest thing I thought, he managed to do.

CLINICIAN: Then you have this fear that you will never heal from a pain that has been so great and so deep.

MARIA: I think that. How will I be? With that hurt and those thoughts, all that he did to me. Because I trusted him and the way that he treated me. I think that if he told me he loved me a lot and he did this to me, what would someone else do who does not love me?

To shift from talking about Maria's distress from the betrayal, the META clinician asked Maria how she was doing now that she was living in a different part of the country, away from her husband, and receiving the support of friends. Maria acknowledged feeling less lonely. She also reported that she was better able to attend to her activities of daily living and that she was comforted by being surrounded by people who responded to her needs. In addition, she identified an important goal (being able to have enough money to live independently) and an important value (her faith in God). With regard to her belief in God, Maria admitted that upon learning about her husband's affair, she lost her faith and began to question whether this was a punishment from God. Nevertheless, she expressed an interest in reviving her faith so that she could "return to be the person she used to be." Upon further questioning, the META clinician learned that Maria aspired to once again feel happiness and optimism, to no longer be apathetic, and to return to attending church and practicing prayer. To elicit additional values and goals from Maria, the META clinician asked an effective, yet provocative question: "How would your life be different, if you were not depressed like you are now?" Maria noted that ideally, she would be working, studying English, spending time with her husband, and cooking.

Once identified, the META clinician was able to build on Maria's values and goals to leverage her motivation for improving her depression and adherence to her treatment. In particular, the META clinician linked Maria's faith in God to her willingness to seek treatment and begin the process of helping herself. Maria expanded this concept by stating that God had not forgotten about her. Instead, he "found people to help her," including the friends that were currently offering her a place to live. The META clinician validated Maria for being able to accept the help that had been offered to her, despite feeling bad. This allowed her to feel more empowered and permitted for internal attributions of success. The ability of the META clinician to shift attributions regarding adherence from external to internal attributions supports the META principle of building self-efficacy.

Maria and the META clinician then explored the effect that the antidepressant medication had on her overall treatment. Maria acknowledged that she responded poorly to the first course of antidepressant treatment. She discontinued it after a few weeks because she felt nausea, stomach pain, dizziness, increased anxiety, and could not sleep well. Nonetheless, Maria had been willing to talk to the psychiatrist about these side effects and try a different class of antidepressant, one that so far had produced fewer side effects and helped her feel "a little bit better."

As a way of expanding the discussion on side effects and providing some psychoeducation, the META clinician elicited the information that Maria already knew about medication and then asked permission to provide additional information. The META clinician was able to inform Maria that the side effects from the antidepressant medication typically last for 3–4 weeks, which is when one's body can begin to acclimate to the medication. She also provided psychoeducation on the best way to take the medication and the effects that it can have on one's mood and state of mind.

Having provided more information on antidepressants, the META session then proceeded by expanding on Maria's ambivalence about the medications. Together, the clinician and client explored her reasons for having decided to try another course of medication despite having had such a negative experience with the original medication, Lexapro. Maria admitted that she "hit rock bottom" during her period of nonadherence, experiencing extreme sadness and an inability to sleep. The clinician again reflected Maria's desire to "feel better" and her wish to "return to the person she used to be" as the motivating factors that helped her decide to take a chance on a new course of medication.

Because an obvious barrier for Maria's adherence to the treatment was negative side effects, the META clinician explored what would happen if Maria began to reexperience side effects while on the new course of medication. At this point, Maria's ambivalence was most evident as she responded that she did not know whether she would discontinue the medication or continue to take it. The META clinician reminded Maria that in addition to choosing between stopping or continuing the medication, she could also talk with her doctor and explore another change in medication, as she had done before.

Aside from dealing with the side effects of the medication, Maria also expressed concern about becoming dependent on the antidepressant. The META clinician dealt with this concern in a similar manner, first by asking her what she knew about this issue and then by providing additional information to clear up misconceptions. This modeled for Maria the importance of acquiring accurate information in order to empower herself, resolve ambivalence, and move toward her goals.

The session concluded with Maria's ratings of the *importance* she places on taking the medication (7 out of 10, the highest), her *confidence* in taking the medication (3.5 out of 10), and her *readiness* to take the medication (7 out of 10). Maria explained that her relatively high rating on the importance and readiness scales was being driven by her wish to "feel better." Her low rating with regard to her confidence in taking the medication was largely attributed to her doubts about the side effects. Nevertheless, Maria acknowledged that if she were to begin to see positive effects of the medication, it would increase her confidence.

Interestingly, following the "importance/confidence/readiness" conversation, Maria did not respond with the expected surge in motivation or increase in change talk. Instead, her depression appeared to worsen as she returned to talking about her lost dreams, her loss of faith, and questioning how God could let her suffer to the extent that she had. This forced the META clinician to re-build Maria's motivation by validating her pain and reminding her of the action she had taken to move past her depression, including calling 911 when she felt suicidal and coming to the various therapy sessions. However, Maria did not respond positively to the clinician's interventions. She was consumed by her de-pression and began to express suicidal ideation ("I wish God would come find me and take me"). This led the META clinician to conduct a thorough risk assess-ment. While Maria was deemed safe enough to leave the clinic, the risk assess-ment revealed additional obstacles to Maria's treatment, including lack of money and insurance.

Second Session

The second META session began with Maria reporting improved mood, improved adherence with the medication, a resurgence of prayer and faith, and no side effects from the new class of antidepressant (Cymbalta). She credited God, the medications, and her META sessions for helping her "feel better" and begin to regain the confi-dence she needed to pursue her goals. In fact, Maria noted that during the course of the week, she was able to go out to eat with friends and search for employment.

The META clinician effectively reflected the apparent contrast in Maria's pre-sentation from the previous week and inquired how she was able to produce such a dramatic turnaround:

Veo la diferencia, en que me esta diciendo que 'me siento mejor, estoy tomando mi medicamento como debe ser, no me esta sentando tan mal, y busque trabajo y encontré uno.' Eso es tremendo . . . y eso, lo hizo usted, nadie se lo hizo, pero usted mismita. ¿De donde saco esas fuerzas?

I see the difference in what you are telling me . . . that you feel better, are taking your medication like you should, not feeling so bad, and that you looked for a job and found one. That is tremendous . . . and that, you did by yourself, nobody but you. Where did you get the strength?

This led to a dialogue in which Maria crystallized her sources of motivation (i.e., her friends and God) as well as her goals (helping herself, helping her mother, achieving independence, feeling comfortable). While Maria continued to feel the pain of her recent betrayal, she and the META clinician were able to observe that the pain did not overpower her and/or keep her from moving toward her goals. Furthermore, Maria noted that the busier she was, the less time she could spend ruminating over her husband. Throughout the session, the clinician specifically focused on Maria's personal strength and the steps she had independently taken to move forward (e.g., following up with her charity care applications, obtaining employment, taking her medication). Interestingly, instead of feeling empowered, it appeared as though Maria was uncomfortable with this level of validation. She responded by minimizing her achievement, stating that she still had periods in which she was suffering, and attributing any success to an external source (God helping her feel better). She also began to question "Why me?" and wonder whether she deserved this type of punishment.

As in the case of Lupe, the META clinician incorporated the use of *dichos* as a way of addressing Maria's faith and level of self-blame. The clinician asked Maria if she had heard of the *dicho* "*Dios aprieta pero no ahorca*" ("God squeezes but does not choke"). In part, this *dicho* stimulated hope within Maria as she remembered that there is "always a way out of a situation." Unfortunately, Maria did not completely respond to this intervention. She was resistant and pushed against the clinician's efforts to build her hope. She questioned whether this *dicho* really applied to her since she had already lost her faith. The clinician and Maria remained stuck in disagreement by arguing about the extent to which she had or had not lost her faith.

As a result of this disagreement, the META clinician was unable to move toward the expected tasks of a typical session 2, like strengthening commitment to improve adherence for antidepressant medication. Instead, she returned to many session 1 type objectives, such as understanding Maria's course of depression, solidifying her source of motivation, and assessing the role that antidepressant medication played in her overall treatment. The clinician asked provocative questions like: "Why did you decide to turn to God again if you had lost your faith?" or "Where do you see yourself in the future (e.g., in a week or in a month)?" and "What are your good days like?" These questions were useful in drawing out Maria's values, goals, and sources of motivation.

Of interest, Maria noted in the second META session that her new course of medication was helping her and not producing any negative side effects. Nevertheless, she continued to be concerned about becoming dependent on the medication. She was also concerned about long-term effects that it could have on her body. As in session 1, it became clear to the clinician that Maria had many questions about the medication. Although the clinician continued to offer some information and clear up misconceptions, she also worked toward empowering Maria to take a greater interest in learning about the medication and sharing her doubts or questions directly with the psychiatrist. In addition, the clinician attempted to anticipate additional barriers (i.e., getting medication despite not having insurance or enough money) and offered Maria alternative options, like obtaining samples from the psychiatrist, accessing low-fee pharmacy programs, and continuing with the application for charity care.

Maria rated an 8 out of 10 for all the scales of *importance, confidence*, and *readiness* to take the medication. She attributed the increase in her ratings (as compared to session 1) to having had a positive response to the new course of medication (Cymbalta). After all, she reported feeling more relaxed, thinking less about the betrayal that precipitated her depression, and sleeping better. She also had the experience of taking the medication for 1 week consistently without having negative side effects. Given these relatively high ratings, the META clinician took advantage of the opportunity to point out to Maria that despite her concerns, she was motivated enough to give the medication another try so that she could attempt to feel better and "return to the person she used to be." The MEMS readings served to reinforce Maria's success in taking the medication, as it demonstrated that Maria had taken her medication every day since switching to Cymbalta.

After the MEMS® reading, the clinician explored with Maria whether she would be willing to make a commitment to taking the medication for an extended period of time (i.e., 3–6 months). This induced a resurgence of ambivalence for Maria. She returned to talking about her concerns of becoming dependent on the medication and predicted that in 3–6 months, she would be "sick and tired" of taking the antidepressant. It appeared that Maria was not yet at the appropriate "stage of change" for that level of commitment or change talk.

Because Maria presented with suicidal ideation during the first META session, the second META session concluded with a brief risk assessment. Maria confirmed that she was experiencing less suicidal ideation and that she would be willing to call emergency numbers if needed. The META clinician reinforced Maria's strengths and reflected her desire to live as evidenced by wanting to take care of her body by not overmedicating it. Maria expressed her genuine appreciation to the META clinician for her concern. The META clinician self-disclosed that she had been worried about Maria over the course of the week, and Maria acknowledged that it made her feel better knowing that others cared about her. Of note, this last exchange was probably the strongest marker of alliance between the clinician and client.

Endpoint Assessment

Maria returned to the research study a week later to meet with the research assistant for her endpoint assessment (T2). While completing the Beck Depression Inventory-II, Maria disclosed that she continued having thoughts of killing herself. She had a vague plan and was unable to contract for safety. The research assistant referred Maria for a psychiatric evaluation, and she ended up being hospitalized in an inpatient psychiatric unit for 2 weeks. This marked her third hospitalization in less than 6 months.

Booster Session

Two months after her second META session, which was a week after her release from the hospital, Maria was invited to meet with the META clinician for a booster META session. She stated that she was doing well, continuing her work in a factory job, and continuing to follow up with her psychiatrist. She also informed the META clinician of her recent inpatient hospitalization and admitted that, at the time, she had been feeling increasingly upset, ruminating about her husband's betrayal, and having strong suicidal ideation. Nevertheless, she noted that since her release, her suicidal ideation had decreased and she was able to keep her goals in sight (i.e., working, taking care of herself, and helping her mother). In fact, staying busy with work was serving Maria well as it kept her distracted from thinking about her husband's betrayal. The META clinician took advantage of this opportunity to reflect that Maria was taking active steps toward helping herself feel better. In addition, she emphasized that her ability to follow up with her psychiatric appointments clearly demonstrated an investment in her treatment.

The role of the medication as part of her treatment was revisited in the booster session. Maria indicated that, while in the hospital, her medication dose of Cymbalta had been increased. She stated that it was "too strong" and complained of feeling "out of it." Despite this side effect, the MEMS® reading revealed that she had been taking the medication almost regularly since being released from the hospital (she only forgot to take it on one day). Her desire to feel better served as her source of motivation despite having doubts about the medication. In fact, Maria revealed that she had learned to manage the side effects by taking the medication at night. That way, if she felt nauseous or dizzy, it would not interfere with her daytime activities. The META clinician commended Maria for figuring out a way of navigating obstacles to treatment.

For the booster session, Maria rated the *importance* of taking medication as an 8/10 and her *confidence* and *readiness* as a 7/10. She attributed the high ratings to the recognition that medication was helping her feel better, that she was more active, and that she was less suicidal. However, her ratings fell short of a 10/10 because she still acknowledged that her mood cycled and she continued to have days in which she felt sad, hopeless, and apathetic. During these days, she wondered whether there was any hope in taking the medication. The META clinician accurately reflected that despite feeling depressed and unmotivated, Maria was somehow able to find the strength to take the medication, which in turn helped her regain energy and feel less depressed. When asked to reflect on this process, Maria once again credited her faith in God as helping her have the strength to "get things done."

Because this was the last META session with Maria, the META clinician attempted to get a sense of Maria's long-term commitment to the antidepressant and anticipate any outstanding barriers to treatment. Maria indicated that she was willing to continue taking the medication until her body could acclimate and she would no longer feel the side effects. The META clinician validated Maria's concerns about side effects and becoming addicted to the medication. Similar to how the clinician had done in the first session, the clinician also provided information on these topics and elicited Maria's reaction. Maria appeared to respond positively, and the clinician encouraged her to follow up with her psychiatrist should she have more questions. She still, however, had clear ambivalence about the medication. Maria admitted that she preferred to go back to the lower dose of Cymbalta since it caused the fewest side effects, even though it made little impact on her depressive symptoms. The session ended with a summary statement of Maria's plan: continuing to take the medication, observe whether or not the side effects decrease, and continue consulting with the psychiatrist.

Ana's Mixed-Outcome Therapy: Assessment, Formulation, and Course

ASSESSMENT OF ANA'S PROBLEMS, GOALS, STRENGTHS, AND HISTORY BACKGROUND

As mentioned earlier, Ana was a 27-year-old, monolingual, Spanish-speaking Guatemalan woman who had immigrated to the United States 8 years prior to her participation in the study. She lived with her partner, their two children (ages 5 and 3), her sister, and brother-in-law in a two-bedroom apartment. Ana had a fifth-grade education. She was pulled out of school so that she could work and contribute to the expenses of her family of origin. After immigrating to the United States, she worked in a factory for about 1 year. At the time of the research study, she was unemployed and caring for her children full time.

History

Ana reported first experiencing depression during her young adolescence, at about the age of 11 or 12, when she became the victim of incest at the hands of her father. In addition, two other men sexually abused Ana during her adolescence. Ana remembered always "being sad," lonely, and crying. She had intrusive nightmares and attempted suicide by overdosing on medication. Ana's abuse lasted until she left home; however, her depression persisted much beyond that time. She continued to fear men, especially when they were drunk. She also had chronic passive suicidal and homicidal ideation. In fact, when pregnant with her son, she considered ending her life by jumping off a bridge.

Ana was referred to the CMHC after expressing suicidal ideation and thoughts of hurting her children while at a general medical checkup at a community health clinic. Her only previous exposure to treatment had been 2 years prior when she had seen a psychiatrist on two occasions. She did not take any medication at that time. By the time of the first interview with the study (T1), she had been reengaged in treatment with a psychiatrist for 3 or 4 months and was taking Lexapro and Seroquel. Ana had no history of psychiatric hospitalizations.

Status at Intake

Based on her history and current presentation, it appeared as though Ana met criteria for a diagnosis of chronic major depressive disorder and posttraumatic stress disorder. Her depressive episode appeared to have some mood-congruent psychotic features, including auditory hallucinations and paranoid ideation. A bipolar presentation was ruled out as Ana did not endorse any manic or hypomanic symptoms and also none were observed by the clinician. Finally, although she did not meet criteria for alcohol or substance abuse at the time of the study, Ana admitted that she drank heavily from the age of 15 to 17 to numb the emotional pain of the sexual abuse.

On the importance and confidence scales, Ana provided ratings of 10/10, stating that the medication and therapy were helping her feel better and reducing the amount of nightmares she was having. Nonetheless, she identified a few obstacles to taking the medication, including difficulty remembering to take it every day, not having enough money or insurance to pay for the treatment (she depended on free samples to get the medication), and some concern about becoming addicted. For these reasons, she provided a rating of 5/10 on her readiness to take the medication.

Most of Ana's attitudes toward the medication were positive. Unlike other clients in the study, Ana did not face any resistance from her family for taking the medication nor did she believe that it would interfere with her ability to work. She was also willing to take it on a long-term basis and noted that in the 30 days prior to the study, she had been taking the medication whether she was feeling better or feeling worse.

ANA'S FORMULATION AND TREATMENT PLAN

Ana's presentation was complicated by comorbid PTSD associated with her experience of sexual abuse. As a result, her depression was characterized by intrusive nightmares, flashbacks, and chronic suicidal and homicidal ideation. She was influenced to take the medication by her relationships with her doctor and therapist, the desire to prevent depressive symptoms from coming back, and the belief that taking the medication would help her achieve certain goals or aspirations in her life. Ana's main barrier to adhering to the antidepressant medication was forgetfulness and confusion over whether or not she had taken the medication on a given day. She was also significantly socially isolated and experienced shame and stigma over her mental illness. Nonetheless, at the time of the research study, Ana was participating in intensive individual psychotherapy at the CMHC, apart from the research study, from which she derived a great deal of support and insight.

ANA'S COURSE OF THERAPY

First Session

The META experience for Ana started in a similar fashion as the cases presented earlier (i.e., with brief chitchat to break the ice followed by agenda setting). However, Ana's case was different in that she was assigned to an META clinician who had also conducted her initial intake for the clinic a few months prior. As a result, the alliance was quickly established. One could also argue that Ana's case was different because she presented in an action-oriented stage of change. She started the session by excitedly updating the clinician on how she had been doing since her intake. She noted that when she originally came for help, she was depressed, isolated, feeling worthless, guilty, and victimized, and having recurrent thoughts of ending her life and the life of her children. She recognized that she was not treating her children well, noting that because of her experience of being sexually abused by her father, she feared that her son would somehow sexually abuse her daughter. As a result, she pushed her son aside and would often hit him or yell at him. He was scared to talk to her or even approach her. However, by the time of the first META session, Ana was no longer feeling or behaving this way. For the 2 weeks prior to the session, she had been happy, not ruminating about her problems, having fewer nightmares, feeling less frightened, no longer turning to suicide as an answer, and confiding in others.

Of particular importance was how Ana's relationship and interactions with her son had improved. A few weeks prior to the META session, she had approached her son and told him not to be scared of her. She apologized for having made the mistake of yelling and hitting him and reassured him that it would not happen again. She offered herself as someone he could go to if he needed something. Her relationship with her children had changed so drastically that they were engaging in activities together, including dancing around the house (something that had never happened before). In addition, Ana's relationship with her partner was changing. She was no longer thinking of leaving the relationship or rejecting her partner's touch. Ana was surprising herself and those around her with her positive behavioral changes and renewed confidence.

Ana expressed gratitude for having been referred to the clinic, noting that at first she was ambivalent about accepting treatment, but was now thankful because she was feeling better. She indicated that the way she was welcomed by the clinic was especially meaningful because in the past, she had been rejected from services for her inability to speak English. She was grateful that she had found a place where she felt supported.

Ana mostly credited her success to the therapy she was receiving at the CMHC. She indicated that her individual therapist taught her that what had happened to her as a child (sexual abuse at the hands of her father) was not her fault. Therapy also provided an outlet for her to talk about her problems, especially because her family and those at home were unaware of the extent to which Ana was suffering. She was learning how to manage psychosomatic symptoms and traumatic flashbacks by naming it as something "psychological." Ana was particularly excited that she had been "symptom-free" for weeks at a time, instead of just a few days. She was motivated to remain this way because her primary goals were to "*seguir adelante*" (move forward), feel worthwhile, no longer feel afraid, enjoy her children, and gain employment.

Pursuing Ana's goals (e.g., employment) was not an easy task, especially because her PTSD produced a higher sensitivity for retraumatization. For example, Ana noted that she was afraid to go back to work because she remembered being frightened when she once found a male in the woman's bathroom at the factory where she was working. Following this incident, she did not return to work. Nonetheless, since feeling better and more motivated to "*seguir adelante*" (move forward), Ana was able to think of other means of employment. She was considering jobs that placed her less at risk, like cooking and baking. In fact, her main motivation to gain employment was so that she could have enough money to take her children out to McDonalds or Burger King. This was something she knew would make them happy.

Since Ana appeared to be in an action-oriented stage and ready for change, the META clinician advanced the session in the direction of increasing change and commitment talk. The META clinician stated:

¿Y como podemos continuar con los avances y lo que ha ganado? ¿Como puede continuar con todo lo que ha progresado?

How can we continue with the advances and that which you have gained?
How can you continue with all the progress you have made?

This type of question allowed Ana to identify and consolidate all the factors that helped her achieve her goals, including her work with her therapist, her work with her psychiatrist, her participation in the research study, and taking the antidepressant medication. Ana noted that the medication had been especially helpful in reducing her rumination of her traumatic past. It also decreased the frequency and intensity of her intrusive nightmares. Because Ana mostly made external attributions of her success, the META clinician attempted to reinforce internal attributions, like her efforts in taking advantage of the treatment that was being offered to her.

Despite all of her gains, Ana noted that she still had moments where she struggled with PTSD symptoms, especially on the days when she came to her individual therapy sessions and spoke about her past. In fact, during the META session, Ana indicated that as she was speaking about her sexual abuse, she felt her body getting warm, as if it (the abuse) was happening to her again. These moments made Ana concerned that her happiness would disappear. After all, in the past, she had only been symptom-free for 1–2 days before the nightmares and negative thoughts emerged. The META clinician normalized this experience for Ana and reinforced that she was beginning to learn the "tools" that could help protect her from experiencing a resurgence of depressive symptoms.

During the first META session, Ana's MEMS® scans revealed that she was taking her medication with 100% adherence. This reflected Ana's dedication and motivation to take advantage of her treatment and achieve her goal to "seguir adelante" (move forward). She noted that her health and happiness had a direct impact on her family's well-being. Her motivation to adhere to her treatment was also reinforced by believing that she was becoming a "good mother" and that nobody else could love her kids in the same way she did.

On the importance and confidence rating scales, Ana rated herself a 10/10. She confirmed her commitment to take the medication, stating that she always carries the pills because they "help me." In addition, she noted that her confidence had been reinforced by individual therapy sessions since they were contributing to all the improvements in her life (i.e., eating and sleeping better, getting along better with her husband, providing for her children, enjoying life, dancing, wanting to work, and improving her ability to tolerate past trauma). As for readiness to take the medication, Ana rated herself an 8/10, citing that one of her barriers to readiness was forgetfulness. Nonetheless, she was able to offer up strategies to remember to take the medication, including pairing it with mealtime. Though Ana's adherence at the time of the first META session was 100%, she continued to be a good candidate for motivational enhancement, as it would help determine whether she could sustain this level of adherence over a long period of time. After all, research shows that adherence to antidepressant medication significantly decreases after the first 30 days, especially amongst socioeconomically disadvantaged Latinos (Olfson et al., 2006).

Although Ana felt rather confident about the antidepressant medication, she presented with more ambivalence about the sleeping pills that the psychiatrist had prescribed to her. On the one hand, the sleeping pills helped her escape the intrusive thoughts she often experienced once she laid down for bed. On the other hand, they caused excessive drowsiness, leaving her too tired to attend to her children the next day. As a way of resolving this ambivalence, she decided to take the sleeping pills only when necessary.

The other area of concern for Ana was her fear of relapsing into a depressive state. She worried that her suicidal ideation would return, and at the same time, she would lose sight of the importance of her children. Despite the apprehension of a setback, Ana remembered that she had resources to help her, including phone numbers to emergency hotlines as well as the continued support of her individual therapist.

Second Session

By the time of the second META session, Ana was experiencing a relapse of symptoms. Her intrusive nightmares had returned, and she was having visions of her children being sexually abused. She was feeling desperate, tired, unmotivated, and was ruminating about the past. With the return of her nightmares came her suicidal ideation, where she lost sight of all those who loved her and only thought about death. According to Ana, the depressive and PTSD symptoms resurfaced 1 week prior to the second META session, with the most intense symptoms occurring the day before. In fact, she reported that if she had been left alone the day before, she might have attempted suicide. She felt grateful for the opportunity to talk to her individual therapist and the META clinician in back-to-back sessions the next day. This, however, was not without ambivalence. On the one hand, Ana recognized that she gained strength from talking with someone about her problems. On the other hand, she felt embarrassed that she continued to struggle with the same problems and ashamed that "strangers" (the treatment team) cared more about her than her own family.

The META clinician attempted to explore with Ana the factors that kept her from harming herself. Ana stated that thinking about her individual therapist helped her feel better as she remembered that there was someone who worried about her and took an interest in her. She also felt strongly connected to the CMHC, noting that it was a place that had helped her heal, a place that she trusted, and a place where she felt like she was treated well. She also noted that being around others, distracting herself with cleaning the house, and evoking her religious beliefs helped keep her safe. The META clinician validated Ana for having put together, albeit unconsciously, a robust safety plan. In addition, the META clinician took advantage of the opportunity to remind Ana of some of the strategies that she had previously used to combat her negative thinking, which she had mentioned during session 1, including reminding herself that "this was psychological." This served to boost Ana's sense of self-efficacy as well as reinforce her own ability to self-soothe successfully. In addition, the META clinician reminded Ana of all her recent achievements (dancing with her son, improved communication with her partner), the personal strength she had gained, and the progress she had made toward her future goals (working). Despite having experienced this setback, Ana was resolved to *"seguir adelante."* She was motivated to return to her symptom-free days.

In addition to trying to strengthen Ana's ego, the META clinician also spent some time validating Ana's experience. The truth of the matter was that she was struggling with very intrusive and disturbing nightmares. She was scared that she had lost her grip on recovery and worried that the symptoms would "overtake her." Because Ana's symptoms were so intense, the META clinician provided Ana with psychoeducation about the general course of a major depressive episode and reminded her that the symptoms would eventually pass.

Despite the clinician's efforts to move Ana past her depressive symptoms, she was very much trapped in a negative self-state. She wondered how she could possibly rid her mind of her intrusive thoughts. The META clinician attempted to dislodge Ana from this state by having her compare her current experience of intrusive thoughts to previous experiences. This approach proved successful as she recognized that, at present, she was a "stronger person," with more confidence and resources to help her manage her symptoms.

Nonetheless, feeling isolated, as though nobody cared about her, was a theme that resurfaced for Ana throughout the session. She was reluctant to turn to others for support because she (1) did not want to make them feel bad, (2) was afraid of not being believed if she were to disclose her history of sexual abuse, and (3) feared that she would be ridiculed or called "crazy." While she was extremely grateful for the support of her individual therapist and the CMHC, she was ashamed that she did not have people in her life to whom she could turn to for help. Ultimately, Ana was willing to push past the shame and embrace the sense of safety and trust that she felt from the clinic.

Ana indicated that she had forgotten to take some of her medication during the last week. She noted that since her nightmares had returned, she found herself more forgetful and had experienced difficulty concentrating. The MEMS® reading, however, revealed that she had nearly 100% adherence, only having missed 1 day. The META clinician reinforced her level of adherence despite feeling forgetful. Even so, Ana appeared to feel guilty that she had failed one day and was observed to be distraught by the confusion she experienced over whether or not she had taken the medication. She also disclosed fear that she was going to be reprimanded by the treatment team for having missed one day. This misconception was immediately cleared when the META clinician stated,

Y aquí estamos, no para castigarla pero para apoyarla en la manera que podemos y ayudarla hacer el plan que, que funcione bien para usted.

We are not here to punish you, but instead to support you in any way we can and help you find a plan that works well for you.

Because Ana presented forgetfulness as a barrier to taking her antidepressant medication, the META clinician spent some time addressing how she could overcome this obstacle. With Ana's permission, the META clinician first solicited Ana's ideas of how to solve this problem. When she was unable to produce any solutions, the META clinician reminded Ana that, in the previous session, she had thought of pairing the medication with meals. Ana noted that this strategy no longer worked because as her anxiety had increased, she craved food all the time and had ceased to have formal mealtimes. She demonstrated renewed motivation to remember her medication, predicting that as she began to feel better, her concentration and memory would improve, allowing her to take her medication as prescribed. Ana increased her change talk by stating, "voy a tratar de seguir como yo estaba/ I am going to try to return to the way I was [i.e., less confused about having taken the medication]." The META clinician reinforced Ana's desire to renew her commitment to taking the medication and took advantage of the opportunity to offer Ana concrete strategies on how to remember the medication, like using a calendar system, setting an alarm, or using a pill box. After presenting these options, the clinician and Ana evaluated each option and created a plan of action.

At the time of the second META session, Ana rated the importance of taking the medication as high, stating that she very much wanted to continue with the medication in hopes of feeling better. She confirmed having complete confidence in returning to feel the happiness she had felt in the previous week. This type of change talk transported Ana to a place where she felt optimistic about her future,

Si, esto lo voy a dejar, algo pasajero, que ahorita voy a salir y voy a ir. Me siento ya contenta.
Yes, I'm going to leave this behind, like something temporary; now I'm going to move forward. I'm feeling happier.

The META clinician reflected that this type of positive attitude would not only help her reach her goals but also protect her from future relapses. By the end of the second META session, she was expressing her motivation to "hechar ganas" (put forth effort) and asserting her commitment to battle her depression, both for herself and in honor of the treatment team.

Booster Session
Ana's presentation at the time of the last META session, which was 2 months after the second META session, was very similar to how she appeared in the first META session. She excitedly reported to the META clinician that she had survived her depressive relapse and was doing well. She had learned to manage her nightmares, had shed her feelings of guilt over her past sexual abuse, built trust in her individual therapist, and was "getting to know" what life was like in a state of happiness. She was pleased that she was no longer yelling or hitting her children,

fighting with her husband, or constantly thinking about death. Over the course of those couple of months, Ana reported discovering a sense of inner confidence and self-worth, which led her to develop a deeper love for herself and her children. In addition, she was becoming more independent and practicing assertive behavior.

Of particular interest, Ana noted feeling younger and stronger. She acknowledged that while depressed, she was often in physical pain and felt "too old to pursue life." However, her psychosomatic symptoms had nearly disappeared, and she was now able to imagine the life that awaited her. Furthermore, she had regained the energy to engage with the world around her, including running, laughing, singing, and "jumping" around with her children.

She again credited having someone to talk to (her individual therapist) as one of the main factors in helping her achieve her gains. She had learned to trust her therapist and unburden herself of the heavy load she was carrying. In addition, she identified that the most important source of motivation to *seguir adelante* (move forward) was so that she could have a presence in the lives of her children. This was of particular significance because her children, which used to be a source of fear, had become a source of strength. Ana was so impressed with the changes in herself that she commented,

Todo es diferente para mí. Todo ha cambiado. Si quiero cantar, canto. Si quiero bailar, bailo. Me llevo bien con mis niños. No les pego y no les grito.

Everything is different for me. Everything has changed. If I want to sing, I sing. If I want to dance, I dance. I get along with my kids. I don't hit them or yell at them.

In addition, others were noticing these positive changes. Some of her relatives were so impressed by her transformation that they began requesting referrals to therapy (even though they had previously disavowed it as something just for "crazy" people).

Whereas in the past, she had only experienced happiness for short periods of time (i.e., a day, two days, or a week at most), she was now feeling confident that the "good times" were going to last. The META clinician reflected Ana's personal strength, her willingness to *"poner de su parte"* (put forth effort), her ability to build a trusting alliance with her individual therapist, and her dedication to practicing what she had been learning in treatment as factors that helped her survive her relapse and get back on track toward her goals. Ana added that the feedback and attention that she had received from participating in the research study, including a letter from the META clinician and several phone calls from her individual therapist, also contributed to her success. In addition to lifting her spirits, these outreach efforts reminded her that she was not alone. In fact, Ana disclosed that one of the reasons she kept from harming herself was because she did not want to disappoint her service providers.

As Ana began to gain more strength, she was able to reflect on her history of abuse and start to consider addressing her emotions in a more meaningful way. For example, Ana began to contemplate having a conversation with her mother about her experience of being sexually abused by her father. She also thought that perhaps, in the far future, she may be able to confront her father. This was a delicate matter for Ana. On the one hand, she was feeling ready to unload some of her anger and have some of her questions answered. On the other hand, she was concerned that revisiting her past would trigger strong emotions and a resurgence of depressive symptoms. Ana was resolved to "take things one step at time" and approach this matter slowly and strategically.

Ana's progress was also unfolding in her dream life. Although she continued to have occasional nightmares, Ana was no longer running away from them or waking up in tears and wanting to end her life. Her dreams continued to include themes of death, guilt, shame, ridicule, and being unappreciated. She saw the people that harmed her in her nightmares, but this time, she was able to see herself getting help in the dreams. The more she took interest in understanding the meaning of her dreams, the more activated she became in addressing her pain. Ultimately, this led her to a deeper state of healing.

The META session concluded by once again checking in with Ana about the role of medication in her overall treatment and consolidating her adherence to the medication. Ana confirmed that both the medication and her individual therapy had equally helped her in achieving her goals. The META clinician and Ana discussed the barrier to adherence that she had identified in previous sessions (i.e., forgetfulness or confusion of whether or not she had taken the pill). Ana reported that she continued to struggle with this issue, especially when feeling very depressed. She noted that the use of a calendar was not too effective, and the META clinician was able to spend part of the session brainstorming new ways to overcome this obstacle (e.g., using a pill box or an alarm). Ana was given the opportunity to evaluate the different options and take ownership over a strategy that best suited her lifestyle.

On the ICR scales, Ana rated the *importance* of taking the medication as 10/10. She maintained 100% *confidence* (rating of 10/10) in her ability to adhere to her treatment, noting that her confidence had increased over time. She had gotten a "taste" of the positive effects of the medication and what it was like to feel better. She stated, "I'm feeling like a new person, as if nothing had happened." This strengthened her commitment to continue her adherence to the medication. As for her *readiness* to adhere to her medication, both she and the META clinician agreed that she was already putting it into practice.

Even though Ana expressed commitment to taking the antidepressant medication, her behavior reflected some level of continued ambivalence. At the end of the session, she disclosed that she was about to run out of medication and was considering going without it for 4–5 days until her next appointment with the psychiatrist. Then again, she expressed concern about what could happen if she were to discontinue the medication, especially if it meant a resurgence of symptoms. She continued to require a significant amount of support in resolving this ambivalence and figuring out ways in which she could get her needs met (i.e., obtain a prescription from her psychiatrist so that she would not go without medication).

Therapy Monitoring and Use of Feedback Information

Clinicians in the study received ongoing feedback via supervision by a doctoral-level psychologist trained in META, as well as an off-site META consultant. Supervision included audio- review and live role-plays. The META consultant listened to transcripts of the session and coded the sessions according to the Motivational Interviewing Treatment Integrity (MITI) scales (Moyers et al., 2005). This allowed clinicians to gauge their level of fidelity to the intervention and improve their technique in areas like empathy/understanding, "MI spirit," use of open-ended questions, and use of reflections. In addition, the consultant provided written feedback to the clinician after the first two sessions of META with comments on strengths, areas of improvement, and potential homework assignments to practice the technique. Employing the ongoing supervision allowed the clinicians to modify the intervention accordingly. For example, after receiving feedback, one clinician was increasingly mindful of creating a collaborative environment with the client, avoiding the role of "expert," watching her tone of voice so that her statements would not be perceived as questions but rather as reflective statements, and deepening her reflective statements to make them more meaningful while still conveying understanding.

Concluding Evaluation of the Therapy Process and Outcome

Lupe's Positive Outcome

It is clear that the META intervention in Lupe's case was a success as measured by her subjective report as well as the results of the final assessments. Lupe dramatically eradicated her depressive symptoms according to her BDI-II scores. When she began the study, she scored a 43 on the BDI, placing her in the severe range and higher than the treatment group mean which was 31.1 (Table 6.1). By the time of the last assessment, 4 months later, her BDI score was a 3. This was not only significantly lower in comparison to her original score, but it was also lower than the mean for the treatment group, which was 18.0 (Table 6.1). Lupe's final BDI score suggests that she ended the study with minimal to no depressive symptoms. In addition, Lupe was able to increase her percentage of adherence to the antidepressant medication from 80% (at T1, the beginning of the study) to 89% (at T3, the time of the last assessment period). This compares to a mean adherence percentage for the treatment group at T3 of 65.7% (Table 6.2).

As for her subjective experience of the META, by the time of the exit interview, Lupe was reporting that she had met her initial goal: returning to her old self. She was back to smiling, singing, and being active. In fact, her improved mood had impacted her family as she reported that her relationships were stronger and the home environment was more relaxed. Her relatives were grateful for these changes, and they validated her efforts at getting better. This, in turn, fueled her motivation to continue her adherence to the medication. Lupe stated:

> Yo voy a continuar a tomar la medicina, aunque me sienta mal (con efectos secundarios) o aumente de peso. Lo mas importante es que me sienta bien (emocionalmente).
>
> I'm going to continue taking the medication, whether or not I feel bad (with side effects) and whether or not it causes weight gain. The most important is that I feel better (emotionally).

Overall, Lupe credited her recuperation to her own efforts, therapy, medication, her treatment team, her belief in God, and her family. With regard to the META sessions, Lupe reported that the ability to confide in someone else and feel as though that person really cared about her was the most therapeutic factor. She felt relief in being able to "unload." In addition, she noted that the outreach efforts and sincere concern from the treatment team—separate from the META sessions per se—left her feeling as though "others cared about her." This motivated her to help herself and take the first step of coming to the appointments. At the appointments, she was able to learn more about herself, clarify misconceptions about medication, and contrast the effects of her depression to the goals she had yet to achieve. Her pleasant experience at the appointments fueled her motivation to adhere to her treatment and to "stick with her plan" of taking the medication. Ultimately, this became an interacting chain, with each component reinforcing the next, resulting in Lupe's improved mood and strong commitment to the medication.

MARIA'S NEGATIVE OUTCOME
In the case of Maria, the META process was very far less successful as compared to that of Lupe's case. At the time of the final assessment, Maria continued to experience severe depression as measured by her BDI-II score, which was 33. She also had elevated levels of suicidal ideation throughout the study, and she required psychiatric hospitalization during the middle of her participation in they study (at the time of the T2 assessment). In addition, there was no lasting effect of the META sessions on improving her adherence to the antidepressant medication. Her adherence dropped from 78%, measured after her two META sessions (which compares to the group mean for the treatment condition of 75%) to 37% at the end of the study (compared to the group mean for the treatment condition of 65.7%; see Table 6.2). In fact, Maria lost her medication bottle for several weeks, and it was not until she was called in for the exit interview that she found it (note that the time period where she reportedly lost the MEMS® bottle was not included in the adherence data). Finally, the META sessions did not produce any change in increasing Maria's *confidence* or *readiness* to take the medication; her ratings remained the same over the course of her participation in the study.

Interestingly, according to Maria's subjective experience, the META sessions were "a good experience." She felt particularly comforted by knowing that the treatment team and the META clinician were concerned about her. She referred to the META clinician as "more than just a doctor," and she was appreciative of how the clinician followed up by calling and sending her letters. While she acknowledged that there were times when she continued to feel sad, she reported that, overall, she had improved as compared to when she first presented to the study. She cited God, the research study, her therapist, and her psychiatrist as the factors that helped her get better.

Maria's main obstacles to adherence at the time of the exit interview were the side effects she felt from the medication (nausea and stomach pain) and the stigma she experienced over her mental illness. She reported that others did not understand her depression and would criticize her for being "too dramatic." For that reason, she was reluctant to confide in others, ask for help, or let someone know when something was bothering her. Given the extent of Maria's shame and social isolation, the opportunity to confide in the META clinician and feel understood was likely one of the most important therapeutic factors.

One marker of progress for Maria was that, by the end of the study, she was starting to access more community resources. Maria acknowledged that her faith had been fundamental in helping her fight her depression. To that end, she decided that it would be helpful to seek support from the church. Increasing her participation in church had the potential to strengthen Maria's spirit and expose her to a network of people that could be good sources of support.

ANA'S MIXED OUTCOME

Ana's outcome with the META sessions had mixed results. Objectively (i.e., as measured by BDI-II scores), Ana had minimal change in her level of depression throughout the course of the study. As shown in Table 6.1, at the time of the final assessment, Ana continued with moderate levels of depression and had only decreased 3 points in comparison to her ratings from the first assessment (from a 26 to a 23). Interestingly, after two sessions of the META intervention, her level of depression actually worsened into the severe range, to a score of 35. Compared to the mean of the treatment group, Ana's depression scores at the beginning of the study were below the mean and above the mean by the final assessment. In addition, her percentage of adherence to the medication decreased over the course of the study (see Table 6.2). She started off with 100% adherence at the outset of the study. By the time of the exit interview, she was 78% adherent, suggesting that the META intervention had a smaller effect on sustaining her level of adherence over time. Nonetheless, Ana's adherence was above the group mean of 65.7% (see Table 6.2).

Ana's subjective experience of the META sessions proved different from her objective results. In the follow-up exit interview she expressed immense gratitude to the study, for it provided her with the opportunity to "move forward," offered her someone to talk to, allowed her to build insight into her mental illness, and gave her the tools to manage her symptoms. As she gained internal strength, she noticed a reduction in the frequency and intensity of her symptoms, particularly suicidal ideation.

She was able to shed her feelings of worthlessness and guilt and discover new passions, interests, and values. Instead of feeling victimized and asking herself "Why me?," she began to view her previous experiences as opportunities to learn and grow. Most important, she credited the study for solidifying her identity as a competent mother and wife. Her transformation was so noticeable that by the time of the last assessment, the research assistant commented that she was "carrying herself with more confidence."

Ana reported that the most helpful component of the treatment "was the way that she was treated." She felt listened to and understood. Ana acknowledged that, at times, the questions that were asked of her were challenging and provoked emotion. However, she was grateful that the clinician took the time to process her reactions. She was also appreciative of the team's outreach efforts (calls and letters). It helped her feel motivated and made her realize that strangers were taking an interest in her. In fact, after receiving a pamphlet from the research study with information about depression, she bought a book to learn more about the origin and course of her illness.

COMPARING THE CASES ON READINESS FOR CHANGE

Analysis of the three cases suggests in part that the success or failure of the META intervention depended heavily on the participants' readiness for change and whether or not the clinician tailored the intervention appropriately. As mentioned earlier, the motivation to change a particular behavior is a dynamic process and people fluctuate through various stages of readiness, including precontemplation, contemplation, preparation, action, and maintenance (Miller & Rollnick, 2002). One could argue that Lupe, the most successful case, responded well to the intervention because she moved quickly through the aforementioned stages of change. When she presented to the first session, she may have been in a contemplation stage. By the end of the intervention she was likely in the action phase. Maria, on the other hand, may have had less success because she entered the study at an earlier stage of change (i.e., precontemplation), and instead of progressing to other stages of change, she more or less vacillated between precontemplation and contemplation.

To that end, it would have been important for the META clinician to respond appropriately to the client's stage of change. For those in a precontemplation stage, it is important to listen carefully, roll with the resistance, offer information if necessary, instill hope, and provide the space for the individual to make his or her own decision (Miller & Rollnick, 2002). When analyzing Maria's course of therapy, it was the second author's (A. P.'s) clinical impression that the META therapist did not consistently "meet" Maria at her stage of change. On the one hand, the clinician appropriately responded to Maria's sense of disempowerment and her lack of information. On the other hand, the META clinician hurried Maria through several key moments of the intervention, like building rapport (e.g., setting the agenda) and exploring her values and goals. For example, while the clinician appropriately elicited Maria's goals and values with a provocative question, "How would your life be different without depression?," she did not spend enough time working with Maria on elaborating the response and eventually developing a state of discrepancy.

Instead, only moments later, the META clinician proceeded to inquire about the role that medication had on her depression. In addition, Maria's resistance was not sufficiently validated, and she seemed rushed to engage in change and commitment talk prematurely. In fact, most of the change talk was actually being produced by the clinician instead of the client. This made it difficult to determine whether Maria was genuinely feeling committed to change or simply being acquiescent.

Likewise, the outcome of Ana's case may have also been affected by the therapist's inconsistent response to her stage of change. Reviewing her course of treatment revealed that a main concern for Ana was the fear of relapsing to depressive and PTSD symptoms. Relapse is a common concern in individuals undergoing change, and according to Miller and Rollnick (2002), clinicians should provide reassurance, help the participants make sense of the resurgence of the symptoms, and help them see the relapse as a learning opportunity rather than a crisis. However, in the case of Ana, the META clinician seemed to hurry her and prematurely focus on issues related to the medication instead of spending more time validating and amplifying her fear of relapse.

COMMON VERSUS SPECIFIC FACTORS

Finally, it's important to note that the META intervention is multifaceted. It involves both *common factors*, such as having been listened to in a nonjudgmental manner; feeling cared for by the treatment team; having the ability to confide in someone; and being able to receive information and clarify misconceptions. And it involves *specific factors*, like developing discrepancies; rolling with resistance; imparting information; providing feedback; facilitating change talk; supporting self-efficacy; and empathically meeting the client at his or her stage of change. The case studies describe how these two sets of factors are intertwined and complementary. Both are needed for MI to be provided properly.

SYNTHESIS OF THE FINDINGS FROM THE RCT AND CASE STUDY APPROACHES

What the RCT and Case Study Types of Knowledge Tell Us

As discussed in the chapter introduction, the RCT and the case studies yield different types of knowledge that are complementary. The RCT focused on only a few variables, but it was able to make a strong inference that the intervention in general caused the improvement in those variables. Specifically, this focus is reflected within the logic model in Figure 6.1, with the relevant components and causal forces outlined in light lines. In particular, the RCT results show that after adjusting for covariates, the clients in the Motivational Enhancement Therapy for Antidepressants (META) condition, as compared with the usual care (UC) only clients, showed significantly higher antidepressant adherence, both at Time 2 (5 weeks after baseline) and at Time 3 (5 months after baseline). In addition, the results indicated a complex impact of the META condition on depression.

Specifically, while the META group did not significantly differ from the UC group on the mean Beck Depression Inventory-II (BDI-II) scores across time, a statistically significantly higher percentage of the META group participants than the UC group participants showed remission from depression at 5 months. Particularly, at 5 months, 50% of META participants achieved symptom remission, compared to only 20.8% of UC participants. More about the meaning of this discrepancy between the group-level and individual-level results will be discussed next.

In contrast, the case studies captured a much broader range of variables, including all the components in Figure 6.1, that is, boxes 1–10 and arrows, A–N. Table 6.3, first presented above, provides examples of some of the ways in which the case studies captured Components 1–8 specifically. In addition, not shown directly in Table 6.3, the case studies captured the intertwining, reciprocally causal relationships among the various components. For example, Lupe's case shows a "virtuous circle" in which (a) she felt relief in being able to "unload" her emotional distress and concerns to an empathetic and sympathetic therapist, leading her (b) to feel that "others cared about her," in turn (c) motivating her to come to her next appointment, during which she clarified her misconceptions about medication, so as to (d) view the medication as helpful in overcoming her depression (in spite of it leading to weight gain) and in meeting her positive personal and life goals, which in turn (e) fueled her motivation to continue taking her medication and activating her to work on her goals, which in turn (f) elicited a positive response from her family, which in turn (g) further motivated her to continue with her medication plan and to work on her goals.

As another example, the less successful cases of Maria and Ana show the points at which such potential virtuous circles break down into "vicious" circles. This is illustrated in Maria's case by (a) her recent experience of a traumatic rejection by her husband, resulting in (b) her now lacking a strong social support system, and (c) in fact having a social support system that stigmatized her depression, all of which (d) decreased her motivation to take her medication and work on her life goals, which in turn led to (e) an increase in her depression, leading to (f) the need for hospitalization between her second and third META session, which precipitated (g) a further rejection by her social support system of her severe depressive experience, with all of the aforementioned leading to (h) a reduction in her motivation for complying with her antidepressant medication.

In sum, the RCT knowledge informs us about the impact of the META intervention in contrast to the control condition of UC only. With the RCT, the emphasis is primarily *variable oriented* and targeted on arrow E, as shown in Figure 6.1. Specifically, as indicated by the components with light lines in Figure 6.1, the focus on the RCT design is on the capacity of the META therapy (box 10)—compared with the control group, which did not receive the META therapy—to increase adherence with antidepressant medication (impacting on box 2), and thus, via E, to reduce depressive symptoms (box 7). Through its use of randomization and a control group, the design allows one to conclude with confidence that the intervention was the cause of the difference in the group means.

In a complementary way, the systematic case studies in the META project are *person oriented* and so focused on *all* the boxes and arrows in Figure 6.1, since these are all captured in the dynamics and complexities of the clinical phenomena that the case study seeks to document and analyze holistically. Thus, the case study knowledge zooms in and provides a detailed, clinical narrative about (a) the actual experiences, behaviors, and life contexts of different patients regarding their major depression, (b) the therapeutic processes of their META sessions, (c) the quantitative and qualitative outcomes of these sessions, and (d) the seeming causal relationships among process and outcome variables. Moreover, the case studies provide the aforementioned knowledge for patients with different outcomes, thus qualitatively and quantitatively contrasting the nature and determinants of success and failure in the experimental META condition.

Putting both kinds of knowledge together tells us that the META intervention is effective to a certain, specifiable degree (from the RCT knowedge); that this is true for particular types of clients (from the case study knowledge); and how and why particularly the META therapy works (from the case study knowledge). Based on this combined knowledge, we can then develop procedures for better matching particular clients—like Lupe—who are particularly suited to the META therapy condition as it is now designed. For those patients who are not well matched to the three-session META intervention—like Maria and perhaps Ana—we can learn from their therapy process to develop alternative types of approaches, such as a longer series of META sessions, and/or adding in additional types of therapy.

An Implication of the Complex Results Concerning the Impact of the META Condition on Level of Depression

Numerical data on groups of clients in an RCT can be analyzed from two perspectives (Eells, 2007). In one approach, the data are first numerically aggregated and then the means calculated and compared (the "aggregate-then-analyze" method). In the other approach, the data are first analyzed within each client, and then the individual results aggregated (the "analyze-then-aggregate" method).

In reviewing the data on the impact of META on depression level, it was found that by the aggregate-then-analyze method, there was not a statistically significant relationship between being in META and having a reduced level of depression. However, by the analyze-then aggregate method, there was such a significant relationship, so that at 5 months, 50% of META participants achieved symptom remission, compared to only 20.8% of UC participants.

Technically, this suggests that the META clients who did not go into remission (like Maria) did more poorly on their group mean than the UC patients who did not go into remission, washing out the overall mean differences between the META and the UC groups. To illustrate this principle, consider a hypothetical situation with two groups of four clients, with all the clients starting with a BDI score of 30, and requiring a drop of 15 points or more to go below the clinical cutoff point of 15. In Group A, all the BDIs drop by 10, and in Group B, two clients' BDIs drop by 20, and two by 0. The average BDI drop is 10 in both, but the remission rate in Group A is 0% compared to a remission rate of 50% in Group B.

The greater degree of impact of the META condition on within-individual symptom remission versus that on mean group differences is consistent with published findings more broadly. For example, Clement (2013) has reviewed 27 published meta-analyses of outcomes between experimental and control groups in psychotherapy research and found a mean effect size of 0.76. He compared this to the results of 18 published meta-analyses of within-patient outcomes (pretherapy versus posttherapy). Here he obtained a mean effect size of 1.35. A one-way ANOVA on the mean effect sizes of these two groups of meta-analyses reveals a highly significant difference between them. Clement concludes that "published meta-analyses of mean ESs [effect sizes] from RCTs have greatly underestimated how much a given patient improves during a course of psychotherapy" (p. 25).

In sum, this discrepancy in findings by the two methods points to the general importance of analyzing data from multiple perspectives (Eells, 2007), as emphasized by the "mixed-methods" model that provides a grounding for this book. More particularly, the positive findings by the analyze-then-aggregate method argues for the value of extending the case studies to contrast the characteristics of the 50% in the META group (like Lupe) who did go into remission with the other 50% (like Maria and Ana) who did not enter into remission.

The Case Studies Reveal That the Three-Session MI in the META Condition Was "Genuine" Therapy

As mentioned above, the tailored, three-session META intervention in the present study was designed as a client-centered therapy that sought to identify and address the unique psychological, sociocultural, and other barriers to adhering to antidepressant medication that are outlined in the logic model in Figure 6.1. The finding that META was associated with symptom remission, but that this symptom remission was not associated with antidepressant adherence, indicates that the META intervention had a direct psychotherapeutic effect, which was not part of our initial research design. We were quite surprised when we found that adherence was not a significant predictor of remission.

The clinically rich and far-ranging details provided in the systematic case studies (as illustrated, in part, by Table 6.3) are very valuable in further understanding such surprising and complex data. Particularly, we believe that the META intervention—even in the instance of Lupe's only two sessions—can be characterized as genuine therapy, not just "preparation" for antidepressant or other therapy (although META can of course be combined with other types of therapy). For example, the case studies illustrate that the META intervention, like other therapies, was grounded in a principle-based manual (Miller & Rollnick, 2002), requiring the therapist to adapt a series of principles to the client's needs and reactions in a manner that was client responsive (Stiles, Honos-Webb, & Surko, 1998). Also, as described earlier, the case studies showed that the META therapy, like other types of therapy, involved a number of both *common factors* and *specific factors*, which are complementary to and causally intertwined with each other.

Moreover, as noted earlier, in the process of doing the Latino cultural adaptation, we learned that the clients were turned off by a discussion of their problems that focused only on medication. Rather, our adaptation was oriented to all of the behaviors and strategies the clients could employ to better cope with their depression, and to working with them to make their adherence an important part of that. Thus, the META intervention applied to a broad range of coping behaviors, although it did emphasize the medication adherence. In practice, as illustrated in the case studies, the other coping skills reinforced during the META sessions were quite varied and dependent on the material elicited in sessions. Examples include clients being behaviorally activated to spend more time with their kids, to find a job, to expand their social support system, to work to repair certain relationships, to be a good mother, to allow oneself to be taken care of by a treatment team, and to get out of the house more. This focus beyond adherence helped to bypass the resistance that "one cannot solve problems by just by taking medications."

In sum, we see from our RCT results that the META intervention did indeed improve antidepressant adherence. For the finding that enhanced rates of depression recovery in the META group was independent of adherence, and thus that the META had an independent psychotherapy effect, the case studies spell out the variety of clinical processes by which this effect took place. And with a vibrant debate on the relative effectiveness of antidepressants versus psychotherapy (e.g., compare Fournier, DeRubeis, Hollon, et al. [2010] on supporting its empirical efficacy versus Kirsch [2014] on disputing its empirical efficacy), the current mixed-methods approach illustrates its utility in more closely examining processes of improvement. In the current analyses, the qualitative therapy process information in the case studies generated additional evidence that META may have had a direct psychotherapeutic effect, in addition to any possible pharmacotherapeutic effect.

The Advantages of a Naturalistic Study

Two of the particular characteristics of the META study that are of great practical importance are its modest requirement of new therapeutic resources (three sessions of manual-based, "add-on" therapy) and its grounding in a CMHC setting, providing a great deal of external validity. That is, the knowledge derived from the META study is particularly generalizable to implementing this intervention within existent community mental health settings, including settings with particular cultural minorities, as shown by the success of the META program's tailored version of the META model in meeting the needs of an underserved Latino population.

The Need for Replication

A clear limitation of this project is that the relatively small numbers in the RCT and the inclusion of only three case studies restrict the ability to generalize from the project's results. However, the fact that the results are very promising argues for investing in replications of both components of the project: the RCT and the case studies. Also, the modest resources required to implement META and its capacity to be tailored to different cultural groups in actual CMHC settings makes it attractive to mental health service developers.

Another concern relates to the fact that 30% (27 out of 92) of the individuals approached for the RCT ultimately did not participate. Although this engagement rate is comparable to those found in other clinical trials, it raises questions as to whether those who did not participant felt they were already adherent or perhaps were among the least adherent.

Finally, the knowledge derived from the case studies in the present project will be very valuable in developing ways to identify, in the future, two types of clients. The first includes those clients like Lupe, who are particularly suited to benefit from three-session META; and the second includes those like Maria and Ana, who need more than three sessions of META (e.g., by including more sessions, by slowing down the pace of the sessions, or spacing out the sessions; and/or by adding other kinds of therapy to the META). Identifying different types of clients who are systematically "matched" to interventions requiring different amounts of resources connects importantly to the emerging "stepped-care" movement of finding the most cost-effective sequence of interventions for treating a particular individual, involving a "stepped series of interventions moving from less intensive and less expensive to more intensive and expensive" (Crow, Agras, Halmi, et al., 2013, p. 306). Kazdin and Blase (2011) emphasize the importance of determining to whom these different sequences of interventions might be applied. We believe from our experience in the META project that case studies provide a very promising approach for accomplishing this task.

REFERENCES

Anglin, D. M., Link, B. G., & Phelan, J. C. (2006). Racial differences in stigmatizing attitudes toward people with mental illness. *Psychiatric Services, 57*, 857–862.

Atdjian, S., & Vega, W. A. (2005). Disparities in mental health treatment in U.S. racial and ethnic minority groups: Implications for psychiatrist. *Psychiatric Services, 56*, 1600–1602.

Beck, A. T., Steer, R. A., & Brown, G. K. (1996). *Manual for the Beck Depression Inventory-II*. San Antonio, TX: Psychological Corporation.

Bem, D. J. (1972). Self-perception theory. In L Berkowitz (Ed)., *Advances in experimental social psychology*, vol. 6 (pp. 1–62). New York, NY: Academic Press.

Byerly, M., Thompson, A., Carmody, T., Bugno, R., Erwin, T., Kashner, M., & Rush, A. J. (2007). Validity of electronically monitored medication adherence and conventional adherence measures in schizophrenia. *Psychiatric Services, 58*, 844–847.

Clement, P. W. (2013). Practice-based evidence: 45 years of psychotherapy's effectiveness in a private practice. *American Journal of Psychotherapy, 67*, 23–46.

Cooper, L. A., Gonzales, J. J., Gallo, J. J., Rost, K. M., Meredith, L. S., Rubenstein, L. V., . . . Ford, D. E. (2003). The acceptability of treatment for depression among African-American, Hispanic, and white primary care patients. *Medical Care, 41*, 479–489.

Crow, S. J., Agras, W. S., Halmi, K. A., Fairburn, C. G., Mitchell, J. E., & Nyman, J. A. (2013). A cost effectiveness analysis of stepped care treatment for bulimia nervosa. *International Journal of Eating Disorders, 46*, 302–307.

DiClemente, C. C., McConnaughy, E. A., Norcross, J. C., & Prochaska, J. O. (1986). Integrative dimensions for psychotherapy. *Journal of Integrative & Eclectic Psychotherapy, 5*, 256–274.

Eells, T. D. (2007). Generating and generalizing knowledge about psychotherapy from pragmatic case studies. *Pragmatic Case Studies in Psychotherapy, 3*(1), 35–54. Available at http://pcsp.libraries.rutgers.edu/. doi: http://dx.doi.org/10.14713/pcsp.v3i1.893

First, M. B., Spitzer, R. L., Gibbon, M., & Williams, J. B. W. (2005). *Structured clinical interview for DSM-IV-TR Axis I Disorders—Patient edition (with psychotic screen).* New York, NY: Biometric Research Department.

Fournier, J. C., DeRubeis, R. J., Hollon, S. D., Dimidjian, S., Amsterdam, J. D., Shelton, R. C., & Fawcett, J. (2010). Antidepressant drug effects and depression severity: A patient-level meta-analysis. *Journal of the American Medical Association, 303*, 47–53.

George, C. F., Peveler, R. C., Heiliger, S., & Thompson, C. (2000). Adherence with tricyclic antidepressants: The value of four different methods of assessment. *British Journal of Clinical Pharmacology, 50*, 166–171.

Givens, J. L., Houston, T. K., Van Voorhees, B. W., Ford, D. E., & Cooper, L. A. (2007). Ethnicity and preferences for depression treatment. *General Hospital Psychiatry, 29*, 182–191.

Hettema, J., Steele, J., & Miller, W. (2005). Motivational interviewing. *Annual Review of Clinical Psychology, 1*, 91–111.

Interian, A. (2010). A brief self-report measure to assess antidepressant adherence among Spanish-Speaking Latinos. *Journal of Clinical Psychopharmacology, 30*, 755–757.

Interian, A., Lewis-Fernández, R., Gara, M. A., & Escobar, J. A. (2013). A randomized-controlled trial of an intervention to improve antidepressant adherence among Latinos with depression. *Depression and Anxiety, 30*, 688–696.

Interian, A., Martinez, I. E., Guarnaccia, P. J., Vega, W. A., & Escobar, J. I. (2007). A qualitative analysis of the perception of stigma among Latinos receiving antidepressants. *Psychiatric Services December, 58*, 1591–1594.

Interian, A., Martinez, I., Rios, L. I., Krejci, J., & Guarnaccia, P. J. (2010). Adaptation of a motivational interviewing intervention to improve antidepressant adherence among Latinos. *Cultural Diversity & Ethnic Minority Psychology, 16*, 215–225.

Kazdin, A. E., & Blase, S. L. (2011). Rebooting psychotherapy research and practice to reduce the burden of mental illness. *Perspectives on Psychological Science, 6*(1), 21–37.

Kessler, R. C., Berglund, P., Demler, O., Jin, R., Koretz, D. Merikangas, . . . Wang, P. (2003). The epidemiology of Major Depressive Disorder. *Journal of American Medical Association, 289*(23), 3095–3105.

Kirsch, I. (2014). Antidepressants and the placebo effect. *Zeitschrift für Psychologie, 222*, 128–134.

Lanouette, N. M., Folsom, D. P., Sciolla, A., & Jeste, D. V. (2009). Psychotropic medication nonadherence among United States Latinos: A comprehensive literature review. *Psychiatric Services, 60*, 157–174.

Melartin, T. K., Rytsala, H. J., Leskela, U. S., Lestela-Mielonen, P. S., Sokero, T. P., & Insometsa, E. T. (2005). Continuity is the main challenge in treating major depressive disorder in psychiatric care. *Journal of Clinical Psychiatry, 66*, 220–227.

Melfi, C. A., Chawla, A. J., Croghan, T. W., Hanna, M. P., Kennedy, S., & Sredi, K. (1998). The effects of adherence to antidepressant treatment guidelines on relapse and recurrence of depression. *Archives of General Psychiatry, 55*, 1128–1132.

Miller, W. R. (1983). Motivational interviewing with problem drinkers. *Behavioural Psychotherapy, 11*, 147–172.

Miller, W. R., & Rollnick, S. (2002). *Motivational interviewing: Preparing people for change.* New York, NY: The Guilford Press.

Miranda, J., Duan, N., Sherbourne, C., Schoenbaum, M., Lagomasino, I., Jackson-Triche, M., & Wells, K. B. (2003). Improving care for minorities: Can quality improvement interventions improve care and outcomes for depressed minorities? Results of a randomized, controlled trial. *Health Services Research, 38*, 613–630.

Miranda, J., Nakamura, R., & Bernal, G. (2003). Including ethnic minorities in mental health intervention research: A practical approach to a long-standing problem. *Culture, Medicine & Psychiatry, 27*, 467–486.

Moyers, T. B., Martin, T., Manuel, J. K., Hendrickson, S. M., & Miller, W. R. (2005). Assessing competence in the use of motivational interviewing. *Journal of Substance Abuse Treatment, 28*, 19–26.

National Institute of Mental Health (NIMH). (2008). *The numbers count: Mental Disorders in America* (NIH Publication No. NIH 99-4584) [Online]. Available at http://www.NIMH. NIH.gov/publicat/numbers.CFM

Olfson, M., Marcus, S. C., Druss, B., Elinson, L., Tanielian, T., & Pincus, H. A. (2002). National trends in the outpatient treatment of depression. *Journal of American Medical Association, 287*, 203–209.

Olfson, M., Marcus, S. C., Tedeschi, M., & Wan, G. J. (2006). Continuity of antidepressant treatment for adults with depression in the United States. *American Journal of Psychiatry, 163*, 101–108.

Opler, L., Ramirez, P., Paul, M., Domínguez, L. M., Fox, M. S., & Johnson, P. B. (2004). Rethinking medication practices in an inner-city Hispanic mental health clinic. *Journal of Psychiatric Practice, 10*(2), 134–140.

Penley, J. A., Wiebe, J. S., & Nwosu, A. (2003). Psychometric properties of the Spanish Beck Depression Inventory-II in a Medical sample. *Psychological Assessment, 15*, 569–577.

Persons, J. B. (2008). *The case formulation approach to cognitive-behavior therapy.* New York, NY: Guilford.

Persons, J. B. (2013). Who needs a case formulation and why: Clinicians use the case formulation to guide decision-making. *Pragmatic Case Studies in Psychotherapy, 9*(4), 448–456. Available at http://pcsp.libraries.rutgers.edu/. doi: http://dx.doi.org/10.14713/pcsp.v9i4.1835

Project MATCH Research Group (1997). Project MATCH secondary a priori hypotheses. *Addiction, 92*, 1671–1698.

Prawda, A. (2010). *Pragmatic case study analyses of motivational interviewing with depressed Latinos.* Doctoral dissertation, Graduate School of Applied and Professional Psychology, Rutgers University. Available at https://rucore.libraries.rutgers.edu/search/results/?key=ETD-RU&rtype%5B%5D=&query=prawda

Rios-Ellis, B. (2005). Critical disparities in Latino mental health: Transforming research into action. *National Council of La Raza*, 1–33.

Rogers, C. R. (1959). A theory of therapy, personality, and interpersonal relationships as developed in the client-centered framework. In S. Koch (Ed.), *Psychology: The study of a science*, vol. 3 (pp. 184–256). New York, NY: McGraw-Hill.

Schnittker, J., Freese, J., & Powell, B. (2000). Nature, nurture, neither, nor: Black-white differences in beliefs about the cause and appropriate treatment of mental illness. *Social Forces, 78*, 1101–1130.

Sleath, B., Rubin, R. H., & Huston, S. A. (2003). Hispanic ethnicity, physician-patient communication, and antidepressant adherence. *Comprehensive Psychiatry, 44*, 198–204.

Stiles, W. B., Honos-Webb, L., & Surko, M. (1998). Responsiveness in psychotherapy. *Clinical Psychology: Science and Practice, 5*, 439–458.

Warden, D., Rush, A. J., Wisniewski, S. R., Lesser, I. M., Kornstein, S. G., Balasubramani, G. K., ... Trivedi, M. H. (2009). What predicts attrition in second step medication treatments for depression? A STAR*D Report. *International Journal of Neuropsychopharmcology, 12*, 459–473.

Warden, D., Trivedi, M., Wisniewski, S. R., Davis, L., Nierenberg, A. A., Gaynes, B. N., ... Rush, A. J. (2007). Predictors of attrition during initial (citalopram) treatment for depression: A STAR*D Report. *American Journal of Psychiatry, 164*, 1189–1197.

Whaley, A. L. (1997). Ethnic and racial differences in perceptions of dangerousness of persons with mental illness. *Psychiatric Services, 48*, 1328.

Wiebe, J. S., & Penley, J. A. (2005). A psychometric comparison of the Beck Depression Inventory-II in English and Spanish. *Psychological Assessment, 17*, 481–485.

Yin, R. K. (2014). *Case study research: Design and methods* (5th ed.). Thousand Oaks, CA: Sage.

COMMENTARY
The Best of Both Worlds

John C. Norcross

The extraordinary contribution by Interian, Prawda, Fishman, and Buerger (this volume) presents and celebrates many of my favorite methods: motivational interviewing (MI), real-world research, cultural adaptations, therapeutic relationships, systematic case studies, and randomized clinical trials (RCTs). The reader may excuse me, then, for my unabashed enthusiasm for the chapter and for its clinical and research underpinnings. As a commentator, however, I will endeavor to highlight an occasional quibble and to offer an alternative hypothesis or two. All that within the context of my rousing burst of "Well done, colleagues! This is precisely what the future of clinical practice and psychotherapy research requires."

What strikes me in reading this chapter is the exponential expansion in understanding that occurs when we adopt multiple perspectives. In practice, our patients profit from both worlds when we conduct MI as both a therapy relationship and a treatment method, when we adopt with fidelity an evidence-based treatment and adapt it with cultural flexibility, and when we combine psychological therapy with a pharmacological intervention for disabling disorders. In research, we progress by conducting both RCTs and systematic case studies and by analyzing results at both the group level and individual level. When we discard the either/or and embrace the both/and, psychotherapy practice and research thrive. The phenomenon becomes fuller, richer, more verdant—and more consequential for those receiving our services.

MOTIVATIONAL INTERVIEWING

Interian and colleagues illustrate how a psychological treatment can be evaluated using two methods—an RCT and systematic case studies. They convincingly demonstrate how this combination capitalizes on the relative advantages of each method and how the ensuing synergy advances both the practice and research base of MI.

Motivational enhancement therapy (MET) served as an early incarnation of MI and was employed in the influential Project MATCH (Miller et al., 1992; Project MATCH Research Group, 1993) for the treatment of alcohol abuse, among other studies. Their particular intervention is characterized as motivational enhancement therapy for antidepressants (META). In Interian et al.'s study, MI was creatively employed in several of its multiple applications: (1) as a prelude to pharmacological treatment in order to enhance client motivation for medication adherence; (2) as a stand-alone brief intervention for adherence; and (3) in combination with the other treatments the patients were receiving in a community mental health center (Miller & Moyers, 2005).

Using a sophisticated additive design, Interian and colleagues randomly assigned chronically depressed patients to either usual care (UC) at the community mental health center or to the UC plus three META sessions provided by the research staff. The UC patients did receive the antidepressant medication but not the META sessions.

Consistent with the expanding body of MI outcome studies (more than 200 controlled studies and counting), the results of the META were impressive. By the final META contact (time 3), rates of medication adherence for participants in the META condition almost doubled those of participants in the UC condition—59.81% versus 33.57%. Such adherence—and importantly—attending psychotherapy led, at 5 months, to 50% of META participants achieving symptom remission, compared to only 21% of UC participants. MI does indeed typically produce large effects in a small number of sessions (Lundahl & Burke, 2009).

The MI may, in fact, account for the group differences. But let me pose two additional, complementary hypotheses: Something almost always works better than nothing, and any relational-based cultural adaptation might have done likewise. As to the first, thousands of psychotherapy research studies now attest that psychotherapy (of practically any variant and duration) invariably outperforms no treatment. Compared to the UC condition, the depressed patients in the META condition certainly received something more: three individual sessions led by passionate, bilingual clinical psychologists and doctoral students specifically trained and continually supervised in MI. That is certainly "something more" than treatment as usual provided by the typically overburdened, underfunded staff at a community mental health center. Without a comparable treatment condition in the research design, we cannot ascertain whether it was the MI itself or the "something more" that accounts for the gains in adherence.

As to the second hypothesis, a close reading of the chapter leads one to be impressed by the robust therapeutic relationships created in the META condition (by clinicians and researchers alike) and by the sensitive cultural adaptations employed. Might these, rather than the MI, be responsible for the patient improvements in adherence that are largely attributed to the MI itself? I will argue next in the affirmative to that question.

Before that, however, my second hypothesis in no way detracts from the MI and, indeed, is perfectly compatible with its methods and spirit. Miller describes his MI as "Carl Rogers in new clothes": a person-centered, directive approach that enhances intrinsic motivation to change by helping clients explore and resolve ambivalence (Rollnick & Miller, 1995). As such, it combines elements of both person-centered style (warmth, empathy, egalitarian relationship) and person-centered technique (key questions, reflective listening). MI expands on person-centered therapy by incorporating therapist goals about desirable changes and by providing specific methods to move the patient toward behavior change. Thus, arguing that patient gains may be largely attributable to a strong, facilitative relationship in which culture is honored is another way of describing MI.

That accounts, in my eyes, for the delicious irony in both humanistic therapists and cognitive-behavioral therapists claiming MI as their own. Those in the humanistic camp and Miller himself favor the view that MI is an extension of person-centered therapy, but many cognitive-behavioral colleagues insist that the operationalization of MI methods, its directive elements, and its voluminous research base render it an alternative to Rogerian treatment (Prochaska & Norcross, 2013). To accommodate both worlds and to roll with the resistance, I will consider here MI as both an alternative to and an extension of person-centered therapy.

REAL-WORLD RESEARCH

Of special note and commendation is that the RCT under consideration was conducted in a naturalistic setting with complex patients suffering from depression and a host of comorbid disorders. The patients suffered from chronic depression, having received an average of 5 to 7 years of antidepressant medication. Although the researchers did not purposefully recruit patients who were ambivalent about their medication—in the contemplation stage of change—they knew from the research literature that low adherence would prove common among these types of clients, and thus the clients in their research were far less likely to achieve their treatment goals than those in the preparation or action stages (Norcross, Krebs, & Prochaska, 2011). The UC condition entailed counseling provided in a community mental health center (CMHC), usually staffed by masters-level, direct-care professionals and serving impoverished patients with few financial resources to seek mental health care elsewhere. CMHCs around the country are notoriously underfunded and struggling to make ends meet in addressing the insatiable need for psychological, pharmacological, and case management services.

Such real-world RCTs are impressive on multiple counts. They redress many of the justifiable criticisms leveled at controlled studies conducted in laboratory or university clinics: unrepresentative patients, unrealistic exclusion criteria, and impractical to apply to other settings, among others. Studies such as this enhance external validity, permit generalization, and provide practitioners with the confidence that the therapy under investigation has been tested under authentic clinical conditions.

Judging from the case histories, the depressed patients in the study suffered from much more than depression. They also experienced the trauma of rape, incest, suicide attempts, immigration, psychotic symptoms, partner infidelity, unemployment, homelessness, and chronic suicidal ideation. One could make a case that many were suffering from chronic posttraumatic stress disorder and mood-congruent psychotic features, with depression the secondary disorder.

These multidisordered patients and the clinical setting provoked a memory of one of my first field experiences, which occurred in a CMHC located in Southern

New Jersey, just 50 miles from central New Jersey, where this study was conducted. My supervisor asked for my diagnostic impressions of a depressed, impoverished woman he had just interviewed. I replied, "Poverty and overwhelming life stress." He nodded his approval but then said, "But that's not in the *DSM*, so we will have to diagnose her with major depressive disorder." Those are the real-world multiple afflictions that Interian, Prawda, Fishman, and Buerger courageously tackled in their research (and conversely, that many researchers tend to neglect in their laboratory studies with patients largely in the preparation and action stages).

CULTURAL ADAPTATIONS

The chapter authors summarize the discouraging evidence on depression among Latinos: They are more likely to underutilize services, and when they do utilize services, experience lower engagement, limited access to culturally and linguistically sensitive treatment, and suffer from high rates of attrition during antidepressant treatment. The confluence of these challenges manifests in low rates of psychotropic medication adherence among Latinos, which reliably predicts higher levels of depressive symptoms and an increased risk of relapse. That's a compelling line of reasoning to conduct an RCT to improve adherence to antidepressant medications for the Latino population.

The authors clearly learned and incorporated lessons from decades of cultural adaptations. They began, not by educating or preaching or correcting, but with empathy and validation. MI effectively addresses ambivalence, especially in the precontemplation and contemplation stages, and the authors (unlike most pharmaceutical companies) honestly acknowledge barriers to medication adherence. Then, instead of unilaterally determining what the clients need, the researchers admirably conducted in Spanish a series of focus groups prior to the study. The focus groups identified cultural values that acted as sources of motivation for the clients, and these values (not the researchers') informed how MI was adapted.

All treatments were conducted in the participants' language of choice, which was usually Spanish. Use of clients' preferred or native language evidences the highest effect size of any single method of cultural adaptation (Smith, Rodriguez, & Bernal, 2011). But the researchers did not stop with language; their cultural adaptation involved cultural values, outreach efforts, and *dichos* (sayings or proverbs). Again, a research lesson worth learning: The more methods of cultural adaptation used, the better the clinical results (Smith et al., 2011).

Reading segments from the session transcripts gives one the distinct impression that another adaptation was occurring for many of these Latinos: a religious adaptation of secular MI. Many of the sayings allude to faith and God as sources of motivation; for example, the *dichos* "A quien madruga, Dios le ayuda" ("God helps he who rises to the occasion") and "Dios aprieta pero no ahorca" ("God squeezes but does not choke"). In three sessions, the META was selectively tailored to culture and religion alike. This is another clinical gem reinforcing the meta-analytic research on the benefits of religious adaptation of therapy (Worthington, Hook,

Davis, & McDaniel, 2011) and highlighting the multiple intersections of personal identities known collectively as "culture."

THERAPEUTIC RELATIONSHIPS

At root, MI is a relational therapy (Norcross & Lambert, 2014). While seeking to increase motivation for antidepressant medication adherence, the META clinicians were conducting good, old-fashioned psychotherapy filled with nonjudgmental feedback, empathic reflections, and deep caring. Those clinicians, in the "spirit" of MI, engaged in considerable outreach and alliance-building behaviors. Multiple contacts, collaborative goal setting, honoring ambivalence, and adapting treatment to the singular patient (e.g., stage of change, culture, religion, preferences) are all associated with, and predictive of, successful treatment outcomes (Norcross, 2011).

My hypothesis that the therapeutic relationship and treatment adaptations accounted in large part for the salubrious outcomes in this study is anchored in the results of decades of psychotherapy research and is supported by the authors' conclusions that the relationship between META and depression remission together with the lack of a relationship between depression remission and antidepressant adherence indicates that META had a direct impact on depression independent of its impact on adherence. The very act of additional psychotherapy, a relational MI, is probably operating here. Specifically, as the authors discuss, psychotherapy appears to have impacted not only on antidepressant adherence (box 2) but also on such factors as motivation to cope with depression (box 3), the ability to elicit social support (box 4), the ability to connect behavioral activation with Latino values (box 5), and the ability to connect with positive life goals (box 8).

In a relational frame as well, clinicians respect a client's resistance and stage of change, instead of treating them as obstacles to be overcome or barriers to be crushed. The work is fundamentally collaborative, as seen in this research study with the instruction to meet the client at his or her stage of change. Tailoring treatment to the stage of change and the MI style beautifully encapsulates the ideal relational stance of a psychotherapist working with patients in the precontemplation and contemplation stages of change. Leading by following, nurturing parent, Socratic teacher, Carl Rogers-ish—all metaphors for meeting clients where they are and helping them move forward on their timeline.

If after the first MI session the client was not ready to change, "the META clinician was instructed to remain in Phase 1, continue to meet him or her at his or her stage of change, and work toward helping the client develop more reasons for change" (p. 276). These are sage instructions, incorporating flexibility into the standard protocol. Moving ahead of the client is a recipe for stage mismatch, perceived invalidation, and resultant premature termination. In the authors' words, "Analysis of the three cases suggests in part that the success or failure of the META intervention depended heavily on the participants' readiness for change and whether or not the clinician tailored the intervention appropriately" (p. 306). Kindly note the two parts: the client's contribution and clinician's adaptation to the stage. Both, of course, prove central to therapy outcome, particularly in the relatively brief context of three sessions (Norcross et al., 2011).

RCT researchers tend to think of psychotherapy in terms of interventions, protocols, and fidelity checks, but our patients routinely experience it as a relationship. We read in the case studies about the relational experience of psychotherapy. "The research assistant had made extensive outreach efforts to recruit and engage Lupe in the study, which made her feel as though someone cared about her" (p. 280). Lupe is quoted as saying, "Well, I feel a little better because she [the research assistant] gave me strength and I feel that it is good. . . ." (p. 280). Maria "felt particularly comforted by knowing that the treatment team and the MI clinician were concerned about her". She referred to the META clinician as "more than just a doctor," and she was appreciative of how the clinician followed up by calling and sending her letters (pp. 304–305). Ana, in turn, "reported that the most helpful component of the treatment 'was the way that she was treated'. She felt listened to and understood" (p. 306). Not the treatment method per se but the therapist qua person. All of our evidence-based treatments come to naught unless the client feels engaged, supported, and understood in a good-enough relationship.

SYSTEMATIC CASE STUDIES

The patients' narratives, almost always missing in reports of RCTs, breathe life into cold group statistics. Tis probably true, as Bertrand Russell once remarked, that a mark of an intelligent person is the ability to read a bunch of numbers and to cry (such as in the tables of an RCT report), but it seems that humans are also hard-wired to respond to the individual story or case. Such has been repeatedly found to be true in the way that psychotherapists acquire their knowledge (e.g., Stewart, Stirman, & Chambless, 2012). I tried to imagine reading only the RCT results without the case studies; it (almost) made me cry.

The three cases illuminate the rich, idiographic material of a positive outcome, a mixed outcome, and a negative outcome of META. The research becomes alive, and I can glean an experience-near sense of what transpired. This enriched presentation, we should immediately note, is a product of a systematic case study, which adheres to the comprehensive outline presented by the volume editors and adopted in the journal *Pragmatic Case Studies of Psychotherapy* (http://pcsp.libraries.rutgers.edu/). Such in-depth studies should not be confused with the cursory, ofttime selectively incomplete case presentations made at training centers and grand rounds.

Those alleged "case studies" rarely present all of the clinical data in a meaningful way that enables clinical conclusions or knowledge transfer. Just last month, at a case presentation during psychiatry ground rounds, an intern made an impressive presentation on a patient treated with six or seven sessions of psychotherapy. Quite a success—for both the patient and the psychotherapist. But I happened to notice that the intern failed to mention if the patient was receiving other simultaneous treatments. The intern sheepishly admitted that the patient had, at the same time as psychotherapy, started an antidepressant, group therapy, and frequent meditation trainings. Like Paul Meehl (1977) in his classic "Why I do not attend case conferences," I have grown increasingly skeptical of the veracity and utility of traditional case studies for improving psychotherapy research, training, or practice.

But in these systematic case studies I get the sense that the clinical data, for good and ill, are presented in a more honest and comprehensive manner. Combined with the cold, hard facts of the RCT, the systematic case studies enable us to integrate the idiographic and the nomothetic, the particular and the general. The mixed-methods paradigm—the best of both worlds—allows us to appreciate the particularities of the individual case and, at the same time, the generalities of the group trends.

The chapter authors assert that the systematic case studies provide an opportunity to examine the causal mechanisms involved in psychotherapy. They argue that case studies enable us to look at "the causal relationships among process and outcome variables." Here I beg to quibble. Like most of my research colleagues, I believe any causal statement requires experimental control of the involved variables. To be sure, case studies allow us to speculate about those causal relationships, but I do not believe case studies, systematic or otherwise, permit any definitive statements about cause and effect. Accordingly, I would have been more comfortable with the authors describing their causal relationships in the text and Figure 6.1 as "hypothesized" or "putative" mechanism of change.

RCTS AND BEYOND

My own clinical and research commitment aims toward methodological pluralism. I worship at the altar of many methodologies depending upon the question posed. As the American Psychological Association's Task Force on Evidence-based Practice (2006, p. 274) concluded: "Multiple research designs contribute to evidence-based practice, and different research designs are better suited to address different types of questions." As Interian, Prawda, Fishman, and Buerger assert in this chapter, "The RCT and the case studies yield different types of knowledge that are complementary" (p. 307).

The RCT results revealed that META positively impacted primarily Spanish-speaking Latinos suffering from depression and other disorders, increasing on average their medication adherence and, in complex ways (the only "ways" that I trust as a clinician), reducing their depression. By employing randomization and a control group, the RCT design permits us to conclude with confidence that the META caused the salubrious difference.

In truth, we know from thousands of outcome studies and hundreds of meta-analyses that psychotherapy, even brief psychotherapy, can and does have these salubrious effects. Imagine what might have happened if the three-session MI gave way, not only to adherence to antidepressant medication but also to a fuller course of relational psychotherapy for chronic depression!

The leitmotif or take-home message of my commentary is the value of informed pluralism in psychotherapy. The complexities of research and practice increasingly demand an integrative, multidimensional look at the phenomenon of interest—be that a particular patient or a research study. Although it might be more satisfying and elegant if the psychotherapy world were not a multiverse, but a universe, this quest will not be realized, at least not soon (Messer, 1992). Let's follow the lead of Interian and colleagues in this chapter and the authors of the other chapters in embracing the best of all worlds.

REFERENCES

APA Task Force on Evidence-Based Practice. (2006). Evidence-based practice in psychology. *American Psychologist, 61,* 271–285.

Lundahl, B. W., & Burke, B. L. (2009). The effectiveness and applicability of motivational interviewing: A practice-friendly review of four meta-analyses. *Journal of Clinical Psychology, 65,* 1232–1245.

Meehl, P. E. (1977). Why I do not attend case conferences. In P. E. Meehl (Ed.), *Psychodiagnosis: Selected papers* (pp. 225–302). New York, NY: Norton.

Messer, S. B. (1992). A critical examination of belief structures in integrative and eclectic psychotherapy. In J. C. Norcross & M. R. Goldfried (Eds.), *Handbook of psychotherapy integration* (pp. 130–168). New York, NY: Basic Books.

Miller, W. R., & Moyers, T. B. (2005). Motivational interviewing. In G. P. Koocher, J. C. Norcross, & S. S. Hill (Eds.), *Psychologists' desk reference* (2nd ed.). New York, NY: Oxford University Press.

Miller, W. R., Zweben, A., DiClemente, C. C., & Rychtarik, R. G. (1992). *Motivational enhancement therapy manual: A clinical research guide for therapists treating individuals with alcohol abuse and dependence.* Rockville, MD: National Institute on Alcohol Abuse and Alcoholism.

Norcross, J. C. (Ed.). (2011). *Psychotherapy relationships that work* (2nd ed.). New York, NY: Oxford University Press.

Norcross, J. C., Krebs, P. M., & Prochaska, J. O. (2011). Stages of change. In J. C. Norcross (Ed.), *Psychotherapy relationships that work* (2nd ed., pp. 279–300). New York, NY: Oxford University Press.

Norcross, J. C., & Lambert, M. J. (2014). Relationship science and practice in psychotherapy: Closing commentary. *Psychotherapy, 51,* 398–403.

Prochaska, J. O., & Norcross, J. C. (2013). *Systems of psychotherapy: A transtheoretical analysis* (8th ed.). Pacific Grove, CA: Cengage-Brooks/Cole.

Project MATCH Research Group. (1993). Project MATCH: Rationale and methods for a multisite clinical trial matching patients to alcoholism treatment. *Alcoholism: Clinical and Experimental Research, 17,* 1130–1145.

Rollnick, S., & Miller, W. R. (1995). What is motivational interviewing? *Behavioural and Cognitive Psychotherapy, 23,* 325–334.

Smith, T. B., Rodriguez, M. D., & Bernal, G. (2011). Culture. In J. C. Norcross (Ed.), *Psychotherapy relationships that work* (2nd ed., pp. 316–335). New York, NY: Oxford University Press.

Stewart, R. E., Stirman, S. W., & Chambless, D. L. (2012). A qualitative investigation of practicing psychologists' attitudes toward research-informed practice: Implications for dissemination strategies. *Professional Psychology: Research and Practice, 43*, 100–109.

Worthington, E. L. Jr., Hook, J. N., Davis, D. E., & McDaniel, M. A. (2011). Religion and spirituality. In J. C. Norcross (Ed.), *Psychotherapy relationships that work* (2nd ed.). New York, NY: Oxford University Press.

PART III

Reflections and Next Steps

Reflections are presented on the four projects as a whole by the well-known RCT researcher, Jacques Barber, and his research team. The book concludes with the editors' summary of themes and guidelines for the future embodied in the knowledge gained by the four projects.

An Outside Perspective

HAROLD CHUI, SARAH BLOCH-ELKOUBY,
AND JACQUES P. BARBER ■

We commend the chapter authors for undertaking the onerous task of conducting randomized controlled trials (RCTs) *and* case studies on various psychotherapeutic interventions. RCTs are time consuming and expensive to run; even the most productive researchers do not typically run more than a few of them across their careers (Barber, 2009). Performing case studies within RCTs may not only "improve the yield" (Silberschatz, 2015) of painstakingly collected data, but it may also add diversity to the methods used in clinical research.

In this commentary, we first highlight strengths across the four chapters. In particular, we use specific examples from the chapters to illustrate how case studies within RCTs can expand our knowledge about psychotherapy. Next, we examine potential challenges in conducting effective case studies within trials. Specifically, we try to distinguish theory-driven conclusions from data-driven conclusions drawn from the case studies. We also discuss the intricacies of case selection because it has the potential to impact what we look at in the first place. We offer our thoughts on what could be done when faced with these challenges.

Note that we come to this commentary as researchers who have been steeped in traditional RCT designs but who have also used mixed-methods research. Nevertheless, we are enthusiastically endorsing the editors' idea of "expanding the gold standard" of the traditional RCT by making systematic case studies a regular part of it, and we are delighted to have the opportunity to do so in this chapter.

BENEFITS

As Gelso (1979) illustrated in his bubble hypothesis, every research design has flaws, just as a bubble between a decal and windshield will move from one spot to another no matter how hard one tries to eliminate it. RCTs try to clarify the causal link between treatment and outcome by imposing rigorous experimental control. However, such control is often seen as compromising generalizability to everyday clinical practice (e.g., Kazdin, 2008). As shown in Chapters 3–6, case studies focus on documenting and illustrating the detailed workings of the complex processes of psychotherapy and their relationship to outcome. Although the conclusions drawn based on a very small sample may be limited in applicability to other patients, the more cases described and analyzed, the greater the power of generalizations about relevant patterns that emerge. Accumulating corroborative evidence from different research paradigms will hopefully improve the shortcomings related to overreliance on any single research method. The recent rise of the pragmatic trial (Patsopoulos, 2011) is an example of researchers attempting to strike a balance between explanatory power and generalizability. Pragmatic trials investigate the effectiveness of interventions in routine clinical practice without the rigorous control of conditions typical of RCTs. Given that funding for RCTs has decreased in recent years (e.g., Barber & Sharpless, 2015), conducting case studies within pragmatic trials may be an attractive and viable alternative.

The four psychotherapy research projects described in Chapters 3–6 of this book illustrate a number of ways in which findings from case studies can complement findings from RCTs. First, findings from case studies may help generate new hypotheses about specific variables. As proposed by the various chapter authors, such hypotheses may be tested in subsequent RCTs and/or investigated using the theory-building case study approach (Stiles, 2007), discussed in Chapter 1.

For example, in Thastum et al.'s Chapter 3, Marius's parents' overprotectiveness appeared to have prevented him from participating fully in therapy and may have contributed to the negative outcome observed. This provides further confirmation to the empirical literature that quality of caregiver engagement in a child's therapy is an important variable to include in future studies of cognitive-behavioral therapy (CBT) for anxiety in children and adolescents. Future RCTs may compare outcomes with or without caregiver overinvolvement or test how caregiver engagement may moderate the effects of treatment. In terms of theory-building case studies, patient outcome can be contrasted across multiple cases with varying levels of caregiver engagement in the context of other clinically important variables and of theories about the role of parental involvement. Should a rigorous effect emerge across different research paradigms, quality of caregiver engagement should be investigated in therapies for other childhood disorders.

Second, case studies can explore multifaceted theoretical hypotheses that emerge from RCTs, as for example, the case studies of Levy et al. in Chapter 5 help to clarify the complex dynamics of patients with borderline personality disorder and the possibilities for successfully treating them. In fact, two particular examples come to mind in the work of the third author (J. P. B.). In one study (Barber, Barrett, Gallop, Rynn, & Rickets, 2012), an RCT was conducted comparing short-term dynamic psychotherapy, psychopharmacology, and placebo for major depressive disorder in a group of "economically disadvantaged, highly comorbid, chronic, recurrently depressed, urban patients" (p. 71). Although no significant difference in outcome was observed among the three conditions, when the full sample was considered, psychotherapy was found to be particularly effective for ethnic minority men. Systematic case studies could be an effective approach for exploring the multiple reasons for why the results for this particular population were different.

In the other study, Barber and Muenz (1996) analyzed the completer data set from the NIMH Treatment of Depression Collaborative Research Program (Elkin et al., 1989) to test the hypothesis that "cognitive therapy (CT) is more effective than interpersonal therapy (IPT) for treatment of depressed patients with an elevated level of avoidant personality, whereas the reverse holds for depressed patients with elevated level of obsessive personality" (p. 951). With the data confirming the hypothesis, Barber and Muenz theorized one likely reason, namely, the "theory of opposites," which posits that helpful therapy for personality disorders "requires the therapist to behave in a way that is antithetical ('opposite') to the interpersonal behavior, personality pattern, and cognitive style of the patient" (p. 952), to bring out the underdeveloped behavioral and personality patterns of the patient. For example, CT would be more likely to provide an avoidant client with exposure to fearful situations, while IPT would provide obsessive patients with situations involving discussing affect and encouraging its expression. In addition, Barber and Muenz suggest an expansion of the theory such that "the therapist's style should be more similar to the patient's at the beginning of treatment [to encourage a good working alliance] but dissimilar at later stages of treatment in long-term therapy [following the logic of the theory of opposites]" (p. 957). Such a complex set of hypotheses seems particularly well suited for investigation with systematic case studies.

Third, qualitative data from case studies may illustrate that it is difficult to perform accurate and comprehensive measurements of outcome using only standardized quantitative instruments. For example, in Interian et al.'s Chapter 6, even when Maria was judged to have a negative outcome based on quantitative criteria, her increased access of community resources over the course of therapy emerged as a significant achievement. Similarly, in Kerner and Young's Chapter 4, treatment success was demonstrated by Menorka's improvement on standardized measures of symptoms, social relationships, and academic functioning, *as well as* her improvement in two qualitative therapy goals: to better express and verbalize her negative emotions and to feel closer to others. Changes toward these goals were documented in the case study and, as far as reported in the chapter, not evaluated through quantitative scales administered in the RCT.

The study of personalized treatment outcome began in the 1960s when measures such as Target Complaints (Battle et al., 1966) and Goal Attainment Scaling (Kiresuk & Sherman, 1968) were developed. These measures assess problems and the severity of problems unique to each individual patient. The personalized approach to the study of treatment outcome has emerged again in recent years with various refinements (e.g., Elliott et al., 2015; Hill, Chui, & Baumann, 2013; Silberschatz, 2015). Case studies research seems especially suited to demonstrate individualized, qualitative, and nonsymptomatic changes through psychotherapy. Such outcomes complement a range of primary and secondary outcomes that are typically quantified in RCTs. For example, in an RCT study, Muran, Safran,

Samstag, and Winston (2005) administered the Target Complaints and Goal Attainment Scale along with other commonly used outcome measures (e.g., Symptoms Checklist-90-Revised, Inventory of Interpersonal Problems). This could be done more frequently in future RCTs.

Finally, by systematically analyzing every session in a case, case study researchers may be able to observe therapeutic processes that occur simultaneously or consecutively in the course of therapy. Such richness in data can help us untangle the sequence of events that occur and generate more refined hypotheses about the mechanisms of change for future testing on a larger sample. For example, in Levy et al.'s Chapter 5, consistent with their transference-focused psychotherapy (TFP) theory, they were able to link Ms. J's improvement in reflective functioning and narrative coherence in the first year of therapy to subsequent engagement in 4 years of additional therapy and associated actual life changes over the course of that therapy (e.g., marriage, friendships, stable career). In the same way, they linked the lack of change in reflective functioning and narrative coherence in Ms. V after the first year of therapy to the lack of observable changes in Ms. V's life and her lack of engagement in subsequent therapy. Levy et al. thus suggested from their case studies that early structural changes may be important for subsequent changes in life functioning. This idea is certainly worth further testing in future studies, for example, using a time-series single-case design (Borckardt et al., 2008). Furthermore, we would argue that the finding that reflective functioning change early in treatment would raise questions about the very nature of reflective functioning. What does it mean if reflective functioning can be changed so quickly? It would be very important for future investigators to show that the change in reflective functioning predicts subsequent change in life functioning over and beyond concurrent change in life functioning or symptoms (Barber et al., 2015).

CHALLENGES

In addition to the advantages associated with using a mixed-methods approach, there are a number of challenges when using case studies within RCTs. We highlight confirmatory bias and case selection as two major areas of concerns and suggest possible solutions to improve the scientific rigor of case studies within trials.

What We Learned From the Case Studies and What We Already Knew

A caveat when using case studies to derive conclusions is that authors may be biased to select and collect observations that are consistent with their theory but perhaps not substantiated by empirical findings. For example, in Chapter 6, Interian et al. attributed differences in outcome among the three cases to patients' different levels of readiness for change and to whether therapists matched interventions to these levels. In particular, "When analyzing Maria's course of therapy, it was the second author's (A. P.'s) clinical impression that the MI therapist did not consistently 'meet' Maria at her stage of change" (p. 306). However, the authors did not report that patients' stages of change were assessed in this study, for example, by systematic coding of therapist interventions in terms of their appropriateness for patients' respective stages of change, or, in lieu of this, by presenting qualitative clinical detail specifically documenting each client's stage of change. Without these types of data, we wondered if those impressions were based on empirical evidence, or whether the authors' explanations for the observed differences in patient outcome may reflect their theoretical adherence to the stages-of-change model as applied in motivational interviewing. Of course, the authors' basic hypothesis could have been correct. However, in our view, the best way to substantiate their interesting hypothesis is to conduct a complex RCT that would take into account the patient's stages of change and different interventions (e.g., Magill, Stout, & Apodaca, 2013).

Another example of possible researcher bias pertains to patients' attachment and defense organization in Levy et al.'s Chapter 5. The authors suggested that Ms. J, the positive-outcome case, had a deep longing for relationships and used denial and derogation of relationships as defenses against assumed disappointment and abandonment. Over the course of therapy, Ms. J was able to reduce her fear of disappointment and acknowledge her strong need for intimacy. On the other hand, Ms. V, the negative-outcome case, was dismissive and resistant to exploring her feelings. Her desire for connection "was consistently muted by representations of relationships organized in terms of predator and prey, as is often the case in patients with comorbid antisocial personality disorder" (p. 233). The characterization of Ms. V's manipulative stance might have been based on theoretical assumptions, rather than on actual assessment of internal representations. In addition, although patients' attachment style was characterized as part of the RCT, no coding of patient defenses was reported in the RCT nor, in its stead, were there sufficient clinical observational data documenting defenses. Case study researchers have to ensure that their clinical characterizations are based on observed data and not only exemplifications of what we already knew or presumed about different constructs of interest.

As mentioned by the editors in Chapter 8, RCTs have been under attack for methodological problems, such as lack of replication, selective publishing of only studies with positive results (known as "the file drawer" problem), and the conforming of results to the expectations of the author; and the field is taking these concerns more and more seriously. In a parallel way, we urge case study researchers to devote careful attention to combatting sources of bias, excessive subjectivity, and drawing definitive conclusions without sufficient data. Spence (2001) reminds us that therapists' (and case study researchers') recall and interpretation of clinical data may be influenced by preconceived theories. As Nickerson (1988) argues, confirmation bias, or "the seeking or interpreting of evidence in ways that are partial to existing beliefs, expectations, or a hypothesis in hand" (p. 175), is a well-known phenomenon in human cognition, affecting both RCT and case study researchers alike.

McLeod (2010) described four strategies to reduce investigators' subjectivity and bias. These include using multiple researchers in case studies, examining qualitative case materials like tapes and transcripts in conjunction with results from quantitative measures, analyzing data using standardized procedures, and reporting of researchers' theoretical allegiance and potential biases. Although the chapter authors have applied the first three strategies in their case studies, they could have done more to qualify their conclusions by acknowledging how researcher bias and the adherence to a certain theoretical frame might have impacted the inductive reasoning process. On the other hand, it should be noted that Fishman (1999) offered that one way to reduce the impact of therapist biases in case studies is to have cases undergo external review and to publish these commentaries along with the case study. He has followed this practice in the journal he founded and edits, *Pragmatic Case Studies in Psychotherapy*. Similarly, this book has included external commentaries for each of the four RCT project chapters, and the present commentary serves as another illustration of such an effort.

Case Selection

Across the four studies, the authors provided thoughtful remarks about how they had chosen the cases to be included in the systematic case studies. For example, in Levy et al.'s Chapter 5, selected cases displayed similar symptomatic gains but differed significantly in personality structural changes. Levy's choice of cases demonstrated the nuances involved in defining outcome and an attempt to match outcome criteria to the goals of treatment. In Chapter 6, Interian et al. presented a mixed-outcome case in addition to the positive- and negative-outcome cases. This method seems well suited to illustrate the clinical complexity that practitioners typically face and should be considered in reports from future case studies. In Chapter 4, Kerner and Young added the importance of looking at representative case studies from the comparison/control group in addition to case studies from the target treatment group to clarify different mechanisms of change. Although such case studies were not performed for Kerner and Young's chapter, in fact, as described in Chapter 8, Young and Moore, one of her present graduate students, are now in the process of conducting these types of case studies.

Despite the fact that much care was taken to select appropriate cases in each chapter, many contextual differences are present that make a simple comparison between positive- and negative-outcome cases difficult. For example, in Kerner and Young, Shelly's bisexual orientation might have presented additional challenges for her psychotherapy. As the authors rightly pointed out, Shelly's sense of worthlessness might be connected to an internalized stigma associated with her sexual orientation. They also noted how minority stress could have limited Shelly's ability to benefit from group treatment due to discomfort, poor self-perception, and low levels of peer trust. What needs greater acknowledgment, in our opinion, is the negative impact of the interaction of multiple minority statuses on patients (Shelly is female, bisexual, and Black). Compared to White

LGB-identified individuals, LGB people of color have reported greater heterosexism within their racial/ethnic communities *and* racism within the LGB community (Balsam, Molina, Beadnell, Simoni, & Walters, 2011). The "triple jeopardy" (Greene, 1996, p. 109) of sexual minority women of color, as in the case of Shelly, therefore accentuates the contextual differences that exist between the positive- and negative-outcome cases in Kerner and Young. Given that the study of cultural differences and their influence on therapy was *not* an explicit goal of the current chapters, comparing more homogenous cases that have fewer contextual confounds may have better illuminated the workings of psychotherapy. On the other hand, both Menorka and Shelly were included in the RCT, and it is important to remember that such cultural differences can be present in RCTs.

At the other extreme, one wonders if the negative outcome of Ms. V in Levy et al.'s Chapter 5 might have been driven primarily by her psychopathy, a notoriously difficult-to-treat pathology where response to psychotherapy may be limited, particularly during adulthood (Salekin, Worley, & Grimes, 2010). Conclusions about the efficacy of TFP for borderline personality disorder might thus be confounded by the specific comorbidity in Ms. V's case. The control for baseline severity and comorbidity appears critical when one attempts to compare and contrast psychotherapy cases, especially in cases where there is good clinical wisdom to suggest that the said comorbidity will likely impact outcome. However, the fact that both Ms. J and Ms. V were included in the experimental condition of the study is a reminder of the heterogeneity typically found in RCT's. Although this has the advantage of enhancing external validity, because the clients mirror the actual world of practice, it can reduce the measured efficacy of the treatment and result in a misleading assessment of a treatment's value.

Besides matching cases on patient characteristics, choosing cases based on the current literature on treatment response may yield useful information. For example, in Chapter 3, Thastum et al. compared a female with generalized anxiety disorder with a male with social phobia. As the authors reviewed, favorable outcome to CBT for anxiety had been linked to male gender and nonsocial phobia anxiety disorders, whereas unfavorable outcome had been linked to female gender and social phobia. By comparing cases that each combined typical characteristics of responders *and* nonresponders, the authors in effect "cancelled out" the contribution of diagnosis and gender to outcome and attempted to uncover other factors that may also predict the outcome of CBT. An alternative approach would have been to examine a female with social phobia who did unexpectedly well and a male with generalized anxiety disorder who did unexpectedly poorly in therapy. If they exist in the sample, these true anomalies could shed light on important moderators of treatment response that do not usually show up in large-scale studies. This example falls under what McLeod (2010) would consider as choosing a deviant case as a way to illustrate some aspects of the work that do not fit the prevailing literature.

All in all, a close look at the positive-outcome and negative-outcome clients chosen for comparison reminds us that, as the editors acknowledge in the final chapter, the limitation of only two or three case studies per study means that these chapters provide only a "proof of concept" for the cases-within-trials paradigm, and that many more case comparisons are needed to properly implement the paradigm.

CONCLUSIONS

The four chapters we have commented on illustrate a variety of ways in which two or three case studies can complement RCT findings. One of the major roles and contributions of case studies is to generate or highlight new and original hypotheses about treatment, mechanisms, and moderators—contributing to the Popperian context of discovery (Popper, 1934/2002). Those hypotheses, however, would require further testing as part of the Popperian context of justification, through RCTs and/or further case studies. Systematic case studies can also shed light on some dimensions of outcome that are not easily or often captured by standardized scaled instruments. Additionally, case studies often involve viewpoints beyond the patient's and the therapist's to include observers' qualitative evaluations of the therapeutic process and outcome. In this regard, the use of case studies in RCTs may provide complementary data and reduce overreliance on quantitative outcome assessment.

Nevertheless, just as methodological problems have become associated with RCT designs, as mentioned earlier, we have also illustrated in this commentary ways (e.g., confirmation bias and bias in case selection) through which case studies may introduce error in the conclusions made about treatment outcome. Researchers therefore need to be aware of both the benefits and challenges inherent in the pursuit of each research method and to seek ways to achieve effective complementarity between them.

REFERENCES

Balsam, K. F., Molina, Y., Beadnell, B., Simoni, J., & Walters, K. (2011). Measuring multiple minority stress: The LGBT People of Color Microaggressions Scale. *Cultural Diversity and Ethnic Minority Psychology, 17*(2), 163–174. doi:10.1037/a0023244

Barber, J. P. (2009). Toward a working through of some core conflicts in psychotherapy research. *Psychotherapy Research, 19*(1), 1–12. doi:10.1080/10503300802609680

Barber, J. P., Barrett, M. S., Gallop, R., Rynn, M. A., & Rickets, K. (2012). Short-term dynamic psychotherapy versus pharmacotherapy for major depressive disorder: A randomized, placebo-controlled trial. *Journal of Clinical Psychiatry, 73*(1), 66–73. doi:10.4088/JCP.11m06831

Barber, J. P., Milrod, B., Rudden, R. G., Solomonov, N., McCarthy, K. S., Sharpless, B. A., . . . Chambless, D. L. (2015, June). *Mediators in the Cornell Penn Panic Psychotherapy Study*. Panel presented at the Society for Psychotherapy Research 46th International Annual Meeting, Philadelphia, PA.

Barber, J. P. & Muenz, L. R. (1996). The role of avoidance and obsessiveness in matching patients to cognitive and interpersonal psychotherapy: Empirical findings from the

Treatment for Depression Collaborative Research Program. *Journal of Consulting and Clinical Psychology, 64*(5), 951–958. doi:10.1037/0022-006X.64.5.951

Barber, J. P. & Sharpless, B. A. (2015). On the future of psychodynamic therapy research. *Psychotherapy Research, 25*(3), 309–320. doi:10.1080/10503307.2014.996624

Battle, C. C., Imber, S. D., Hoehn-Saric, R., Stone, A. R., Nash, C., & Frank, J. D. (1966). Target complaints as criteria of improvement. *American Journal of Psychotherapy, 20*, 184–192.

Borckardt, J. J., Nash, M. R., Murphy, M. D., Moore, M., Shaw, D., & O'Neil, P. (2008). Clinical practice as natural laboratory for psychotherapy research: A guide to case-based time-series analysis. *American Psychologist, 63*(2), 77–95. doi:10.1037/0003-066X.63.2.77

Elkin, I., Shea, M. T., Watkins, J. T., Imber, S. D., Sotsky, S. M., Collins, J. F., & . . . Parloff, M. B. (1989). National Institute of Mental Health Treatment of Depression Collaborative Research Program: General effectiveness of treatments. *Archives of General Psychiatry, 46*(11), 971–982. doi:10.1001/archpsyc.1989.01810110013002

Elliott, R., Wagner, J., Sales, C. D., Rodgers, B., Alves, P., & Café, M. J. (2015). Psychometrics of the Personal Questionnaire: A client-generated outcome measure. *Psychological Assessment*, doi:10.1037/pas0000174

Fishman, D. B. (1999). *The case for a pragmatic psychology*. New York, NY: New York University Press.

Gelso, C. J. (1979). Research in counseling: Methodological and professional issues. *The Counseling Psychologist, 8*(3), 7–35. doi:10.1177/001100007900800303

Greene, B. (1996). Lesbian women of color: Triple jeopardy. *Journal of Lesbian Studies, 1*(1), 109–147. doi:10.1300/J155v01n01_09

Hill, C. E., Chui, H., & Baumann, E. (2013). Revisiting and reenvisioning the outcome problem in psychotherapy: An argument to include individualized and qualitative measurement. *Psychotherapy, 50*(1), 68–76. doi:10.1037/a0030571

Kazdin, A. E. (2008). Evidence-based treatment and practice: New opportunities to bridge clinical research and practice, enhance the knowledge base, and improve patient care. *American Psychologist, 63*(3), 146–159. doi:10.1037/0003-066X.63.3.146

Kiresuk, T. J. & Sherman, R. E. (1968). Goal attainment scaling: A general method for evaluating comprehensive community mental health programs. *Community Mental Health Journal, 4*, 443–453. doi:10.1007/BF01530764

Magill, M., Stout, R. L., & Apodaca, T. R. (2013). Therapist focus on ambivalence and commitment: A longitudinal analysis of Motivational Interviewing treatment ingredients. *Psychology of Addictive Behaviors, 27*(3), 754–762. doi:10.1037/a0029639

McLeod, J. (2010). *Case study research in counselling and psychotherapy*. London, UK: Sage.

Muran, J. C., Safran, J. D., Samstag, L. W., & Winston, A. (2005). Evaluating an alliance-focused treatment for personality disorders. *Psychotherapy: Theory, Research, Practice, Training, 42*(4), 532–545. doi:10.1037/0033-3204.42.4.532

Nickerson, R. S. (1998). Confirmation bias: A ubiquitous phenomenon in many guises. *Review of General Psychology, 2*(2), 175–220. doi:10.1037/1089-2680.2.2.175

Patsopoulos, N. A. (2011). A pragmatic view on pragmatic trials. *Dialogues in Clinical Neuroscience, 13*(2), 217–224.

Popper, K. R. (1934/2002). *The logic of scientific discovery*. London, UK: Routledge.

Salekin, R. T., Worley, C., & Grimes, R. D. (2010). Treatment of psychopathy: A review and brief introduction to the mental model approach for psychopathy. *Behavioral Sciences & The Law, 28*(2), 235–266. doi:10.1002/bsl.928

Silberschatz, G. (2015). Improving the yield of psychotherapy research. *Psychotherapy Research* http://dx.doi.org/10.1080/10503307.2015.1076202

Spence, D. P. (2001). Dangers of anecdotal reports. *Journal of Clinical Psychology, 57*(1), 37–41. doi:10.1002/1097-4679(200101)57:1<37::AID-JCLP5>3.0.CO;2-S

Stiles, W. B. (2007). Theory-building case studies of counselling and psychotherapy. *Counselling and Psychotherapy Research, 7*(2), 122–127. doi:10.1080/14733140701356742

Themes and Lessons Learned

DANIEL B. FISHMAN, STANLEY B. MESSER,

DAVID J.A. EDWARDS, AND FRANK M. DATTILIO ∎

Each of the four project chapters (Chapters 3–6) contains a wealth of information and analysis about the randomized controlled trial (RCT) design and study findings, about the process and outcome in the two or three case studies drawn from the RCT experimental condition in each study, and about how to synthesize the RCT and case study knowledge within each study. Chapter 7 presents an outside perspective on the four projects from a research team highly experienced in conducting and thinking about traditional RCTs. In this chapter we conclude by highlighting some of the themes that emerged for us from the previous chapters.

KNOWLEDGE GAINED FROM THE RCT STUDIES

The RCT design has provided an invaluable contribution to enhancing scientifically rigorous information about the efficacy of psychotherapy, as a massive published literature demonstrates (e.g., Society of Clinical Psychology, 2015; The Cochrane Library, 2015).[1] As described in Chapter 1 and by William Piper, one of the commentary authors, as interest in RCTs grew in the 1970s, the initial model was the "thin" RCT. Here the emphasis was on reducing the complexity of naturalistic psychotherapy in order to identify foundational change outcomes for a particular type of therapy, maximizing efficacy and internal validity. Toward the

---

1. It is true that there have been a very recent series of critiques in terms of methodological problems in the body of published RCTs, such as the selective publishing of RCTs (the "file drawer" problem), the lack of precise replicability of most RCTs, and the "allegiance effect" (results conforming to the expectations of the author) (Cuijpers & Cristea, 2015; Nosek et al., 2015). However, these problems are not intrinsic to the logic of the RCT but are only the result of poor practice in designing and administering them and in policies regarding their publication; and importantly, efforts are being conducted to remediate these poor practices (Pashler & Wagenmaker, 2012; Tolin et al., 2015; Winerman, 2013).

goal of attaining experimental rigor, Piper (2001) describes the "thin" RCT and some of its implicit limitations:

[The "thin" RCT] only focuses on pre-therapy to post-therapy efficacy in averaged form, only reports results in terms of statistical significance and effect size, and only studies atypical patients [e.g., those with only a single diagnosis], therapists [e.g., those who are inexperienced and in training], and therapies [e.g., those that use highly structured manuals involving sequentially specific procedures]. (p. 60)

As described by investigators like Piper (2001), researchers carrying out these "thin" RCT designs soon found that their immersion in the multidimensional and situationally specific clinical phenomena of the psychotherapy being studied led them to move away from "thin" to "thick" designs, which (a) involved systematically studying therapist, client, and therapy process variables, rather than trying to hold these variables constant through random assignment, and (b) emphasized questions of effectiveness and external validity rather than questions of efficacy and internal validity only.

Critiques of "thin" RCTs and arguments for the need to move to "thick" ones were anticipated in two highly cited articles from the 1960s. Kiesler (1966) emphasized the importance of studying patient and therapist variables when he identified two "myths" in psychotherapy research: the "patient uniformity assumption," which states that "patients at the start of treatment are more alike than they are different" (p. 110), and the "therapist uniformity assumption," that "therapists are more alike than different" (p. 112). This article was immediately followed by Paul's (1967) famous statement that the goal of psychotherapy research is to answer the question: "*What* treatment [identifying the importance of treatment variables], by *whom* [emphasizing the importance of therapist variables], is most effective [emphasizing the importance of types of outcome measures] for *this* individual [emphasizing the importance of patient history and personality variables] with *that* specific problem [emphasizing the importance of symptom and disorder variables], and under *which* set of circumstances [emphasizing the importance of other contextual variables]?"

As a result of the forces that Kiesler and Paul anticipated 50 years ago and that Piper (2001) and other researchers subsequently lived through, RCT designs have become more elaborated. This is reflected in the projects described in Chapters 3–6. At the same time, each project attains the core goal of all successful RCT studies: demonstrating the statistically and clinically significant advantage of the experimental condition over a control condition (Chapters 3, 4, and 6), or the statistical and clinical equivalence of the experimental condition as compared with an already empirically established alternative therapy condition (Chapter 5). An example of these findings for each of the projects is illustrated in Table 8.1. In line with being a "thick" design, each of these RCTs also offers a number of distinctive elements not included in the early "thin" designs. Some examples are outlined next.

Table 8.1 ILLUSTRATIVE FINDINGS IN THE RCT STUDIES

Project	Problem Addressed	Name of Treatment in Experimental Condition	Type of Treatment in Experimental Condition (Modality)	Control Condition (Modality)	Sample Outcome Measure	Sample Result
Thastum et al. (Chapter 3)	Youth anxiety	The "Cool Kids/Chilled Adolescents" (CK/CA) program	Cognitive-behavioral treatment (group therapy)	Wait list (NA)	Independent clinician's rating of a client's primary anxiety disorder on the Anxiety Disorder Interview Schedule for *DSM-IV* (ADIS)	The experimental group and control group were not statistically significantly different at pretreatment, but the experimental group showed significantly greater reduction at posttreatment with a pre- to posteffect size of 1.98.
Kerner and Young (Chapter 4)	Adolescent depression	The Interpersonal Therapy-Adolescent Skills Training (IPT-AST) program	Interpersonal therapy (group therapy)	Usual individual school counseling (UC) (individual therapy)	Parental report on the Center for Epidemiological Studies-Depression Scale (DES-D)	The experimental group was not statistically significantly different from the control group at pretreatment, but the experimental group showed a significantly greater reduction in depressive symptoms at posttreatment, with a pre-to-post effect size of .81.

(continued)

Table 8.1 CONTINUED

Project	Problem Addressed	Name of Treatment in Experimental Condition	Type of Treatment in Experimental Condition (Modality)	Control Condition (Modality)	Sample Outcome Measure	Sample Result
Levy et al. (Chapter 5)	Adult borderline personality disorder	Transference-focused psychotherapy (TFP)	Psychoanalytic therapy (individual therapy)	One of two formally established, bona fide treatments: dialectical behavior therapy [DBT] or supportive psychotherapy[SPT] (individual therapy)	Independent clinician's rating of suicidality on the Overt Aggression Scale-Modified (OAS-M)	The experimental group was not statistically significantly different from the control groups at pre-treatment, but the experimental group showed a statistically significant reduction at the .05 level in pre-to-post, in comparison to a similar level of reduction in the DBT control group and a nonsignificant reduction in the SPT group.
Interian et al. (Chapter 6)	Adult depression in monolingual, disadvantaged Latino women	Motivational enhancement therapy for antidepressants (META)	Motivational interviewing individual therapy, plus community mental health center treatment (individual therapy)	Community mental health center treatment only (individual therapy)	Client self-report on the Beck Depression Inventory (BDI)	The experimental group was not statistically significantly different from the control group at pretreatment, but in the experimental group, the participants had nearly six times the odds of achieving symptom remission than the control group, a highly statistically

Described in Chapter 3, Thastum et al.'s RCT on cognitive-behavioral therapy (CBT) for youth anxiety included a "stepped-care" (Crow et al., 2013) component, so that clients who were nonresponders in the group-therapy RCT study then received custom-tailored individual therapy, a procedure that increased the overall success rate from 73% to 89%. It also had two built-in replication aspects. First, their "Cool Kids/Chilled Adolescents" treatment RCT was a cross-cultural replication in Denmark of the original CK/CA RCT study in Australia. Thastum et al. document both very similar quantitative results between the two countries, and also qualitative evidence of similarities of CK/CA as implemented in two different cultures. Second, they built in an informal replication within their study, in that the waiting-list control group later received the same treatment as the experimental group, showing that the control group improved only after receiving the CK/CA treatment, and at a rate similar to the initial experimental group.

In light of their focus on prevention of full-blown depression, Kerner and Young's RCT on interpersonal therapy (IPT) for adolescent depression described in Chapter 4 included extensive follow-up periods, which revealed the limits of the amount of time during which treatment had a distinctive impact relative to the control group.

The RCT described in Levy et al.'s Chapter 5 on transference-focused psychotherapy (TFP) for borderline personality disorder (BPD) involved comparisons with two other, bona fide treatments. This meant that it can be thought of first, as a "noninferiority trial," in which TFP was compared to dialectical behavioral therapy, the previously established benchmark for empirically supported treatments of BPD. Second, it can be thought of as a "superiority trial," in which TFP, a psychoanalytic therapy focused around transference interpretation, was compared with supportive psychotherapy (SPT), a psychoanalytic therapy with an explicit exclusion of transference interpretation. Thus, in this comparison, the explicit addition of transference interpretation was predicted to create an advantage in outcome based on TFP theory. The RCT described in Levy et al.'s chapter also included a number of design elements explicitly oriented to facilitate generalization to routine practice settings, such as seeing clients in the therapists' private practice offices, and providing clients the opportunity for therapy lasting the typical multiyear length of TFP, after the 1-year course of therapy in the formal RCT was completed.

In each of these three chapters, the experimental condition was contrasted with one or more control conditions. In the fourth study, by Interian et al., the experimental condition of motivational enhancement for antidepressants (META) was an add-on, with all the patients receiving real-world, individualized medication and therapy treatment at a community mental health center (CMHC), and the experimental group receiving, in addition, META therapy in a separate clinical setting. This design had three particularly important effectiveness elements that facilitated generalization to routine practice. First, the patients all received individualized medication and psychotherapy treatment at the CMHC, so that the META condition imposed no experimental constraint on patients' CMHC experiences. Second, the META treatment was designed to be very brief, increasing the feasibility of applying it in real-world settings. Third, the META treatment was conducted in Spanish to facilitate work with monolingual Spanish patients, and also the content of the treatment was adapted to Latino culture, increasing the chance that it would apply to the context of real-world settings involving Latino clients.

KNOWLEDGE GAINED FROM THE CASE STUDIES

Table 8.2 presents some of the contrasts between the positive-outcome and negative-outcome clients within each of the four RCT projects. The table illustrates how case studies make at least two important, interrelated contributions to the development of clinical knowledge. First, they contribute to theory-building by instantiating the meaning of general theoretical concepts, that is, as mentioned in Chapter 1, by concretizing them with specific, real-world-embedded, narratively structured examples of case material (Messer, 2011).

Second, the case studies reflect the contextually complex conditions under which a particular therapy for a particular type of disorder does and does not work, and allow for the detection of different patterns of response to the intervention. For example, across the four studies we see the same broad theme played out in different contexts. This is the contrast between clients who are ready for change because they are oriented, motivated, and psychologically equipped to engage in the positive-change processes stimulated by a particular therapy model versus those clients who are not so ready. Thus, in Thastum et al.'s project, Lisa was emotionally drawn to the therapy group and eager to try out new cognitive restructuring strategies, while Marius was repelled by the therapy group because of his social phobia and was highly resistant to cognitive restructuring seemingly because of his developmental level. In Kerner and Young's project, Menorka's positive history of social connections drew her enthusiastically into the group and its activities and processes that were designed to stimulate positive interpersonal change, while Shelly's discomfort in social relationships and distrust of others, exacerbated by the alienation she felt because of her sexual identity issues, kept her distrustful of, and thus detached from, the group's capacity to induce change. In Levy et al.'s project, Ms. J's initial intense distress fueled her capacity to go beyond her layers of defensive resistance and to be open to a transference relationship with the therapist, which in turn allowed her to take advantage of this major vehicle for therapeutic change in the TFP model. By contrast, Ms. V's relative comfort in being taken care of in her role as "professional patient"—that is, the secondary gain she achieved from her psychopathology—closed her off to any changes in her highly defensive stance to the world. Finally, in Interian et al.'s project, the cyclical nature of a client's life events and life circumstance as they interact with therapy is illustrated by how the META therapy was able to stimulate a *virtuous circle* in Lupe's life, whereas it could not combat a *vicious circle* in Maria's life.

This theme of differential readiness for taking advantage of therapeutic processes that facilitate positive change is just one example of what we can learn from case studies drawn from RCTs. Other examples are discussed in the next section.

Table 8.2 CONTRASTS BETWEEN THE POSITIVE-OUTCOME AND NEGATIVE-OUTCOME CASES

Project	Positive-Outcome Case	Negative-Outcome Case
Thastum et al., CBT for Youth Anxiety	*Engagement in the group therapy.* "Lisa and her parents were in many ways ideal clients and instantiate, that is, embody, some of the mediators of positive change in CK/CA therapy. Both Lisa and her parents were from the beginning motivated for the therapy. Lisa understood quickly the main principles of the therapy, realistic thinking and gradual exposure; she used the central therapeutic methods, including doing her homework; and she participated actively in the group. Her parents worked actively to combat their tendency toward overprotection, they used the other parents in the group, and they were happy about the group setup. In addition, the alliance between the graduate student therapist (ST) and the family seemed very good" (p. 96). *Cognitive aspect of the therapy.* As mentioned, Lisa was very responsive to the cognitive aspect of the therapy. *Parents.* As mentioned, Lisa's parents were a very positive resource in Lisa's therapy.	*Engagement in the group therapy.* "The reasons for the limitations of the group therapy were exemplified by the case study of Marius, whose social phobia 'scared him off' from participating in and benefitting from the group, a process exacerbated by his parents' overprotectiveness. The follow-up individualized therapy with Marius showed how the same CBT principles behind the manualized therapy could be adapted and tailored to the needs of Marius and his parents to yield a positive result" (pp. 101–102). *Cognitive aspect of the therapy.* "In Marius's case, there might have been too much focus on cognitive restructuring, with the therapy therefore not meeting Marius's developmental level. Marius reacted with great resistance to the therapist's and parents' attempts to make him verbalize his feelings and thoughts. It was apparently not before the therapists gave up this endeavor in the beginning of the nonresponder treatment course that positive change began to emerge. Thus, to successfully treat Erik [another published case by Thastum's research team] and Marius, a modification of the CK/CA manual was required, where more focus was on exposures as a less direct means to challenge their maladaptive cognitions. Both youth were either not motivated or not able to engage in cognitive restructuring as an exercise detached from the exposure. When doing exposures, it was possible to challenge their erroneous cognitions, as they could more readily see the relevance of having realistic thoughts during anxiety-provoking situations" (p. 97). *Parents.* Marius's mother suffered from an anxiety disorder herself, which exacerbated Marius's problem through modeling and overprotectiveness. Marius's parents did not have "the resources and/or did not get enough support to change their maladaptive behavior toward Marius during the manualized group treatment . . . [and] in this case parental anxiety therefore may have decreased the efficacy of the therapy" (p. 98).

(continued)

Table 8.2 Continued

Project	Positive-Outcome Case	Negative-Outcome Case
Kerner & Young, IPT-AST for Adolescent Depression	*Engagement in the group therapy.* Menorka's success was moderated by factors like "her positive attitude toward change, eagerness to utilize the skills, sociotropy, and a history of positive interpersonal relationships" (p. 174). *Sexual identity issues.* Menorka did not manifest any sexual identity issues.	*Engagement in the group therapy.* Shelly's lack of success was moderated by her "absences [from the group], interpersonal deficits, social anxiety, . . . and negative cognitive style, which made it difficult for her to fully engage and practice skills with the group to increase her relationships. Shelly's challenges with trust were also apparent in the group as a whole and even extended to group members' feelings of support and trust within the school" (p. 174). *Sexual identity issues.* Shelly's challenges with trust were associated with her "sexual identity issues and her emerging bisexuality", which also appeared "to be significant contributors to her social anxiety and her interpersonal avoidance" (p. 185).
Levy et al., TFP for Adult Borderline Personality Disorder	*Resistance.* Ms. J showed a high "capacity to respond and overcome layers of resistance and defensiveness" (p. 238), and thus to open up to a transference relationship. *Structural variables.* Ms. J's responsiveness was associated with impressive movement on the structural variables over the course of the year of the therapy. She "moved from the lowest score on reflective functioning of −1.00 to a 6.00 at 1 year, above the clinical cutoff of 5.00; and from 2.50 to 4.00 on narrative coherence" (p. 254).	*Resistance.* Ms. V showed a low capacity to respond to and overcome layers of resistance and defensiveness (p. 238). *Structural variables.* Ms. V's lack of responsiveness was associated with "essentially no change" (p. 238) on the structural variables of reflective functioning, narrative coherence, and attachment, and this lack of movement was associated with very little change in her distress level and functioning at 1 year, and with her dropping out of the therapy after one year after only a few months (p. 231). *Qualitative outcome.* From the detailed data about Ms. V's course of therapy, the therapist viewed V as making no movement in her highly defensive stance to the world over the 1 year of therapy, and then refusing to continue in the therapy. Some of this difference is reflected in the pre-post standardized measures. For example, at the end of therapy, both J and V had substantial decreases in the secondary symptoms. However, on the anger-during-the-previous-month measure, J had a substantial decrease (from 42 to 13), while V actually increased over the same period (from 12 to 18) (see Table 5.4, p. 212).

Table 8.2 Continued

Project	Positive-Outcome Case	Negative-Outcome Case
	Also, concerning attachment, J had begun therapy with the "incoherent and disorganizing effect of 'vacillating between two opposing styles'" . . . [while] "over the course of the year she organized around a consistent style . . . [that was] an intact (albeit not secure) strategy for getting one's attachment needs met, and thus . . . [served a more] adaptive function" (p. 229). *Qualitative outcome.* "From the detailed data about Ms. J's therapeutic process, it seems clear that these structural changes she made in the first year of treatment . . . provided the tools she was able to use in the next 4 years of therapy to move beyond symptomatic change to completely transform her life such that she established a healthy, mutually compatible marriage; obtained a master's degree; became steadily employed in a full-time position; and developed genuine friendships and meaningful interests in the arts" (pp. 238–239). *Secondary gain.* J showed relatively little secondary gain derived from her symptoms.	*Secondary gain.* "It seemed clear from V's case study that the secondary gain associated with her illness was a strong force in her resisting openness to the pain and distress associated with change. Specifically, for the 10 years before the RCT, V had been treated in just about every inpatient, partial hospitalization, and outpatient program in the hospital associated with the RCT. Although this did not result in change, it did legitimize her disability payments and subsidized housing, creating an equilibrium she did not seem motivated to change" (p. 238).

(continued)

Table 8.2 Continued

Project	Positive-Outcome Case	Negative-Outcome Case
Interian et al.'s META Project for Adult Depression	*Cycle of change.* Lupe's case shows "a 'virtuous circle'" in which (a) she felt relief in being able to 'unload' her emotional distress and concerns to an empathetic and sympathetic therapist, leading her (b) to feel that 'others cared about her,' in turn (c) motivating her to come to her next appointment, during which she clarified her misconceptions about medication, so as to (d) view the medication as helpful in overcoming her depression (despite it leading to weight gain) and in meeting her positive personal and life goals, which in turn (e) fueled her motivation to continue taking her medication and activating her to work on her goals, which in turn (f) elicited a positive response from her family, which in turn (g) further motivated her to continue with her medication plan and to work on her goals" (p. 308).	*Cycle of change.* Maria's case shows "a 'vicious circle' . . . illustrated by (a) her recent experience of a traumatic rejection by her husband, resulting in (b) her now lacking a strong social support system, and (c) in fact having a social support system that stigmatized her depression, all of which (d) decreased her motivation to take her medication and work on her life goals, which in turn led to (e) an increase in her depression, leading to (f) the need for hospitalization between her second and third MI session, which precipitated (g) a further rejection by her social support system of her severe depressive experience, with all of the above leading to (h) a reduction in her motivation for complying with her antidepressant medication" (p. 308).

SYNTHESIZING THE RCT AND CASE STUDY KNOWLEDGE

Table 1.1 in Chapter 1 illustrates the fact that RCTs are designed to assess whether *on average* a particular experimental treatment is efficacious. Thus, in the results of the hypothetical RCT in Table 1.1 in Chapter 1, 60% of the clients in the experimental condition have positive outcomes as opposed to 20% in the control condition. However, the group results do not describe *how* or explain *why* some clients in the experimental condition are successful and others are not, and likewise for the control condition. It is just this kind of knowledge that the case comparisons in the four project chapters are able to provide. In this discussion we draw out how this kind of knowledge is generated from within case studies and from comparisons between them, showing how the methodology of the systematic case study presented in Chapter 2 is able to contribute kinds of knowledge not available from multivariate research such as RCTs.

How the Case Studies Add Knowledge to the RCT's Guiding Conception

In Chapter 2 we presented the Disciplined Inquiry model of best practice in psychotherapy, which is illustrated in Figure 2.1 of Chapter 2 (p. 31). Central to this model is the guiding conception—that is, the theoretical framework—which guides the clinician through the process of assessment, case formulation, and treatment planning. The final step in the process is a concluding evaluation (Box L), which consists of (a) outcome data and (b) process data relating the outcome data to the guiding conception underlying the treatment (Box B; Fishman, 2013). As shown in the figure, if the results of the evaluation are consistent with the guiding conception, the feedback loop J adds confirmation to the guiding conception via a process of assimilation. If the results of the evaluation are not consistent with the guiding conception, the feedback loop K leads to a revision of the guiding conception via a process of accommodation.

In this context, quantitative and qualitative analysis of the four positive-outcome cases presented evidence (a) that treatment in the experimental condition worked very well for each of these clients, and (b) that the process of change was consistent theoretically with the theoretical rationale on which the experimental treatment was based. Thus, in these instances the results of the case studies add confirming evidence to the change mechanisms identified in the guiding conception; in other words, evidence that the therapy worked "as advertised."

Moreover, for the positive clients, the case studies add new dimensions to the theoretical guiding conception by highlighting the importance of contextual variables in creating the conditions for the change mechanisms to be activated. For example,

- in Thastum et al.'s study of CBT for youth anxiety, Lisa's positive response to the cognitive-restructuring and exposure exercises seemed dependent upon two traits that she brought to the therapy: (a) social interest and comfort in engaging with others, which helped her to positively join and participate in the group process of the therapy; and (b) psychological-mindedness, which helped her to engage in and learn from the cognitive and exposure tasks.

- in Kerner and Young's study in preventing adolescent depression, Menorka's interest in making social connections, reinforced by a history of trusting interpersonal relationships, provided her with the motivation to engage in the group openly and to subsequently to learn the new interpersonal skills that were taught in the group.

- in Levy et al.'s study of adult borderline personality disorder, Ms. J entered the therapy with an underlying capacity and motivation to engage with the therapist and to expose her interpersonal vulnerabilities to him. This allowed her to respond to the therapist's transference interpretations, in turn facilitating her learning about how to be more self-reflective and to rework her schemas to facilitate a healthier attachment style.

- in Interian et al.'s study of adult depression in monolingual Latina women, Maria manifested a dramatic capacity to quickly form a very close relationship with the therapist. This, together with her having an existing strong social support system, provided her with an emotional base from which to explore positive changes in her thinking and behavior.

In contrast, quantitative and qualitative analysis of the negative-outcome cases in which the treatment did not work well provided valuable information for expanding the guiding conception to include factors that had not initially been attended to. It also brought into focus three possible problems with the guiding conception on which the treatment manual was based. First, the negative outcome could have been due to the quantity or *dose* of the treatment being too small, meaning that more treatment of the same or a different type—via a "stepped-care" model involving a "stepped series of interventions moving from less intensive and less expensive to more intensive and expensive" (Crow, Agras, Halmi, et al., 2013, p. 306)—was more likely to be successful. Second, the negative outcome could have been due to a poor *match* between the *type of client* and the *type of treatment package* provided, such that another treatment package would have been more successful with that type of client. And third, the outcome might have been positive if the content of the treatment theory and/or procedures had been *adapted* to suit the needs for this particular type of client. The way in which these processes apply to the four negative-outcome cases is discussed next. (Note that there are other hypotheses about why the treatment might not have been working, such as the participation of a mediocre therapist or a poor match between the person of the therapist and the client. However, in the four RCT projects, there did not seem to be evidence supporting either of these hypotheses.)

MARIUS'S NEGATIVE OUTCOME

Regarding the second hypothesis about why the treatment failed in some instances, Marius's personality was a poor match for the group therapy format, since his social anxiety intruded into his constructive participation. Moreover, he resisted the cognitive restructuring task and his parents reinforced his avoidance of some of the other therapeutic tasks. Because Marius was a nonresponder, using a stepped-care model, he was followed up with therapy that was individual and individualized, with an emphasis on exposure rather than cognitive restructuring and a particularly active and responsive effort to engage the parents and change their behavior. This was actually an alteration in the dosage of the therapy (by adding more therapy) and a modification in the theoretical nature of the therapy (by having individual rather than group therapy, by deemphasizing the cognitive restructuring component, and by more active engagement with the parents). On the other hand, Thastum et al. point out that there are common CBT theoretical principles behind both the individual and the group treatments, and thus Marius's two treatments had related guiding conceptions.

Marius's case study reveals important insights not contained in Thastum et al.'s group data, namely, it reveals why Marius responded so poorly to the group CBT, and it shows how to design a successful individual and individualized therapy. As discussed by Thastum et al., qualitative case knowledge from Marius's case complements the quantitative research finding that youth with social phobia do less well in group CBT than youth with other anxiety disorders, suggesting that youth with social phobia might be better treated with individual therapy.

SHELLY'S NEGATIVE OUTCOME

Likewise, Shelly's personality was a poor match for the group process. The case study reveals some of the theoretical reasons why. For example, Shelly was mistrustful about revealing herself to others, particularly because of social anxiety over her emerging bisexuality; she had a negative cognitive style that put others off; and she did not have a friend in the group, as did Menorka. Although at the end of the group Shelly was starting to get more engaged, thus suggesting that an increase in the dosage of therapy would have been helpful, it is also likely that modifying the type of therapy would have been particularly helpful for Shelly, by, for example, following up the group therapy with individual therapy, as in the case of Marius. Such individual therapy would have allowed for a more explicit focus on Shelly's anxiety about her emerging bisexuality without the concern of having to share her thoughts and feelings in a group of peers.

Ms. V'S NEGATIVE OUTCOME

Ms. V. was a poor match for the theory behind the TFP model. She resisted recognition of the development of a transference relationship and rejected transference interpretations, one of the core elements of the theory. The reason why she was resistant is suggested by the case study: Ms. V seemed to achieve secondary gain from her illness, as mentioned in Table 8.2, seeming to lock her into retaining her symptoms and way of thinking. In other words, a client will not be motivated to change unless her present equilibrium is sufficiently distressing, and Ms. V's pretherapy equilibrium, along with her subsequent equilibrium during her 1 year and 3 months of therapy, did not seem to meet that criterion. In addition to being a poor initial match, Ms. V quit the additional therapy offered at the end of the first year after 3 months, thus making it clear that an increase in the dosage of TFP was not what was needed. Levy et al. suggest that because of the mismatch with TFP in Ms. V's case, the two other types of therapy in the RCT, perhaps in part as integrated with TFP, might have been a more successful match for her, offering therapy that was more supportive, less challenging, and more focused on interpersonal skill building. In their words,

> Supportive psychotherapy (SPT) would likely have done more to understand V's "refractory depression" as a reality of her subjective experience, and worked to help her understand her experience of being abused and manipulated by others. . . . Dialectical behavior therapy . . . likely would have approached the . . . question regarding acceptance of V's more modest goals versus substantial change in her level of functioning not as a dichotomy, but as a dialectic within which both needs could be respected and understood. The DBT therapist would likely have sought to validate V in her current experience of feeling abused and exploited, while also questioning whether she was working toward "a life worth living." . . . Perhaps most fruitful for V may have been a more integrative approach that combined elements of DBT, such as joining a skills group, to supplement her work in TFP. (pp. 233–234)

Maria's Negative Outcome

Maria was not a good match for the three-session META therapy. Although she established a positive relationship with the therapist, she remained at the contemplation phase of change, and her lack of a strong social support system led to a "vicious circle" of events regarding her depression. Because she did have good rapport with the therapist, it seems that a stepped-care approach might have worked for her. This would have meant increasing the number of her motivational enhancement sessions to help her to reach the action phase and then, because of the depth of her problems, perhaps an additional type of therapy for depression would have been needed.

Note that the theoretical factors and patterns that surfaced in each of the negative-outcome case studies just mentioned are based on only one case, and so their generality is quite limited. On the other hand, as described earlier, in all four cases there were general patterns in terms of factors like client "match" to the particular therapeutic conditions offered by each type of therapy, and the need for a more individualized approach to each case. This highlights the importance of therapist responsiveness, which will be elaborated on in the next section. More broadly, as discussed later, generalizations from case studies are strengthened as the number of case studies involved increases—much like the concept of "power" in the statistical analyses in quantitative group research—so that common patterns inductively emerge across subtypes of large numbers of cases.

THE ROLE OF RESPONSIVENESS

Chapter 1 mentioned the concept of therapist "responsiveness" (e.g., Kramer & Stiles, 2015), which means the clinician being flexible in adapting treatment to the individual client based on the distinctive idiographic aspects of the client, the contextually specific aspects of the client's life, and what emerges in the ongoing therapy process. In the words of Kramer and Stiles, "responsiveness is ubiquitous and creates serious problems for a ballistic, cause-effect understanding of how therapy works" (p. 277). On the face of it, this concept goes against the protocol-based treatment manuals and the principle-based manuals discussed in Chapter 1, although more flexibility is designed into the principle-based manuals (Girio-Herrera & Ehrenreich-May, 2014).

One example that maximizes a therapist's flexibility is Persons's (2008) individualized case formulation model, mentioned in Chapter 1. In this model, general theoretical principles in the CBT guiding conception are employed to develop a distinctive initial case formulation and associated treatment plan for each client. In line with Peterson's (1991) disciplined inquiry model outlined in Figure 2.1, the Persons model is designed to adapt the case formulation and associated treatment plan to the ongoing process of therapy, that is, to obstacles and/or new pathways that develop over the course of therapy, again a form of responsiveness.

Responsiveness provides a helpful perspective on the three reasons mentioned earlier for why some clients have poor outcomes in the experimental condition. To recall, the reasons included an insufficient amount of therapy requiring an increase in the *dose* of therapy; a mismatch between the *type of client* and the *type of treatment manual* employed requiring the use of another treatment manual; and a mismatch in the content of the treatment manual and the client's clinical condition and other characteristics, requiring a *change in the content* of the manual. Each of these three reasons is a call for greater responsiveness, that is, for changing the therapy in certain ways so as to adapt it to the idiographic realities of the individual clients. A good example of this is the way in which the therapists in the Thastum et al. study in Chapter 3 were responsive to those clients who did poorly in the manualized group research by developing an altered, individualized case formulation and treatment plan for them. In recent years, there has been an emerging dialectic in the psychotherapy field between, on the one hand, a focus on treatment responsiveness, and, on the other hand, a focus on *therapist fidelity* to a manual, meaning a focus on ensuring that clinicians closely follow a therapy manual. As illustrated by the cases in Chapters 3–6, case studies are uniquely designed to explore this dialectic, documenting and exploring what actually happened in a particular case, and, thus, this can reveal, for example, (a) instances in which the manual in fact allows flexibility, the different varieties of flexibility that actually occur, and the process results (positive, negative, and neutral) of that flexibility; (b) instances in which the therapist deviates from the manual for good clinical reason with good clinical results; and (c) instances in which the therapist deviates from the manual for a poor clinical reason with poor clinical results. These types of data can be of great value in enhancing the development of better theoretical conceptions that guide therapeutic work and better case examples of successful treatment among similar types of clients receiving similar types of therapy.

Note that a similar concept to responsiveness has emerged in the discussion of APA's evidence-based practice in psychology model (EBPP; APA Presidential Task Force on Evidence-Based Practice, 2006), mentioned in Chapter 1. In this model, best professional practice is viewed as integrating RCT-based and related empirical treatment research with the therapist's clinical expertise and the patient's characteristics and preferences. Tolin et al. (2015) interpret this integration as a "filtering" of the results of that research "through the clinician's and patient's 'lenses'" (p. 319); in other words, "the best available research evidence forms the basis of clinical decisions and is interpreted, adjusted, and implemented through clinical expertise and patient characteristics" (p. 332). The process of this filtering and adjusting would seem to be identical to what Kramer and Stiles (2015) identify as the therapist's responsiveness to the client.

An Example of How the Case Studies Capture the Multidimensional, Reciprocally Interactional Nature of the Therapy Process

The RCT presented in Chapter 6 was designed to use motivational enhancement therapy for antidepressants (META) to increase the adherence to antidepressant medication in depressed, disadvantaged, primarily monolingual Latino women. It was not expected that the META would be therapeutic in itself. The outcome of the RCT was unexpected, therefore, since it showed that, while the META did increase antidepressant adherence, this increased adherence *did not* lead to reduced depressive symptoms. Furthermore, the META intervention itself *did* have a positive impact on reducing depressive symptoms.

By looking at the details of specific cases, the authors were able to generate hypotheses to explain these findings and, in particular, the way in which the META intervention could in and of itself have had a therapeutic effect. This enabled them to develop a "logic model" (Yin, 2014) that would encompass and conceptualize both the original focus of the project—to increase medication adherence—and the finding that the META intervention was therapeutic in itself.

Their model is described in Chapter 6 and outlined in Figure 6.1 of that chapter. This is a biopsychosocial model based on the hypothesis that many different, reciprocally interacting components simultaneously impacted to create a therapeutic impact in the Interian et al. study, including the client's history; biochemical, psychological, interpersonal support, and Latino-sociocultural mechanisms underlying the client's behavior; precipitating events leading to the client's depressive symptoms and other problems; the client's strengths; and the client's social support system. This kind of biopsychosocial model does not assume that any causal factor is primary and provides a basis for understanding how the META therapy could have had a distinctive therapeutic effect. Thus, Lupe's case study shows us how the META therapist was able to achieve an independent therapeutic effect by positively engaging her psychological mechanisms and strengths and by motivating her to engage her support system—all facilitated by the effective use of powerful Latino cultural values, as reflected in *dichos* (sayings) like "*Grano a grano, la gallina llena el buche*" ("Grain by grain, the hen gets a mouthful").

It's also important to note that in line with the logic model's multifaceted nature, the META intervention involves both

> *common factors*, such as having been listened to in a nonjudgmental manner; feeling cared for by the treatment team; having the ability to confide in someone; and being able to receive information and clarify misconceptions; and . . . *specific factors*, like developing discrepancies; rolling with resistance; imparting information; providing feedback; facilitating change talk; supporting self-efficacy; and empathically meeting the client at his or her stage of change. (p. 307)

The three case studies Interian et al. present illustrate how these two sets of factors are intertwined and complementary in creating effective META treatment.

The logic model in Figure 6.1 embodies the principles of Peterson's (1991) disciplined inquiry, Persons's (2008) individualized CBT case formulation approach, and other individualized case formulation models collated by Eells (2007). As such, the logic model is designed to be applicable to other types of therapy—including those used in the other RCT projects in Chapters 3–5. The point the model illustrates is that any course of therapy impacts on a life lived within many reciprocally interacting factors that must be understood in context—and it is this kind of knowledge that systematic case studies are uniquely qualified to provide.

Perspectives From the Commentaries Regarding the Value Added by Case Studies

HOFFMAN, ZENDEGUI, AND CHU'S COMMENTARY CONCERNING THASTUM ET AL.'S CHAPTER ON CBT FOR YOUTH ANXIETY

Hoffman et al. emphasize how Thastum et al.'s successful follow-on individual therapy with nonresponders depended on qualitatively individualized case formulations; that is, Thastum et al. adapted the *universal principles* built into a packaged RCT to the *local needs* of each particular client. Hoffman et al. then argue the merits of this same methodological strategy in meeting the challenge of internationally implementing CBT programs for anxious youth across very different cultures, namely, by using a mixed-methods approach to collect qualitative knowledge about local cultures to aid in adapting the empirically supported universal principles of CBT to the local needs of those different cultures.

DIETZ'S COMMENTARY CONCERNING KERNER AND YOUNG'S CHAPTER ON IPT-AST FOR PREVENTING ADOLESCENT DEPRESSION

Dietz points out the ways in which group research methods and case study methods can work together in a complementary manner, by triangulation, in identifying the underlying moderators and mediators of adolescent depressive symptoms. She cites the example of correlational findings that IPT-AST group treatment has been more effective in depressed adolescents who initially report high parent–child conflict and/or affiliative behavior. Dietz then points out that in the contrasting cases of Menorka and Shelly, these two variables did seem associated with their differential outcomes. At the same time, the case studies explored the specific circumstances of how these mechanisms of change worked in these particular clients and how these variables complexly interacted with other relevant variables also present in these two clients.

PIPER AND HERNANDEZ'S COMMENTARY CONCERNING LEVY ET AL.'S CHAPTER ON ADULT BORDERLINE PERSONALITY DISORDER

As mentioned earlier, in their commentary Piper and Hernandez describe the movement from "thin" RCTs in the 1970s to the "thick" RCTs that we see today, particularly as experienced by Piper (2001) in his own research. These authors point out that the move from group-research-only to a combination of group and case study research is part of the natural progression from thin to thicker and thicker RCTs.

NORCROSS'S COMMENTARY CONCERNING INTERIAN ET AL.'S CHAPTER ON MOTIVATIONAL ENHANCEMENT FOR ADULT DEPRESSION

As mentioned earlier, in Interian et al's RCT, the clients in the experimental group showed higher antidepressant medication adherence and, independent of adherence increases, decreased depression. In his commentary, Norcross points out that while the RCT group design emphasizes the addition of motivational interviewing (MI), which Interian et al. call "META," as what differentiated the experimental group's difference from the control group, there were actually many specific elements in the META group that were associated with the therapeutic effect of the META intervention. Moreover, these multiple elements were only apparent by reading through the three case studies from the META group in qualitative, narrative detail the three case studies presented that were drawn from the META group. Three of the examples of these elements Norcross provides are listed here.

First, the META treatment was "led by passionate, bilingual clinical psychologists and doctoral students specifically trained and continually supervised in ME[TA]" as compared with "treatment as usual provided by the typically over-burdened, underfunded staff at a community mental health center" (p. 317). In other words, it was the particular enthusiasm, commitment, time availability, and relationship skills of the META therapist team that were part of its therapeutic effectiveness, in addition to their just following the META treatment manual.

Second, the Latino cultural adaptation of the META manual was distinctive and powerfully connected to the META clients, with a particular focus on religious imagery, again going beyond just following the standard META manual. In Norcross's words, "Reading segments from the session transcripts [indicated that what was taking place was] . . . a religious adaptation of secular META. Many of the sayings allude to faith and God as sources of motivation; for example, the *dichos* 'A quien madruga, Dios le ayuda' ('God helps he who rises to the occasion') and 'Dios aprieta pero no ahorca' ('God squeezes but does not choke')" (p. 291).

Third, the META therapists, in the "spirit" of motivational interviewing, "engaged in considerable outreach and alliance-building behaviors, [including] multiple contacts, collaborative goal setting, honoring ambivalence, and adapting treatment to the singular patient (e.g., [in terms of each client's] stage of change, culture, religion, preferences)" (p. 320). Norcross emphasizes that all of these therapy activities are associated with, and predictive of, successful treatment outcomes, again going beyond the specifics of the motivational interviewing manual typically used in RCTs.

CHUI, BLOCH-ELKOUBY, AND BARBER'S COMMENTARY ON THE FOUR PROJECTS

Barber and his research teams have a long history of traditional RCT research, and we welcome their balanced commentary on the benefits and challenges of routinely adding systematic case studies in a formal way to RCT group designs. These authors show an openness to move away from the exclusive group quantitative thinking of traditional RCTs to consider the complementary advantages of case-based, idiographic analysis that can capture the rich complexity of clinical phenomena and can thus add to both the theory and the pragmatic effectiveness of the psychotherapy. As discussed in the introductory chapter, such analysis has been formally developed by a variety of qualitative researchers, such as Eells (2007), Flyvbjberg (2006), Kramer and Stiles (2015), Persons (2008), Stiles (2009), Taylor and Bogdan (1998), and Wertz et al. (2011).

FUTURE DIRECTIONS

Expansion of the Number of Cases Analyzed in the Experimental Conditions

The nine clients described in Chapters 3–6 and summarized in Table 8.2 are only a small fraction of the 149 clients in the experimental conditions of the four projects (see Table 1.2 in Chapter 2). This means that only a small part of the qualitative data collected on each of these 149 clients has been examined in any depth. These include audio or video recordings of all therapy sessions, therapists' clinical notes, and notes from supervision. These rich clinical records could be used for further qualitative investigations, including other case studies that could throw greater light on the important clinical questions raised by each study.

As mentioned in the discussion of Table 1.1 in the first chapter, it is important to look at multiple examples of positive-outcome and negative-outcome clients in

an RCT's experimental condition because it is very possible that there are different causal patterns behind the success of different clients, and likewise, different
causal patterns behind the failure of different clients. For example, as described in
Chapter 3 about Thastum et al.'s work with anxious youth, the researchers followed
up with individual therapy for 14 nonresponders to the manualized CBT group
therapy who were appropriate for and accepted the subsequent therapy. Eleven of
these had positive outcomes. To achieve success in the various cases, the therapists needed to employ different, individualized case formulations (Lundkvist-
Houndoumadi, Thastum, & Hougaard, 2015). This finding is consistent with the
model put forth by the cognitive-behaviorist Persons (2008), which states that
typically the generic case formulations that are built into protocol-based therapy
manuals are insufficient for successful cognitive-behavioral therapy, and that in
best practice, individualized case formulations that reflect different causal models
of psychopathology and change are the rule, not the exception.

It is also relevant here to remember the discussion of Interian et al.'s "mixed -
outcome" case of Ana, which reminds us that clients typically fall somewhere on
a continuum where clear positive outcome and clear negative outcome are only
the poles. Investigating varieties of "mixed-outcome" cases will help to complete
our understanding of individual differences in the reactions to therapy and the
need to be responsive to these. For example, Ana started the META in a very
positive frame of mind:. She quickly established a positive relationship with the
META therapist, she was 100% medication adherent, and she appeared to be in
an action-oriented stage of change. Yet unlike Lupe, who showed excellent progress as reflected in both her quantitative and qualitative data, Ana's outcome data
reflected inconsistencies. Specifically, from the beginning of treatment to follow-
up, on the Beck Depression Inventory Ana showed basically no change (26 and
23, respectively, in the moderate depression range); and on the percent-of-medi-
cation-adherence measure, she showed a substantial decrease (from 94% to 78%,
respectively). On the other hand, at follow-up, Ana's subjective report about her
experience of the META sessions was quite positive. For example, in the follow-up
exit interview Ana

> expressed immense gratitude to the study, for it provided her with the oppor-
> tunity to "move forward," offered her someone to talk to, allowed her to build
> insight into her mental illness, and gave her the tools to manage her symp-
> toms. As she gained internal strength, . . . she was able to shed her feelings
> of worthlessness and guilt and discover new passions, interests, and values.
> Instead of feeling victimized and asking herself "Why me?", she began to
> view her previous experiences as opportunities to learn and grow . . . [and]
> credited the study for solidifying her identity as a competent mother and
> wife. (pp. 305–306)

Ana's case illustrates new ways in which case studies can inform us, for example, with conflicting results between quantitative and qualitative indicators—
suggesting both (a) the need to use multiple methods for measuring outcome,

and (b) the need to better understand the meaning of a conflict between the results of quantitative and qualitative indicators. Investigating varieties of "mixed-outcome" cases will help to complete our understanding of individual differences in the reactions to therapy and the need to be responsive to these.

Analyzing the Cases in the Control Conditions

Moreover, as we know from previous research with "spontaneous recovery" (Cross, 1964), for the 157 individuals in the control conditions of the four projects (see Table 1.2 in Chapter 2), there will be examples of individuals with positive outcome along with individuals with negative outcome, all documented with the RCTs' quantitative measures. In one instance (Levy et al.'s Chapter 5), there were audiotapes or videotapes and supervision notes available for each of the clients in the control conditions, which consisted of bona fide therapies, to provide a rich clinical record in order to conduct systematic case studies. In the other three studies, while audiotapes or videotapes were not available, it would have been feasible to follow up each of these clients with retrospective clinical interviews to provide a qualitative understanding of their changes over the time of the RCT. This could be done for the control group participants both in regard to other members of the control group and relative to their respective experimental group, as documented by the data from the RCTs, which have information on the same quantitative measures across all of the participants. (For a related type of retrospective study, see Hansen et al., 2015.)

In general, investigating the change mechanisms associated with positive versus negative outcomes in the control condition of an RCT can reveal important additional knowledge about how positive change can occur outside of the experimental condition. A specific example of how case studies of the control condition can be of particular value emerged from the RCT research discussed in Chapter 4 by Kerner and Young. The control condition was "school counseling" (SC), which consisted of 30- to 45-minute supportive individual counseling focusing on topics like caregiver relationships and academic issues. In the RCT described, there was evidence suggesting the effectiveness of the SC condition in helping the SC group over time to catch up in functioning with the IPT-AST group. This finding is consistent with other studies. For example, in a meta-analysis of 32 randomized trials that directly compared evidence-based treatments (EBTs) versus usual care (UC), like individual or group school counseling, Weisz, Jensen-Doss, and Hawley (2006) found that while overall the EBTs were better, this advantage was modest, and that in five of the studies the UC was found to be superior to EBTs. In this context, Young's doctoral dissertation student, Katie Moore (2016), pursued this finding by conducting comparative systematic case studies of a successful UC group and an unsuccessful UC group, each drawn from the control condition of one of Young's RCT studies on the prevention of depressive symptoms in youth. Moore found substantial and clinically important differences between the two groups on a variety of interrelated factors, including: (a) setting characteristics, like conducting group sessions during or after school; (b) the behavior and attitudes of the group leaders, e.g., more vs. less directed and structured; (c) the therapeutic processes involved, like encouraging group cohesiveness, establishing and reviewing goals, using role-playing, using self-disclosure, and focusing on affect; and (d) the therapeutic content of their interventions, like behavioral activation, problem solving, and exploring the past.

As another example, in Chapter 5 Levy et al. point out that the bona fide models in their RCT—Transference-Focused Psychotherapy (TFP), Dialectical Behavior Therapy (DBT), and Supportive Psychotherapy (SPT)—are each based on a different theory of change. TFP focuses on integrating representations of self and others as they become active in the therapeutic relationship, by means of a particular use of transference interpretation; DBT focuses on direct, behavioral skills training and the concept of dialectics in understanding the world; and SPT focuses on a supportive relationship, with the therapist as a model of reflection without the use of transference interpretation. The overall finding in the RCT of the equivalence of TFP, DBT, and SPT as reported by Levy et al. suggests that there may be different theoretically based routes to improvement, although an alternative hypothesis is that it is the common elements among the three that are of equal or more importance. Case studies of the "control cases" would be an excellent way of starting to test these hypotheses.

The Nine Cases Presented as a "Proof of Concept"

An overall point we want to emphasize is that the more cases one is comparing, the stronger the degree of generalization from the results, since more and more cases sample more and more of the range of contextual complexity in real-world therapeutic situations (Fishman, 1999; Flyvbjerg, 2006; Iwakabe & Gazzela, 2009). Thus, we recognize the limitations of the small number of cases (9) presented in Chapters 3–6, and in line with this we see them as a "proof of concept" of the full case-study-knowledge potential that is built into RCT study designs. Adding to this proof of concept is the wide span of the different RCTs and associated case studies reviewed in Chapters 3–6, on dimensions like age; type of psychopathology; modality of therapy (individual versus group); type of therapy theory involved (cognitive-behavioral therapy, interpersonal therapy, psychoanalytic therapy, and client-centered therapy); and length of therapy (from three sessions [for the META clients in Chapter 6] to the 5 years [for the case of Ms. J in Chapter 5).

Conclusion

One of the inspirations for this book has been the late Gordon Paul's (1967) classic and aforementioned framing of the question that psychotherapy research should aim to answer: "What treatment, by whom, is most effective for this individual, with that specific problem, under which set of circumstances, and how does it come about?" Over the years, RCTs have provided important parts of the answer to that question, with a specific focus on "what treatments" are "most effective" for "specific problems," as illustrated by the types of findings in Table 8.1 for the four projects reviewed in this book.

As we have documented, early attempts to create "thin" RCT designs (Piper, 2001) that would be as elegant and scientifically rigorous as possible, emphasizing efficacy and internal validity, collided with the qualitative, narrative richness and complexities of real-world clinical phenomena. This resulted in the other elements in Paul's question to emerge: "by whom" (emphasizing the therapist-as-a-person factors); "for this individual" (emphasizing patient history, life situation, and personality factors); "under which set of circumstances" (emphasizing the importance of other contextual variables, such as the culturally related factors of the client's ethnicity, race, religion, economic status, educational status, vocational status, gender identity, and sexual orientation); and "how does it come about" (emphasizing the nature of psychotherapy process and underlying mechanisms of change). Paying attention to these parts of Paul's question are important if the results of RCT studies are to maximize their external validity, that is, to be relevant to effectiveness questions of how different types of therapy work in real-world settings of naturalistic practice.

Incorporating these latter parts of Paul's question into RCT designs has led to the development of the "thick" group research designs that are illustrated in Chapters 3–6. However, there are intrinsic limitations to the group research methods at the heart of traditional RCT designs. Group research methods are best at exploring linear relationships among a relatively small set of discrete and precisely operationally defined variables. In contrast, clinical phenomena frequently include large numbers of variables arrayed in complex patterns involving nonlinear and often reciprocally causal relationships (Fishman, 1999; Flybjerg, 2006, Stiles, 2009), that is, in Flyvbjerg's (2006) words, "concrete, practical (context-dependent) knowledge" (p. 221). This is the arena in which systematic case studies demonstrate particular strength, as illustrated in the nine case studies presented in Chapters 3–6. Thus we have argued that adding systematic case studies to the group-research component of contemporary RCT designs crucially complements the type of knowledge yielded by the latter.

We believe that the RCT projects in Chapters 3–6 provide "proof of concept" evidence in favor of expanding the traditional RCT "gold standard" of research on the efficacy of psychotherapy. We argue that the gold standard needs to be a mixed-methods research approach in which RCTs are not reported alone but in conjunction with systematic case studies and a discussion synthesizing the results of the group research component with the case studies component. We propose that the full realization of this agenda will require four crucial elements.

- the continuing improvement of case study methodology so that systematic case studies become of higher and higher quality, paralleling recent efforts to increase the methodological quality of RCTs, as mentioned in footnote 1;

- the creation of more and more numbers of such high-quality case studies, far exceeding the number of 1,200 already published, as mentioned in Chapter 2, remembering that the field of law as an example is based on tens of thousands of cases.
- the growing accessibility of such case studies in highly searchable collections parallel to what exists for legal cases, such as proprietary databases like Westlaw (www.westlaw.com) and open-access databases like the Legal Information Institute at Cornell Law School (www.law.cornell.edu); and
- the increasing expansion of methodologies—like theory-building case studies (Stiles, 2009), the metasynthesis of case studies (Iwakabe & Gazzola, 2009), and the meta-analysis of qualitative research focused on the same topic, such as clients' experiences of psychotherapy (Levitt, Pomerville, & Surace, 2016)—for the rigorous cross-comparative analysis of multiple case studies and related qualitative research.

We look forward to efforts to further advance this vision!

REFERENCES

The Cochrane Library (2015). Mental health reviews. Available at http://www.cochraneli-brary.com/topic/Mental%20health/, accessed December 5, 2015.

Crow, S. J., Agras, W. S., Halmi, K. A., Fairburn, C. G., Mitchell, J. E., & Nyman, J. A. (2013). A cost effectiveness analysis of stepped care treatment for bulimia nervosa. *International Journal of Eating Disorders, 46,* 302–307.

Cuijpers, P. & Cristea, I. A. (2015, September 28). How to prove that your therapy is effective, even when it is not: A guideline. *Epidemiology and Psychiatric Services,* pp. 1–8. doi: 10.1017/S2045796015000864

Fishman, D. B. (1999). *The case for pragmatic psychology.* New York, NY: NYU Press.

Fishman, D. B. (2013). The pragmatic case study method for creating rigorous and systematic, practitioner-friendly research. *Pragmatic Case Studies in Psychotherapy,* 9(4), 403–425. Available at http://pcsp.libraries.rutgers.edu. doi: http://dx.doi.org/ 10.14713/pcsp.v9i4.1833

Flyvbjerg, B. (2006). Five misunderstandings about case study research. *Qualitative Inquiry, 12,* 219–245. http://dx.doi.org/10.1177/1077800405284363

Girio-Herrera, E. & Ehrenreich-May, J. (2014). Using flexible clinical processes in the uni-fied protocol for the treatment of emotional disorders in adolescence. *Psychotherapy, 51,* 117–122.

Hansen, B. P., Lambert, M. J., & Vlass, E. N. (2015). Sudden gains and sudden losses in the clients of a "supershrink": 10 case studies. *Pragmatic case studies in psychotherapy,* 11(3), 154–201. Available at http://pcsp.libraries.rutgers.edu. doi: http://dx.doi.org/ 10.14713/pcsp.v11i3.1915

Iwakabe, S. & Gazzola, N. (2009). From single case studies to practice-based knowl-edge: Aggregating and synthesizing case studies. *Psychotherapy Research, 19,* 601–611.

Kiesler, D. J. (1966). Some myths of psychotherapy research and the search for a para-digm. *Psychological Bulletin, 65,* 110–1365.

Levitt, H. M., Pomerville, E., & Surace, F. I. (2016). A qualitative meta-analysis examining clients' experiences of psychotherapy: A new agenda. *Psychological Bulletin, 142,* 801–830. doi: http://dx.doi.org/10.1037/bul0000057

Lundkvist-Houndoumadi, I., Thastum, M., & Hougaard, E. (2015). Effectiveness of an individualized case formulation-based CBT for non-responding youths with anxiety disorders. *Journal of Child and Family Studies, 25,* 503–517. doi:10.1007/s10826-015-0225-4.

Messer, S. B. (2011). Theory development via single cases: A case study of the therapeutic relationship in psychodynamic therapy. *Pragmatic Case Studies in Psychotherapy,* 7(4), 440–448. Available at http://pcsp.libraries.rutgers.edu. doi: http://dx.doi.org/10.14713/pcsp.v7i4.1112

Moore, K. (2016). *Understanding usual care in schools: A mixed methods approach.* Unpublished doctoral dissertation, Rutgers University-New Brunswick.

Nosek, B., et al. (2015). Estimating the reproducibility of psychological science. *Science,* 349, aac4716. doi:10.1126/science.aac4716

Pashler, P. & Wagenmakers, E-J. (2012). Editors' introduction to the special section on replicability in psychological science: A crisis of confidence? *Perspectives on Psychological Science, 7,* 528–530.

Paul, G. L. (1967). Strategy of outcome research in psychotherapy. *Journal of Consulting Psychology, 31,* 109–118.

Persons, J. B. (2008). *The case formulation approach to cognitive-behavior therapy.* New York, NY: Guilford.

Piper, W. E. (2001). Collaboration in a new millennium. *Psychotherapy Research,* 11, 1–11.

Society of Clinical Psychology (2015). Research-supported psychological treatments. Available at http://www.div12.org/psychological-treatments/, accessed December 5, 2015.

Stiles, W. B. (2009). Logical operations in theory-building case studies. *Pragmatic Case Studies in Psychotherapy,* 5(3), 9–22. Available at http://pcsp.libraries.rutgers.edu. doi: http://dx.doi.org/10.14713/pcsp.v5i3.973

Tolin, D. F., McKay, D., Forman, E. M., Klonsky, E. D., & Thombs, B. D. (2015). Empirically supported treatment recommendations for a new model. *Clinical Psychology: Science and Practice, 22,* 317–338.

Weisz, J. R., Jensen-Doss, A., & Hawley, K. M. (2006). Evidenced-based youth psychotherapies versus usual clinical care. *American Psychologist, 61,* 671–689.

Winerman, L. (2013). Interesting results: Can they be replicated? In the wake of scandal, psychologists are encouraging more data sharing and replication studies. *Monitor on Psychology, 44,* p. 38.

Yin, R. K. (2014). *Case study research: Design and methods* (5th ed.). Thousand Oaks, CA: Sage.

INDEX

Note: Page numbers followed by italicized letters indicate *notes, figures* or *tables.*